Causal Modelling in Nonexperimental Research

Causal Modelling in Nonexperimental Research

**An Introduction to the
LISREL Approach**

Willem E. Saris
L. Henk Stronkhorst

SOCIOMETRIC RESEARCH FOUNDATION
Amsterdam, The Netherlands

Series on Linear Structural Equation Models

1.   T.K. Dijkstra: *Latent Variables in Linear Stochastic Models. Reflections on the "Maximum Likelihood" and "Partial Least Squares" Methods*

2.   A. Boomsma: *On the Robustness of LISREL Against Small Sample Size and Non-Normality*

CIP-INFORMATION:
SARIS, W.E.
CAUSAL MODELLING IN NONEXPERIMENTAL RESEARCH: AN INTRODUCTION TO THE LISREL APPROACH/ W.E. SARIS AND L.H. STRONKHORST.
—AMSTERDAM: SOCIOMETRIC RESEARCH FOUNDATION
—(STRUCTURAL EQUATIONS MODELS; NR.3)
WITH REF., INDEX.
ISBN 90—70947—04—8
SISO 300.6 UDC 303.7
SUBJECT HEADING: NONEXPERIMENTAL RESEARCH: CAUSAL MODELLING
© COPYRIGHT 1984 SOCIOMETRIC RESEARCH FOUNDATION.

Sociometric Research Foundation
Blauwburgwal 20
1015 AT Amsterdam
The Netherlands

Preface

In experimental research the analysis of variance has a very important place due to the fact that it allows the testing of hypotheses with respect to the causal effects of variables on each other. In nonexperimental research where interval variables are studied, *"covariance structure analysis"* serves this purpose. Of major importance in this procedure is the formulation of causal models and their evaluation, the topics which are simultaneously treated in this book. Just as in the case of the analysis of variance, the proper use of the procedures is a requirement for the advancement of the disciplines which have to rely on this type of analysis. In a recent paper, Louis Guttman strongly criticized causal modelling with his statement that:

"There has been a flowering of causal discoveries in sociology at a pace un-heard of in the history of science. Virtually every month, current journals publish new "causal analyses" and "causal modelling" which undoubtedly put sociology at the forefront of all the sciences in terms of frequency of discovery of fundamental relationships".

This cynical quote is only one of the critiques of causal modelling which can be found in the literature. This criticism cannot simply be brushed aside. A secondary analysis of the data reported in journals specializing in many research areas shows that the majority of the models presented as final causal theories should not have been accepted. Furthermore models are often ob-tained by data fitting, and are consequently very likely candidates for rejection in replication studies. But replications of such studies are seldom done. Also, the proportion of explained variance is very low most of the time, which means that the results presented do not provide very strong evidence for the causal arguments hypothesized.

This unsatisfactory situation is not necessary. Since 1973 the statistical tools for the estimation and testing of causal models have been readily available in programs such as LISREL, developed by Jöreskog and his co-workers. The procedure in this program provides very efficient methods for the estimation and testing of causal models. This is even more true since the development of LISREL VI, released in 1983, in which several estimation procedures are provided and in which new facilities are offered for the analysis of categorical data as well. The procedure is not restricted to those models traditionally discussed under the heading of causal modelling, such as recursive and non-recursive models without latent variables. With this method one can also analyze measurement models, factor analytic models, multi-trait-multi-method models, variance-covariance component models, causal models with latent

V

variables and models for panel data. All of these models can be analyzed using a single estimation and testing procedure with the same program. This feature makes this approach very efficient.

Although the usefulness of the LISREL approach has been recognized by the methodologists in the social sciences, LISREL has so far not been used very frequently in substantive research. No doubt, one of the problems has been the level of abstraction with which the method has been presented. In general the expositions have been too technical for most substantive investigators.

After the first author of this text became convinced of the importance of the LISREL approach for the nonexperimental sciences, he started to write a text in which the LISREL approach and program were introduced to researchers. This text took the reader from the formulation of models, through their estimation, testing and correction, and provided a discussion of the large variety of models that can be analyzed using this approach and program. However, in practice, courses based on this text turned out to be too demanding for those people who had to grasp both the general methodology as well as the specifics of the different models. Therefore the authors decided that a text was necessary which could explain the methodology that is used in LISREL without confusing the readers too much with the large variety of possibilities offered by the LISREL system.

For this reason the authors have chosen to explain the methodology of causal modelling for nonexperimental research using the LISREL approach. In this way it is also possible to make a link between the earlier approaches which have been used for this purpose, such as path analysis, regression analysis, partial correlation and econometric approaches.

Our experience with teaching introductory courses in causal modelling to second year university students using this book has been very favorable so far. This text has been successfully used at the Free University in Amsterdam and the University of Amsterdam. We were also requested to present the same course several times at the Summer School of the European Consortium for Political Research at the University of Essex. The reactions of the more advanced students of this Summer Program have also been very favorable.

Apart from studying the textbook, students are advised to work on the exercises which are presented at the end of each chapter. It has also proven to be a valuable learning experience when a secondary data analysis is performed on the basis of published research papers within the student's own field of interest (a list of papers can be obtained for this purpose from the publisher). Using these three teaching tools simultaneously, the introduction of this topic turned out to be very successful. Most students accept that research should be done more or less along the lines presented in the text and that statistics plays an important role in this endeavor. The secondary analysis, for which all students had to use LISREL, did not present any serious problems for those involved. The reason that the reactions to this course are much more favorable than to the normal courses in inferential statistics (for which this course can be a substitute), is that the required activities are closely related to the theoretical activities that these students are mostly concerned with during their studies.

But we do not think that this book is only useful for students. One of the reasons that we have written this book was, that we were concerned about the quality of the research done in the disciplines that use nonexperimental data. As we have indicated above, a lot of the criticism made of published research is justified. We have therefore also written this book for those researchers who are willing to reconsider their present approaches, with the aim of improving their research. For this purpose we have chosen to explain the approach in a way which is in agreement with the commonly used approach as much as possible.

Our experiences at the University of Essex, at the Universities in Amsterdam and at the Netherlands CBS have convinced us that after the study of this text one can fairly easily adopt the full LISREL approach with all its possibilities. Although in this text the use of matrix algebra has been completely avoided, matrix representations are very frequently used so that the step to the formal use of matrix algebra, necessary for the formulation of the full system, is no longer difficult.

The writing of this book is not only the work of the authors. Many others provided helpful feedback. In this respect we must mention all the students whom we have tought on this topic. It is partially due to them that we have been inspired to continue with the efforts to complete this book.

We wish to thank Marius de Pijper and Irmtraud Gallhofer for their cooperation in the many stages which the publication of this book went through. We are grateful to Martin Bulmer and Alberto Satorra for their useful comments on the last version. The corrections of our English suggested by Derek Coleman were very important even though it might prove impossible to make our language perfect.

This book has been produced by Kees Aarts using the program TEX (Knuth, 1979), in collaboration with Elise van Vliet, John Faase and Emiel Bon. Especially Kees Aarts we have to thank for his dedication to finish this work.

Finally, as TEX requires masters and grandmasters, we are also very grateful to Rob Veldhuyzen van Zanten, who helped us out of the most complicated problems.

Even though a large group of people helped us to avoid errors in the book we can not blame them for any mistakes which still remain. Comments in this respect are always appreciated by the authors.

Willem E. Saris
L. Henk Stronkhorst

CONTENTS

IX

Introduction

In this introduction various issues are discussed which precede the systematic treatment of the subject matter. In this way an introduction is provided to the idea of causality before more concrete arguments on the specification of causal theories are presented. Experimental and nonexperimental research designs are compared. It is indicated that under certain conditions causal hypotheses can also be tested on nonexperimental data. The steps to come to an acceptable causal theory are indicated and it is shown how the various themes that concern us, are organized in this text.

Causality

Throughout the centuries people have tried to find causal explanations for what was happening in the world around them. This preoccupation with causal explanations seems to be the result of at least three different concerns. First of all, people who are looking for causal explanations are often convinced that such explanations represent the most fundamental understanding of the process they are studying, and that such knowledge is relatively invariant through time and space (Goldberger, 1973; Duncan, 1975). Secondly, from a practical point of view it is evidently far more interesting to know that one phenomenon (X) is a cause of another phenomenon (Y), than to know merely that these phenomena always appeared together. Potentially, knowledge of cause and effect makes it possible to influence reality in an intelligent way, while this is not true in the case of knowledge about covariation of phenomena only. For policy implications then, causal theories are more interesting. Finally, theories which are stated in terms of causal relationships between the variables can be derived, which means that not all relationships need to be specified separately (see Blalock,1969a). Such derivations are not so straightforward for theories which are based only on covariation statements (Costner and Leik, 1964). This also allows a more parsimoneous statement of scientific theories.

Despite the evident attractiveness of the use of causal theories, from the beginning of this century, philosophers have criticized their use. The main criticism was that one can only observe that two events occur together, or at most follow one another. According to this argument, one can not prove that one phenomenon is the actual cause of another. This would imply that causal

1

theories could never be verified and therefore the causal approach should be abandoned, according to this criticism. However, the situation with respect to causal theories is not different from the one encountered for any other kind of theory: it is never possible to prove that a theory is correct, since there are always many different theories which can describe the same observations (Popper, 1959). The question that should be raised is whether or not theories—including causal theories—can be rejected on the basis of observations. Probably most people would agree that as a means of testing causal hypotheses the experiment is a more efficient design than nonexperimental research. Some (such as Campbell and Stanley, 1963) argue that the experiment is the only way to settle the disputes on such points as to whether or not variable X has influence on variable Y. Unfortunately, a large number of substantive areas exists in which experiments are simply impossible and where one has to rely on nonexperimental research. Although this nonexperimental research may seem to be less convincing or conclusive, it can still be used in tests of causal hypotheses. Before it is indicated what the special problems of nonexperimental research are and how these problems can be overcome, a brief introduction to experimental designs is provided.

The Experimental Design

A typical aim in experimental research is that one wants to show that a particular variable will change, whenever another variable is changed. However, the fact that one can observe the expected order of events does not in itself prove that one is dealing with a causal process. The problem is that many other explanations might be given for the same order of events if not all other relevant variables are kept under control so that all possible alternative explanations are excluded. In physics this is done by keeping the whole experimental situation under control. This means that one tries to keep all relevant factors exactly the same, except for the one variable the effects of which one wants to study. If the control is indeed efficient (this will always remain an assumption) and the order of events is as expected, one does not reject the causal hypothesis. If the expected effects do not happen, one has to reject the causal hypothesis, provided one is convinced that all variables were under control. The use of this procedure seems to give the hypothesis a fair chance of being rejected and therefore this type of experimental research is accepted as very appropriate to the test of causal hypotheses.

In social science experiments an extra complication occurs in the fact that living subjects are not always interchangeable. Therefore the natural science design has to be adjusted. In general, one is not working with individuals, but with groups which are formed so as to resemble each other in important aspects. In the simplest design two groups are formed. One is called the *"experimental group"* and the other the *"control group"*. Subjects are distributed over the two groups at random. In this way the groups are believed to be identical, except for differences by chance. After this is done, the purpose of the experimental design is again accomplished: while all other variables are kept constant, a change in variable X is introduced in the experimental group, but not in the control group. Subsequently one checks whether the two groups differ from each other by more than can be expected by chance with respect to the effect that was predicted. If the difference is significant, the causal hypothesis is not rejected. If the difference is not significant, the causal hypothesis has to be rejected. It will be clear that, using this design, causal hypotheses have a fair chance of being rejected and therefore this design seems to be appropriate for the test of causal hypotheses.

In order to avoid the possibility that an effect of another important variable is confused with the effect of the causal variable of interest, one can also use matching procedures. This is done by first looking for pairs of subjects which are identical in most important aspects and randomly assigning one of each pair of subjects to either one of the two groups (i.e., experimental and control group). In that way it is known for sure that the two groups are identical in most important aspects. This approach, the combination of matching and randomization, represents an even stronger design than that based on randomization alone. It is important to keep these principles of experimental research in mind when moving to the nonexperimental designs which are used in many of the social sciences.

Nonexperimental Research

The major characteristic of *nonexperimental research* is that none of the relevant variables can be manipulated by the investigator. This has two consequences. First, it means that one does not obtain evidence concerning the causal ordering of events. The causal ordering of variables should be settled in a different way and requires extra theoretical work, since a sequence of events can not be derived from the data. Given a chosen causal ordering (as posited in a theory) the tenability of a causal theory can be tested with nonexperimental data. But direct inference about the causal ordering without making prior assumptions is impossible.

A second consequence is that the subjects which are studied in nonexperimental research, may be different with respect to many characteristics, and not only in the isolated aspect for which we want to establish an effect. Therefore it is not clear if a relationship found between the causal variable and the effect variable should be attributed to a causal effect or—partly or entirely—to the effect of other variables.

However, this situation is not so dramatically different from the situation in the experiment as it may seem at first. In experiments one also has to control variables in order to exclude competing explanations. This control is executed by either random assignment of subjects to the experimental and the control group, or by matching of subjects. In nonexperimental research one can not form an experimental and control group by definition, so the first approach of experiments is not feasible. By contrast, matching can be used and this has been done in the past. It consists of the pairwise matching of individuals after the data have been collected. Since this design looks quite similar to the experiment, it has sometimes been referred to as an *"ex post facto* experiment" (Greenwood, 1945; Chapin, 1947). A problem with *ex post facto* experiments is that the number of people eventually studied is reduced considerably compared to the number observed originally. For example, in one study the number of cases reduced from 1194 in the original study to 46 in the final test. It is questionable whether the results on the final 46 people are representative of the total group. For this reason the application of matching procedures in nonexperimental research has not been entirely satisfactory.

The Simon-Blalock approach is a procedure in which the control by matching is replaced by a more efficient statistical control of all important variables. The procedure was introduced by Blalock in 1962 and was derived from the work of Simon (1954). In this approach a causal theory is specified which includes all variables that are important according to the investigator. From such a theory certain testable conclusions can be derived with respect to the covariations between variables. The theory cannot be correct if these derived conclusions do not hold for the data. In that case the theory has to be rejected. Using this approach, causal theories can be falsified in nonexperimental research.

Boudon (1965) and Duncan (1966) have suggested a somewhat different procedure which is indicated with the names *analysis of dependence* or *path analysis*. This path analysis approach is based on the work of the genetecist Sewall Wright (1934). In this approach causal theories are specified including all important variables. Furthermore, procedures have been developed to establish the relationship between the causal effects specified in the theory and the measures for covariation between the variables. These relationships were then used to obtain estimates of the causal effects. The same relationships could also have been used for the test of the causal theories, but the emphasis was on estimation of effects at that time and not on the testing of the theories.

Since 1973 the program *LISREL* is available which not only provides an efficient estimation procedure for the causal effects but also a test of causal theories. This test is based on the relationship between the measures of covariation between variables (covariance and correlation) and the causal effects. If the theory is correct, the measures for the covariation derived from the estimated effects should be the same as the measures of covariation obtained from the data, apart from sampling fluctuations. If they are not the same, the causal theory on which the computations are based has to be rejected.

This discussion illustrates that there are certainly possibilities to test causal hypotheses on nonexperimental data. But a fundamental difference from experimental studies is that random assignment of people to different treatment groups (experimental and control groups) is not possible. Therefore all important variables which could provide an alternative explanation of the causal hypothesis of interest have to be taken into account explicitly by matching, by statistical control or by comparison of the derived measures of covariation and the obtained covariation from the data. This means that one has to pay more attention to theory formation in nonexperimental research than in experimental research. If important variables have been omitted in a nonexperimental study the conclusions from the analyses of the data are questionable, while this is not necessarily true in experimental studies. In the latter randomization can make the different groups approximately identical without explicit matching on this variable. It will be clear that the possibility to control by randomization is an important advantage of experimental research. On the other hand, it is one of the exciting aspects of nonexperimental research that one is required to specify a more complete theory for the research field of interest. It means that one can gain more in this way if the theory is not rejected than in experimental research where, in general, one is only concerned with one hypothesis at a time.

This discussion of designs indicates that causal hypotheses can also be tested on nonexperimental data, but it indicates as well that a book on causal modelling with nonexperimental data should not only consider technical testing procedures but also discuss extensively the phase of theory formulation.

The Plan of the Book

Given that causal hypotheses are of interest to many social scientists and that experiments are not always possible to test these hypotheses, the purpose of this volume is to show how causal hypotheses can be tested using nonexperimental data. Since the LISREL approach is at present the most general and efficient procedure, this approach will be introduced and the analyses will be done with the most recent version of the program, LISREL VI (Jöreskog and Sörbom, 1983). For information about other programs we refer to the last chapter. In this volume the discussion will be very elementary; neither matrix algebra nor prior statistical knowledge is required. In order to give an overall perspective on the potential of the LISREL approach, all steps necessary in substantive research are discussed and illustrated using one eleborate example. The various steps are discussed in the more or less chronological order of the research process. A flow chart of the plan of the book is given in Figure I.1. If the reader is loosing track because of a detailed discussion in a particular chapter, he or she is advised to return to this flow chart to pick up the main line of argument again.

In *chapter 1* the basic elements of causal theories are introduced. Using these elements a researcher can formulate a testable causal theory. How this can be done, is the topic of *chapter 2*. The next step is the transition from a verbal theory to a structural equation model in the course of which it becomes evident how the causal effects should be specified (*chapters 3 and 4*). From the model,covariances between the variables can be derived, assuming for the moment that the theory is correct (*chapter 7*). Since the covariances are used as the data base for estimation of the effects as well as the test of the theory, one should investigate whether the parameters can be determined and the model tested before proceeding with the research (*chapter 8*). If this is not possible, the theory should be corrected until estimation and testing are possible. So there is a loop at this point in the flow chart.

If the effects can be estimated and the theory can be tested one can in principle start the data collection (*chapter 5*) and the covariances or correlations between the variables can be computed from the data (*chapter 6*). A special problem in this respect is the fact that one does not usually have data for the whole population but only for a sample from the population, which makes the results less certain (*chapter 9*).

Having obtained information about the covariances between the variables from the data and having established the relationships between the covariances and the causal effects from the theory, the causal effects can be estimated (*chapter 10*) and the model tested (*chapter 11*). If the model does not hold against the data, the theory is rejected and should be corrected (*chapter 12*), which brings us back to the beginning. If the model is acceptable according to the test, it is still possible that a simpler theory also fits the same data (*chapter 13*).

Having found a parsimonious theory which fits the data, an interpretation of the final result should be tried and possible practical consequences can be derived (*chapter 14*). Furthermore the question should be raised whether or not the result obtained is acceptable from a theoretical point of view. The answer to this question also implies what one has to do next: to make a new study of the same problem or a part of it, or to accept the theory as it stands (*chapter 15*). Finally, in the *Epilogue*, we want to make some methodological remarks connecting this approach with other work in the field.

One can not, in our view, learn this approach without doing it. A large

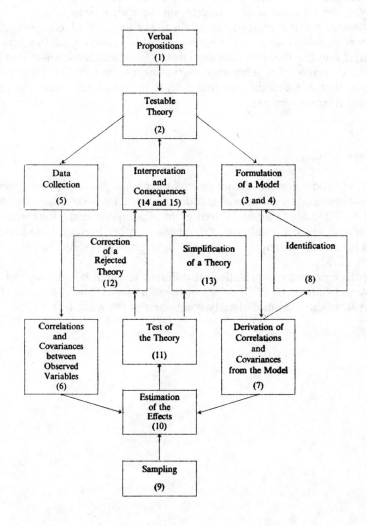

Figure I.1 A Flow Chart of the Testing of Causal Hypotheses on Nonexperimental Data and the Plan of the Book (Chapter Numbers Are Added in Parentheses)

number of exercises is therefore included in the text. In addition the reader is strongly advized to choose an article from the international journals for secondary analysis. It is necessary that the paper contains a correlation matrix for the variables of interest. Suggestions for activities with respect to secondary analyses are included in the exercises on the appropriate places.

Although we strongly recommend the use of the LISREL computer program, the text in this volume is not so specific that the study of this text is only useful if one has this program available. Other programs could also be used for the exercises. The advantage of the use of the LISREL program at this stage is that one becomes familiar with it in a situation where the problems are still relatively simple. *

Further Reading

In this introduction we did not discuss the philosophical problems concerning the use of causal hypotheses in any detail. For a more complete discussion we refer to Blalock's "Causal Inferences in Nonexperimental Research" (1964), which also gives a number of references to other literature. Other relevant texts have been written by Simon (1952), Stegmuller (1960), Suppes (1970) and Vetter (1972).

With respect to the evaluation of different research designs we can refer to Cook and Campbell (1979) as one of the more recent publications in this field, apart from the literature already mentioned in the main text.

---

* Information on the acquisition of the program can be obtained from 1. Scientific Software, P.O. Box 536, Mooresville, IN 46158 USA; tel. (317) 831-6296; 2. SPSS Inc., Marketing Department, Suite 3300, 444 North Michigan Avenue, Chicago, IL 60611, USA; tel. (312) 329-2400.

Chapter 1
Basic Elements of Causal Theories

There are various kinds of research problems. An important distinction can be made between research problems which require descriptive studies and research problems which call for explanatory studies. If, for example one raises the problem whether violence in the streets has increased in recent years, one is clearly dealing with a research problem which asks for a descriptive study. The same is true if one asks the question whether there are equal opportunities on the schools for children of different socio-economic status. An example of a research problem asking for an explanatory study is: "Does the amount of violence on the television influence the amount of violence in the streets?", or: "Why have children from lower socio-economic status less opportunities to go to college than children with higher status?". The last two questions call for theories which specify the causal mechanisms which produce violence in the streets and the unequal opportunities in the schools.

In this text we will restrict the discussion to the explanatory type of research. This means that the study of causal mechanisms is the central topic. The basic concepts which are necessary to formulate causal theories are "units", "variables" and "relationships". These basic concepts will be introduced in the next sections, while the formulation of causal theories will be the topic of chapter 2.

Units

Units or research elements, are the carriers of the characteristics or properties one is interested in. In the "equal opportunity study" suggested above, the unit would be the individual child, while in the "violence study" the unit would be an area during a certain period. The choice of the type of research unit is an important decision, since it may influence the sort of properties and relationships one can study. If one were to choose the school instead of the individual child as the unit in the "equal opportunity study", the theory would turn out to be different. In that case one would be trying to explain why schools with high percentages of people with low socio-economic status will also have a high percentage of people not going to college. But reasons for this relationship are not necessarily the same as reasons for the relationship that individuals from lower classes are less frequently going to college than

Table 1.1   Units in Social Science Research

Level of Aggregation	People	Language	Type of unit Time	Space
low	individual	word	hour	neighbourhood
	dyad	sentence	month	city
up to	small group	paragraph	year	region
	collectivity	chapter	decade	country
high	society	book	century	continent

people from higher social classes. Therefore the choice of the unit is a basic part of the formulation of the research problem.

One can distinguish between at least four types of units that are used widely in one or more of the social sciences. They are listed in Table 1.1. For each type five concrete examples of units are presented, ranked in an increasing order of *aggregation*. The first type of unit deals with human beings directly. In many social sciences the individual is used as the unit of research. Sociologists dealing with survey research, political scientists engaged in opinion polls and business promotors doing marketing research, are all interested in the characteristics of individual people. Social psychologists are especially interested in the behavioral processes which go on in groups of between five and twenty five people. They study what happens in such small groups. In between the individual and the small group one may wish to distinguish the dyad, composed of the relationship between two units (in itself an important unit in a specialization like marriage counseling). Collectivities are larger groups of people, ranging from voluntary associations to huge business organizations. The study of the dynamics of such collectivities is the subject of many disciplines. Finally, a study may focus on total societies. Social and cultural anthropology can be thought of as a science with a long tradition in the comparative study of overall societies.

A different type of unit is language. Words and sentences are the units of interest in various branches of linguistics dealing with more formal aspects of languages. Using some form of content analysis, sociologists have studied letters, political scientists have investigated party programs and other documents of decision makers, while specialists in foreign and domestic literature have studied and compared total books of particular authors and novelists.

Time is another type of unit, obviously giving a dynamic flavour to the studies in which this unit is used. In economic research, *time series analysis* deals with the performance of an economic system through time. For example the supply and demand of a particular consumer good may be followed over a period of several months or years.

Space is the final type of unit to which reference is made in Table 1.1. The importance of spatial patterns per se is especially recognized in the study of social geography, but other social sciences have also organized many of their empirical data on the basis of geographic areas (societies are often equated with countries for example).

The units which are entered in Table 1.1 represent examples of units which are used in actual research. The discussion suggests that some sciences are specialized around the study of a particular unit, but there are also many social sciences in which various types of units and levels of aggregation of those units are in use.

Variables

The units can be described by number of characteristics. If there is no variation in a characteristic across units, one is dealing with a *constant*. The incest taboo is a constant for all human societies. If on the other hand, different units assume different values or scores, one has to do with a *variable*. Marriage forms differ widely across societies (looking at one aspect, there are monogamous and polygamous marriages). Age is another example. On this variable the scores can go from 0 to about 110. If all units in a study have the same value on a characteristic, this characteristic can never be used as an explanation for difference between the units on other characteristics, that is, a constant cannot explain a variable. Therefore we have little interest in such constants and all interest centers on variables. Many variables are routinely measured for individuals from their birth onwards, starting with length, body temperature, skin complexion and sex, but eye color is ignored at the outset since that is a constant and consequently not interesting.

Variables vary in the number of values they can obtain. Some variables like sex can only have two values and are called "*dichotomous variables*". Other variables like skin complexion, can have several values and are therefore called "*polytomous variables*". Furthermore, some variables, such as "number of participants" or "education level" can take on a number of discrete values without anything in between. These variables are called "*discrete* variables". Others, like the variables "length" and "temperature" can take on any value within a certain continuum. Such variables are called "*continuous* variables". Some further distinctions will be made in later chapters where their use is called for.

Discussions about variables are facilitated by giving the variables appropriate names, such as "length" and "body temperature". Naming variables is not always easy. The process of thinking about an appropriate name is sometimes identical to getting a firm grasp on how a social system works or what, for a particular research, is important in such a system.

A mistake which is sometimes made, is that scores on a variable are treated as variables themselves. For example, "rich" and "poor" are not two different variables, but two values of the single variable "income". The same is true for the terms "school dropout" and "graduate", which are values of the single variable "school achievement", and not variables themselves.

Another mistake which is often made is that complex processes are described and labelled as single variables. Discrimination is an example of such a case. According to us, it is a complex process by which certain groups in society obtain less opportunities and rewards (such as income, jobs and education) than other groups. Nevertheless, this process is often treated as if it was a variable. Certainly in the early stages of research this is very confusing and should be avoided.

Relationships

A very common observation is that certain phenomena tend to go together and others do not. For example, we all know that, in general, rich people live in nice houses. As another example, we often will have fever if we are sick, and so on. In fact we know even more than is expressed in such statements. We also know that, in general, poor people live in bad houses and also that we have no fever if we are healthy . Probably most people will even agree with statements like "the richer people become, the nicer the houses they live in" and "the sicker we are, the higher the temperature will be".

Translating such informal statements into the *"variable language"* introduced in the last section, we can say that in each statement two variables are involved, namely "income" and "quality of the house" in the first type of statement and "temperature" and "health" in the second. It is further indicated that certain scores on one variable are often associated with certain scores on the other variable. In such cases it is said that two variables have a *relationship* with each other. So we can state that the variables "income" and "quality of the house" have a relationship with each other, and similarly that there is a relationship between "health" and "temperature".

Scientific theories consist for a large part of statements which indicate the relationships between variables. In some sciences the formulation of such relationships is in the form of the first two statements we have given in this section, in which the scores of variables are emphasized. In general, however, the formulation in variables is preferred. We will follow this practice and specify theories as sets of statements indicating relationships between variables. But in doing so, various formulations are possible. We want especially to make a distinction between covariation and causal relationships.

Covariation and Causation

An essential element of the notion of *causation* is that of "production" or "force". This means that it is hypothesized that a change in one variable (the cause) actually produces a change in another variable (the effect). By contrast, *covariation* merely refers to the fact that certain scores on one variable are often going together with certain scores on the other variable.

Consider the following two variables: "number of cars" and "number of telephones". If one collects information on these two variables for a large number of countries (units) it will turn out that in general a large number of cars goes together with a large number of telephones, and a small number of the first with a small number of the other. So the two variables *covary* clearly with each other, but no causal interpretation should be given to this relationship.

Next consider the following two variables: "number of smokers" and "amount of smoke". If one collects information on these two variables for a large number of rooms it will turn out that large numbers of smokers go together with large amounts of smoke and small numbers of smokers with small amounts of smoke. Thus these variables also covary with each other, but now most people (except the smokers maybe) will agree that a change in the number of smokers will cause a change in the amount of smoke, and that is a causal statement.

The essential difference between the two is that in addition to covariation of the variables, one can argue convincingly that changes in one variable do lead to, i.e. produce or force, changes in the other in case of causal relationships.

Since the idea of production or force is an essential part of the concept of cause, we think this aspect should be made explicit in the verbal formulation of causal hypotheses. An example of such a causal hypothesis is:

(1.1)   Scholastic achievement affects the choice of secondary school

In this hypothesis two variables are encountered: "Scholastic achievement" and "Choice of secondary school". The relationship between the two is expressed in such a way that scholastic achievement is clearly seen as the causal variable, while choice of secondary school is considered as the effect variable.

This causal hypothesis and the meaning of the variables deserves a little more attention since we are going to use it in subsequent sections as well. The unit of analysis that we have in mind is the 11 to 13 years old teenager, leaving the elementary school and about to continue an educational career on a secondary school. In the long run this transition is an important one, at least in Europe, since the choice of secondary school determines to a large extent what kind of job one can obtain later on. The reason for this is that secondary schools differ from each other with respect to the kind of jobs they are giving access to. The lowest-level schools only prepare for technical-manual work, the middle-level schools give access to administrative and semi-professional work and the highest-level schools give access to highly skilled jobs, and usually attendance at and completion of the latter type of school is required for entry to the university.

One might expect that in such an important decision with respect to the future career of pupils qualifications play an important role. That is why we have hypothesized that the scholastic achievement affects this choice. The meaning of the causal hypothesis may now be clarified. It is saying that the scholastic achievement of final-grade elementary school pupils affects the decision to which school type the pupils will go in the following autumn.

An alternative presentation of the causal hypothesis is shown in Figure 1.1. We follow the convention of picturing variables in rectangles, while the causal effect is symbolized by an arrow pointing from cause to effect variable.

The verbal form of a covariation statement is different from the one used for causal hypotheses. An example, for the same two variables as used in the causal statement, is as follows:

> The higher the scholastic achievement, the more advanced the type of secondary school

This hypothesis does not have the causal characteristics of the previous statement. Only an association of scores of the two variables, i.e. covariation of the two variables, is specified without indicating that one causes the other. When the two parts of a statement (before and after the comma) can be interchanged, chances are that one is dealing with a covariation statement. In a causal statement this is not possible. In causal statements the verbs "affect", "influence", "produce" and "determine" are often used.

Unfortunately sometimes the formulation for a covariation is used while causal interpretation is given. In such cases the first variable is the causal variable and the second one the effect variable. This practice is confusing since even in the context of a causal analysis there is a need for covariation statements. So one should not exhaust one's means of expression. A clear distinction between the two types of statements is therefore maintained throughout

Figure 1.1   The Causal Diagram of Hypothesis (1.1); a Direct Causal Relationship

this text and the causal characteristic is clearly specified if the intention is to formulate such a hypothesis.

For practical applications of research findings causal statements are more useful than covariation statements. If policy agencies know, through research, what the causes are of an undesirable situation, manipulation of these causes to improve the situation is possible. If merely covariaton statements are made available through research, the same agencies will have to guess what the effects will be of their policies. One of the difficulties is that covariation of variables does not necessarily imply a causal relationship between the variables. In order to show this a new type of relationship has to be introduced, i.e., a "spurious" relationship.

Spurious Relationships

The elementary form of a causal relationship and covariation relationship involves only two variables. In a *spurious* relationship at least three variables are involved. A spurious relationship refers to the existence of covariation between two variables, which is due, totally or partially, to a common cause of the two variables.

In the last section it was hypothesized that the covariation between scholastic achievement and choice of secondary school was due to a causal effect of the first variable on the second. However, this effect might be completely or partially spurious because of a common cause of both variables. For example the quality of the secondary school could play this role.

In case the covariation between the two variables is completely spurious, the theory consists of only two causal statements:

(1.2a)   Quality of the elementary school determines scholastic achievement

(1.2b)   Quality of the elementary school determines choice of secondary school

The variables "scholastic achievement" and "choice of secondary school" have been introduced earlier. "Quality of the elementary school" is a new variable, which refers to how good the teachers are, how well-equipped the school is and so on. The theory is presented in Figure 1.2.

Note that nothing has been said about the effect of scholastic achievement on the choice of secondary school. This means, by convention, that it is supposed that the direct effect does not exist. Nevertheless one may expect a relationship between these two variables. This inference follows from the theory specified in (1.2a) and (1.2b), since:

> A low-standard elementary school will lead to a low level of scholastic achievement and also to a relatively simple type of secondary school,

while

> A high-standard elementary school will lead to a high level of scholastic achievement and also to a relatively advanced type of secondary school.

Thus, because of these effects of the elementary school, it follows that:

> The higher the level of scholastic achievement, the more advanced type of secondary school training is chosen

This covariation statement follows from the two causal statements (1.2a) and (1.2b). Therefore, according to this theory the covariation between these two variables does not indicate a causal process, but is due to the common causal effect of a third variable. Since this relationship does not idicate a causal process, but can be explained by other variables, it is called a "spurious" relationship. It is important to realize that one will observe covariation between variables of which the relationship is said to be spurious.

The distinction between spurious and causal relationships is very important. Erroneous inferences from the theory are likely if the two are confused. In the school career example—if for the time being we assume the theory as it was formulated in this section to be correct—extra-curricular activities of a child would not change its educational prospects. For the effect of such activities on the child's scholastic achievement is not carried over in the choice of secondary school, since the last relationship is spurious. Extra-curricular activities will have effect only if the variables are causally related.

In general one can summarize that a causal relation between two variables implies that the variables covary (all other variables being equal), but the opposite statement is not true. Covariation between variables does not necessarily imply that the two variables are causally related. As was shown in this section, the relation can also be spurious.

Figure 1.2   Causal Diagram of Hypotheses (1.2); a Spurious Relationship

Direct and Indirect Causal Relationships

Up to this point only *direct* effects were encountered. In *indirect* causal relations the effect of a causal variable on an effect variable is mediated by a third variable. One way to look at *intervening* variables is that they clarify the way in which a causal variable produces changes in an effect variable, i.e. the causal mechanism is made more explicit by intervening variables.

To illustrate indirect causation, a theory is formulated containing the two following statements:

(1.3a)   Quality of the elementary school determines scholastic achievement

(1.3b)   Scholastic achievement determines the choice of secondary school

A causal or path diagram of this theory is presented in Figure 1.3. Note that this time the effect of quality of the elementary school on the choice of secondary school is not specified. By convention, this means that we hypothesize no direct effect between these variables. Nevertheless, according to the present theory, there is a causal effect, but it is mediated through the intervening variable "scholastic achievement" and therefore called an indirect effect.

Suppose for a moment that we would have ignored "scholastic achievement" in our design. In that case we would definitely find a relationship between elementary school quality and secondary school choice. But, someone might ask, what is the causal mechanism underlying that relationship? This is a request for intervening variables, and one of these is the scholastic achievement of students.

The example illustrates clearly that there is no need, fortunately, to verbally specify indirect effects between variables, since these can be inferred from the direct causal effects. This simplifies the theories considerably.

One may come across situations in which a particular causal variable has a direct as well as indirect effect on some effect variable. This is illustrated

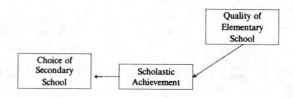

Figure 1.3   Causal Diagram of Hypotheses (1.3); Indirect Causal Relationship

by an extension of our example. We now argue that the process of transition from the elementary school to secondary school can not only be described by statements (1.3a) and (1.3b), but that statement (1.4) should be added, thus creating a fourth theory:

(1.4)   Quality of the elementary school determines the choice of secondary school

This theory is presented in Figure 1.4. Clearly, the quality of the elementary school has both a direct, as well as an indirect effect on the choice of secondary school type.

Reciprocal Causal Relationships

In the causal relationships which we have discussed so far, causation was a one-way process, that is, cause and effect were clearly distinguished and the cause produced the effect. For some theoretical questions the distinction between cause and effect may become blurred. In that case one may be dealing with *reciprocal causation*. A reciprocal (as opposed to one-way) causal relationship is one in which two variables influence one another. The reciprocal effects may also be either direct or indirect.

Apart from the substantive theory the question of whether an investigator has to specify a reciprocal causal relationship between variables depends on the research design within which the variables were measured. As an example, consider the course of social conflicts, in which two parties (students and police, workers and managers, oppositions and regimes, and so on) face each other. Actions from one side are reacted upon by the other party in the conflict. The two parties affect each other's behavior sequentially through time. The actions and reactions can follow one another in a short time period, while the research design might only allow measurement of actions and reactions

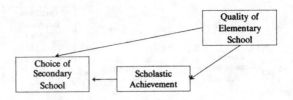

Figure 1.4   Causal Diagram of Hypotheses (1.3) and (1.4); Direct and Indirect Causal Relationship

for each month. Then the investigator may use reciprocal relations as an approximation of the real causal process, since accuracy of the data does not allow the specification of one-way relations.

Another substantive area, in which reciprocal relations are often specified is what sometimes is referred to as "small group research". Homans' studies in particular are famous in this tradition. A rudimentary version of a small-group theory is presented in the following two statements:

(1.5a) The opinion of a respondent influences the opinion of his best friend

(1.5b) The opinion of the best friend influences the opinion of the respondent

Figure 1.5 gives a graphical representation of these statements. The reciprocal relationship is denoted by two seperate arrows, each representing one statement.

In this example the use of reciprocal causation is more or less forced, because a research design in which the conversation of the two friends would be interrupted at certain intervals to ask questions about their opinions at successive points, would be quite artificial. Thus we approximate the causal process by the formulation of reciprocal causation.

The reciprocal causation can also be indirect. An example of such a theory is once more obtained from small group research and deals with the adaptation of a newcomer to the norms of a group:

(1.6a) Deviation from the norms leads to isolation

(1.6b) Isolation leads to knowledge of the norms

(1.6c) Knowledge of the norms decreases the number of deviations from the norms

Figure 1.5 Causal Diagram of Hypotheses (1.5); Reciprocal Relationship

The reciprocal character of this theory is revealed clearly in Figure 1.6.

Note that in the verbal theoretical statement the reciprocity of the relations is not made explicit. Verbal hypotheses as well as path diagrams only express direct causal relations. Covariation of variables, spuriousness, indirect effects and reciprocal effects all result by combining several direct effects.

Conditional Relationships

So far, several types of relations between causal and effect variables have been discussed. Now it is time to introduce a new type of variable, called *conditional variable*. Conditional variables determine the size of causal effects, up to the point that effects which were substantial may disappear once the conditional variable is taken into consideration.

An example of a conditional variable is provided by the theory of the previous section. There, in statement (1.6c), it was said that a person's knowledge of group norms would reduce his deviations from these norms. However taking into account an additional consideration, we now wish to emphasize that this effect will occur only when a newcomer is eager to become a member of the group. This condition on the original effect can be made explicit as follows:

(1.7)   Knowledge of the norms will reduce the deviations from these norms, provided the person wants to become a group member.

This statement is represented graphically in Figure 1.7. The arrow from the conditional variable is not directed towards another variable, but towards another arrow. This indicates that the conditional variable influences the size of the causal effect.

One may argue that causal effects are always conditioned by other variables, i.e. variables which specify the situation in which a process

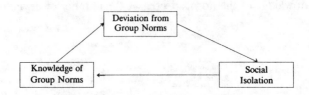

Figure 1.6   Causal Diagram of Hypotheses (1.6); Indirect Reciprocal Relationship

can occur. Thus, persons and the groups in which they act are situated in time and space. In general, such conditions are taken for granted and often they are not made explicit. It also happens that the research is restricted to those units for which the causal effects hold true.

Some Final Remarks

Having discussed the main concepts used for the formulation of causal theories, let us return for a moment to the research problems mentioned in the introduction. The following problems were formulated: (1) Does the amount of violence on the television influence the amount of violence in the streets ? and (2) Why have children of lower socio-economic status less opportunities to go to college than children of high socio-economic status?

Using the concepts introduced in this chapter we can say that in the first research problem two variables are mentioned: "amount of violence on the television" and "amount of violence in the streets". The research question is whether the first variable is a cause of the second variable. The answer to this question is simply yes or no, but to give such an answer is not very simple as we will see in this text.

In the second research problem also two variables have been specified, i.e. "socio-economic status" and "level of secondary school", but now the question is not whether the one has an effect on the other but how this effect comes about. This is a question which asks for an explanation of an already established causal effect. The answer has to be a causal theory which specifies the causal mechanism by introducing intervening variables through which the effect is postulated to occur.

Both examples illustrate that the use of the basic concepts clarifies the research problems. Another important point to mention is that it is not possible to obtain the answers to these two questions by means of experimental research. This is a very common situation in the social sciences. The way in which non-experimental research can give an answer to such questions about

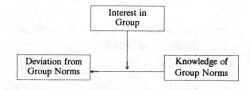

Figure 1.7   Causal Diagram of Hypotheses (1.6c) and (1.7); Conditional relationship

cause and effect is the topic of this book. The first step one has to take is that
the theoretical ideas which can be formed on the basis of the literature should
be formulated as a causal theory which is suitable for testing. This is the issue
of the next chapter.

Further Reading

With respect to the basic concepts: units, variables and relationships, discussions can be found in many methodology textbooks. A good example is Riley
(1963). A basic introduction to the concepts of causal theories is hard to find,
since most of the time the discussion is already put in mathematical form.
At least two texts, however, give a brief nontechnical introduction. These are
Blalock's book on "Causal Inferences in Nonexperimental Research" (1964),
especially the introduction, and his book "Theory Construction" (1969a),
mainly chapter 2. The problem of conditional relationships is discussed especially by Heise in the first chapter of his book "Causal Analysis" (1975).
However, a disadvantage of this text is that it is set in a somewhat different
conceptual framework, which could be confusing.

With respect to the formulation of reciprocal causal relationships a debate
was held in econometrics. Wold argued in defense of one-way causal relationships. Although his ideas were very stimulating, reciprocal causal relationships
have nevertheless been accepted as approximations of processes which develop
too fast to obtain measurements for each point in time (Basman 1963, Fisher
1969 and 1970, Strotz and Wold 1960). A rather nontechnical discussion of
this topic can be found in Blalock (1969a) and in Schmidt (1977). In our
text no special attention is given to reciprocal relationships because they do
not provide further problems in the LISREL approach, except with respect to
identification as we shall see.

Exercises

1.1 A list of six hypotheses is presented. Can you indicate the variables in
these statements and suggest the units of research which could be used to
obtain data and test these hypotheses?
(*a*) Income partially determines voting behavior.
(*b*) The scholastic achievement of an elementary school pupil affects his or her
teacher's recommendation of a secondary school.
(*c*) The teacher's recommendation of a certain secondary school determines
the pupil's choice of secondary school.

(d)The policies of multinational corporations influence the behavior of governments.

(e)Birth rates of countries have strong effects on rate of economic growth.

(f)The frequent use of a particular word in a text is an indication of the importance attached to this word by the author.

1.2 Translate the following propositions into statements which specify relationships between variables.

(a) Older people are more often ill than younger people.

(b)Quite often older people have had less schooling than younger people.

(c) Usually children from higher class families obtain better positions in society than children from lower class families.

(d)Violence on TV is probably one of the factors which has led to more violence in the streets.

(e) Pollution is a danger to the human race.

(f) The USSR and USA are involved in an arms race.

1.3 Are the relationships which you have specified to answer question 2 covariation statements or causal statements? If you have formulated a causal hypothesis, try now to formulate the same relationship as a covariation statement, and vice versa.

1.4 Do you think that any of the propositions in question represents a spurious relationship? If so, specify the common cause

1.5 A number of questions are asked with respect to the following causal diagram:

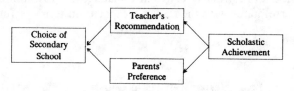

(a)Formulate all direct causal effects.

(b) What are the indirect effects which can be derived from these direct effects?

(c)Indicate all spurious relationships. Which variables produce (or, which variable produces) the spurious relationships?

(d)Could you imagine that a reciprocal relationship occurred somewhere in this theory?

(e) This theory does not hold in general. Can you indicate some of the conditions which are probably required?

Chapter 2
Formulation of Causal Theories

The basic elements of causal theories were mentioned in the first chapter. In this chapter the formulation of causal theories will be discussed. First of all the translation from verbal reports of a particular empirical process to a set of causal hypotheses will be illustrated. Next the general structure of valid tests of such causal hypotheses is discussed. Statistical tests can only be carried out after the data have been gathered. Yet it is important to discuss testing at this point, since a correct test at the stage of data analysis presupposes that the data collection and formulation of causal theories has been carried out in certain specified ways. A valid test of the theory may only be possible when some additional variables are introduced in the model. Therefore, in the next sections the discussion of the initial causal theory is extended first by considering whether additional variables have to be incorporated and second by checking if additional causal effects have to be specified. The possibility of conditional relationships and the problem of disturbances in the relationships are also discussed. Finally some procedures are suggested to simplify the causal theories in order to arrive at a manageable research design, that is one which corresponds with the research capacity in terms of funds, time and manpower.

From Verbal Reports to Causal Hypotheses

The starting point of causal modelling is in general a process about which an investigator wants to get more information. For example, as part of the more general field of social mobility studies, there has been special interest in the transition process from the elementary school to the secondary school. Obviously there are many more of such processes in the social sciences.

Information about processes like these can often be found in reports of experts in the particular field of interest. Such reports are rarely written in a form in which concepts like units, variables and causal effects are used. Much ingenuity is often required to make the transition from the verbal reports to causal hypotheses. There are no fixed rules which can be given to do this, since it depends very much on the substantive topic of interest. The example which follows illustrates one way to arrive at an initial causal theory.

The verbal report we have used for our study of school career was given by a test bureau which also plays a role in this process. This bureau suggested the following sequence of events to come to a decision concerning the choice of a secondary school:

> In January the head of the elementary school gives a recommendation concerning the type of secondary school which seems appropriate for the pupils. This recommendation is made available to the parents and the test bureau. Subsequently the parents apply for a place in the school of their choice for the child. The application consists of some personal data (sex of pupil and occupation of the parents) and the teacher's recommendation. In February or March a school achievement test is administered. About a month later the score on this test is made available to the school. The school informs the assignment committees of the secondary schools about this result. In these committees the final decision with respect to the choice of secondary school is made.

This example shows that there can be quite a difference between such verbal reports and the causal hypotheses which should be the building blocks of our causal theory. At this point it is not even evident what the relevant variables are in this process.

This example shows that the first thing which has to be done is to determine the list of variables which are important in the process to be studied. In the text above various parties have been mentioned which influence the process. Actions of each party which influences the process can be seen as the relevant variables. This approach suggests the following variables: the "teacher's recommendation"; the "parents' preference" (expressed in the application); the "pupil's school test results" and the "committee's decision", which we will call the "choice of secondary school".

The next step is the determination of the *causal order* of the variables. Indicators for the causal order can be found in the sequence of the events as reported. Another source of information is an analysis of the flow of information or material or people through the system. In our example the causal order of the variables is rather simple and clearly indicated in the verbal report. The process starts with the teacher's recommendation, followed by the parents' preference, when they send in an application. Subsequently the school test becomes available and finally the choice of the secondary school is determined by the assignment committee.

Now the causal hypotheses can be specified. At this point, *causal diagrams* can be very useful. First of all, the names of the variables are written down with the position of the variables indicating the causal order, then the causal hypotheses are specified by introducing arrows between the variables for which one expects direct causal effects. For our example this process leads to the causal diagram presented in Figure 2.1. This causal theory can be summarized with two statements:

(2.1a) The choice of secondary school is influenced by teacher's recommendations, parents' preference and the school test score

(2.1b) The parents' preference is influenced by teacher's recommendations

It is a convention that effects which are not specified are supposed to be zero. It can be seen that no effects of teacher's recommendation and parents' preference on the school test score have been specified, despite the fact that this last variable appears later in the causal ordering. There simply are no theoretical arguments for including these effects.

After this free translation of the verbal account in a causal theory, it is often very useful to check whether or not the preliminary theory seems complete. In the theory set out so far, no causal effect was specified relating the teacher's recommendations and the test result. Yet one may certainly expect covariation between these two variables. We could be satisfied with an unexplained covariation as we see later, but thinking about the reason underlying this covariation we come up with a variable which can not be left out of the theory; this is "scholastic achievement". This variable is very crucial in the whole process, as is reflected in the following extension of the theory:

(2.1c) Scholastic achievement has direct causal effects on the teacher's recommendation, the parents' preference and the school test score

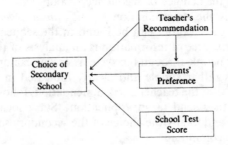

Figure 2.1   Causal Diagram Representing the Causal Hypotheses for the School Career Example

Introduction of these effects in the diagram leads to Figure 2.2.

It should be clear from the discussion in the first chapter that the introduction of this new variable affects the interpretation of the relationships considerably. One consequence is that the relationship between teacher's recommendation and parents' preference is not only hypothesized as a direct causal effect, but also as a spurious relationship due to the common cause, scholastic achievement. Similar remarks can also be made for most of the other relationships between the original variables. Therefore this variable has to be introduced in the theory, even though the verbal report does not refer to this variable explicitly. Clearly, theory formulation is an active process.

The illustration shows that it is very difficult to present general rules for the formulation of causal theories. The process depends very much on the topic of concern. The following steps can be recommended: (1) make a list of all variables which might be relevant; (2)indicate the causal ordering of the variables; (3)specify the causal hypotheses. The way in which one actually proceeds with these three steps depends largely on the substantive research undertaken and prior knowledge in the area.

Testing Causal Hypotheses

Evidently there is no guarantee that the ideas which resulted in a particular causal theory, are totally or even partially correct. Empirical data have somehow to be used to correct any errors of judgment. For example, both the verbal report of the school transition as well as our causal hypotheses concerning this process, suggest that the teacher's recommendation affects the parents' preference. However, the parents might as well have so much information on the child's prospects, that they formulate their preference independently from

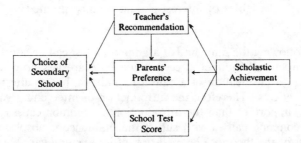

Figure 2.2.   Causal Diagram of a More Complete Causal Theory for the
School Career Example

the teacher. This argument would imply a zero effect of teacher's recommendation on parents' preference and the observable covariation would represent
a spurious relationship (the reader may want to check this). By contrast it is
possible that the parents do not trust their own judgment and completely rely
on the teacher's recommendation. This would mean that the effect of scholastic achievement on parents' preference is indirect and not direct. Which one
of these alternatives is correct is unclear without data and without a test of
these hypotheses.

A problem with causal hypotheses is that the "causal force" is not observable, since this is a theoretical notion. Only the degree of covariation can be
determined from data. But we have seen in the first chapter that covariation
is not a proof for a causal relationship since covariation can also be produced
by common causes of the variables of interest.

Although there is no proof of the existence of causality, causal hypotheses
can still be falsified. In general one can say that *a causal hypothesis is falsified
if the strength of the spurious relationship between the variables of interest is equal
to the observed covariation between these variables*. This rule is based on the
fact that an alternative explanation has been given for the observed relationship. In case the covariation and the spurious relationship are not equal, there
are two possible explanations: either there is a causal effect between the variables (and this is what we usually want to establish), or an important common
cause has been omitted from the research. This last possibility, the omission
of relevant common causal variables, is an important obstacle in testing. It
indicates that a researcher should take care from the start to introduce as
many common causes as possible in the research, in order to make the test of
the causal hypotheses a valid one, and to avoid criticism after the research has
been done. A formal test of these hypotheses will be discussed in chapter 11.
Here we merely indicate that such tests are possible and that in order to do
a valid statistical test, all important common causes (sometimes called *control
variables*) of the variables of interest should be incorporated in the research
design.

Roughly following the same line of argument, a test can be constructed with
respect to direct and indirect effects. Such tests are less crucial since they
do not lead to a falsification of a causal hypothesis, but to alternative interpretations of effects. Therefore the introduction of intervening variables in a
theory is less important than the introduction of common causes. The incorporation of common causes with substantial influence is absolutely essential
for a fair test of the theory. The inclusion of intervening variables refines the
interpretations which can be given. Further details of tests will be given in
chapter 11.

Necessary Extensions of Causal Theories

From the previous discussions on theory testing, it follows that the common causes for each pair of cause and effect variables have to be introduced in a complete causal theory. If this is not done, tests of the causal effects are invalid and the estimates of the sizes of the effects will be incorrect. This test requirement introduces a new and unavoidable problem. The problem is that the incorporation of a common cause implies the introduction of two new causal hypotheses in the theory, for which one has to start the search again for common causes. To illustrate, suppose the original hypothesis consists of a causal variable x, which influences dependent variable y. Subsequently a variable T is entered as a common cause of both x and y, that is, there are now two additional hypotheses maintaining that T causes x and that T causes y. But now following the same strategy, one has to search for variables that affect both T and x, and also for variables that affect both T and y. A second configuration arises when two common causes of x and y have entered the theory; T_1 and T_2. Here one may wonder if the common causes of T_1 and T_2 have to be incorporated in the theory in order to derive a valid test. We will treat these two situations separately, i.e. a distinction is maintained between common causes of (1) a new variable—T—and one of the variables in the original hypotheses—x or y—, and (2) of two new variables on T_1 and T_2. We start by discussing the first type.

In the earlier example it was hypothesized that scholastic achievement affected the teacher's recommendation. However at least a part of this relationship may be spurious because of an additional variable. We think that it is plausible to advance the following hypothesis:

(2.1d) The quality of the elementary school affects the pupil's scholastic achievement and the teacher's recommendation

Having introduced the effect of quality of the elementary school on scholastic achievement, one other additional variable comes to mind: the socio-economic status of the pupil's parents. The impact of this variable is reflected in the following hypothesis:

> The socio-economic status of the parents affects the choice of elementary school (which equals the quality of elementary school), and the scholastic achievement of the pupil

Now that the variable socio-economic status has been entered one can go on to ask for a variable which might be a common cause of socio-economic status of the parents and scholastic achievement of the child. In this process one is forced backwards down the causal chain of events. In this particular example, one can argue that the status of the grandparents affects the status of the pupil's parents, but it is very unlikely that this 'grandparent'-variable has any direct effect at all on the scholastic achievement of the student. Consequently this variable is not a common cause of both variables. The same applies to other variables. For this reason we think that the inclusion of socio-economic status of the parents suffices.

We see that the time distance between the newly introduced variables (T_i) and the variables of the original hypotheses (x or y) is becoming larger and larger. Consequently the introduction of new variables will come to a natural end, since the new variables do not cause the x and the y variables and thus are unlikely to be a common cause.

The same phenomenon will not occur if we shift our attention to the introduction of common causes of pairs of variables which are both new (T_1 and T_2). The variables "quality of elementary school" and "parents' socio-economic status" are an example. Both are newly introduced variables, and we have hypothesized that the status affects the type of schooling. According to the principle that all common causes have to be introduced in order to create a valid test and estimate of the effect from status to elementary school quality, the cycle of theory formation has to start all over again at this point. But having introduced the new variables, the common causes of the new variables have to be introduced which is an endless process. Therefore the investigator has to decide where to stop with the introduction of new variables. For the last introduced causal variables, the causal effects can not be tested correctly because the common causes have not been introduced. Therefore it is better not to specify causal effects between these variables but rather leave the covariation between these variables unexplained. These variables, which are not explained by other variables in the theory are called *predetermined* or *exogenous* variables. (In general the two names indicate the same kinds of variables but strictly speaking the class of predetermined variables is broader since it also contains effect variables measured at an earlier point in time, that is, lagged endogenous variables.) By contrast the other variables which one does try to explain are referred to as *endogenous* or *jointly dependent* variables.

According to the last principle we have decided to split up the last hypothesis into two elements, one causal hypothesis:

(2.1e)   The socio-economic status of the parents affects the scholastic achievement of the pupil and one covariance statement:

(2.1f) The predetermined variables socio-economic status and quality of elementary school covary with each other.

In diagrams covariation statements like (2.1f) are usually symbolized by lines connecting the variables with arrows pointing in both directions (see Figure 2.3). It should be noted that these two-way curves create a new type of relationship which has not been distinguished yet. In chapter 1 it was indicated that the covariation of two variables could be the result of direct effects, indirect effects and spurious relationships. But now it is apparent that the covariation between some variables may be produced by either spurious relationships or indirect effects. For example, in Figure 2.3 the covariation between "socio-economic status" and "scholastic achievement" can be partially a spurious relationship as a result of variables which are the common causes of the two predetermined variables, and partially an indirect effect from socio-economic status via school quality to scholastic achievement. Since it is unclear what these covariations are and from which variable they come, they are called *joint effects*. This is the price for not having specified the causal mechanism that links the predetermined variables.

Completeness Check with an Effect Matrix

After the introduction of a number of new variables in a causal theory it is fruitful to check whether the theory is complete in terms of relationships. Therefore, we shall concentrate now on the detection of omitted causal effects.

A useful tool for this purpose is the *"effect matrix"*, one of which is presented in Table 2.1. The matrix is constructed by listing all the variables of a causal

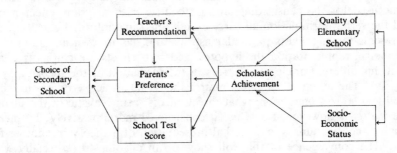

Figure 2.3   Causal Diagram of the Extended Causal Theory of School Career

Table 2.1   Effect Matrix of the Preliminary School Career Theory

Variable as Effect		SA	TR	PP	SS	CS	Variable as Cause Quality of Elementary School	Socio- Economic Status
Scholastic Achievement	SA	–	0	0	0	0	1	1
Teacher's Recommendation	TR	1	–	0	0	0	1	0
Parents' Preference	PP	1	1	–	0	0	0	0
School Test Score	SS	1	0	0	–	0	0	0
Choice of Secondary School	CS	0	1	1	1	–	0	0

0 means no causal effect specified;
1 means causal effect hypothesized.

theory in the column headings and names of all effect variables in front of the rows. Since the predetermined variables are, by definition, not considered as effect variables in a particular theory, they need not to be listed in the rows. It is convenient to list the predetermined variables as the extreme right hand columns. Once the variable names are listed in this way, the matrix is filled with zeros and ones. If one hypothesizes a direct effect from a causal variable to an effect variable, the number 1 is entered in the relevant cell. If no direct effect is expected a 0 is entered.

Specifically, looking at the first row of Table 2.1, one starts thinking which variables mentioned in the column headings could be direct causes of scholastic achievement. Because of the time order of the variables we think that only "parents' status" and "elementary school quality" can have a direct effect on "scholastic achievement". Therefore we fill in a 'one' in the last two cells of the first row and elsewhere zeros. In the same way all rows can be filled with ones and zeros depending on whether one expects a direct causal effect or not.

The construction of an effect matrix is especially helpful in realizing where one has omitted direct causal effects. The zero restrictions of a causal theory are made very explicit, more so than in a *"path diagram"*, which is another name used for the causal diagram. Of course, path diagram, effect matrix and the verbal formulation all carry exactly the same information. Yet, each representation highlights particular aspects and has its own advantages. In the matrix representation the hypothesized zero effects are emphasized and from this different angle some errors in the formation of the theory may be avoided. The filling of the effect matrix should be an active pocess in which one hypothesizes once more what direct effects seem realistic in the theory. The matrix is however also of use if constructed more 'passively', by merely copying the diagrammatic or verbal presentation of a theory in another format. The convenience of this will show up in chapter 10 (especially when dealing with the LISREL program).

Returning to the school career example, we now come to realize that one effect has been omitted. We have not specified the possibility that the

(2.1g) Parents' socio-economic status influences the parents' preference

The diagram and effect matrix should be changed accordingly.

At this point we think that all important effects have been introduced in the theory. Many additional effects could have been suggested, but probably these effects would be very small. Since *parsimony* of theories is attractive, they have been omitted.

Conditional Relationships

The last check in the formulation stage is a check on conditional relationships. In the school career example, the region did establish such conditional effects in the past. In that time the relationship between scholastic achievement and choice of secondary school was different in regions with many schools as opposed to few schools. However, several measures have been taken to ensure equal access to secondary schools in all regions of the Netherlands and consequently the effect may now only exist in very few regions. Therefore the effect is ignored.

Having gone through all these steps, one can be quite sure that the theory is complete according to current knowledge. However, this does not mean that all the causal relations will operate without exceptions. In general, one should anticipate disturbances in the relations. The next section explores the nature of these disturbances in more detail.

Disturbances

Four main arguments point to the presence of disturbances in scientific theories. The first three are especially relevant for theories dealing with social phenomena. First, the lack of explanatory power of many social science theories may indicate that the right questions have not been raised yet and the right variables have not been identified. Reformulations of existing problems have caused revolutionary changes in other sciences. Secondly, in certain areas of social science research the number of relevant variables which are needed for exact description of social processes may be overwhelming. For reasons of parsimony the less important variables may be ignored, thus introducing uncertainty in relationships. A third argument which leads towards the expectation of disturbances is that there will be, next to predictability, also an element of unpredictability in human behavior. Finally, the measurement of social variables is usually a hazardous process, in which one may anticipate numerous errors. There is a tremendous difference between the care, precision and perfection used in measurement of the natural science variables compared to the average social science survey. Such unreliability in measurement is a source of disturbance and may even cause explanatory errors.

There is some truth in all four arguments. In order to deal with these arguments, the *disturbance* term is introduced into our theory. In summary, the disturbance term may represent: (1) the effect of unknown variables, (2) the effect of known but omitted variables, (3) the randomness of human behavior, and (4) measurement error. If relationships contain a disturbance term they are called *stochastic relations*. By contrast, relationships without disturbances which are exactly specified are referred to as *deterministic relations*.

In social science theory such as developed in this chapter, the relationships are stochastic even after all of the steps of the previous sections have been carefully followed. To have gone through these procedures ensures that all important variables have been incorporated, but several minor variables may still have been ignored. Therefore, the disturbance term should be considered as a new type of variable representing all of these omitted variables. In general it should be plausible to argue that:

(2.1h) The omitted variables have only minor effects on the endogenous variables, they are unrelated with each other, and they are unrelated with the predetermined variables

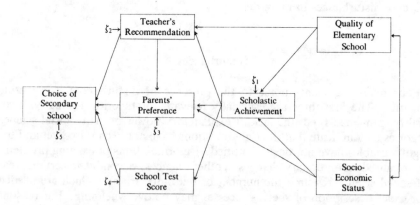

Figure 2.4   The Causal Diagram of the Complete Theory of School Career developed in this Chapter

Evidently, this hypothesis is only trustworthy if one has devoted enough time to finding the most important variables and entering the common causes for all pairs of variables in the theory except the predetermined ones. But certainty can never be obtained. Only further research, in which different sets of variables are used, can establish whether the last statement is correct.

In causal diagrams the disturbance "variables" are not shown in rectangles. Since they cannot be identified with names, a short symbol is chosen. For each endogenous variable the disturbance is represented by ζ_i (pronounce "zeta sub i"), where the subscript i differs for the different variables. In Figure 2.4 the disturbance terms have been entered. This path diagram represents the complete school career theory.

Simplification of Causal Theories

In this chapter we have seen that a large number of variables have to be introduced in causal theories in order to make causal hypotheses testable. This process can lead to very complex theories for which data collection becomes too expensive or time consuming within a single research project. Sometimes the complexity is a consequence of an ambitious starting point chosen by the investigator. In such a case the investigator may come to reconsider his initial point of departure. However, if the starting point cannot be changed, there is still another option which may help to solve the problem: the deletion of variables from the theory. Clearly, in view of the discussion in this chapter, one cannot omit variables arbitrarily. The arguments have indicated that this could lead to invalid tests of the theory. Instead the following rules for simplification of theories are suggested: (1) Common causes of variables which are related by direct causal effects cannot be left out of the theory; (2) Intervening variables can be omitted from the theory without harming the test procedures of causal hypotheses in the theory; (3) Variables which influence either cause or effect variables but not both, can be omitted without harming the test procedures of causal hypotheses in the theory.

The first rule follows directly from the earlier discussions and does not need any further comments. Ommiting intervening variables will change some indirect effects into direct effects. This simplification will not reduce the possibilities to test these causal hypotheses. Of course, the test to determine whether the effects were indirect or direct will not be possible anymore after the deletion of intervening variables. The third rule is also in line with the arguments of this chapter. The price one has to pay for this kind of simplification is not in the field of testing, but possibly in the extent with which some dependent variables can be explained by the introduced explanatory variables.

A theory which is simplified according to these rules will reveal the minimum number of variables that should be measured in the data-gathering stage, in order to assure a valid empirical test of the causal hypotheses of interest.

In the school career example, simplification is not really needed, since this theory is rather simple. In part, this is the result of the fact that we have applied the third rule from the start. In this way pupil's "IQ" is left out as a variable, even though this variable will certainly affect scholastic achievement. But pupil's IQ cannot directly affect any of the other variables. Therefore this variable does not produce any spurious relationship and can thus be omitted. As a negative result of this omission, we may expect that differences in scholastic achievement will not be explained as well as it would have been possible otherwise.

With respect to the second rule it can be seen in the causal diagram of the theory that simplifications are possible. If one is mainly interested in the size of the effect of scholastic achievement on choice of secondary school, the intervening variables "teacher's recommendation", "parents' preference" and "school test score" could be left out of the theory without harming the validity of test and estimation of the size of the effect of scholastic achievement on choice of secondary school. The causal theory which results after these simplifications is presented in Figure 2.5. This form indicates the minimum number of variables which have to be measured in order to test this set of causal hypotheses. The reader should check that some new direct effects appear in this theory after the simplification, since some indirect effects are changed into direct effects.

Having discussed the formulation of verbal causal hypotheses, the next step will bring us from the verbal statements to mathematical formulations of the hypotheses. In this step the precision with which the hypotheses are formulated will be increased. It will also allow more formal derivations from the theory, which are needed for the confrontation of the theory with empirical data.

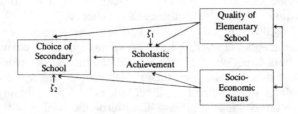

Figure 2.5   The Causal Diagram of the Simplified Theory of School Career derived from Figure 2.4

Further Reading

The best reference for a non-technical discussion of the topic of this chapter can be found in Blalock's book on "Theory Construction" (1969a). Chapters 2 and 3 in particular provide some more information. The topic is discussed from a different starting point and some more examples from the social science literature are given. A non-technical discussion of the testing of causal models is very hard to find. Again Blalock's "Causal Inferences in Nonexperimental Research", chapter 1, is close to what we have said in this chapter. The transition of verbal reports into causal models has been studied by Axelrod et.al. (1976). The reader might find in his book useful suggestions for this otherwise very unstructured task.

Exercises

2.1 Often it is very difficult to recast a verbal report of a process directly into a causal theory. As an exercise we present parts of the text which Richardson (1960) has used to formulate his famous arms race theory. For this purpose Richardson used a number of texts of political decision makers of this time. He starts with a speech of the Defense Minister of Jedesland:

"The intentions of our country are entirely pacifist. We have given ample evidence of this by the treaties which we have recently concluded with our neighbors. Yet, when we consider the state of unrest in the world at large and the menaces by which we are surrounded, we should be failing in our duty as a government if we did not take adequate steps to increase the defenses of our beloved land".

Next, Winston Churchill is cited on a point of view which presents another aspect of the picture of arms races. In 1923, Churchill spoke about the constraints which exist with respect to armaments:

"Believing that there are practically no checks upon German naval expansion except those imposed by the increasing difficulties of getting money, I have had the enclosed report prepared with a view to showing how far those limitations are becoming effective. It is clear that they are becoming terribly effective".

These two statements give an indication of the way nations decide about their defense budgets. Try to formulate on the basis of these two verbal reports a causal theory which might explain arms races. Restrict the theory to only two groups of nations which behave in the same way.

2.2 Verbal reports are not always available. That does not mean that in such cases theory formation is impossible. As an exercise, we will try to develop a theory for an organization which wants to gain some benefit for its members (for example, a trade union or civil rights group). In its efforts to meet the targets, the organization has to choose between a number of different actions, from "very violent" to "nonviolent". In the choice of a particular type of action, the organization has to take into account that the members are less willing to participate in more violent actions.

(*a*)Formulate this last proposition in a causal hypothesis.

(*b*) We think that *expected success* and *expected risk* also play a role in the decision to participate. Formulate a causal theory with these four variables.

(*c*)Present this theory in a causal diagram.

(*d*)What kind of relationship do you forsee between "expected success" and "expected risk"?

(*e*) Do you expect a direct effect from the variable "action violence" to "willingness to participate"? Why?

(*f*) Can we ever prove that "action violence" affects "willingness to participate in the action"?

(*g*)What do we have to do to give this hypothesis a fair chance of being rejected?

(*h*)Do you think that all important variables have been introduced in the theory?

(*i*)Are all important effects introduced in the theory? (The reader can check this by use of an effect matrix).

(*j*)If all important variables are introduced, what can we say about the disturbance terms?

(*k*) Between which of the four variables do you expect covariation according to your theory?

2.3 Scientific reports are a third source of information on causal hypotheses. Select an article for secondary analysis from a scientific journal. It is necessary that the paper contains a correlation matrix for the variables of interest.

(*a*)Read the theoretical introduction of the paper and try to formulate the causal theory suggested by the author. Present the theory in verbal as well as diagrammatical form.

(*b*) Indicate whether you think that the theory of the author is complete. If not, specify your own ideas.

(*c*)Summarize your findings as if it was the first part of a paper like the one of the author. Indicate clearly why you have introduced changes in the original theory. (If there are other authors who have stated the same point as you, it is necessary to make a reference to them).

Chapter 3
Formulation of
Linear Structural Equations

So far we have discussed whether one variable had an effect on another or not. In order to determine and test the effects, however, the form of the relationships has to be established. With respect to these relationships, it is important to know whether or not the size of the effect depends on the value of the causal variable. If not, the effect is simply proportional to the change in the causal variable and the relationship will be linear; if the size of the effect depends on the value of the causal variable, the form of the causal relationship may be more complicated.

It is also important to determine whether the size of an effect associated with one particular causal variable depends on the value of other causal variables. If it does, the effects of the two variables are not additive; if, on the other hand, the impact of one variable is independent of the value of other variables the effects are additive.

Often the same substantive variables can be measured or expressed in a number of different scales. An income variable can be expressed in pounds, dollars or other currencies; temperature can be measured in degrees centigrade, or Fahrenheit as well as by other temperature scales; age in months, years or 5-year intervals. In order to determine the existence of any effects between such variables in one particular research project, the type of scale that is used is quite arbitrary. Yet one may have to translate the results to other measurement scales for purposes of comparison across studies. This can be done by transformation of the variables. It may also affect the parameter values which describe a relationship. A transformation, consisting of two steps, which is applied frequently in social science research, is standardization. The procedure is introduced briefly in this chapter.

Linear Relations

The relationship between variables can take on different forms. There is an important distinction between linear and nonlinear forms. *Linear* forms are used very frequently in research and this text will soon concentrate entirely on such linear forms. The reason is that several empirical relationships are indeed

Table 3.1   Some Hypothetical Data on Monthly Income (y) and Years of
Employment(x), summarized in Equation $y = 300 + 20x$

Monthly Income in Dollars y	Years of Employment x
300	0
320	1
340	2
360	3
500	10
520	11
700	20
720	21

linear in form. In addition, it has been shown that various nonlinear relationships can be either approximated by or transformed into linear relationships.
We now review some basic characteristics of the linear form.

As an example consider the causal hypothesis that "job experience" influences someone's "income". More specifically, the following statement illustrates what is meant by a linear relation:

> An employee earns $300 per month during the first year of employ-
> ment and receives a raise of $20 per month for each year that he/she
> works in the same job.

"Number of years of employment" and "income" are the two variables that
we are concerned with here. For the sake of convenience, we indicate the
variable "income" with the symbol y and the variable "years of employment"
with x.

Some data points, corresponding with the above statement, are presented in
Table 3.1. These data points can be plotted in a graph in which each point
represents the combination of a value of y and a value of x. Figure 3.1 gives
a graphical representation of the data.

A straight line can be drawn to connect the various points of Table 3.1.
Note that it was not necessary to plot all the data points of Table 3.1 because
a straight line is determined by only two points. Apart from the geometric
representation, the data points can also be summarized by an equation, i.e.
by

$$y = 300 + 20x \qquad (3.1)$$

Equation (3.1) is a mathematical representation of the relationship which
was described earlier in verbal form. For, according to the equation, even
without job experience, the employee's income will be $300, but if he has

worked 10 years ($x = 10$) in a job he will earn 10 times 20 dollars more. This relationship is called linear because of the form—a straight line—as shown in Figure 3.1.

A characteristic feature of a linear relation is that the same change in x (the cause, in terminology of chapter 1) will produce an equal amount of change in y. This is illustrated clearly in Table 3.1 as well as in Figure 3.1: the increase in the number of years of employment from 0 to 1, 1 to 2, 10 to 11 or 20 to 21, all result in a fixed increase ($20) in monthly income. The constant "20" indicates the effect on y of a one unit change in x. This constant is called the *slope* of the plotted line and refers to the degree to which the line slopes. The other number in the equation, 300, is called the *intercept*; it indicates at what point the vertical axis is intercepted when the x-value is zero. Given the constant 20 (the slope) and the value $y = 300$ for $x = 0$ (the intercept), the linear function is determined which in this case is the linear equation (3.1). Figure 3.1 can be drawn directly from knowledge of the slope and intercept, i.e., if we know equation (3.1). This graphic method is an alternative to plotting any two points from Table 3.1.

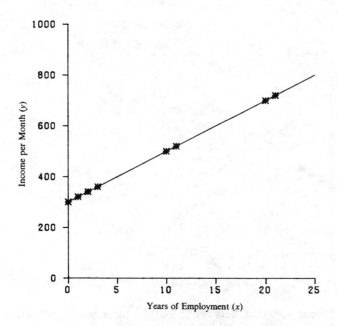

Figure 3.1   Linear Relation between Monthly Income (y) and Years of Employment(x), where $y = 300 + 20x$

Table 3.2   Some Hypothetical Data on Monthly Income (y) and Years of
Employment (x), Summarized in Equation $y = 250 + 30x$

Monthly Income in Dollars y	Years of Employment x
250	0
280	1
310	2
340	3
550	10
580	11
850	20
880	21

Although the slope and intercept are constant for all employees of one
particular institution, they are not necessarily the same across institutions.
Therefore, they are called *parameters*. In a second institution a corresponding
statement could be:

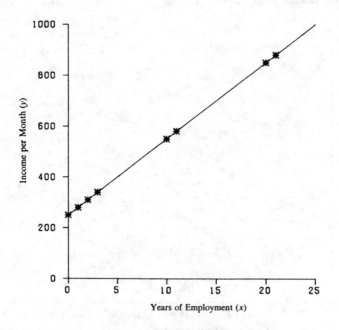

Figure 3.2   Linear Relation between Monthly Income (y) and Years of
Employment (x), where $y = 250 + 30x$

An employee earns $250 per month during the first year of employment and receives a raise of $30 per month for each year that he works in the same job.

This statement can be translated into the following mathematical form:

$$y = 250 + 30x \qquad (3.2)$$

Table 3.2 gives eight pairs of values for the variables and Figure 3.2 represents the relationship graphically. Both of the relationships in equations (3.1) and (3.2) are linear, but they have different parameter values. In the second relationship the employee starts with a lower income, but the effect of experience is larger. An infinite number of linear relationships can be formulated. Their verbal form will always be:

An employee earns an amount α during the first year and receives a raise of amount γ in each additional year he/she works in the job.

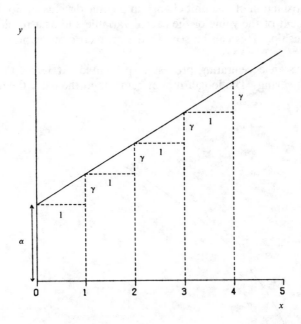

Figure 3.3 General Form of Linear Relation $y = \alpha + \gamma x$, where y and x are Variables, and α and γ are Parameters representing Intercept and Slope

In mathematical form this is presented as:
$$y = \alpha + \gamma x \tag{3.3}$$
Equation (3.3) gives the general mathematical formulation of a linear relationship. This formulation of the relationship can be used in any case where it is realistic to argue that:

> A change of one unit in x will result in a change in y of γ, whatever the value of x itself.

Here γ represents the effect of x on y and α represents the value of y when x is equal to zero. A geometric representation of this general case is given in Figure 3.3

Obviously the form of the relationship is not always linear. There are many cases in which the effect of a variable depends on the value it assumes. Three empirical examples of this from the social sciences are given in Figure 3.4, 3.5 and 3.6.

In Figure 3.4 a levelling-off effect is shown. When the income increases, the effect on satisfaction of one unit change in income decreases. So this effect is not independent of the value of the causal variable and as a result it is not a linear relationship. This can be seen in the geometric representation given in Figure 3.4.

In Figure 3.5 an accelerating process is presented. It refers to the well known effect of saving. The longer money remains in the bank the larger the

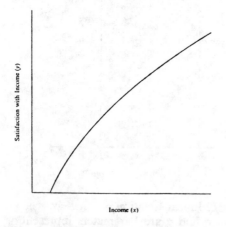

Figure 3.4   The Decreasing Effect of Income Increments on Satisfaction

yearly increment will be. Apparently the effect also depends on the value of the causal variable. Once again the relationship is not linear, as Figure 3.5 shows.

Finally a combination of the previous two effects can be found in Figure

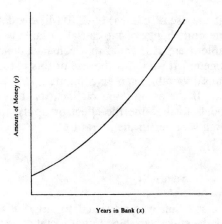

Years in Bank (x)

Figure 3.5   The Increasing Effect of Interest on Amount of Saving

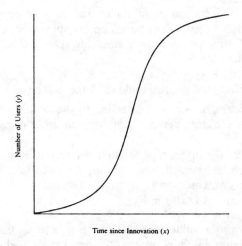

Time since Innovation (x)

Figure 3.6   The Increasing and Decreasing Diffusion Process

3.6, which indicates that diffusion processes first accelerate and then level off after some time. This process is also described by a nonlinear relationship.

There are of course many more examples of such nonlinear relationships. Nevertheless, this book is focussed entirely on linear relationships. The reasons for this restriction were given earlier. First, the linear relation can serve as an approximation of reality in many cases. Secondly, it is quite often the case that transformations of the variables can be performed, which make the relationships linear.

The main issue here is that the use of a linear equation like equation (3.3) implies that the effect of a one unit change of the causal variable is independent of the value of this variable itself; it is equal to a constant denoted by γ, which we call the effect parameter. If we know the size of this parameter, the effect of any change in the causal variables can be computed, i.e. γ times the change in the causal variable. If the assumption of linearity does not hold, one should use different models to describe the effect or apply appropriate transformations. For this topic we refer to the literature.

Additivity

In the previous section the discussion was restricted to situations in which one causal variable influences the effect variable. Often social science theories contain several causal variables for each effect variable. Thus the problem of how different effects should be combined arises. In this text it will be assumed that the effects can be added.

An example of additive effects can be found in the study of opinions. In many studies it is found that a respondent builds up his opinion as a weighted average of the opinions of other persons. In mathematical form this statement can be presented as follows:

$$y = \gamma_1 x_1 + \gamma_2 x_2 + \gamma_3 x_3 + \cdots + \gamma_k x_k \qquad (3.4)$$

where y represents the opinion of the respondent, x_i the perceived opinion of the ith person and γ_i the weight which is attached to the opinion of the ith person. The effects of the different persons' opinion can differ depending on the weight attached to it.

If a respondent evaluates the opinion of the first person as twice as important as the opinion of a second person, while he/she does not take any other person's opinion into account, equation (3.4) would become:

$$y = (2/3)x_1 + (1/3)x_2 + 0x_3 + \cdots + 0x_k$$
$$\text{or } y = (2/3)x_1 + (1/3)x_2 \qquad (3.5)$$

If we had information about the values of the variables x_1 and x_2, the value of the variable y could be computed. Suppose that the first person had a score of 60 and the second person had a score of 30, then the score of the respondent would be

$$y = (2/3)60 + (1/3)30 = 50$$

Clearly, the effects of both variables are added to compute the respondent's score.

A characteristic of additive relations is that the effect of one causal variable does not depend on the value of another causal variable. For example, in equation (3.5), the effect of x_1 on y does not depend on the value of x_2. For,

$$\text{if } x_2 = 0, y = (2/3)x_1 + 0;$$
$$\text{if } x_2 = 30, y = (2/3)x_1 + 10;$$
$$\text{if } x_2 = 60, y = (2/3)x_1 + 20;$$
$$\text{if } x_2 = 90, y = (2/3)x_1 + 30.$$

These equations are presented in Figure 3.7 Clearly, the effect of x_1 on y is the same (2/3) for all four values of the x_2 variable.

Not all relationships are additive. There are relations which are different for various values of a third conditional variable, as we have seen in the first two chapters. In the school career theory we expect the student's scholastic achievement to have a proportional effect on the teacher's recommendation with respect to the secondary school training. Suppose the achievement score

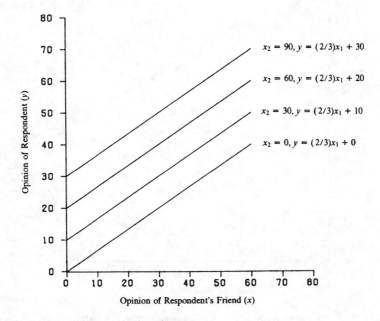

Figure 3.7   The Effect of x_1 is the Same for Different Values of x_2

ranges from 0 to 100 and the teacher's recommendation from 0 to 6. In that case the relationship would be ideally equal to

$$y = \gamma x_1, \text{ with } \gamma = (6/100) \qquad (3.6)$$

since the points $(x_1 = 0, y = 0)$ and $(x_1 = 100, y = 6)$ should lie on the line. But suppose that the size of the effect parameter (γ) depends on the value of another variable, which is "the highest level of secondary school available in the area" which is denoted by x_2. If $x_2 = 3$ in a region, the highest recommendation will be 3 and not 6. Consequently the effect of x_1 will reduce to $(3/100)$. If $x_2 = 1$, the maximum advice is 1 and the effect (γ) of x_1 will only be $(1/100)$. A geometric representation is given in Figure 3.8. The discussion of this example suggests that the effect parameter (γ) depends on the value of another causal variable (x_2), in particular

$$\gamma = (1/100)x_2 \qquad (3.7)$$

Substitution of this form in equation (3.6) gives

$$y = (1/100)x_2 x_1 \qquad (3.8)$$

It is clear from equation (3.8) that the two variables x_1 and x_2 are not added but multiplied. Thus, instead of additive effects, we are dealing with multiplicative effects in this example. There exist many other types of nonadditive

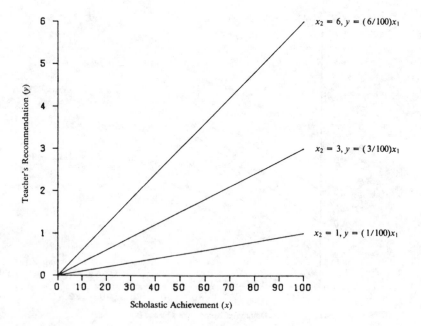

Figure 3.8   The Effect of x_1 is Different for Different Values of x_2

effects, but we will not discuss them here.

In the remainder of this text, the discussion is restricted to additive effects. This means that the effects of variables are independent of each other and that they can therefore be added. Once again two reasons can be given for this choice. The first is that additive relations often represent a good approximation of reality. The second reason is that many nonadditive effects can be made additive by a suitable transformation. If the assumption of additivity does not hold, one should use a different approach or use an appropriate transformation. For this topic we refer to the literature.

Using only linear equations like equation (3.4) where the effects are additive, implies that the effects are assumed to be independent of each other. The effect parameters γ_i are interpreted as *the effects of a one unit change of x_i, when all other variables are held constant*. Thus, if one knows the size of this parameter, the effect of any change in x_i, everything else being constant, can be computed as γ_i times the change in x_i.

The Effect of Disturbances

In the last chapter it was argued relationships in social science are never deterministic, as there are always reasons to expect disturbances in these relationships. It was also suggested to summarize all these disturbances into one variable called the "disturbance term" and denoted by "ζ". As this variable represents an essential part of social science theory, it should also be included in the equations which represent these theories. But then the question arises whether the effect of the disturbance term should be additive or not. As we have assumed up to now that all effects are additive, we shall also opt for the assumption that the effect of the disturbance term is additive. Thus, for the simple case of a relationship between two variables, the equation would become

$$y = \alpha + \gamma x + \zeta \qquad (3.9)$$

An example of such a relationship is presented in Figure 3.9, where the relationship between "years of experience" and "income" is specified. It is assumed that variation in income is not only due to the number of years of experience, but also to various other variables such as "amount of work done", "work productivity", "the circumstances in which the work is done" and so on. All these explaining variables have minor effects and therefore they are not explicitly mentioned in the theory. These omitted variables will become a part of the disturbance term and therefore the relationship can no longer be described by a single straight line but, due to the disturbance term, income will be spread about the line.

In Figure 3.9 the score of a person with 10 years of experience is depicted. According to the original theory this person should earn $(300 + 10.20) = 500$ dollars, but due to this individual's disturbance term his salary is 50 dollars higher. From this Figure we can read the meaning of the additivity assumption. This disturbance term must be additive for all individuals, but its magnitude can vary across individuals. Thus for some people the observed income is higher than expected according to the original theory and for some it is lower.

It will be clear that hardly any prediction of the income variable is possible if the disturbances are too large. Therefore one must try to include all important variables explicitly in the equations, in order to make the disturbances as small as possible. But due to the fact that uncertainty will remain, a disturbance term must always be added to the model.

When the theory contains several causal variables, the form of the equation becomes

$$y = \alpha + \gamma_1 x_1 + \gamma_2 x_2 + \gamma_3 x_3 + \cdots + \gamma_k x_k + \zeta \qquad (3.10)$$

Also in this case the effect of the disturbance term is added to the effects of

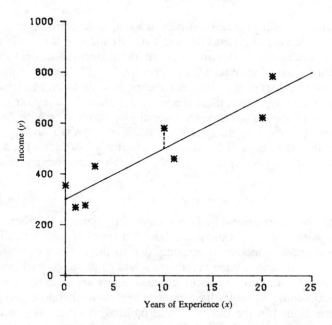

Figure 3.9   The Relationship between "Years of Experience" and "Income", taking Disturbances into Account

Table 3.3   Various Scoring Schemes of the Variable "Teacher's Recommendation"

School Level	Raw Scores y	Transformed Raw Score y'	Deviation Score y^d	Standardized Score y^s
first	1	0	-3	-1.5
second	2	.5	-2	-1.0
third	3	1.0	-1	-.5
fourth	4	1.5	0	0
fifth	5	2.0	1	.5
sixth	6	2.5	2	1.0
seventh	7	3.0	3	1.5
mean	4	1.5	0	0
standard deviation	2	1.0	2	1

the other variables.

In later chapters we will discuss the problem of estimating the spread of the the disturbance term, which is important when we want to make statements concerning the precision of a formulated theory.

Unit of Measurement and Transformations

In the first example discussed in this chapter, the variables were expressed in dollars and years of experience. Such units of measurement are arbitrary. One can also express the scores for the same variables in dimes and half year periods or any other unit of measurement that seems appropriate. For example, if we change the unit of measurement to dimes we get for equation (3.1)

$$y' = 3000 + 200x \qquad (3.1')$$

where y' is the same variable as before, but now expressed in dimes: $y' = 10y$. We see now that the effect seems larger as well (200 instead of 20), but this is only due to the different measurement unit. The effect of one more year of experience is 200 dimes, which is still 20 dollars.

So the magnitude of the effect is changed due to the measurement unit, but not in a way which is substantively meaningful. The changes in the variables indicated here are called *transformations*. This example shows that the coefficients can change with the transformation of the variables. In this case equation (3.1') can be obtained from equation (3.1) by multiplying both sides by 10 (the reader may check this).

In economics there is considerable consensus about the scales which should be used for the measurement of variables. This is not true for the other social sciences. In Table 3.3 four possible scales have been presented for the vari-

Table 3.4   Various Scoring Schemes of the Variable "Achievement Level"

Achievement Level	Raw Score	Transformed Raw Score	Deviation Score	Standardized Score
	x	x'	x^d	x^s
zero	0	0	-50	-5
first	10	.1	-40	-4
second	20	.2	-30	-3
third	30	.3	-20	-2
fourth	40	.4	-10	-1
fifth	50	.5	0	0
sixth	60	.6	10	1
seventh	70	.7	20	2
eigth	80	.8	30	3
nineth	90	.9	40	4
tenth	100	1.0	50	5
mean	50	.5	0	0
standard deviation	10	.1	10	1

able "teacher's recommendation" and in Table 3.4 the same is done for the variable "achievement level". In column 1 of Table 3.3 the different categories of the variable "teacher's recommendation" are presented. Assuming a distance of 1 unit between the different levels, the scores in column 2 are obtained. These are the scores actually used in the study. In another study only 3 levels are distinguished and the value 3 is used for the highest level. The scale for this transformed variable is presented in the third column and the transformed variable is denoted by y'. It can be verified that the transformation of y to y' can be described as $y' = -(1/2) + (1/2)y$.

Another commonly used scale is that the scores are expressed as deviations from the mean. The mean is the value around which the scores are centered. If we denote the variable in *deviation scores* by y^d and the mean by μ_y, then it follows that $y^d = y - \mu_y$. As we see in Table 3.3, the scores look quite different in this case. Finally there is a measure of the spread of the scores around the means, which is called the *standard deviation* and is denoted by σ_y. If the scores of the variable as expressed in deviation scores are divided by the standard deviation of this variable, the *standardized scores* are obtained, such as are presented in the last column of Table 3.3. If this standardized variable is denoted by y^s, then

$$y^s = \frac{y - \mu_y}{\sigma_y}$$

It should be clear that, whatever the transformation, the distance between all levels remains the same in each scale, although the distance itself might differ from scale to scale.

In Table 3.4 the same kinds of transformations are performed on the variable "scholastic achievement". For both examples it is hard to say which scale should be preferred. Since the choice will affect the specific form of the relationship between the variables as has been shown in Figures 3.11 to 3.13 for the first two columns of Tables 3.3 and 3.4, assuming that the relationship is linear, and that the lowest score on the scale is concurrent with the lowest score on the other scale and the highest score on the one with the highest score on the other. In these Figures the equation is specified and it can be seen that in each case the equation is different, due to the change in the scales in which the variables are expressed. Taking into account the scale transformations made, one can easily verify that all equations really represent the same relationship and can easily be obtained from each other.

These examples also illustrate that one should be very careful with the interpretation of the effect parameters. The size of the parameters depends on the scale of the variables. In all these cases we are dealing with the same relationship but the value of the effect parameter can nevertheless be quite different. This phenomenon interferes with a comparison of the sizes of the effects. For this purpose one should always use the same scales or one should standardize the variables, which we shall discuss in the next section. But before going on to this topic, there is more to be said about the use of deviation scores.

In Figure 3.10 we have presented the same relationship for the same two variables in deviation scores. In this Figure we see that effect parameter γ remains the same as when the raw scores were used (see Figure 3.11). On the other hand, we see that $\alpha = 0$ in this case, due to the fact that the equation

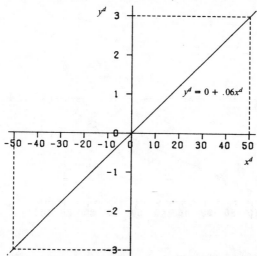

Figure 3.10 The Relationship between "Teacher's Recommendation" (y^d from Table 3.3) and "Scholastic Achievement" (x^d from Table 3.4)

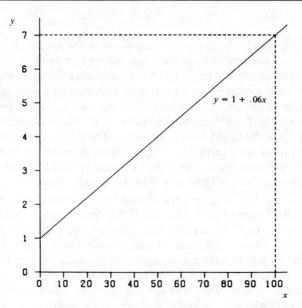

Figure 3.11   The Relationship between "Teacher's Recommendation" (*y* from Table 3.3) and "Scholastic Achievement" (*x* from Table 3.4)

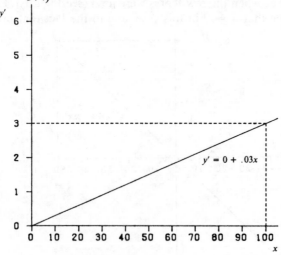

Figure 3.12   The Relationship between "Teacher's Recommendation" (*y'* from Table 3.3) and "Scholastic Achievement" (*x* from Table 3.4)

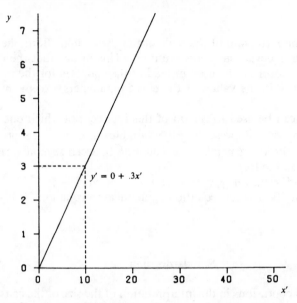

Figure 3.13 The Relationship between "Teacher's Recommendation" (y' from Table 3.3) and "Scholastic Achievement" (x' from Table 3.4)

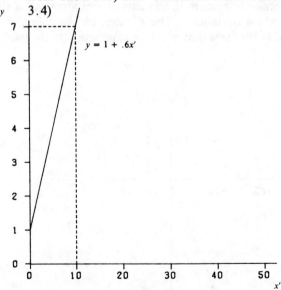

Figure 3.14 The Relationship between "Teacher's Recommendation" (y from Table 3.3) and "Scholastic Achievement" (x' from Table 3.4)

passes through the zero point of the scale of the y^d variable. Both phenomena will always occur if deviation scores are used. This means that the equation for the deviation scores can be used instead of the equation for the raw scores without any change in the values of the effect parameters, except that α will become zero.

This notation can be used to get rid of this intercept in which one is often not interested anyway. Representing the variables in deviation scores by y_i^d and x_i^d, we can write the general linear equation between several variables in deviation scores in the form

$$y^d = \gamma_1 x_1^d + \gamma_2 x_2^d + \gamma_3 x_3^d + \cdots + \gamma_k x_k^d + \zeta \qquad (3.11)$$

The reader can verify that this equation is identical to equation (3.10), except that α is left out.

Standardization

In order to avoid confusions in the interpretation of the size of the causal effect of variables, the variables are often standardized in the way we have shown in Tables 3.3 and 3.4. The effect of standardization on the scores is that the scores are not expressed anymore in the unit of measurement of the original scales, but in standard deviations. The division by the standard deviation, which is expressed in the same unit as the original scores in the numerator, has

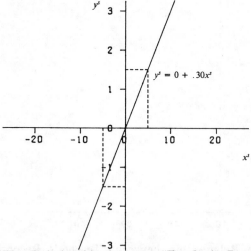

Figure 3.15   The Relationship between "Teacher's Recommendation" (y^s from Table 3.3) and "Scholastic Achievement" (x^s from Table 3.4)

a similar effect as division of an income variable expressed in dimes by ten. The new unit is then the dollar. In this case it is for all variables the standard deviation and by this standardization the scores become identical, as can be checked in Table 3.3. If we use the raw scores of y in the second column, the mean is assumed to be 4 and the standard deviation 2. Standardization of the scores gives us the scores in the last column. For example, the score 1 of y will become $(1 - 4)/2 = -1.5$ for the standardized variable y^s. This means that this value 1 is 1.5 standard deviations away from the mean. As this score is lower than the mean a minus sign appears. The same calculation is used to derive other scores.

If the starting point was the variable y' in column 3 of Table 3.3, the mean would of course be obtained for a lower level (1.5) and the standard deviation would be 1. Computation of the standardized score for the value 0 of the variable y' gives $(0 - 1.5)/1 = -1.5$ which is exactly the same score as the score obtained for the value 1 of y. The rule, that by standardization the scores become identical for the same categories expressed on different scales of the same variable, holds in general as long as the scales are linearly related with each other.

Therefore, if the variables are standardized, only one equation will be obtained that is independent of the scales which have been used to measure the variables. This is of course a very desirable consequence of standardization. This equation is presented in Figure 3.15 for the two variables discussed before. This Figure indicates that now the effect is .30. The interpretation of this effect is that if x^s increases by one standard deviation, then y^s will increase by .30 standard deviations. The general equation for two standardized variables is

$$y^s = \gamma^s x^s + \zeta'$$

This equation indicates that if x^s increases by one standard deviation, y^s will increase by γ^s standard deviations. In this equation the disturbance term is not standardized. In general this is not done, even though it is possible in principle. But due to the fact that these scores are transformed the "prime" is used to indicate that a transformation is introduced. For further details we refer to the next section. The relationship between the standardized coefficient γ^s and the unstandardized coefficient γ can be derived as

$$\gamma^s = \gamma \frac{\sigma_x}{\sigma_y} \qquad (3.12)$$

The standard deviations σ_x and σ_y will never be zero because this would mean that the variables have only one value. They would then be constants instead of variables. Therefore it follows that whenever $\gamma = 0$, then also $\gamma^s = 0$ and if $\gamma \neq 0$ then $\gamma^s \neq 0$. Consequently, we can test whether the causal effect is zero just as easily using the standardized coefficient γ^s as the unstandardized coefficient γ.

The results obtained here can be generalized to any number of variables. If the standardized variables and coefficients are indicated with a "s" we can rewrite the general linear equation (3.10) for standardized variables as follows

$$y^s = \gamma_1^s x_1^s + \gamma_2^s x_2^s + \gamma_3^s x_3^s + \cdots + \gamma_k^s x_k^s + \zeta \qquad (3.13)$$

The form of the equation has remained the same as the one of equation (3.10), only the interpretation has changed. All the parameters are standardized and the interpretation of γ_i^s is that y^s will change by γ_i^s standard deviations if x_i^s changes by one standard deviation and all other variables remain the same.

In the next section we will prove the relationship between the standardized and unstandardized coefficient. This section can be skipped if one is not interested in this technical aspect.

* The Relationship between γ^s and γ

In order to derive the relationship between γ^s and γ, we start with the equation where the variables are expressed in deviation form, that is equation (3.11), which is repeated here

$$y^d = \gamma_1 x_1^d + \gamma_2 x_2^d + \cdots + \gamma_k x_k^d + \zeta$$

In order to standardize y^d we have to divide y^d by σ_y. Then the right hand side should also be divided by σ_y:

$$y^s = \frac{y^d}{\sigma_y} = \gamma_1 \frac{1}{\sigma_y} x_1^d + \gamma_2 \frac{1}{\sigma_y} x_2^d + \cdots + + \gamma_k \frac{1}{\sigma_y} x_k^d + \frac{1}{\sigma_y} \zeta$$

In order to standardize $x_1^d \ldots x_k^d$, we have to divide each variable by its own standard deviation (σ_{x_i}), but in that case the effect parameter γ_i should be multiplied by the same constant σ_{x_i}. This leads to

$$y^s = \gamma_1 \frac{\sigma_{x_1}}{\sigma_y} \left(\frac{x_1^d}{\sigma_{x_1}} \right) + \gamma_2 \frac{\sigma_{x_2}}{\sigma_y} \left(\frac{x_2^d}{\sigma_{x_2}} \right) + \cdots + \gamma_k \frac{\sigma_{x_k}}{\sigma_y} \left(\frac{x_k^d}{\sigma_{x_k}} \right) + \frac{1}{\sigma_y} \zeta$$

Note that all x and y variables are standardized while ζ is not, but only transformed by multiplication by $\frac{1}{\sigma_y}$. Therefore, we shall not write ζ^s but ζ' in the equation for the standardized variable. Substitution of x_i^s for $\frac{x_i^d}{\sigma_{x_i}}$ gives

$$y^s = \left(\gamma_1 \frac{\sigma_{x_1}}{\sigma_y} \right) x_1^s + \left(\gamma_2 \frac{\sigma_{x_2}}{\sigma_y} \right) x_2^s + \cdots + \left(\gamma_k \frac{\sigma_{x_k}}{\sigma_y} \right) x_k^s + \zeta'$$

In this equation we see that the coefficient of the standardized variable x_i^s is equal to $\gamma_i \frac{\sigma_{x_i}}{\sigma_y}$. So we get

$$\gamma_i^s = \gamma_i \frac{\sigma_{x_i}}{\sigma_y} \text{ for all } i,$$

which is the result also presented in equation (3.12).

Some General Remarks

In this chapter we have shown that the γ_i coefficient is the parameter which indicates the effect of the ith causal variable on the effect variable if the effects are proportional and additive. This means that we should try to find the value of this parameter in order to determine whether this effect exists. If the effect is zero, it does not exist; for all other values it does exist. We also saw that the size of the effect parameters depends on the scale of measurement. In order to avoid confusion in interpretation, two solutions are possible: one either uses the same scales all the time or variables must be standardized. As a result of standardization, the parameters change in size, but the test of whether the effect exists or not remains the same. One has to check whether the standardized effect parameters γ_i^s are zero or not. So far we specified only one equation. In the next chapter we will discuss more complete theories.

Further Reading

There are several series of school books in which the topic of the form of relations and of mathematical equations is discussed at length and in which exercises are given to enable the reader to become familiar with transformations. The reference that may very well be most helpful is the textbook from which you learned your first algebra and geometry.

A book which covers many other mathematical techniques and which may be useful to consult is Bishir and Drewes' "Mathematics in the Behavioral and Social Sciences" (1970).

An argument for additive effects in case of opinion formation can be found in the work of Anderson (for example Anderson (1974)) who has shown that, in general, integration of information by subjects can be described by simple linear additive models.

Exercises

3.1 Denote the defense budget of the USSR by x and the defense budget of the USA by y.

(a) Formulate an equation for the relationship between x and y, assuming that the USA want to increase their budget with the same amount as the USSR while the USA yearly spend $100 billion no matter what the USSR is spending.

(b) Illustrate the relationship between the two variables with a table and with a line in a graph.

(c) What is the size of γ and α in this case?

(d) What would happen if γ were smaller than 1?

(e) What would happen if γ were larger than 1?

3.2 An insurance company has to pay \$500,000 for each insured person who is killed in an accident. In order to evaluate the potential claims on the company's funds, the company studies the total costs (y) for different sizes of accidents, measured by the number of people killed (x).

(a) Indicate the relationship between x and y in a table and in a figure.

(b) Is this a linear relationship?

(c) It might seem strange, but respondents who were asked to rate the seriousness of accidents do not see the seriousness as a linear function of the number of people who got killed in them. The increase in seriousness by going from 10 to 11 victims is larger than by going from 100 to 101 victims. Indicate in this case the form of the relationship by means of a curve.

(d) Is it in this case impossible to use linear equations?

3.3 Going back to the arms race example, imagine that the USA want to be able to defend themselves not only against the USSR but also against China. Suppose y is the defense budget of the USA, x_1 is the defense budget of the USSR and x_2 is the defense budget of China.

(a) How should the relationship between these three variables be formulated?

(b) How does the equation change if we take into account that the USA do not have to carry out the military task on their own, but that the NATO partners will also bring in their share?

(c) Are the effects in this model additive?

(d) What are the sizes of the γ-coefficients?

3.4 Exams can be evaluated in different ways. In this and the next exercise two different procedures are given. In both cases the exam consists of two parts which are both rated on a scale of 0 (very bad) to 10 (very good). One possible way to compute a total score (y) is to take the weighted average of the two parts, where the first part (x_1) is weighted three times more than the second part (x_2).

(a) Specify the relationship between these three variables.

(b) What are the values of the different parameters?

(c) Indicate in a figure the relationship between y and x_1 for different values of x_2.

(d) If a person obtains a score of 3 on the second part, can he or she still obtain a total score of 6 (which means that the exam was passed)?

3.5 An alternative procedure to determine the total score would be that (1) a person should have at least a 6 on the second part to pass the exam, while (2) in that case he or she will obtain a score for the total exam which is identical to the score on the first part. We will suppose that he or she gets a zero as long as the second part has not been finished correctly.

(a) For the two conditions of x_2 specify the relationship between y and x_1.

(b) Is the relationship additive or not?

(c) Can you think of a way to formulate the relationship between all three variables in one equation?

3.6

(a) Rewrite the original relationship of 3.1a, if we recognize the fact that the budget of the USSR is expressed in roubles (the rate of exchange is supposed to be 1 rouble = $2).

(b) In this formulation $\gamma \neq 1$. Does this mean that the USA will spend more than the USSR?

(c) How large should γ be in the case where the USA do not react to the USSR-budget?

(d) Rewrite the same equation knowing that the USA-budget is expressed in units of 1 million.

(e) How large should γ be if the USA do not react to the USSR-budget in this case?

3.7 In Table 3.3 the scores for y^s are computed from the scores of y. Standardization should make the different scales identical.

(a) Show that calculation of y^s from y' leads to the same scores as the scores calculated from y in Table 3.3.

(b) Show that calculation of x^s from x' leads to the same scores as the scores calculated from x in Table 3.4.

(c) If we know that $\gamma = .06$, $\sigma_x = 10$ and $\sigma_y = 2$, what do you expect γ^s to be?

(d) Give a presentation of this relationship in formula form and give a verbal interpretation.

(e) Suppose $\gamma^s_= .3$, $\sigma_x = 10$ and $\sigma_y = 2$. How large is γ in this case?

(f) Write out the equation for the variables in deviation form and give an interpretation of this equation.

Chapter 4
Formulation of
Linear Structural Equation Models

In the previous chapter the formulation of linear structural equations was discussed. In general theories contain more than one endogenous variable and need therefore also to be formulated in a set of equations. However, the model specification is not only a matter of the transformation of a causal diagram into a set of equations. The formulation of a structural equation model requires that the researcher plays an active role in specifying the causal mechanism which might have produced the observed data. The more time that is spent in this phase of formulation of the model, the less uncertainty remains which requires testing in a later stage.

First, the notation for the models is introduced. This notation is in agreement with the notation of the User's guide to LISREL. Next, the formulation of a causal model is illustrated by the example of the school career model. Finally, in the last two sections the transformation of scores into deviation scores and the use of standardized scores is again discussed.

Notation of Linear Structural Equation Models

"Linear structural equation models" represent causal theories with proportional and additive effects. If the theory contains only one effect variable, then only one equation is needed and the form of the equation is the one presented in equation (3.10). In general however, theories are composed of more than one effect variable, and there may be various causal links between the variables in the theory. This leads to models with several equations which are connected in a system. For this reason, such systems are also called simultaneous equation models.

Some conventions in the notation of the various equations follow. The variables which the model should explain or account for, have been called *endogenous* or *jointly dependent* variables. The ith endogenous variable is denoted by y_i. The variables that are not explained by other variables in the theory are called *predetermined* variables; the ith predetermined variable is denoted by x_i.

The effect on the ith endogenous variable from the jth endogenous variable is denoted by β_{ij}. The effect on the ith endogenous variable from the jth predetermined variable is denoted by γ_{ij}.

In chapter 2 four reasons were stated for introducing a disturbance term into the theory. This variable, denoted by ζ, may represent the effect of unknown variables, the effect of known but omitted variables the randomness of human behavior and measurement error. Since it is hard to ignore these four factors, a disturbance term is introduced in each equation of the model. In general it is assumed that the effect of the disturbance term is additive.

Using this notation, the general form of a set of linear equations can be specified. If there are p endogenous variables and q predetermined variables in total and the effects are assumed to be proportional and additive, the general system will be of the following form:

$$y_1 = 0y_1 + \beta_{12}y_2 + \cdots + \beta_{1p}y_p + \gamma_{11}x_1 + \cdots + \gamma_{1q}x_q + \alpha_1 + \zeta_1$$
$$y_2 = \beta_{21}y_1 + 0y_2 + \cdots + \beta_{2p}y_p + \gamma_{21}x_1 + \cdots + \gamma_{2q}x_q + \alpha_2 + \zeta_2$$
$$\vdots \qquad \vdots \qquad \vdots$$
$$y_p = \beta_{p1}y_1 + \beta_{p2}y_2 + \cdots + 0y_p + \gamma_{p1}x_1 + \cdots + \gamma_{pq}x_q + \alpha_p + \zeta_p \quad (4.1)$$

All linear structural equation models with p endogenous variables and q predetermined variables are special cases of this general system. Note that in the case of p endogenous variables the system consists of p equations, since each endogenous variable is explained in terms of the other variables in the system.

The variation of and the covariation between endogenous variables are partially determined by the variation of and the covariation between predetermined variables. Therefore, the variation within each predetermined variable as well as the covariation between the predetermined variables are essential components of a structural equation model. The amount of variation of the ith predetermined variable is denoted by ϕ_{ii} and the amount of covariation of the ith and the jth predetermined variable is denoted by ϕ_{ij}. The exact definitions and computations of these coefficients will be discussed in chapter 6. The emphasis at this point is on the notation.

Finally, the variation in the disturbance term and the covariation between the disturbance terms are fundamental components of a structural model. The amount of variation in the ith disturbance term is denoted by ψ_{ii}. The amount of covariation between the ith and j^{th} disturbance term is denoted by ψ_{ij}. Once again, the statistical methods to determine the amount of variation and covariation are discussed in chapter 6.

The notation of this section will be used throughout this text to write linear structural equation models, so it is worth spending a little more time to become completely familiar with it.

Specification of Linear Structural Equation Models

A structural equation model is not merely a set of linear equations. An important requirement is that the equations should represent the *causal mechanism which has produced the observable values of endogenous variables and therefore also the covariations between these variables*. Unfortunately this point has not always received full attention in research practice. Yet it is crucial in the process of developing a structural model to take time to search for an understandable mechanism for each equation specified. As long as the empirical process is not clear to the investigator, alternative formulations should be contemplated. The problem with this suggestion is that it is difficult to define what is meant by 'understandable'. This depends on the topic being studied. Therefore we can only illustrate the process with a discussion of the example used in the earlier chapters.

The suggested approach is no guarantee for the formulation of a correct theory, but the chances are certainly higher compared to theory formation in which a number of causal effects are entered mechanically. Reasoned theory is in general simpler and can be tested more easily than superficial, ad hoc theories. Furthermore, the time spent in formulating the theory can lead to more appealing theories. This would mean that both the investigator and other scholars will be more likely to continue along similar lines of study, leading to more cumulative results in the social sciences than it is the case at present. However, all this is rather vague. Let us look at an example to see what we mean by the formulation of an understandable mechanism.

In the school career theory presented in the second chapter, five endogenous variables and two predetermined variables were distinguished. We will not repeat the verbal arguments concerning the hypothesized direct effects between

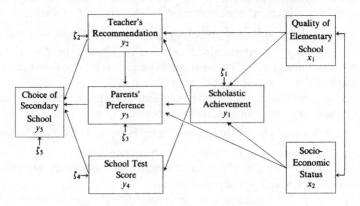

Figure 4.1   The School Career Theory of Chapter 2

the variables. A condensed presentation of the theory can be seen in Figure 2.4 which is represented again in Figure 4.1.

In order to specify a structural equation model of this theory, one has to indicate the causal mechanism which produced the values of endogenous variable. In doing so, one specifies which variables play an important role and whether or not their effects are proportional and additive. Let us start the discussion with the variable "choice of secondary school". The scores on this variable are determined by assignment committees. According to the verbal report, these committees have information for each pupil about the teacher's recommendation, the preference of the parents, the school test score, the social background of the pupils, their sex and the elementary school attended. The simplest mechanism which we can suggest for the explanation of the choice of secondary school is that the committees take a weighted average of the opinions concerning the school choice from (1) the teacher, (2) the parents and (3) the opinion which the committee itself can form on the basis of the school test score. The opinion of the teacher is the same as the teacher's recommendation, the opinion of the parents is given as their preference. We expect a linear relationship between the school test score and the committee's opinion based on this test. The diagram in Figure 4.2 presents this theory.

It is hard to imagine how the variables "socio-economic status", "sex" and "quality of the elementary school attended" can play a role in this process. It seems strange to assume that the committee determines the school choice by a weighted average of three opinions which are all formed specifically in the process of deciding about this school choice and at the same time to assume an effect of socio-economic status. Such a mechanism is unclear. However, it might be possible that socio-economic status, sex and quality of the elementary school have an indirect effect due to the fact that they affect the causal variables.

Another possibility is that these variables have a conditional effect. For example, the weight of the teacher's recommendation might be higher if the pupil comes from a high quality elementary school. This might be a reasonable

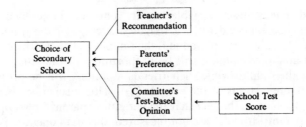

Figure 4.2   The Explanation of the Variable "Choice of Secondary School"

mechanism. However, for reasons of parsimony, this formulation is avoided and only introduced later if necessary. It should be stressed that scholastic achievement can not have any direct effect at all because this information is not known to the committee.

A final problem is that the opinion of the committee, based on the test score is unknown to us as this opinion was not measured separately. Therefore this variable is omitted, leading to a direct effect of the school test score on the choice of secondary school.

Given these arguments, we expect that the causal mechanism for this variable can be formulated as in statement 4.1:

(4.1)   The choice of secondary school (y_5) is proportionally affected by the teacher's recommendation (y_2), the parents' preference (y_3) and the school test score (y_4), and these effects are assumed to be additive.

This statement can be formulated in the following equation which includes the disturbance term:

$$y_5 = \beta_{52}y_2 + \beta_{53}y_3 + \beta_{54}y_4 + \alpha_5 + \zeta_5 \qquad (4.2a)$$

The fourth endogenous variable is the school test score (y_4). The tests are constructed in such a way that they only measure what the are supposed to measure. In this case it is scholastic achievement. This means that the school test score is supposed to be determined only by scholastic achievement and not by any other variables. Normally these tests should have a linear relationship with the variable of interest. Given this argument statement 4.2 should hold for variable y_4:

(4.2)   The school test score (y_4) is proportionally affected by scholastic achievement (y_1).

This relationship, including the disturbance term, is translated into the following equation:

$$y_4 = \beta_{41}y_1 + \alpha_4 + \zeta_4 \qquad (4.2b)$$

The third endogenous variable is the parents' preference (y_3). This preference is also expected to be a weighted average of the teacher's recommendation (y_2), their own opinion and the opinions of their friends. We argue that the parents' own opinion will be proportional to the scholastic achievement (y_1) of their child, while their friends' opinions will be proportional to the socio-economic status of the parents (x_2). This mechanism is represented in Figure 4.3. Due to the fact that the variables "parents' own opinion" and "opinion of parents' friends" are not measured, this path diagram is simplified, omitting the intervening variables 'parents' own opinion' and 'opinions of parents' friends'. This argument leads to the following statement:

(4.3)   "Parents' preference" (y_3) is proportionally affected by "teacher's recommendation" (y_2), "scholastic achievement" (y_1) and "socio-economic status" (x_2), and these effects are expected to be additive.

The equation which corresponds with statement 4.3, including the disturbance term, is:

$$y_3 = \beta_{31}y_1 + \beta_{32}y_2 + \gamma_{32}x_2 + \alpha_3 + \zeta_3 \qquad (4.2c)$$

We now will discuss the second endogenous variable, the teacher's recommendation. We expect that the teacher normally gives the average recommendation to the pupil, except when the pupil deviates considerably in achievement from the average. This means that we can say that the teacher's recommendation is equal to the sum of the average recommendation given by his school and the deviation from the average for the specific pupil. Furthermore, we can expect that the "devation from the average recommendation" is determined by the "deviation from the average achievement" or the "scholastic achievement score minus the average scholastic achievement score". Finally we expect that the "average recommendation per school" and the "average scholastic achievement score" will be determined largely by the quality of the elementary school. These arguments are summarized in Figure 4.4. In this formulation the variables "socio-economic status" and "sex" do not occur. It is of course possible that these variables have an effect on scholastic achievement and in this way they have an indirect effect on the teacher's recommendation. Another possibility is that socio-economic status is related to the quality of the elementary school because of the fact that pupils with lower SES-background attend schools of lower quality than pupils from higher status families. In this case an indirect effect is specified as well. Given these arguments, we do not see any reason to specify any direct effects of these variables on the teacher's recommendation. In Figure 4.4 the only observed variables are "teacher's recommendation", "quality of the elementary school"

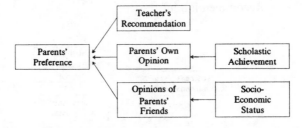

Figure 4.3   The Causal Mechanism Assumed to Hold for Parents' Preferences

and "scholastic achievement". Fortunately, all the other variables are intervening variables which clarify the process but are not essential to the model. Therefore they can be omitted without harm. This simplification leads to the theory depicted in Figure 4.5. Because we expect all effects to be proportional and additive, the theory can be summarized in statement 4.4:

(4.4)   The teacher's recommendation (y_2) is affected proportionally by the quality of the elementary school (x_1) and by scholastic achievement (y_1) and it is expected that these effects are additive.

This statement, including the disturbance term, can be formulated as
$$y_2 = \beta_{21}y_1 + \gamma_{21}x_1 + \alpha_2 + \zeta_2 \qquad (4.2d)$$
Finally the mechanism which we can expect to operate for the variable scholastic achievement (y_1) is specified. It seems plausible to argue that the scholastic achievement of a child improves as the amount of training it gets increases. Up to the secondary school level, this training is obtained predominantly in the family and at school (from the secondary school period onwards the influence of peers is a third influential source of training). The

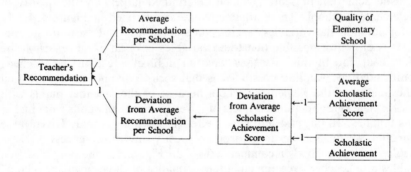

Figure 4.4   The Causal Mechanism for the Variable "Teacher's Recommendation"

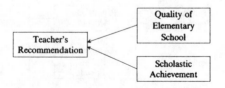

Figure 4.5   The Simplified Theory for the Explanation of "Teachers Recommendation"

effects of this training in school and at home will be additive. Also, we expect the training to be proportionally better in families of higher socio-economic status (x_2) and within elementary schools of higher quality (x_1).

Furthermore we expect intelligence to have an effect on scholastic achievement. This leads to the path diagram of Figure 4.6. Notice that the variable "intelligence" only appears in this diagram and did not need to be introduced at other places in the theory. This means that the variable "intelligence" cannot produce spurious relationships; it is not a common cause. Therefore intelligence can be omitted if we want to simplify the theory. Furthermore, the variable "amount of training" has not been measured, but this variable is an intervening one and can also be omitted. This leaves an explanation of scholastic achievement by the variables "quality of elementary school" and "socio-economic status". In sum:

(4.5) Scholastic achievement (y_1) will be proportionally higher when the quality of the elementary school (x_1) is higher and when the socio-economic status of the parents (x_2) is higher, and it is expected that these effects are additive.

Statement 4.5 can be translated into the following equation in which disturbances are also taken into account:

$$y_1 = \gamma_{11}x_1 + \gamma_{12}x_2 + \alpha_1 + \zeta_1 \qquad (4.2e)$$

Having specified the mechanisms which in our opinion produce variation in the endogenous variables, we formulated the equations of the models for these variables also. According to the specified mechanisms all effects are proportional and additive.

Furthermore, since this theory seems complete, we think it is realistic to formulate statement 4.6 which has already been mentioned in chapter 2:

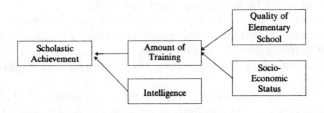

Figure 4.6 The Causal Mechanism to Explain the Variable "Scholastic Achievement"

(4.6)   The omitted causal variables for each endogenous variable have only minor effects, they are unrelated to each other and to the predetermined variables. The omitted causal variables of the different endogenous variables are also unrelated to each other.

Since the disturbance terms represent the omitted variables, this statement can be translated into the following assumptions:

$$\mu_{\zeta_i} = \text{ mean of } \zeta_i = 0 \text{ for all } i\,(i = 1\ldots 5) \tag{4.2f}$$

$$\text{Cov}(\zeta_i x_j) = \text{ covariation of } \zeta_i \text{ and } x_j = 0$$
$$\text{for all } i,j\,(i = 1\ldots 5, j = 1 \text{ or } 2) \tag{4.2g}$$

$$\psi_{ij} = \text{ covariation of } \zeta_i \text{ and } \zeta_j = 0$$
$$\text{for all } i \neq j\,(i = 1\ldots 5, j = 1\ldots 5) \tag{4.2h}$$

The first assumption says that the mean of the ith disturbance term schould be zero. This will be true if the omitted variables in each disturbance term are not related to each other and have minor effects only, so that any effects which there are cancel each other out. This does not mean that in each specific case the disturbance should be zero. This point will be clarified in chapter 6.

The second assumption is that the ith disturbance term does not covary with the jth predetermined variable. This assumption is only justified if no variables are omitted which are common causes of the ith endogenous variable and the jth predetermined variable. If this assumption is violated, that is if such a common cause has been omitted, its effect will be a part of the disturbance term ζ_i of the ith endogenous variable, and the result will be that the covariation of ζ_i and x_j does not equal zero.

The third assumption is that the covariation of the disturbance terms should be zero. This is a translation of the statement that no common causes of the different endogenous variables have been omitted. Note that ψ_{ii}, which is the amount of variation of a single disturbance term, is normally not equal to zero. Otherwise the disturbance term would be either a constant value or zero, which is unlikely. In other words, only the mean of a single disturbance term should be zero, not its variation around that mean.

All these assumptions are only realistic if all important variables have been introduced into the theory. That is why the theory formulation phase is so important in this approach. If not enough time is given to theory formulation, the assumptions might not be realistic which can result in models which do not fit the data.

To complete the formulation of the structural equation model something has to be said about the relationship between the predetermined variables. These relationships are not explained by other variables and a relatively simple statement will suffice to describe these relationships (as suggested in chapter 2):

(4.7) The predetermined variables "quality of elementary school" (x_1) and "socio-economic status" (x_2) might covary with each other.

The translation of such a statement in the notation of this chapter is
$$\phi_{ij} \neq 0 \text{ for all } i,j\,(i = 1 \text{ or } 2, j = 1 \text{ or } 2) \qquad (4.2i)$$
which means that the variation within the predetermined variables (ϕ_{ii}) and the covariations between the predetermined variables (ϕ_{ij}) will possibly not be equal to zero.

Having gone through all these steps, we can summarize the linear structural equation model for the school career theory in the following form:
$$y_1 = 0y_1 + 0y_2 + 0y_3 + 0y_4 + 0y_5 + \gamma_{11}x_1 + \gamma_{12}x_2 + \alpha_1 + \zeta_1$$
$$y_2 = \beta_{21}y_1 + 0y_2 + 0y_3 + 0y_4 + 0y_5 + \gamma_{21}x_1 + 0x_2 + \alpha_2 + \zeta_2$$
$$y_3 = \beta_{31}y_1 + \beta_{32}y_2 + 0y_3 + 0y_4 + 0y_5 + 0x_1 + \gamma_{32}x_2 + \alpha_3 + \zeta_3$$
$$y_4 = \beta_{41}y_1 + 0y_2 + 0y_3 + 0y_4 + 0y_5 + 0x_1 + 0x_2 + \alpha_4 + \zeta_4$$
$$y_5 = 0y_1 + \beta_{52}y_2 + \beta_{53}y_3 + \beta_{54}y_4 + 0y_5 + 0x_1 + 0x_2 + \alpha_5 + \zeta_5 \qquad (4.2)$$
$$\mu_{\zeta_i} = 0 \text{ for all } i\,(i = 1\ldots5)$$
$$\text{Cov}(\zeta_i, x_j) = 0 \text{ for all } i,j\,(i = 1\ldots5, j = 1 \text{ or } 2)$$
$$\psi_{ij} = 0 \text{ for all } i \neq j\,(i = 1\ldots5, j = 1\ldots5)$$
$$\phi_{ij} \neq 0 \text{ for all } i,j\,(i = 1 \text{ or } 2, j = 1 \text{ or } 2)$$

A few words should be said about this final result. A lot of effort was put into formulating a plausible model, looking for various specifications and possible alternatives. Given these efforts, one may expect this result to be very close to the real situation. Therefore the model will only be rejected if there are obvious reasons to do so. Second, we are quite convinced that all important variables have been introduced. The only exception is in the explanation of scholastic achievement, in which the variable "intelligence" is missing. Therefore it is reasonable to be very reluctant about the introduction of any remaining covariation between the disturbance terms and x-variables and between the disturbance terms themselves. Third, we also believe that all effects of the endogenous variables on each other have been introduced. Consequently, β-parameters should not be entered too quickly if the model turns out to be incorrect. In contrast, the arguments about the effects of the predetermined variables on the endogenous variables are not as well-grounded. If the model is not acceptable, the introduction of γ-coefficients ought to be considered, but not without a reasonable interpretation. Fourth, the model as it is formulated in equations is in complete agreement with the path diagram and the verbal theory given before. But during this exercise we have provided additional ideas about the form of the various relationships. Finally, the formulation above is clearly a special case of the general system (4.1). The difference is that a large number of effect parameters are specified to be zero. The reader should also notice the similarity between this representation and the matrix representation discussed in the last chapter. The only difference is that the Γs in the effect matrix are substituted by the symbols indicating the effect.

Structural Equations with Variables in Deviation Scores

In this chapter the general form of linear structural equations and the specific model which was developed to illustrate the process of model building have been shown with variables expressed in their original scores, that is, untransformed and unstandardized. The transformation of variables which is discussed in this section is the transformation of the raw scores to scores that represent deviations of the raw scores from their mean values. In chapter 3 the symbols y^d and x^d were introduced for variables in deviation scores. In general,

$$y_i^d = y_i - \mu_{y_i} \text{ for all } i$$
$$x_i^d = x_i - \mu_{x_i} \text{ for all } i$$

where μ_{y_i} and μ_{x_i} are the means of the variables y_i and x_i.

In Figure 3.14 and equation (3.11) it was illustrated that the application of this transformation does not change the values of the effect parameters. The only difference is that the intercept α disappears from the equations. Usually this coefficient is not the main interest of investigators, so its disappearance is no problem. Also, it can be easily recovered when the need arises. Another useful feature is that the means of all variables are zero in this form, that is $\mu_{y_i} = 0$ and $\mu_{x_i} = 0$ for all i.

With this transformation and its consequences, the formulation of the school career model becomes:

$$y_1^d = \gamma_{11}x_1^d + \gamma_{12}x_2^d + \zeta_1 \tag{4.3a}$$
$$y_2^d = \beta_{21}y_1^d + \gamma_{21}x_1^d + \zeta_2 \tag{4.3b}$$
$$y_3^d = \beta_{31}y_1^d + \beta_{32}y_2^d + \gamma_{32}x_2^d + \zeta_3 \tag{4.3c}$$
$$y_4^d = \beta_{41}y_1^d + \zeta_4 \tag{4.3d}$$
$$y_5^d = \beta_{52}y_2^d + \beta_{53}y_3^d + \beta_{54}y_4^d + \zeta_5 \tag{4.3e}$$
$$\mu_{y_i^d} = \mu_{x_i^d} = \mu_{\zeta_i} = 0 \text{ for all } i \tag{4.3f}$$
$$\text{Cov}(\zeta_i, x_j^d) = 0 \text{ for all } i,j \tag{4.3g}$$
$$\psi_{ij} = 0 \text{ for all } i \neq j \tag{4.3h}$$
$$\phi_{ij} \neq 0 \text{ for all } i,j \tag{4.3i}$$

It is important to note the differences between these equations and equations (4.2a) to (4.2i). First, the change in symbols indicates that the variables are transformed to deviation scores, i.e. y^d and x^d are used instead of y and x. Second, the intercept parameters α_1 to α_5 have disappeared from equations

(4.2a) to (4.2e). Third, an additional to equation (4.3f) says that the mean of all the variables have become zero, due to the transformation.

Because of the simplification involved this formulation of structural equation models in deviation form is attractive and is used very frequently. As before, the parameters which characterize this model are: β-coefficients, γ-coefficients, ϕ-coefficients and ψ-coefficients. Only the α-coefficients have vanished. But if one is interested in their values they can easily be computed using the means of the original variables as will be indicated later.

Structural Equations with Standardized Variables

In the social sciences, standardized variables and coefficients are sometimes preferred over unstandardized variables and coefficients which have been discussed up to this point in this chapter. The reasons behind such a choice will be discussed at the end of this section. First we apply the standardization procedure which was introduced in chapter 3 to a complete set of structural equations. Standardized variables may always be recognized by the s that is attached to them. With this notation they are defined as follows:

$$y_i^s = y_i^d/\sigma_{y_i} \text{ and } x_i^s = x_i^d/\sigma_{x_i} \qquad (4.4)$$

Note that the variables are expressed in deviation form (written as y_i^d and x_i^d), and subsequently divided by their standard deviations.

This transformation of variables affects the parameters of the structural equation. The way in which these coefficients are transformed through standardization of variables is illustrated by equation (4.3b) of the previous section, which was written in deviation form. This equation was

$$y_2^d = \beta_{21}y_1^d + \gamma_{21}x_1^d + \zeta_2$$

When the variables are standardized this equation becomes

$$y_2^s = \beta_{21}^s y_1^s + \gamma_{21}^s x_1^s + \zeta_2'$$

where y_i^s and x_i^s are constructed according to the definition in equation (4.4) and where

$$\zeta_i' = \frac{\zeta_i}{\sigma_{y_i}}$$

$$\beta_{ij}^s = \beta_{ij}\left(\frac{\sigma_{y_j}}{\sigma_{y_i}}\right)$$

$$\gamma_{ij}^s = \gamma_{ij}\left(\frac{\sigma_{x_j}}{\sigma_{y_i}}\right)$$

The form of the equation is exactly the same, but the interpretation of the parameters has changed. All the parameters have now been standardized as well and the interpretation of β_{ij}^s is that y_i^s will change by β_{ij}^s standard deviations if y_j^s would change by one standard deviation, while all the other variables remain unchanged. Similarly, γ_{ij}^s means that y_i^s will change by γ_{ij}^s standard deviations if x_j^s changes by one standard deviation and all other variables remain constant.

Applying the standardization on the structural model for the school career theory, the following result is obtained:

$$y_1^s = \gamma_{11}^s x_1^s + \gamma_{12}^s x_2^s + \zeta_1' \tag{4.5a}$$

$$y_2^s = \beta_{21}^s y_1^s + \gamma_{21}^s x_1^s + \zeta_2' \tag{4.5b}$$

$$y_3^s = \beta_{31}^s y_1^s + \beta_{32}^s y_2^s + \gamma_{32}^s x_2^s + \zeta_3' \tag{4.5c}$$

$$y_4^s = \beta_{41}^s y_1^s + \zeta_4' \tag{4.5d}$$

$$y_5^s = \beta_{52}^s y_2^s + \beta_{53}^s y_3^s + \beta_{54}^s y_4^s + \zeta_5' \tag{4.5e}$$

$$\mu_{y_i^s} = \mu_{x_i^s} = \mu_{\zeta_i} = 0 \text{ for all } i \tag{4.5f}$$

$$\text{Cov}(\zeta_i', x_j^s) = 0 \text{ for all } i,j \tag{4.5g}$$

$$\psi_{ij}' = 0 \text{ for all } i \neq j \tag{4.5h}$$

$$\phi_{ij}^s \neq 0 \text{ for all } i,j \tag{4.5i}$$

$$\sigma_{y_i^s} = \sigma_{x_i^s} = 1 \text{ for all } i \tag{4.5j}$$

The discrepancies between these equations and equations (4.3a) to (4.3i) will be briefly reviewed. First, the s denote that the variables are standardized. Second, all of the coefficients also have a s, meaning that they are standardized too. Third, a tenth equation has been added, equation (4.5j), which indicates that the amount of variation of all the variables in the model has become identical (and equal to one) as a result of the standardization. But despite the changes in the interpretation of the coefficients, the test of the model with standardized variables can be carried out in exactly the same way as for the alternative forms.

The discussion has shown that a causal model with standardized variables can be characterized by the following coefficients: (1) the β_{ij}^s coefficients, indicating the change in y_i^s for a change in y_j^s by one standard deviation; (2) the γ_{ij}^s coefficients, which indicate the change in y_i^s for a change of one standard deviation in x_j^s; (3) the ϕ_{ij}^s coefficients, which indicate the amount of covariation between the standardized predetermined variables i and j; (4) the ψ_{ij}' coefficients, which indicate the amounts of covariation between the disturbance terms and the variances of the disturbance terms.

Now that the three forms in which causal models can be presented have been discussed the relative advantages and disadvantages of the different forms can be evaluated. In the past this topic has provoked heated debates, but since it is very easy to go from one form to the other there is no need for a serious argument. The unstandardized coefficients have the advantage that they are unmixed. This means that the unstandardized coefficients may remain the same from one population to the other even though the variation in the variables may change. By contrast standardized coefficients will change in such situations, since they are functions of the standard deviations (see equation 3.12). Thus, for comparisons ascross populations, the unstandardized coefficients should probably be chosen. However, the measurement scales used in various investigations and for different variables may be very different. In such cases the unstandardized coefficients are not comparable while the standardized coefficients are. In this case, the standardized coefficients are preferable.

Some General Remarks

To summarize, we have demonstrated that some causal mechanisms imply effects of causal variables which do not depend on the values of the causal variables themselves. In these cases structural equation models which represent such causal processes can be specified in linear structural equation models which are special cases of the general system (4.1).

Furthermore we have seen that the coefficient γ_{ii} represents the size of the direct effect on y_i of a one unit change in x_i, while β_{ij} represents the size of the direct effect on y_i of a one unit change in y_j, holding all other variables constant. Consequently, *if the sizes of these coefficients can be obtained one can test whether or not the variables really have direct effects on one another*. If a coefficient turns out to be zero, the conclusion would be that the causal effect does not exist. In chapter 2, where we used only verbal statements of the causal hypotheses, it was not very clear how the hypotheses could be tested. Now we know that the sizes of the β and γ coefficients (or β^s and γ^s if the variables are standardized), are the important issue. This is also the reason why the formulation of theories in equations is so important. The estimation of the values of the effect parameters (β and γ) will be considered in detail in the subsequent chapters. Of course, the actual estimation of the effect parameters is somehow based on empirical data. The type of information that can be derived from such data will be discussed in the next chapter. Although the discussion has had to be very brief, we hope to have shown that the formulation of a structural equation model is an active process. In doing so, one can discover new effects that might clarify the mechanism or eliminate others as unrealistic. This activity can thus lead to changes in the previously formulated, verbal causal theory. If this process of formulation is treated as a routine—transforming causal hypotheses automatically in linear structural equation models—it can lead to misleading results since the coefficients do not represent what one wants them to represent. We will return to this problem in later chapters.

Further Reading

The specification of models is the most neglected of all issues in the social science methodology literature. It seems as if it is assumed that all scholars are familiar with the decision problems discussed in this chapter, or that they are considered to be unimportant. Both points of view are wrong. Therefore we have elaborated on this matter at some length. In the economic literature the discussion of this topic is more frequently found. A relatively simple but nevertheless good introduction to this topic is given by Christ (1966) in "Econometric Models and Methods".

Concerning the choice between standardized and unstandardized coefficients, we refer to Wright (1960), Blalock (1964, chapter 4, and 1967), Tukey (1954), McGinnes (1966) and Duncan's (1975) book. In this literature the standardized coefficients are often called path coefficients. A conclusive article about the advantages and disadvantages of standardized and unstandardized coefficients has been written by Kim and Ferree (1981) The reader should look in this article for further details on this point.

Exercises

4.1 A simplified form of Richardson's arms race model is presented below. It deals with the defense budgets of two nations, the USSR and the USA, at various points in time.

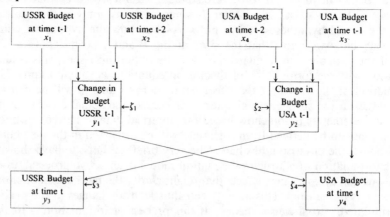

(a) Assuming linear additive effects, how would you translate this theory in a set of equations ignoring disturbance terms ?

(b) If $\beta_{32} = \beta_{41} = 1.2$ and $\gamma_{31} = \gamma_{43} = .99$, while $x_1(1951) = \$110$ billion (10^9 is one billion), $x_2(1950) = \$100$ billion, $x_3(1951) =$

$140 billion, and $x_4(1950)$ = $130 billion, the values for y_1 and y_2 in the year 1951 and the values for y_3 and y_4 in the year 1952 can be calculated. Using these values again as the new x_1 and x_3 and taking the old values of x_1 and x_3 as the new values for x_2 and x_4, the values for the next year can be computed. Show by computing the values for several years that the described process does indeed lead to an arms race between two nations.

4.2 In exercise 2.2 a causal theory was developed for the participation in actions. Starting from the same causal diagram, we ask the following questions:

(a) Is it plausible to assume that the effects among these variables are linear and additive?

(b) Assuming that the effects are proportional and additive, specify the verbal hypotheses and the model.

(c) Assuming that all important variables have been introduced, what can we say about the disturbance terms?

(d) Which coefficients should be zero if this theory is correct?

4.3 In exercise 2.3 you have formulated the theory of another author. This author has tested this theory assuming that the effects of the variables on each other were linear and additive.

(a) How can this theory be formulated in a set of equations, if these assumptions are correct?

(b) Which coefficients should be zero, if the theory is correct?

(c) Do you think that the assumptions of additivity and linearity are realistic in this case?

(d) Why do you think it is important to check these assumptions?

Chapter 5
Information Obtainable from Research

In the previous chapter it was shown that information about the size of the effect parameters β and γ is crucial for a test of causal theories which can be represented in linear structural equation models. Some of the potential effects were fixed at zero a priori, but the effects which are considered to be relevant have to be estimated in empirical research. This chapter starts with a brief exposition of how empirical data may be gathered and assembled in a data matrix. Next, a common sense, graphical method is used to obtain rough estimates of the coefficients in the linear equations and the question is raised whether these estimates of the coefficients can be equated with the structural parameters one is seeking. The problems which have to be faced in this respect are discussed in the remainder of this chapter.

Note that the discussion of the data is directed towards population information. Problems of a different nature, such as those caused by taking samples of units from the population, are addressed in chapter 9.

Collection of Data

Data concerning human beings can be obtained through verbal communication (either spoken or written) or by observation of nonverbal behavior. In interviews as well as questionnaires, respondents are asked directly about their opinions, attitudes, their economic position, religious affilation, political preference and so on. Each answer to questions like these represents the score on a variable for a particular respondent. For nonverbal behavior some kind of coding scheme is usually developed which indicates the kinds of behavior that should be observed to obtain scores on relevant variables. The same kind of activity has to be undertaken in order to transform texts into scores on relevant variables. All of these three approaches are discussed in a number of books referred to at the end of this chapter.

Human beings are the units for which information is usually gathered, but there are several other types of units that may be relevant in a substantive field of interest. In principle the methods to analyze data which are proposed here apply to all types of units. It would be a diversion to go into details about all the different approaches to collecting data about them. The main point is that it is possible, in principle, to obtain information about the scores of the units of research on the variables of interest, i.e. the variables in the causal theory. Exactly how this can be done is discussed in textbooks on data collection and measurement procedures.

In the school career study which we are using as an example, the information about the variables of the theory have been collected by two questionnaires which have been sent to the headmasters of a sample of Dutch elementary schools. In the first questionnaire, which was sent to them before the school test score of the children was reported to the schools, information was collected about the variables socio-economic status (x_2), scholastic achievement (y_1) and the teacher's recommendation (y_2). After the school test score was reported to the schools, a second questionnaire was sent to the headmasters of the schools. In this questionnaire information was asked about: the parents' preference (y_3), the school test score (y_4) and finally the choice of secondary school (y_5). A translation of the questions in these questionnaires with the categories used can be found in Table 5.1. The headmasters were asked to answer these questions about the children for whom it was relevant. In this way information about the scores of all units on six out of the seven relevant variables could be obtained. No information was collected directly for the variable "quality of elementary school" (x_1). This variable was constructed by taking the mean of the scores of all children of each school on the variable school test score (y_4). In this way scores for all individuals on all variables have been obtained.

A distinction can be made between observations, i.e. measurements obtained during data collection, and data, i.e. the information actually used in data analysis. For example, it very often happens that different questions with respect to a particular research topic are combined into one index, while the variables that constitute the index are not used in the analysis itself. We speak of data only when we deal with scores that are used in the analysis. The school career study observations were obtained for six variables, but the data set consists of seven variables.

After the collection of information for all units, and possibly after the construction of new variables from them, a matrix of all the relevant scores can be formed, which is called the *data matrix*. In Table 5.2 a part of such a data matrix is presented for a number of research units in the school career study. Each row in the matrix consists of the scores of one student. Each column represents the scores on one variable. Therefore each cell contains the score of one unit on one variable. Respondent 5 in Table 5.2 received a score of "3" on the variable "teacher's recommendation" (y_2). This means that he or she was advised to go to a school preparing for lower employee work, as can be checked in Table 5.1. It can also be seen that the first five units have the same score on the variable "quality of elementary school" (x_1). The reason is that they attended the same elementary school and therefore the scores on

Table 5.1   The Questions and the Answer Categories Used in the School
                  Career Study

*Questions asked in the first questionnaire, with classification of the answers used
in the coding schedule:*

Name of the child: . . . . .

1. What is the occupation of the father of the child? . . . . .
(Classification of the answers:
    1 unskilled labourer,   4 small businessman,
    2 skilled labourer,   5 higher employee,
    3 lower employee,   6 professional.)

2. What kind of advice has been given to the parents of the child with respect
   to the choice of secondary school? . . . . .
(Classification of the answers:
    1 technical training school,
    2 technical training school or school preparing for lower employee work,
    3 school preparing for lower employee work,
    4 school preparing for lower or higher employee work,
    5 school preparing for higher employee work,
    6 school preparing for higher employee work or university education,
    7 school preparing for an university education.)

3. What do you think the child's score will be on the school test? . . . . .
(Precise predictions are impossible. Therefore we ask you to give a rough estimate expressed in a number between 0 and 100, but it may be easier for you
to round off to five percentage points.)

Questions asked in the second questionnaire:

Name of the child: . . . . .

4. What was the child's score on the school test? . . . . .

5. What kind of school did the parents prefer? . . . . .
(For the classification of the answers see question 2.)

6. What kind of school did the child finally go to? . . . . .
(For the classification of the answers see question 2.)

Table 5.2   Part of the Data Matrix of the School Career Study

Respondent Number	y_1	y_2	y_3	y_4	y_5	x_1	x_2
1	70	6	6	80	6	74	6
2	80	6	7	90	7	74	6
3	90	6	7	90	7	74	6
4	50	6	3	60	3	74	5
5	40	3	3	50	3	74	4
⋮	⋮	⋮	⋮	⋮	⋮	⋮	⋮
15	30	1	1	60	1	60	3
16	30	1	6	80	6	60	2
17	30	3	3	40	3	60	4
⋮	⋮	⋮	⋮	⋮	⋮	⋮	⋮
22	60	3	3	60	3	67	3
23	60	3	3	60	3	67	4
24	70	3	3	80	3	67	3
25	60	2	3	50	3	67	3
26	90	7	7	90	7	67	4
27	80	6	3	90	3	67	4
28	60	3	3	40	3	67	2

y_1 = Scholastic Achievement.
y_2 = Teacher's Recommendation.
y_3 = Parents' Preference.
y_4 = School Test Score.
y_5 = Choice of Secondary School.
x_1 = Quality of Elementary School.
x_2 = Socio-Economic Status.

this variable, which was the mean school test score, have to be identical.

Obviously there is a great deal more to say about the data collection stage and preparation of the data for final analysis, but this is not the topic of this chapter. It would require a lengthy discussion which might easily distract the reader's attention from the main purpose: how is knowledge of the data matrix transferred to knowledge about the sizes of the effect parameters β and γ?

The Best Fitting Line

The reader may now wonder if all coefficients of interest can be derived directly from the data in the data matrix. Let us start with an informal discussion of how this could be done. We are then in a position to better appreciate the problems connected with this procedure.

Starting with a complete data matrix, the scores for all units on each pair of variables can be plotted in a *scattergram*. In Figure 5.1 a scattergram is presented for the variables "scholastic achievement" (y_1) and "school test score" (y_4), and in Figure 5.2 for the variables "school test score" and "choice of secondary school" (y_5). The sizes of the octagons indicate the concentration of data points found in a certain area. Both figures indicate that the relationship between each pair of variables tends to be linear and positive, meaning that an increase in one variable is accompanied by an increase in the other. In both figures a line has been drawn which is the best single line which describes the main trend in the data. There are computational procedures which determine, in some sense, the best fitting line, i.e. the line that gives the closest correspondence with the concentration of data points around it. Such a line is called the *regression line*. As soon as this line is drawn, it can be described by its slope and intercept (if necessary, refer back to chapter 3), meaning that the sizes of the coefficients are known.

The general form of a linear equation, written for the variables in Figure 5.1 (compare equation (3.3)), is

$$y_4 = \alpha_4 + \beta_{41}y_1 \tag{5.1}$$

The value of α_4 is equal to the value of y_4 if y_1 is equal to zero. It turns out that $\alpha_4 = -.15$, as can roughly be checked in Figure 5.1. The value of β_{41} is equal to the increase in y_4 if y_1 increases by one. In this instance $\beta_{41} = 1.0$.

The equation for the line in Figure 5.2 has the form

$$y_5 = \alpha_5 + \beta_{54}y_4 \tag{5.2}$$

For this Figure $\alpha_5 = .56$ and $\beta_{54} = .53$. Alternatively the two relationships can be formulated as follows:

$$y_4 = -.15 + 1.00y_1 + \zeta_4 \tag{5.3}$$
$$y_5 = .56 + .53y_4 + \zeta_5 \tag{5.4}$$

This discussion illustrates that, as soon as the data for the relevant variables have been gathered, it is a relatively simple step to derive the values of the

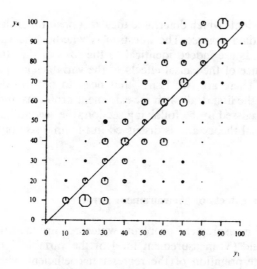

Figure 5.1 The Scattergram and Regression Line for Scholastic Achievement (y_1) and School Test Score (y_4) as obtained from the School Career Study. The Sizes of the Octagons in the Plot indicate the Frequencies with which the Points occur.

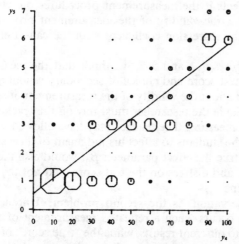

Figure 5.2 The Scattergram and Regression Line for School Test Score (y_4) and Choice of Secondary School (y_5) as found in the School Career Study. The Sizes of the Octagons indicate the Frequencies with which the Points occur.

slope and intercept coefficients which determine the exact position of the linear relationship among the data points. The question is whether the values of these regression coefficients are indeed identical to the sizes of the structural parameters, in this instance of the causal effects of the variables y_1 and y_4 on y_4 and y_5, respectively. There are two issues that need to be considered in evaluating this problem: the first deals with measurement problems during the data collection and is discussed in the following section; the second has to do with the form of the causal theory and is discussed in the final section of this chapter.

The Effects of Measurement Error

There are three types of measurement problems which require attention: (1) validity, (2) reliability and (3) measurement level of the variables. Each of them may affect the interpretation of the regression coefficient which was derived with the procedure described in the previous section.

Validity is the first problem. A measurement procedure is said to be valid if the scores which are obtained in the measurement in fact represent what one wants to measure. If this condition is not met, the measurement procedure is said to be invalid. Clearly, the regression coefficients can never be appropriate estimates of the causal effects if the measurement procedures on which they are based are invalid. Thus the validity of the measurement procedure is a prerequisite for equating the regression coefficient with the causal effect that we want to discover.

For the variables in Figures 5.1 and 5.2, we think that the measurement procedures for the school test score and choice of secondary school are valid, but questions can be raised about the validity of the measurement of scholastic achievement. For this variable the researcher must rely on the teacher's judgment, which is an indirect measure. The teacher may have allowed some personal feelings concerning the students to affect his judgment of their scholastic achievement. If this were true the effect parameter β_{41} would also include the effect of the teacher's likes and dislikes on the test score, and not the effect of scholastic achievement alone.

Unreliability of the observations is the second problem. Unreliability of a measurement procedure occurs when a repeated measurement of the same variable on one unit leads to different results, while the "true score" of this unit is not changed. If the deviations among the observed scores are large from one occasion to the other, i.e. if the reliability of the instrument is low, the relationships between variables that were obtained in this way can appear to be completely different at different times. Consequently, the coefficients which can be derived from such data are not very useful. The regression coefficient can only be meaningful if the reliability of the measurement instruments is high.

For the variables in Figures 5.1 and 5.2 it seems that the choice of secondary school has been measured very reliably. The two other variables may contain some measurement errors, but we believe that they are not substantial.

There are elaborate procedures to compute the reliablility of measurement instruments and to resolve some of the problems of measurements errors. For these topics we refer to the literature. In this text we will ignore measurement errors until chapter 15. This means that we assume that the variables are measured without measurement error. If this assumption is not realistic, serious errors in the interpretation of the results of the analysis can occur.

The *measurement level* of the observed variables is the third and final problem which has to be discussed. In general a distinction can be made between *ratio, interval, ordinal* and *nominal scales* according to the criteria advanced by Stevens (1957). Length, measured in centimeters, is an example of ratio variable; there are equal distances between the centimeters and there is a natural zero point on the scale. Such variables do not occur very often in the social sciences except for variables like "the number of participants" or similar counting variables. Temperature, measured in degrees Celsius or Fahrenheit, is a typical interval variable; there are equal distances between the grades, but the zero point is chosen arbitrarily (Kelvin's scale is a ratio scale). Interval scales are also not often used in the social sciences (Thurstone scales and psychophysical scales are examples), but many scales are used as if they were interval scales although there is no strict proof that this is permitted. Most of the measurement procedures that are widely used in the social sciences lead to ordinal scales; for example, Guttman scales, Mokken scales and Likert scales. A characteristic of ordinal scales is that the scores on them indicate an ordering of the categories, but the distances between the scores and the zero point are unknown. All opinion questions with answer categories as "—strongly agree, —agree, —don't know, —disagree, —strongly disagree", are of this nature. Finally there are variables for which the answer categories can not be ordered at all; these are called nominal scales. "Sex" and "religious denomination" are typical examples of nominal variables. Strictly speaking, the analysis of linear structural equation models discussed in this text requires that the endogenous variables are measured on an interval or higher level scale. The reason why this is so is rather complex. For this point we refer to the literature. But here we can at least clarify the problem if no interval level measurement is used. If a variable is measured on an ordinal scale, rank order numbers are attached to the different categories of the variable. However, rank order numbers are arbitrary as long as they preserve the ordering between the categories. Table 5.3 shows an imaginary ordinal variable with seven categories ranging from A to G, in that order. Distances between the categories do not need to be

Table 5.3   Three Different Sets of Category Values Permissable as Scores
for the Ordinal Variable y

Category Labels of Variable y	Category Values Set 1	Category Values Set 2	Category Values Set 3
A	1.0	1.0	1.0
B	1.1	2.0	3.3
C	1.5	3.0	4.8
D	2.2	4.0	5.8
E	3.2	5.0	6.5
F	4.3	6.0	6.9
G	7.0	7.0	7.0

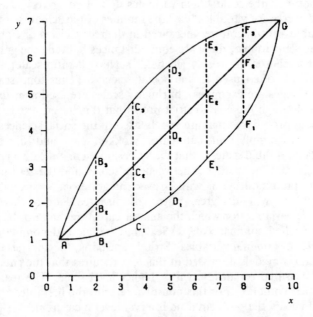

Figure 5.3   The Relationship between Two Variables which are perfectly
related but one of which is ordinal and scaled in three different
ways as presented in Table 5.3

equal. In order to measure this variable on an interval scale, one has to assign numbers to the categories. Three sets of category numbers are presented in Table 5.3, which all preserve the rank ordering of the categories. Figure 5.3 illustrates that the effect of choosing a different set of category numbers has a considerable effect on the form of the relationship. Using the first set of values, we can conclude that the effect of x is not independent of its value, but increases with it. Using the second set of values, we conclude that the effect is proportional, while use of the third set leads to the conclusion that the effect declines as the value of x increases. Clearly uncritical use of the category labels and scores can lead to considerable misinterpretations. Given an ordinal measurement of the dependent variables, we must conclude that no further inferences about the sizes of the causal effects are possible unless one is willing to make further assumptions with respect to the numbers assigned to the categories. Although the requirements with respect to the measurement level of the variables are not very high in this approach, a problem does exist as most social science variables are measured at an ordinal measurement level.

Two fundamentally distinct reactions to this problem can be found in the literature. One reaction is that the attention is directed towards procedures of analysis which are appropriate for the observed ordinal variables; the method of analysis is adjusted to the measurement level of variables. The other reaction is to try to raise the measurement level of the variables; the measurement level of variables is adjusted to the method of analysis. We consider that the second approach is the better one. The reason for this is that only in the latter case can the theories, specified according to the rules discussed before, be tested. When one uses analyses which require only an ordinal measurement level or less, the theories can not be tested completely, and in fact weaker hypotheses than those formulated originally will be tested.

There is also a third, less fundamental, but more practical approach. One can make assumptions from which the category values can be derived. Two approaches have been used. The first is that linearity of the relationship is assumed and the scale values are adjusted if the relationship between the observed variables is not linear. The second approach is that one assumes a certain distribution of a variable (for example a normal distibution; see chapter 6 for this concept) If the distribution of the observed variable deviates from the expected distribution, the scale values are adjusted so that the normal distribution is approximated as far as possible. It will be clear that these two approaches are just as good as the assumption which is made to derive the scale values. For more details about these two approaches we refer to chapter 9.

In the school career example the first approach was chosen. It was assumed that all hypothesized relationships were linear. But given this decision, the category values can be adjusted in such a way that the assumption is fulfilled, i.e. that the observed relationships are linear. However, in this specific case such adjustments were not necessary because all relationships were already approximately linear. Thus, in this example the scores remain as they were presented in Table 5.1. It should be clear that the measurement level can be a serious problem and that the solution used here is only an ad hoc solution. It is of course much better to improve the measurement of the variables. On the other hand, the requirements with respect to the measurement level are not so high that this approach is as impossible as some people might think.

All three points mentioned in this section—validity, reliability and measurement level—have to do with the effect of measurement problems on the interpretation of information obtained from the data. Measurement problems are extremely important and the LISREL approach is also designed to tackle these problems. However, measurement problems are for the most part ignored in this book. The observed variables are assumed to be valid and reliable measures of the theoretical variables, and at least the endogenous variables are assumed to be measured on an interval scale. This section suggests that if these assumptions are far from realistic, the previously discussed approach for obtaining estimates of the parameters can not be used.

Regression Coefficients and Direct Causal Effects

Even when the condition of valid and reliable interval measurement of the variables is met, the interpretation of the regression coefficients (for example, as obtained from the data in Figures 5.1 and 5.2) as estimates of direct causal effects, is not always correct. This point becomes obvious if it is realized that the figures and coefficients can be obtained for any pair of variables which appears in the data matrix, while only for a limited number of them have direct effects been specified. Thus the coefficients so obtained from the data represent something other than the direct effects. The plots indicate how the two variables *covary*, but as we have seen already in chapter 1, the covariation between variables can result from different sources: it can occur because of the direct effect of one variable on another (for example, between y_4 and y_1), but also because of a spurious relationship, or because of a combination of direct, indirect and spurious relationships (as is the case for y_5 and y_1), or as a result of a joint effect (as in case of y_1 and x_1).

Overall, it should be evident that, apart from problems arising from the measurement conditions, direct causal effects can not directly be obtained from the data. Several solutions to this estimation problem have been suggested in the past. The procedure which is discussed below uses measures of the strength of the covariation between the variables. These covariations can be computed for each pair of variables. We will discuss the computation of these measures in the next chapter.

Further Reading

The topics of this chapter require a much fuller discussion than it is possible in this text. Therefore we give a number of references to literature which we think is appropriate for the various topics. First for coverage of measurement procedures used in interviews, see the texts of Torgerson (1958), Coombs (1964) and Dawes (1972) and for practical examples, see Robinson et al. (1968) and Robinson and Shaver (1969). In the field of text analysis Holsti (1969) and Krippendorf (1980) give a good overview of the possibilities and difficulties. On observation techniques see Medley and Mitzel (1967) and Speier (1973). Index construction on the basis of statistical material is discussed in the text of Gurr (1974), Taylor et al. (1972) and Morrison et al. (1972).

In most of the texts mentioned above, the problems of reliability and validity are mentioned. For a more complete overview of this literature which is very elementary, see Carmines and Zeller (1979), although we do not agree completely with their approach. A more complete discussion of this topic can be found in the more complex book of Lord and Novick (1969).

Efforts made by some scientists to raise the measurement level of the variables in social science research can be found in Hamblin (1974), Stevens (1975), Lodge et al. (1976 and 1979) and Lodge (1981). Technical details of this approach are discussed in Saris et al. (1980).

The estimation of regression coefficients is discussed in most statistics books. A simple introduction is given by Wonnacott and Wonnacott (1972) and by Wallpole (1974). Hanushek and Jackson (1977)have clearly indicated why lower level effect variables are a problem and what can be done about it. Similar information is given by Theil (1971) and many others.

In the past, efforts have also been made to develop procedures for ordinal variables analogous to those discussed here for interval variables. This approach can be found in papers of Hawkes (1971), Smith (1972 and 1974) and Somers (1968 and 1974). This approach has been criticized especially by Wilson (1974a, 1974b, 1974c), while the logit, probit and loglinear analysis procedures have made this approach obsolete (see the epilogue).

Furthermore Jöreskog and Sörbom have also introduced procedures in the LISREL approach in order to deal with categorical variables. In chapter 9 a brief introduction of these procedures will be given. For a more elaborate discussion, see Olsson (1979) and Muthen (1984).

Exercises

5.1 Below you will find a list of possible actions which can be done to improve the grants for university students. (These grants have not been increased during several years while inflation was quite high.) We have denoted the violence involved in the first action, a refusal to pay tuition, arbitrarily by 100.

Actions	Violence	Expected Success	Expected Risk	Willingness to Participate
(1) Refusal to pay tuition	100	100	100	100
(2) Protest meeting				
(3) Occupation of the administration				
(4) Blocking the entrance by sitting				
(5) Petitions				
(6) Occupation of the university				
(7) Writing protests on the walls				
(8) Demonstration				
(9) Boycott of lectures				
(10) Sending of protest letters				

Now it is your task to evaluate the violence of the other actions. If you think that the violence of the second action, attending a protest meeting, is twice as high as of the first action, you give the value 200. If the second action is 1/3 in violence of the first action, you should indicate the violence by 33. In the same way all possible actions should be evaluated. After all actions have been evaluated with respect to violence, the same can be done for the expected success, expected risk and the willingness to participate in these actions. Each time the first action is evaluated as 100. The evaluation procedure should be the same for each aspect. Do not look at earlier evaluations while making a new one. If this task has been done, it is clear that a data matrix has been obtained where the research units are the actions and the variables are "violence" (x_1), "expected success" (y_1), "expected risk" (y_2) and "willingness to participate"

(a) Present the relationship between x_1 and y_1 in a scattergram (idem for x_1 and y_3).

(b) Are the two relations approximately linear?

(c) Draw the best fitting straight lines.

(d) What are the coefficients of the two equations?

(e) Do you think that the measurement procedure used will provide you with valid measures of the variables in which we are interested?

(f) Do you think that the measurement procedure used will provide you with reliable measures of the variables? (If you are in doubt, repeat the same procedure without looking at the old evaluations.) (y_3).

(g) What is the measurement level of the variables?

(*h*)Given the answers to the questions *e*, *f* and *g*, what has to be the evaluation of the obtained relationship between the variables?

(*i*)Could the coefficients estimated in *d* represent the direct effects of the variable x_1?

(*j*)If not, what do they represent?

(*k*)Is there a relationship between two other variables which could provide us with an estimate of a direct effect? If so, estimate the effect parameter.

(*l*)Can you also estimate the regression coefficient between y_1 and y_2? What does this coefficient represent?

5.2 With respect to the secondary analysis the reader can ask the following questions:

(*a*)How are the different variables in the study measured?

(*b*)Is something known about the validity, reliability and measurement level of the different variables?

(*c*)On the basis of your evaluation, would you say that the assumption of valid and reliable measurement is realistic?

(*d*)Do the variables in this study fulfill the measurement level requirement suggested in the text?

(*e*)Can the effects be derived immediately from the relationship between pairs of variables?

Chapter 6
Description of Data from a Population

Causal effects are estimated in this book from information about the strength of the covariations between the variables of the theory. Two measures for the degree of covariation between variables are commonly used: the covariance and the correlation coefficient. In order to explain these measures, the mean, variance and standard deviation have to be introduced as well. In this chapter the discussion will be restricted to population data. In chapter 8 the problem of sampling will be introduced. A useful starting point is the introduction of the univariate probability distribution.

Univariate Probability Distribution

In the discussion on the formulation of theories in chapter 2, arguments were presented to the effect that social processes can never be described in a completely deterministic manner, and that there will always be some unpredictability in such processes. However, this does not mean that they are completely unpredictable. For each variable in the theory, one generally expects that certain values are more likely to occur than other values. This means that we could summarize our knowledge about a variable by specifying the *probabilities* of the different values of the variable. Such information is summarized in a *"probability distribution"*. If reference is made to the distribution of one variable at a time, it is called a *"univariate* probability distribution". A variable which can take on various values, while the probabilities of these values are specified by its probability distribution, is called a *"random variable"*. This intuitive definition of a random variable will serve our purposes. For a more general mathematical definition the reader is referred to the literature.

In order to discuss the probability distribution, a distinction has to be made between discrete and continuous random variables. We begin with the discussion of discrete random variables.

Table 6.1 The Absolute and Relative Frequencies and Probability Distribution for the Variable "Choice of Secondary School"

Choice of Secondary School y_5	Number of Students per Value $f(y_5)$	Relative Frequency per Value $f(y_5)/N$	Probability for Each Value $Pr(y_5)$
1	10,000	.100	.100
2	12,100	.121	.121
3	17,800	.178	.178
4	20,200	.202	.202
5	17,800	.178	.178
6	12,100	.121	.121
7	10,000	.100	.100
Total	100,000	1,000	1,000

Discrete Random Variables

A *discrete* random variable is a variable which can take on only a limited number of values. An example is the variable "Choice of secondary school" (y_5) from the school career study, which can take on values from 1 (technical training schools) to 7 (schools preparing for higher employee work or university education).

The question now is how to obtain the probability associated with each value of such a variable. This question can be answered very simply if we have complete information on all units of the population, which is what we assume in this chapter. Let us suppose that the complete data matrix for the population of the school career study is known. Then the data for the variable "choice of secondary school" could be summarized in an absolute frequency distribution as presented in the first two columns of Table 6.1. In the first column the values of the variable y_5 are mentioned and in the second column, the *absolute frequencies*. These frequencies can be obtained by counting the number of units in the population with each value. With $f(y_5)$ we denote the absolute frequency distribution of variable y_5. A specific element of the distribution is denoted by $f(y_5 = k)$, where k can vary from 1 to 7. In this population the total number of units is 100,000, which is denoted by N.

The *relative* frequency distribution is directly obtainable from the absolute frequency distribution by dividing the absolute frequency by the total number of units in the population. The relative frequencies represent the proportions of units with certain values. The relative frequencies are given in the third column of Table 6.1

After these two steps the probability distribution follows immediately. The probability of selecting a unit with a value k (if the unit is chosen by chance from the total population) is equal to the relative frequency of this value, since there are N possible outcomes of this experiment out of which $f(y_5 = k)$ have a score on y_5 of k. Thus the probability distribution is identical to the relative frequency distribution. The probability distribution is presented in the fourth column of Table 6.1. The probability that y_5 is equal to k is denoted by $p(y_5 = k)$, while the probability distribution of the variable y_5 is denoted by $p(y_5)$ (The notation employed here differs slightly from that commonly used in textbooks on statistics. In such texts the distinction between the *values* of a variable and the *variable* itself is emphasized by using different symbols for each of them. Although this would be useful for this chapter, we have decided not to follow this common notation in order to reduce the number of symbols used).

A probability distribution can also be represented in graphical form. Figure 6.1 gives the graphical representation of the probability distribution of y_5 from Table 6.1. Note that the length of the lines represents the size of the probabilities and that the lengths of the lines add up to 1, as should be true for the sizes of the probabilities.

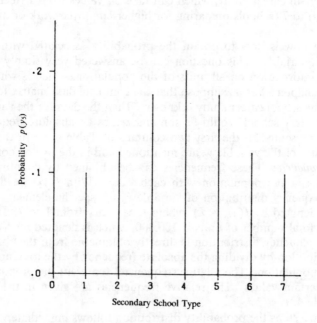

Figure 6.1   The Graphical Representation of the Probability Distribution of y_5 from Table 6.1

Table 6.2 The Absolute and Relative Frequencies and the Densities for a Continuous Variable

Classes	Absolute Frequencies	Relative Frequencies	Probabilities	Densities	Size of Surface
0 – 10	2,000	.02	.02	.002	.02
10 – 20	7,000	.07	.07	.007	.07
20 – 30	11,000	.11	.11	.011	.11
30 – 40	14,000	.14	.14	.014	.14
40 – 50	16,000	.16	.16	.016	.16
50 – 60	16,000	.16	.16	.016	.16
60 – 70	14,000	.14	.14	.014	.14
70 – 80	11,000	.11	.11	.011	.11
80 – 90	7,000	.07	.07	.007	.07
90 – 100	2,000	.02	.02	.002	.02
Total	100,000	1.00	1.00	—	1.00

Continuous Random Variables

Continuous variables can take on an infinite number of values. In the school career example the "test score" is such a variable. This score is based upon the proportion of correct answers and can be expressed with varying degrees of precision: for example, to two, three or four digits after the decimal point. This means that between 0 and 1 alone an infinite number of values could be specified.

To be able to present a table that clearly illustrates how the units are distributed over the various values of a continuous variable, it is necessary to form a number of classes within which values are grouped together. In Table 6.2 the school test scores (y_4) have been categorized in ten classes, each with equal width. The second column of the table presents the absolute frequencies and in column 3 and 4 the relative frequencies and probabilities are given. So far the procedure is the same as for discrete variables. But the graphical representation introduces something new. The probability can not be represented by a line for a continuous variable, since an infinite number of values is possible within each class. Therefore the probability will be represented by a surface: the width of the surface is the width of the class and the height is the *density* in a class. The density is defined as the probability divided by the width of the class. In this way the sizes of the surfaces are equal to the probabilities, and the sum of the sizes of the surfaces is again equal to 1. Figure 6.2 gives a graphical display of the probability distribution of the continuous variable in Table 6.2.

The use of a class width of ten points is arbitrary. Reducing the width to smaller values will result in a more regular shape of the distribution provided that enough information is available. Therefore smooth probability density curves can be used for continuous variables. An example is given in Figure

6.3. The probabilities represented by the surfaces below the curve can be approximated with any preferred precision, by the use of smaller and smaller classes. Usually integral calculus is used for this approximation. In fact all the theorems that we shall state for discrete variables (using summation signs)

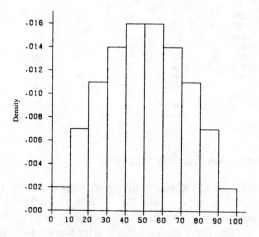

Figure 6.2   The Graphical Representation of the Density of the Continuous Variable of Table 6.2

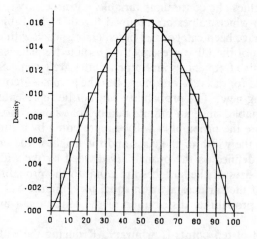

Figure 6.3   The Graphical Representation of the Density of Figure 6.2 by a Smooth Density Function

can be duplicated by theorems for continuous variables (using integral signs). In order to avoid tedious duplication, we shall only discuss the theorems for discrete variables, and leave it to the reader to consult the literature for the analogous form with continuous variables, whenever it is needed.

Mean, Variance and Standard Deviation

For a number of purposes the absolute frequency distribution, the relative frequency distribution and the probability distribution are too detailed representations of the data. It is often necessary to reduce the information to merely two distinctive numbers: (1) the mean (also called the arithmetic average, expectation or expected value) as a measure of the *central tendency* of the distribution, indicating a point around which the other values are centered, and (2) the variance as a measure of the *dispersion* of the distribution, indicating how widely the units are spread around the mean. The *mean* is equal to the sum of all values of the variable of interest in the population divided by the total number of units. The population mean is denoted by μ, or, in order to indicate for which variable the mean is computed, μ_x or μ_y, i.e. with the variable added in the subscript.

According to the definition, the mean of a variable can be computed directly from the data matrix. But the mean can also be computed from the absolute frequency distribution for a discrete variable. In that case each possible value of the variable is multiplied with its absolute frequency and these products are summed, which leads to the sum of all values in the population. Finally, dividing by N gives the value of the mean. Formally this procedure can be formulated as follows for variable y:

$$\mu_y = \frac{\sum yf(y)}{N} \text{ or } \mu_y = \sum y \frac{f(y)}{N}$$

where the summation is over all possible values of y.

The first formula using absolute frequencies is identical to the form in which the relative frequencies are used and thus also identical with a form which uses probabilities. This form is:

$$\mu_y = \sum yp(y) \tag{6.1}$$

where the summation is all possible values of y.

In statistics textbooks the last form is used to define the population mean, being the most general one.

The *variance* of a variable is defined as the mean of the squared deviations from the mean of the variable. If the deviation from the mean is written as $(y - \mu_y)$, then these terms have to be squared and added for all values of y, and finally divided by N, in order to obtain the mean squared deviation or variance. This measure of dispersion is denoted by σ_{yy} in this text.

Table 6.3   The Computation of the Mean (μ_{y_5}), the Variance ($\sigma_{y_5y_5}$) and the Standard Deviation (σ_{y_5}) for the Data of Table 16.1

Choice of Secondary School y_5	Probability Distribution $\Pr(y_5)$	$y_5 \Pr(y_5)$	Deviation from the Mean $y_5 - \mu_{y_5}$	$(y_5 - \mu_{y_5})^2$	$(y_5 - \mu_{y_5})^2 \times \Pr(y_5)$
1	.100	.100	-3	9	.900
2	.121	.242	-2	4	.484
3	.178	.534	-1	1	.178
4	.202	.808	0	0	.000
5	.178	.890	1	1	.178
6	.121	.726	2	4	.484
7	.100	.700	3	9	.900

$$\mu_{y_5} = \sum y_5 \Pr(y_5) = 4.000 \qquad \sigma_{y_5y_5} = \sum (y_5 - \mu_{y_5})^2 \Pr(y_5) = 3.124$$
$$\sigma_{y_5} = \sqrt{\sigma_{y_5y_5}} = 1.768$$

If one uses summary tables to compute the variance of a variable the following form can be used.

$$\sigma_{yy} = \frac{\sum (y - \mu_y)^2 f(y)}{N} \text{ or } \sigma_{yy} = \sum (y - \mu_y)^2 \frac{f(y)}{N}$$

where the summation is over all possible values of y.

Since the relative frequencies are identical to the probabilities, an alternative form is:

$$\sigma_{yy} = \sum (y - \mu_y)^2 p(y) \qquad (6.2)$$

where the summation is over all possible values of y. This is the definition commonly used in textbooks.

In Table 6.3 the mean and variance have been computed for the data of Table 6.1. The different steps of the computation are illustrated in the different columns of the table. It turns out that the mean of the secondary school choice variable was 4 and the variance 3.124. The usefulness of these statistics can be illustrated by comparing the means and variances of different distributions. In Figure 6.4 two more distributions for the same variable are given. These distributions might represent the situation in two different school districts. In situation (a) the mean choice of secondary school is lower than in situation (b) but the dispersion around the mean is the same in both situations. Comparing Figure 6.4b with Figure 6.1 we see that in Figure 6.4b the means of the distributions are the same but the dispersion is in Figure 6.4b much smaller. As can be seen from Figure 6.4, these conclusions on the basis of the mean and variance convey quite accurately what can be learned from a comparison of the total distributions. Thus the mean and the variance are useful as summary measures. Note that the mean of a variable is not necessarily a value which occurs in reality.

From the variance another measure has been derived which is very widely used: the *standard deviation*, denoted as σ_y. This measure is equal to the square root of the variance:

$$\sigma_y = \sqrt{\sigma_{yy}} \qquad (6.3)$$

In chapter 3 we have seen that this measure is used to standardize the scores of variables.

Normal Distribution

The *normal distribution* is a probability distribution of a continuous random variable which is used frequently. One of the reasons for the popularity of this distribution is that some variables may be seen as the sum of a large number of independent random variables. *Independent random variables* are variables which do not covary. The *central limit theorem* says that the distribution of a

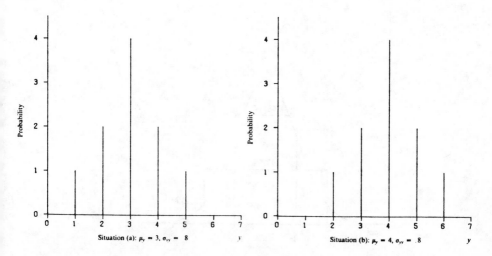

Figure 6.4   Two Different Distributions for the same Variable

variable which is a sum of a large number of independent random variables will approach the normal distribution.

This theorem is very useful because the normal distribution is completely known as we can see in Figure 6.5 . In the so called z-table , printed in Appendix A, precise information of the normal distribution is readily available.

For any normally distributed variable it is known that 68.3% of the observations will fall within a distance of one standard deviation from the mean, while 95.5% of the observations will fall within a distance of two standard deviations from it. The probabilities for any interval can be derived from the z-table.

In order to use the z-table one has to express the values of the variable of interest in deviations from its mean and to divide by the standard deviation. For example, suppose it is known that y is normally distributed with $\mu_y = 5$ and $\sigma_y = 2$, and we want to know the probability that y is larger than 7.5. First we have to determine the distance from the mean in standard deviations (z_0). The distance from the mean is $7.5 - 5$ and the distance in standard deviations is

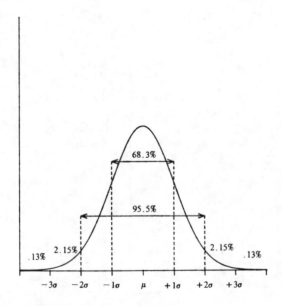

Figure 6.5   Areas below the Normal Curve

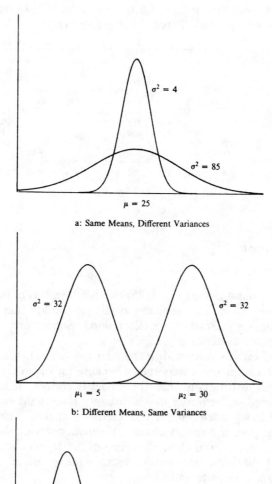

a: Same Means, Different Variances

b: Different Means, Same Variances

c: Different Means, Different Variances

Figure 6.6   Distributions with Different Means and/or Standard deviations

Table 6.4   The Joint Probabilities for the Variables "Choice of Secondary
                  School" (y_5) and "Parents' Preference" (y_3)

Values y_3 y_5	1	2	3	4	5	6	7	Pr(y_5)
7						.009	.092	.101
6					.015	.097	.009	.121
5				.020	.142	.016		.177
4			.020	.162	.020			.202
3		.016	.142	.020				.177
2	.009	.097	.015					.121
1	.092	.009						.101
Pr(y_3)	.101	.121	.177	.202	.177	.121	.101	1.000

$$z_0 = \frac{7.5 - 5}{2} = 1.25$$

Further we know that

$$p(y > 7.5) = p(\frac{y - \mu_y}{\sigma_y} > \frac{7.5 - 5}{2}) = p(z > 1.25)$$

In the z-table it is found that $p(z > 1.25) = .1056$, and from this it follows
that $p(y > 7.5) = .1056$. In a similar way the probability that an observation will fall within any interval can be determined. Some more examples will
be encountered in the exercises.

For the kind of models discussed in this text the normal distribution and
the central limit theorem are of importance because the disturbance term will
approach a normal distribution when the model is correct. If no important
variables are omitted in the theory the disturbance term is the sum of a large
number of small independent effects and therefore approximately normally
distributed. Therefore, if one can obtain information about the mean and
standard deviation, predictions about the values of the dependent variables can
be made even with the disturbance terms present in the equations. Illustrations
of this possibility will be given in the exercises.

Figure 6.6 illustrates the variety of normally distributed variables showing
differences in the mean and/or the standard deviation or variance. This is
the reason why the transformation in standard deviations from the mean (z-
scores) is necessary to reveal the similarity between the different distributions
and to determine the probabilities.

Bivariate Distributions

So far attention has been concentrated on only one variable at a time, that
is, looking at only one   column of the data matrix. In this section the *joint*

distribution of two variables is discussed. The exposition could be arranged in a similar way to the treatment of univariate distributions, i.e. first with the absolute frequency distribution, then with the relative frequency distribution and finally, with the probability distribution. However, in order to shorten the exposition, the probability distribution of the variables "choice of secondary school" (y_5) and "parents' preference" (y_3) is presented immediately in Table 6.4. In this table each cell represents the so called "*joint probability*" of the occurrence of a combination of values for the two variables. The probability of finding a combination of a value 3 on both variables is .142. The probability of finding a combination of a 3 on y_3, and a 4 on y_5, is only .020. The probability of a combination of a 3 on y_3, and a 7 on y_5, is zero and is not entered in the table. Table 6.4 clearly exhibits a strong relationship between the two variables, because only certain combinations of values occur and other combinations do not exist. A typical feature of this case is that combinations for which the two variables have the same value occur very frequently. Therefore the table clearly indicates that the relationship is linear with approximately $\gamma = 1$ and $\alpha = 0$ (the reader should check this). The same point can be illustrated

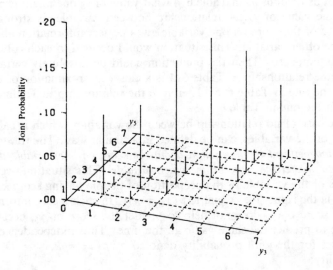

Figure 6.7 The Geometric Representation of the Joint Probability Distribution of y_5 and y_3

Table 6.5 The Joint Probability Distribution for the Variables "Choice of Secondary School" (y_5) and "Teacher's Recommendation" (y_2)

Values y_2 / y_5	1	2	3	4	5	6	7	Pr(y_5)
7				.001	.008	.027	.064	.100
6			.001	.011	.039	.048	.022	.121
5		.001	.012	.051	.073	.036	.006	.178
4	.001	.009	.049	.084	.049	.009	.001	.202
3	.006	.036	.073	.051	.012	.001		.178
2	.022	.048	.039	.011	.001			.121
1	.064	.027	.008	.001				.100
Pr(y_2)	.093	.121	.182	.209	.182	.121	.093	1.000

graphically in Figure 6.7. The heights of the lines on the plane formed by y_5 and y_3 indicate the sizes of the probabilities. Therefore the heights of the different lines should add up to one.

The covariation between variables is not always as strong as in the previous example. In Table 6.5 another example is given where the relationship is somewhat weaker. The relationship between the variables "teacher's recommendation" (y_2) and "choice of secondary school" is said to be weaker because it is not as obvious as in Table 6.4 what value of y_5 one might expect if one knows the value of y_2. A relationship between variables is strongest when knowledge of the score on one variable gives perfect information about the score on the other variable. This situation would occur if in each column only one cell is non-zero. Then the prediction could be absolutely certain. It is seen that the relationship in Table 6.4 is a closer approximation of this situation than the one in Table 6.5. Therefore the relationship in Table 6.4 is stronger than the one in Table 6.5.

The opposite case of no relationship between the variables, which is called "*independence*" of the variables, can be defined in a similar way. The *variables are said to be independent if information about the score on one variable does not help at all to predict the score on the other variable*. This situation occurs if for all values of the variable y_2 the proportion of people having score k on the variable y_5 is the same (i.e. equal to $p(y_5 = k)$). In such a case information about the score on y_2 does not help to predict the score on y_5, because we would have to predict the same value all the time. Thus independence of variables implies for the joint probability denoted by $p(y_5 = k, y_2 = 1)$ the following equality:

$$p(y_5 = k, y_2 = 1) = p(y_5 = k)p(y_2 = 1) \text{ for all } k, 1 \quad (6.4)$$

Table 6.6 has been constructed using this rule. The *marginal* (i.e. univariate)*distributions* are identical to the probability distribution of y_5 and y_2 presented in Table 6.5. Table 6.6 clearly differs from Table 6.4 and 6.5. In

Table 6.6   An Imaginary Probability Distribution for Two Variables which are Independent, while the Univariate Distributions are equal to the Distributions of y_5 and y_2

Values y_2 y_5	1	2	3	4	5	6	7	Pr(y_5)
7	.009	.012	.018	.021	.018	.012	.009	.100
6	.011	.015	.022	.025	.022	.015	.011	.121
5	.017	.021	.032	.037	.032	.021	.017	.178
4	.019	.024	.037	.042	.037	.024	.019	.202
3	.017	.021	.032	.037	.032	.021	.017	.178
2	.011	.015	.022	.025	.022	.015	.011	.121
1	.009	.012	.018	.021	.018*	.012	.009	.100
Pr(y_2)	.093	.121	.192	.209	.182	.121	.093	1.000

Table 6.6 all combinations of values have at least a low probability and the rule of proportionality just mentioned holds for this table, apart from rounding off errors. This is certainly not true for the other two tables (the reader should check this). Before continuing we have to warn the reader that in the literature the term "independent variables" is also used for variables at the right hand side of an equation. In such cases it is not meant to say that these variables do not covary with each other . Only the context can indicate the meaning of the term.

So far we have defined the two extreme cases of perfect relationship and no relationship for the joint probability distribution. No measure has yet been developed for the degree of relationship between the variables. This will be done in the next two sections.

Covariance

In order to introduce the measures of the degree of linear relationship between variables, consider the product of the deviations from the means for two variables y_i and y_j: $(y_i - \mu_{y_i})(y_j - \mu_{y_j})$. If, for a particular unit, y_i and y_j are larger than the means of these variables, the product is positive. If one value is smaller and the other is larger than the mean of the variable, the product is negative. If they are both smaller than the means, the product is positive again. Let us now look at the sum of this product over all units (individuals) in the analysis. If the deviations from the means on both variables move in the same direction for large numbers of research units, the sum over all possible products will become very large. If the deviations on the two variables move in different directions for a majority of research units, the sum of the products will also be very large, but will be negative. If the deviations do not covary

Table 6.7 The Computation of the Covariance between the Variables y_5 and y_3 given that $\mu_{y_5} = 4.0$ and $\mu_{y_3} = 4.0$ and the Joint Probability Distribution of Table 6.4

Values of $y_5\, y_3$	Joint Probability $Pr(y_5 y_3)$	Deviation $y_5 - \mu_{y_5}$	Deviation $y_3 - \mu_{y_3}$	Product	$(y_3 - \mu_{y_3})$ $\times (y_5 - \mu_{y_5})$ $\times Pr(y_5 y_3)$
1 1	.092	−3	−3	9	.828
1 2	.009	−3	−2	6	.054
2 1	.009	−2	−3	6	.054
2 2	.097	−2	−2	4	.388
2 3	.016	−2	−1	2	.032
3 2	.015	−1	−2	2	.030
3 3	.142	−1	−1	1	.142
3 4	.020	−1	0	0	.000
4 3	.020	0	−1	0	.000
4 4	.162	0	0	0	.000
4 5	.020	0	+1	0	.000
5 4	.020	+1	0	0	.000
5 5	.142	+1	+1	1	.142
5 6	.015	+1	+2	2	.030
6 5	.016	+2	+1	2	.032
6 6	.097	+2	+2	4	.388
6 7	.009	+2	+3	6	.054
7 6	.009	+3	+2	6	.054
7 7	.092	+3	+3	9	.828

$$\sigma_{y_5 y_3} = 3.05$$

(that is the products are sometimes positive and sometimes negative) they may well cancel each other out if they are added. Given this characteristic of the sum of the products of the deviations, the mean of these products is used as a measure for the degree of covariation of variables. This measure is denoted by $\sigma_{y_i y_j}$ and will be referred to as the covariance. In order to give a formal definition of the *covariance*, one can write out the sum of the products of the deviations and divide it by the total number of cases in the population. Alternatively, the joint probabilities can be used immediately to define the covariance. This is more in line with the statistical definition in equations (6.1) and (6.2). Thus the formal definition is

$$\sigma_{y_i y_j} = \sum (y_i - \mu_{y_i})(y_j - \mu_{y_j}) p(y_i, y_j) \qquad (6.5)$$

where the summation is over all possible combinations of values of y_i and y_j.

Table 6.7 gives an example of the computation of a covariance, between the variables "choice of secondary school" (y_5) and "parents' preference" (y_3) given in Table 6.4. In discussing Table 6.4 it was indicated that this relationship should be very strong. This can also be seen in the computation: the deviations have the same sign most of the time, and therefore do not cancel each other out when they are added after their multiplication. In this case

Table 6.8 The Joint Probability Distribution for the Variables "Choice of Secondary School" (y_5) and "School Test Score" (y_4)

Values y_4 y_5	10	20	30	40	50	60	70	80	90	100	Pr(y_5)
7			.001	.002	.004	.008	.012	.016	.017	.040	.100
6		.001	.003	.007	.012	.018	.021	.021	.017	.021	.121
5	.002	.004	.009	.017	.026	.031	.031	.025	.017	.015	.178
4	.007	.010	.019	.029	.035	.035	.029	.019	.010	.007	.202
3	.015	.017	.025	.031	.031	.026	.017	.009	.004	.002	.178
2	.021	.017	.021	.021	.018	.012	.007	.003	.001		.121
1	.040	.017	.016	.012	.008	.004	.002	.001			.100
Pr(y_4)	.085	.067	.095	.119	.134	.134	.119	.095	.067	.085	1.000

$\sigma_{y_iy_j} = 3.05$.

For the relationships presented in Tables 6.5, 6.6 and 6.8 we have also computed the covariances. The covariance of y_5 and y_2 in Table 6.5 is 2.63. The covariance in Table 6.6 for the imaginary example is 0.00, and $\sigma_{y_5y_4}$ from Table 6.8 is 29.80. The first two results for Tables 6.4 and 6.5 are not suprising. As the relationship between y_5 and y_2 is weaker than that between y_5 and y_3, and second result, the relationship between the variables of Table 6.6 was constructed to produce independence between the variables. The result for Table 6.8 is somewhat surprising because, merely looking at the probability distribution the relationship does not appear to be stronger than the relationship between y_5 and the other two variables. This observation is indeed correct and the difference in covariance between Table 6.8 and the other tables is due to something else. It involves the scale of the variable y_4 which has a much wider range than variables y_2 and y_3. Since the size of the covariance is dependent upon the scale in which the variables are expressed, it is not easy to compare the covariances for variables with different scales. If there is no relationship the covariance will always be zero, but the maximum value depends on the scale of the variables. For some purposes it may not be practical to use the covariance. If so, another measure is available: the correlation coefficient.

Correlation

The *correlation coefficient* is a measure of the degree of a linear relationship between standardized variables. Standardized variables (y_i^s) are computed from unstandardized variables (y_i) by subtracting the mean (μ_{y_i}) and dividing the

Table 6.9   The Computation of the Correlation between the Variables y_5 and y_3 given the Joint Probability Distribution of Table 6.4 and knowing that $\mu_{y_5} = 4.0$, $\mu_{y_3} = 4.0$, $\sigma_{y_5} = 1.769$ and $\sigma_{y_3} = 1.769$

Values of $y_5\,y_3$	Joint-Probability $\Pr(y_5^s, y_3^s)$	y_5^s	y_3^s	Product $y_5^s y_3^s$	$y_5^s y_3^s \Pr(y_5^s, y_3^s)$
1 1	.092	-1.696	-1.696	2.876	.264
1 2	.009	-1.696	-1.131	1.917	.017
2 1	.009	-1.131	-1.696	1.917	.017
2 2	.097	-1.131	-1.131	1.279	.124
2 3	.016	-1.131	-.565	.639	.010
3 2	.015	-.565	-1.131	.639	.010
3 3	.142	-.565	-.565	.319	.045
3 4	.020	-.565	.000	.000	.000
4 3	.020	.000	-.565	.000	.000
4 4	.162	.000	.000	.000	.000
4 5	.020	.000	.565	.000	.000
5 4	.020	.565	.000	.000	.000
5 5	.142	.565	.565	.319	.045
5 6	.015	.565	1.131	.639	.010
6 5	.016	1.131	.565	.639	.010
6 6	.097	1.131	1.131	1.279	.124
6 7	.009	1.131	1.696	1.917	.017
7 6	.009	1.696	1.131	1.917	.017
7 7	.092	1.696	1.696	2.876	.264

$$\rho_{y_5 y_3} = .97$$

result by the standard devation (σ_{y_i}):

$$y_i^s = \frac{y_i - \mu_{y_i}}{\sigma_{y_i}}$$

To compute the correlation coefficient between two standardized variables y_i^s and y_j^s, we once more consider the products in deviations from the mean: $(y_i^s - \mu_{y_i^s})(y_j^s - \mu_{y_j^s})$. However, in this case the means $\mu_{y_i^s}$ and $\mu_{y_j^s}$ are zero (the proof of this equality is requested in exercise 6.7) and so this product reduces to the term $y_i^s y_j^s$. A statistical definition of the *correlation* coefficient, which is denoted by $\rho_{y_i y_j}$, is that one should take the sum of the products of the deviations divided by their standard errors and divide it by the total number of units in the population. More in line with the definition of the covariance in equation (6.5), one can write

$$\rho_{y_i y_j} = \sum y_i^s y_j^s p(y_i^s, y_j^s) \tag{6.6}$$

with the summation over all possible combinations of the values of y_i^s and y_j^s. Since for each term in this product the scale values of the original variables have been transformed to standardized values, the correlation is independent of the scales of the constituent variables.

Table 6.9 continues the example of Table 6.7 on the association of the variables y_5^s and y_3^s and shows an application of equation (6.6). The correlation between these two variables turns out to be .97. In Table 6.7 their covariance was computed as 3.05. The next question is: is there a more direct relationship between these two measures? Yes. The correlation is identical to the covariance divided by the product of the standard deviations of the two variables:

$$\rho_{y_i y_j} = \frac{\sigma_{y_i y_j}}{\sigma_{y_i} \sigma_{y_j}} \tag{6.7}$$

where $\rho_{y_i y_j}$ represents the correlation coefficient, $\sigma_{y_i y_j}$ represents the covariance, σ_{y_i} represents the standard deviation of y_i, and σ_{y_j} represents the standard deviation of y_j

A distinctive feature of the correlation coefficient is that the maximum and minimum values are bounded and have a clear interpretation. If two variables have a perfectly positive linear relationship, all points fall on the line and the correlation coefficient will be equal to 1. If two variables have a perfectly negative linear relationship, all points fall on the line and the correlation coefficient is equal to -1. Furthermore, if two variables are independent of each other, the correlation coefficient is zero. Because of these useful characteristics the correlation coefficient is often preferred to the covariance. Nevertheless the covariance has some other advantages which will be discussed later.

In order to see how this measure of covariation works in practice we have computed the size of the correlation coefficient for the relationships from Table 6.4 to 6.8. Since we have already seen that $\sigma_{y_5 y_3} = 3.05$, $\sigma_{y_5 y_2} = 2.63$ and $\sigma_{y_5 y_4} = 29.80$ and because the standard deviations are $\sigma_{y_5} = 1.77$, $\sigma_{y_2} = 1.73$, $\sigma_{y_3} = 1.77$, $\sigma_{y_4} = 26.2$, the correlation coefficients can be computed with formula (6.6). It turns out that the correlations are as follows: $\rho_{y_5 y_3} = .97$, $\rho_{y_5 y_2} = .86$ and $\rho_{y_5 y_4} = .64$, while the correlation for the data in Table 6.6 is equal to zero, as expected. These results clearly show that standardization allows the comparison of the degree of relationship between variables even when the scale units for the variables differ.

The Bivariate Normal Distribution

The bivariate normal distribution is an example of a bivariate distribution of two continuous random variables. Three characteristics of the distribution may be noted: (1) both constituent variables have an univariate normal distribution; (2) the distribution of any of the two variables for a given value of the other variable is normal; (3) the distribution is exactly known, and is determined by the means, standard deviations of the variables and the correlation between the two variables. A graphical representation of a bivariate normal distribution is given in in Figure 6.8.

When the correlation between the variables is zero, the units will be spread out over the whole surface of the plane formed by the two variables. If the correlation becomes higher the probability of finding the points close to the regression line becomes higher as well. This phenomenon can be illustrated by crosscutting the distribution of the two variables and exhibiting the contour of the area within which 95% of the units can be found. In Figure 6.9 four such contour lines are shown.

The Multivariate Distribution

Once the bivariate distribution has been considered, the discussion of the *multivariate distribution* is straightforward. Again a joint probability distribution for several variables can be specified if we have full information about the population data matrix. In Table 6.10 a part of the joint probability distribution for the variables of the school career example is given. A graphical representation becomes impossible since we would have to draw an eight-dimensional picture.

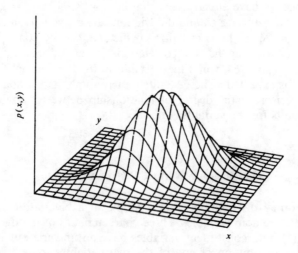

Figure 6.8   Bivariate Normal Distribution

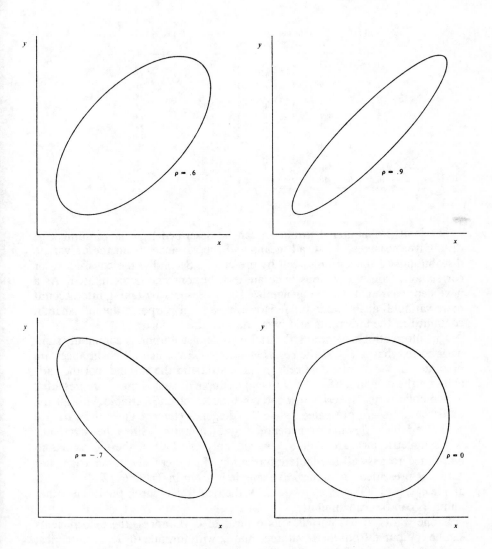

Figure 6.9   The 95% Contours for Bivariate Normal Distribution with Different Correlations between the Variables

Table 6.10   A Part of the Joint Probability Distribution Describing the
                   Multivariate Distribution of x_1 to y_5 for the School Career
                   Example

x_1	x_2	y_1	y_2	y_3	y_4	y_5	$\Pr(x_1, x_2, y_1, y_2, y_3, y_4, y_5)$
			Values of				
1	1	1	1	1	1	1	.020
1	1	1	1	1	1	2	.011
1	1	1	1	1	1	3	.006
1	1	1	1	1	1	4	.000
1	1	1	1	1	1	5	.000
1	1	1	1	1	1	6	.000
1	1	1	1	1	1	7	.000
1	1	1	1	1	2	1	.010
1	1	1	1	1	2	2	.015
⋮	⋮	⋮	⋮	⋮			⋮
10	6	10	7	7	7	6	.003
10	6	10	7	7	7	7	.005

The joint probability distribution can be described by a large number of distinctive measures. First, all means and the variances from the univariate distributions of the variables can be presented. Secondly, the covariances or correlations from the various bivariate distributions can be computed. As a next step one might want to generalize such measures by taking into account more variables at the same time. However, for our purposes the information contained in the univariate and bivariate measures suffices.

The information concerning the multivariate distribution is commonly summarized in what is called the *covariance matrix*, in which all covariances are presented in the off diagonal cells of the matrix and the variances of the variables on the diagonal. Table 6.11 is an example of such a matrix represented in symbolic form. In each row the covariances of one variable with all the other variables are presented, while the diagonal element gives the variance of the variable. This matrix is denoted by Σ (capital σ). Since the covariance is a symmetric measure, i.e. $\sigma_{y_i y_j} = \sigma_{y_j y_i}$ only one half of the matrix has to be printed to pass all available information. In general the lower triangular matrix is presented. A numerical example is given in Table 6.12. In this example $\sigma_{y_5 y_3} = 3.798$ and $\sigma_{y_3 y_2} = 3.272$ (the reader can check this). The other numbers can be read similarly.

If one wants to use correlations instead of covariances, these coefficients can be computed from the covariance matrix with formula (6.7). A numerical example is given in Table 6.13. The correlations are computed frome Table 6.12 by dividing the covariance of two variables by the product of the standard deviations of the two variables. The correlation matrix is symbolized by Σ^s and may be interpreted as a covariance matrix of the standardized vari-

Table 6.11   The Symbolic Representation of a Covariance Matrix(Σ)

y_1	$\sigma_{y_1y_1}$	$\sigma_{y_1y_2}$	$\sigma_{y_1y_3}$	$\sigma_{y_1y_4}$	$\sigma_{y_1y_5}$	$\sigma_{y_1x_1}$	$\sigma_{y_1x_2}$
y_2	$\sigma_{y_2y_1}$	$\sigma_{y_2y_2}$	$\sigma_{y_2y_3}$	$\sigma_{y_2y_4}$	$\sigma_{y_2y_5}$	$\sigma_{y_2x_1}$	$\sigma_{y_2x_2}$
y_3	$\sigma_{y_3y_1}$	$\sigma_{y_3y_2}$	$\sigma_{y_3y_3}$	$\sigma_{y_3y_4}$	$\sigma_{y_3y_5}$	$\sigma_{y_3x_1}$	$\sigma_{y_3x_2}$
y_4	$\sigma_{y_4y_1}$	$\sigma_{y_4y_2}$	$\sigma_{y_4y_3}$	$\sigma_{y_4y_4}$	$\sigma_{y_4y_5}$	$\sigma_{y_4x_1}$	$\sigma_{y_4x_2}$
y_5	$\sigma_{y_5y_1}$	$\sigma_{y_5y_2}$	$\sigma_{y_5y_3}$	$\sigma_{y_5y_4}$	$\sigma_{y_5y_5}$	$\sigma_{y_5x_1}$	$\sigma_{y_5x_2}$
x_1	$\sigma_{x_1y_1}$	$\sigma_{x_1y_2}$	$\sigma_{x_1y_3}$	$\sigma_{x_1y_4}$	$\sigma_{x_1y_5}$	$\sigma_{x_1x_1}$	$\sigma_{x_1x_2}$
x_2	$\sigma_{x_2y_1}$	$\sigma_{x_2y_2}$	$\sigma_{x_2y_3}$	$\sigma_{x_2y_4}$	$\sigma_{x_2y_5}$	$\sigma_{x_2x_1}$	$\sigma_{x_2x_2}$
	y_1	y_2	y_3	y_4	y_5	x_1	x_2

Table 6.12   A Numerical Example of a Covariance Matrix(Σ)

y_1	5.731						
y_2	3.698	3.573					
y_3	3.710	3.272	3.844				
y_4	5.708	3.683	3.695	8.501			
y_5	3.736	3.274	3.798	3.788	3.815		
x_1	1.064	.695	.705	1.059	.709	1.930	
x_2	.937	.605	.756	.934	.751	.312	2.133
	y_1	y_2	y_3	y_4	y_5	x_1	x_2

Table 6.13   A Numerical Example of a Correlation Matrix(Σ^s), Derived from Table 6.12

y_1	1.000						
y_2	.817	1.000					
y_3	.790	.883	1.000				
y_4	.818	.668	.646	1.000			
y_5	.799	.887	.992	.665	1.000		
x_1	.320	.265	.259	.261	.261	1.000	
x_2	.268	.219	.264	.219	.263	.154	1.000
	y_1	y_2	y_3	y_4	y_5	x_1	x_2

ables. If one is using the correlation matrix, it is a good custom to present the variances or standard deviations of the unstandardized variables, since it is otherwise impossible for other researchers to do a secondary analysis on the basis of the covariance matrix. If the variances are published seperately, the covariances can be reconstructed from the correlation matrix. The reader may want to check this using equation (6.7).

The *multivariate normal distribution* is a special case of a multivariate distribution. Such a distribution is characterized by the same features as the bivariate normal distribution: (1) all variables have a univariate normal distribution; (2) all variables are normally distributed for given values of the other variables; (3) the distribution is exactly known and can be completely described by the means and the standard deviations of the different variables and the correlations between the variables.

This section completes the discussion of descriptive measures for the information obtainable from the population. In the next chapter we discuss how this information can be used to obtain the effect parameters of the theory in which we are interested.

* Simplification of the Notation

In this chapter the following formulas for the mean, the variance, the covariance and the correlation were encountered:

$$\mu_y = \sum yp(y) \text{ summing over all values of } y$$

$$\sigma_{yy} = \sum (y - \mu_y)^2 p(y) \text{ summing over all values of } y$$

$$\sigma_{y_i y_j} = \sum (y_i - \mu_{y_i})(y_j - \mu_{y_j}) p(y_i, y_j)$$
$$\text{summing over all combinations of values of } y_i \text{ and } y_j$$

$$\rho_{y_i y_j} = \sum y_i^s y_j^s p(y_i, y_j)$$
$$\text{summing over all combinations of values of } y_i \text{ and } y_j$$

Each of these formulas represents the mean for some random variable or for a product of random variables which is again a random variable. The first form represents the mean of the variable y, the second form the mean of the variable $(y - \mu_y)^2$) or the squared deviation from the mean, the third form represents the mean over the product of two deviations from the means $(y_i - \mu_{y_i})(y_j - \mu_{y_j})$, and the last form represents the mean of the same product but now divided by the respective standard deviations.

In order to simplify the notation, the operator E is used to indicate that the mean or *expectation* is taken for the random variable which is specified in brackets after the E. According to this notation the four formulas become:

$$\mu_y = E(y) \tag{6.8}$$
$$\sigma_{yy} = E(y - \mu_y)^2 \tag{6.9}$$
$$\sigma_{y_i y_j} = E(y_i - \mu_{y_i})(y_j - \mu_{y_j}) \tag{6.10}$$
$$\rho_{y_i y_j} = E(y_i^s y_j^s) \tag{6.11}$$

These equations illustrate that the use of the operator E leads to a reduction in writing.

The advantage of the E operator becomes even more evident if the theorems are used which have been derived for this operator. Three such theorems are especially relevant:

(I)   The expectation of a random variable which is a constant times any other random variable is equal to the constant times the expectation of the random variable:

$$\text{if } y = bx$$
$$\text{then } E(y) = E(bx) = bE(x) \tag{6.12}$$

(II)   The expectation of a random variable which is equal to another random variable plus a constant is equal to the expectation of the random variable plus the constant:

$$\text{if } y = x + c$$
$$\text{then } E(y) = E(x + c) = E(x) + c \tag{6.13}$$

(III)   The expectation of a random variable which is the sum of two other random variables is equal to the sum of the expectations of the random variables:

$$\text{if } y = x_1 + x_2$$
$$\text{then } E(y) = E(x_1 + x_2) = E(x_1) + E(x_2) \tag{6.14}$$

The usefulness of these theorems can be illustrated in an example. Suppose one wants to determine the mean of variable y_5 which is a linear function of four other random variables, such that

$$y_5 = \beta_{52}y_2 + \beta_{53}y_3 + \beta_{54}y_4 + \alpha_5 + \zeta_5$$

In this case, knowing that $\mu_{y_5} = E(y_5)$, it follows that

$$\mu_{y_5} = E(y_5) = E(\beta_{52}y_2 + \beta_{53}y_3 + \beta_{54}y_4 + \alpha_5 + \zeta_5)$$

Applications of theorems II and III lead to

$$\mu_{y_5} = E(\beta_{52}y_2) + E(\beta_{53}y_3) + E(\beta_{54}y_4) + \alpha_5 + E(\zeta_5)$$

According to theorem I this result can be rewritten as

$$\mu_{y_5} = \beta_{52}E(y_2) + \beta_{53}E(y_3) + \beta_{54}E(y_4) + \alpha_5 + E(\zeta_5)$$

or

$$\mu_{y_5} = \beta_{52}\mu_{y_2} + \beta_{53}\mu_{y_3} + \beta_{54}\mu_{y_4} + \alpha_5 + \mu_{\zeta_5}$$

This means that the mean of y_5 is equal to a linear function of the means of the other variables plus the constant. This derivation is much quicker than if we had to use formula (6.1) and had to make the derivation without the theorems. Incidentally, so far we have said that α is the value (or better mean value) of the effect variable given that the causal variables are equal to zero. Here we see that alternatively one can say that

$$\alpha_5 = \mu_{y_5} - (\beta_{52}\mu_{y_2} + \beta_{53}\mu_{y_3} + \beta_{54}\mu_{y_4} + \mu_{\zeta_5}).$$

Further Reading

The topics discussed in this chapter are discussed in all introductory textbooks in statistics. We only want to mention two for which we know that they have been very useful for our own students to pick up the necessary information on their own. The first text is written by Wonnacott and Wonnacott and is called "Introductory Statistics" (1972), the other is written by Wallpole and is called "Introduction to Statistics" (1974). Obviously, there are many more of these texts. For a more complete overview the book of Hays, named "Statistics for the Social Sciences" (1973), is still very useful.

Exercises

6.1 In exercise (5.1) we have seen that the evaluations of the different actions will be unreliable. This means that each person will give different scores for the same action at different points in time. In the table we represent a summary of the scores for the action "demonstration"; the table gives the probability of occurrence of a particular score.

Score	$p(y)$
50	.05
60	.10
70	.20
75	.30
80	.20
90	.10
100	.05

(a)Give a graphic representation of this distribution.
(b)Compute the mean, variance and standard deviation.
6.2 For the action "blocking the entrance by a sit-in", the probability distribution is as follows:

Score	$p(y)$
100	.05
110	.10
120	.15
130	.20
140	.20
150	.15
160	.10
170	.05

(a)Give a graphic representation of this distribution.

(b)Compute the mean, variance and standard deviation.

(c)What are the differences between the distributions for the two actions?

(d)What is the substantive meaning of these technical differences?

(e)Given these distributions, are these random variables discrete or continuous random variables?

6.3 If the same judgment task would have been done expressing the judgments in lines instead of numbers, the scores would be normally distributed with for "demonstrations", for example, $\mu = 75$ and $\sigma = 5.2$.

(a)What is the probability of a judgment larger than 85?

(b)What is the probability of a judgment smaller than 65?

(c)What is the probability of obtaining a judgment between 65 and 85?

(d)Between what values do we find 95% of the scores?

(e)Between what values do we find 50% of the scores?

6.4 If the defense expenditures of the USA (y) were determined mainly by the expenditures of the USSR (x), while all the other variables would have only minor effects and do not covary with each other,

(a)what can we say in that case about the equation?

(b)what can we say about the distribution of the disturbance terms?

6.5 If we know that $\mu_\zeta = 0$ and $\sigma_\zeta = 1.5$ billion, while $\gamma = 1$ and $\alpha = 10$ billion for the equation formulated in the last exercise,

(a)How large are the following probabilities:
$$\Pr(-3 \text{ billion } < \zeta < 3 \text{ billion })$$
$$\Pr(-1.5 \text{ billion } < \zeta < 1.5 \text{ billion })$$
$$\Pr(-0.5 \text{ billion } < \zeta < 0.5 \text{ billion })$$

(b)What value of y do you expect if $x = 100$ billion ?

(c)If $x = 100$ billion , how large are the probabilities
$$\Pr(107 \text{ billion } < y < 113 \text{ billion }$$
$$\Pr(108.5 \text{ billion } < y < 111.5 \text{ billion }$$
$$\Pr(109.5 \text{ billion } < y < 110.5 \text{ billion }$$

(d)Between which values should the value of y be with a probability of 99% if $x = 150$ billion, $\mu_\zeta = 0$ and $\sigma_\zeta = 3$ billion?

6.6 In exercise 5.1 of the previous chapter you have given a large number of judgments with respect to violence, expected success, expected risk of different actions and your willingness to participate in these actions. These judgments contain, of course, measurement error. If we repeat the different judgments over and over again, the following results could have been obtained for the two pairs of variables:

violence x_1	expected success y_1	$p(x_1, y_1)$	violence x_1	willingness to participate y_3	$p(x_1, y_3)$
50	60	.05	50	125	.10
50	70	.20	50	150	.10
50	80	.05	50	175	.10
100	90	.10	100	125	.10
100	100	.20	100	100	.20
100	110	.10	100	75	.10
150	120	.05	150	50	.10
150	125	.20	150	60	.10
150	130	.05	150	70	.10

(a)Can you say without computations which relationship is stronger: the one between violence and expected success or the relationship between violence and willingness to participate? Why?

(b)Compute the covariance for the first pair of variables, if you know that $\mu_{x_1} = 100$ and $\mu_{y_1} = 98.5$.

(c)If you know that the covariance ($\sigma_{x_1 y_3}$) between "violence" and "willingness to participate" is ₁350, while you have $\sigma_{x_1 y_1} = 900$, can you tell on the basis of these measures whether your answer in (a) is correct? Why?

(d)Compute also the correlation coefficients for these two relationships, knowing that $\sigma_{x_1} = 54.8$, $\sigma_{y_1} = 24.13$ and $\sigma_{y_3} = 38.61$

(e)Can you say on the basis of these measures whether your answer in (a) is correct? Why?

(f)How do you think the regression lines in these cases will look?

(g)The regression coefficients do not represent the same information as correlation coefficients. What might be the difference?

6.7* Three theorems on the algebra of expectations have been presented at the end of the chapter.

(a)Prove that these three statements are correct.

(b)Show that if $y = x - \mu_x$, then $E(y) = 0$ and $\sigma_{yy} = \sigma_{xx}$

(c)Show that if $y = (x - \mu_x)/\sigma_x$, then $E(y) = 0$, $\sigma_y = 1$ and $\sigma_{yy} = 1$.

Chapter 7
The Relationships between
Covariances and Structural Parameters

In chapter 4 it was shown that information about the size of the structural parameters β and γ was essential in order to determine whether causal hypotheses should be accepted or rejected. Chapter 5 and 6 indicated that direct analysis of the empirical data was unable to provide this information concerning the size of the coefficients. The kinds of information obtained from these data were means, variances, covariances and correlations of the variables. So, if we want to make use of these data to test causal hypotheses, a link has to be made between this information, that we can calculate from these data, and the structural parameters, which are the basic features of causal theories. This link is explained in this chapter.

Expressed mathematically, the simplest relationship to be found is that between the correlation coefficients and the parameters of the model. This assumes that variables and parameters have been standardized. Therefore this chapter reiterates the formulation of a model in standardized form, a topic which was discussed in chapter 4. There are two ways to explain the relationships between the covariances or correlations and the parameters: an intuitive and a formal way. The intuitive derivation is provided first and is required reading material for anybody interested in causal modelling. The formal derivation is postponed to the final sections of this chapter and represents optional reading.

Model and Data for Standardized Variables

At the end of chapter 4 a linear structural equation model for the full School Career Theory was discussed. In this chapter we will simplify the discussion

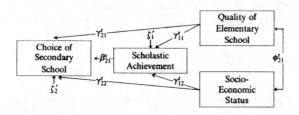

Figure 7.1   Causal Model for the Simplified School Career Theory

119

Table 7.1   Correlation Matrix for the Variables of Model (7.1)

x_1	$\rho_{x_1x_1}$			
x_2	$\rho_{x_2x_1}$	$\rho_{x_2x_2}$		
y_1	$\rho_{y_1x_1}$	$\rho_{y_1x_2}$	$\rho_{y_1y_1}$	
y_2	$\rho_{y_2x_1}$	$\rho_{y_2x_2}$	$\rho_{y_2y_1}$	$\rho_{y_2y_2}$
	x_1	x_2	y_1	y_2

and therefore use the simplified School Career Theory as presented in Figure 2.5 and repeated here in Figure 7.1. This model contains four observed variables. The reader should note that y_2^s was called before y_5^s. Such a change in notation is necessary for the LISREL program which always expects the variables to be numbered from y_1 to y_n without interruption. If these variables are standardized the model can be represented in the equations (7.1a) to (7.1g):

$$y_1^s = \gamma_{11}^s x_1^s + \gamma_{12}^s x_2^s + \zeta_1' \qquad (7.1a)$$
$$y_2^s = \beta_2^s y_1^s + \gamma_{21}^s x_1^s + \gamma_{22}^s x_2^s + \zeta_2' \qquad (7.1b)$$

where

$$\mu_{\zeta_i'} = 0 \text{ for all } i \qquad (7.1c)$$
$$\mu_{y_i^s} = 0, \mu_{x_i^s} = 0 \text{ for all } i \qquad (7.1d)$$
$$\sigma_{y_i^s} = 1, \sigma_{x_i^s} = 1 \text{ for all } i \qquad (7.1e)$$
$$\sigma_{\zeta_i'x_j^s} = 0 \text{ for all } i,j \qquad (7.1f)$$
$$\psi_{ij}' = 0 \text{ for all } i \neq j \qquad (7.1g)$$

Equations (7.1a), (7.1b), (7.1f) and (7.1g) are in agreement with the causal diagram in Figure 7.1. The three remaining equations cannot be recognized in such graphs. Equations (7.1d) and (7.1e) are always true for standardized variables: their mean is zero and their standard deviation (and also the variance is one. Equation (7.1c) is an assumption; the mean of the disturbance term will only be zero if the main causal variables have been incorporated and if the relationships are linear and additive.

There are four observed variables in Figure 7.1. From the data the correlation between each pair of variables can be computed from a data matrix like the one provided in Table 5.2 and organized in a correlation matrix, such as the one in Table 7.1: After this discussion the link will now be established between the information from the data—variances, covariances, or correlations—and the parameters which are characteristic for the causal models.

The Intuitive Approach

In chapter 1 and 2 various sources of covariation between variables were discussed. Now a general rule can be formulated describing the relationship between the correlation coefficient of two variables and the parameters of the model. It is called the *first "Decomposition" rule* since it decomposes the correlation between variables in the four components of covariation.

FIRST DECOMPOSITION RULE

The correlation coefficient between two variables is equal to the sum of the direct effects, the indirect effects, the spurious relationships and the joint effects.

If one is able to specify the indirect effects, spurious relationships and joint effects in parameters of the model, the correlation coefficient can be expressed in the parameters of the model. In the next section the following result will be derived:

Each indirect effect, spurious relationship and joint effect can be expressed as the product of the parameters which connect the two variables of interest.

Using the first decomposition rule one can write out the relationship between the correlation coefficients and the parameters of the model directly from the path diagram. This is illustrated by applying the rule to the model of Figure 7.1.

The first decomposition rule is applied to the off-diagonal elements of the matrix. The correlation between the predetermined variables obtained from the data is not explained in the model and can therefore only be equal to the parameter representing this correlation coefficient in the model

$$\rho_{x_2 x_1} = \phi_{21}^s \qquad (7.1.1)$$

The correlation between y_1 and x_1 is equal to the direct effect (γ_{11}^s) plus the joint effect of x_1^s and x_2^s $(\gamma_{12}^s \phi_{21}^s)$:

$$\rho_{y_1 x_1} = \gamma_{11}^s + \gamma_{12}^s \phi_{21}^s \qquad (7.1.2)$$

The last term is a joint effect since it is unclear whether it is an indirect effect of x_1^s, or a spurious relationship due to x_2^s. The correlation between y_1 and x_2 is equal to the sum of the direct effect (γ_{12}^s) and the joint effect of x_1^s and x_2^s $(\gamma_{11}^s \phi_{21}^s)$:

$$\rho_{y_1 x_2} = \gamma_{12}^s + \gamma_{11}^s \phi_{21}^s \qquad (7.1.3)$$

The correlation between y_2 and x_1 is equal to the direct effect (γ_{21}^s) plus the indirect effect $(\beta_{21}^s \gamma_{11}^s)$ plus two joint effects of x_1^s and x_2^s $(\gamma_{22}^s \phi_{21}^s$ and $\beta_{21}^s \gamma_{12}^s \phi_{21}^s)$:

$$\rho_{y_2 x_1} = \gamma_{21}^s + \beta_{21}^s \gamma_{11}^s + \gamma_{22}^s \phi_{21}^s + \beta_{21}^s \gamma_{12}^s \phi_{21}^s \qquad (7.1.4)$$

The correlation between y_2 and x_2 is equal to the direct effect (γ_{22}^s) plus the indirect effect $(\beta_{21}^s \gamma_{12}^s)$ plus two joint effects of x_1^s and x_2^s $(\gamma_{21}^s \phi_{21}^s$ and $\beta_{21}^s \gamma_{11}^s \phi_{21}^s)$:
$$\rho_{y_2 x_2} = \gamma_{22}^s + \beta_{21}^s \gamma_{12}^s + \gamma_{21}^s \phi_{21}^s + \beta_{21}^s \gamma_{11}^s \phi_{21}^s \qquad (7.1.5)$$
Finally the correlation between y_2 and y_1 is equal to the direct effect (β_{21}^s) plus the spurious relation due to x_1^s $(\gamma_{21}^s \gamma_{11}^s)$ plus the spurious relation due to x_2^s $(\gamma_{22}^s \gamma_{12}^s)$ and two spurious relations from x_1^s and x_2^s $(\gamma_{22}^s \phi_{21}^s \gamma_{11}^s$ and $\gamma_{21}^s \phi_{21}^s \gamma_{12}^s)$:
$$\rho_{y_2 y_1} = \beta_{21}^s + \gamma_{21}^s \gamma_{11}^s + \gamma_{22}^s \gamma_{12}^s + \gamma_{22}^s \phi_{21}^s \gamma_{11}^s + \gamma_{21}^s \phi_{21}^s \gamma_{12}^s \qquad (7.1.6)$$
Having specified all the elements off the diagonal of the correlation matrix in the parameters of the model, we now look at the elements on the diagonal, which represent the variances of the observed variables. Here another rule turns out to be useful.

First, something can be said about the variances of the predetermined variables. These variables are not explained by other variables in the model, and they are taken for granted. Since there is no explanation for them, the variance of such a variable obtained from the data can only be identical to the variance specified in the model. Thus, in the example we have:
$$\rho_{x_1 x_1} = \phi_{11}^s \qquad (7.1.7)$$
$$\rho_{x_2 x_2} = \phi_{22}^s \qquad (7.1.8)$$
Since these variables are standardized we know that both coefficients have to be 1.

Next we turn to the variances of the endogenous variables. For them another rule is very useful.

SECOND DECOMPOSITION RULE

The total variance of an endogenous variable is equal to the amount of variance explained by the causal variables of this endogenous variable, plus the amount of unexplained variance.

If the observed variables have been standardized, the variances equal unity. Consequently, the second decomposition rule says that the variance of the standardized endogenous variable is equal to the sum of the *proportion of variance explained* by the causal variables and the *proportion of unexplained variance*.

The unexplained variance in the endogenous variables (y_i) when they are expressed in deviation scores is equal to the variance of the disturbance term (ψ_{ii}). When standardized variables y_i^s are used, ψ_{ii}' represents the *proportion* of unexplained variance, since $\psi_{ii}' = \psi_{ii}/\sigma_{y_i y_i}$, which is the ratio of unexplained variance and the total variance of variable y_i.

In general the proportion of variance explained by a number of variables is denoted by the symbol $R^2_{y_i.y_1,\ldots,x_1,x_2,\ldots}$, which is called the *"squared multiple correlation coefficient"* or the *"coefficient of determination"*. In order to indicate which variable is explained and which are the explaining variables, one uses subscripts with a point in between. The first index denotes the effect variable, the variables after the point denote the explaining variables. Thus, in the example, one may write for y_1 and y_2:

$$\rho_{y_1 y_1} = 1 = R^2_{y_1.x_1,x_2} + \psi_{11}' \qquad (7.1.9)$$

$$\rho_{y_2 y_2} = 1 = R^2_{y_2.y_1,x_1,x_2} + \psi_{22}' \qquad (7.1.10)$$

The multiple correlation coefficient is a function of the parameters of the structural model and not a parameter of that model itself. The following result will be shown in the next section:

> For any endogenous variable, the proportion of variance explained can be obtained by adding the product of the direct effect and correlation coefficient of that endogenous variable and each of its causal variables.

Applying this rule to y_1 we get

$$R^2_{y_1.x_1,x_2} = \gamma^s_{11}\rho_{y_1 x_1} + \gamma^s_{12}\rho_{y_1 x_2}$$

and to y_2

$$R^2_{y_2.y_1,x_1,x_2} = \beta^s_{21}\rho_{y_2 y_1} + \gamma^s_{21}\rho_{y_2 x_1} + \gamma^s_{22}\rho_{y_2 x_2}$$

Since the different correlation coefficients have already been expressed in the parameters of the model, the last two equations show that the R^2 is not necessary as a new parameter of the model. If one wants to compute the proportion of explained variance for variable y^s_i, the easiest way to do so is by use of the following equation, which is a rewritten version of equations like (7.1.9) and (7.1.10):

$$R^2_{y_i.\text{causal variables}} = 1 - \psi_{ii}'$$

Using the two decomposition rules, we can specify the relationships between the correlation coefficients which are obtainable from the data, and the parameters of the structural model. In the example, this activity has led to ten different equations expressing the distinct elements of the correlation matrix in the parameters of the model. For a model with n observed variables (both x and y variables) the total number of distinct equations expressing the variances and covariances or correlations in parameters of the model, is equal to $\frac{1}{2}n(n+1)$. It is not equal to $n \times n$ since the equations for ρ_{ij} and ρ_{ji} are identical.

The advantage of the decomposition rules is the intuitive understanding which they provide. It is clear that, even in a simple example, the forms of

Table 7.2   Covariance Matrix for the Variables of Model (7.2)

x_1	$\sigma_{x_1 x_1}$			
x_2	$\sigma_{x_2 x_1}$	$\sigma_{x_2 x_2}$		
y_1	$\sigma_{y_1 x_1}$	$\sigma_{y_1 x_2}$	$\sigma_{y_1 y_1}$	
y_2	$\sigma_{y_2 x_1}$	$\sigma_{y_2 x_2}$	$\sigma_{y_2 y_1}$	$\sigma_{y_2 y_2}$
	x_1	x_2	y_1	y_2

the equations become rather complex, which means that there is a possibility of error. Also, the decomposition rules do not give a solution for all models; in particular it is unclear how reciprocal effects should be treated. For this reason we will go on to derive the relationships by means of more formal procedures. But the intuitive rules are nevertheless useful since they indicate better the meaning of the results which can be derived formally. The discussion in the next two sections is rather technical and formal. It is presented for completeness of the argument, but if the reader wants to skip these sections, this is possible without loosing track of the line of argument. The interpretation of the relationships between the measures of covariation which resulted from the data, and the structural parameters of the model, has already been presented in this section.

* The Formal Derivation for Unstandardized Parameters

In order to avoid too abstract an argument, the formal derivation of the relationship between the variances and covariances on the one hand and the structural parameters on the other hand will be given by discussing the example used in this chapter. But it will be clear that the procedure used for this specific case can be used for any other model as well. The starting point is the model in its mathematical form as specified in the set of equations (7.1a) to (7.1g), but with variables which are expressed in deviation from their means. The equations are printed as the set of equations (7.2):

$$y_1^d = \gamma_{11} x_1^d + \gamma_{12} x_2^d + \zeta_1 \qquad (7.2a)$$
$$y_2^d = \beta_{21} y_1^d + \gamma_{21} x_1^d + \gamma_{22} x_2^d + \zeta_2 \qquad (7.2b)$$

where

$$E(\zeta_i) = 0 \text{ for all } i \qquad (7.2c)$$
$$E(y_i^d) = 0, E(x_i^d) = 0 \text{ for all } i \qquad (7.2d)$$
$$E(\zeta_i x_j^d) = 0 \text{ for all } i,j \qquad (7.2e)$$
$$\psi_{ij} = E(\zeta_i \zeta_j) = 0 \text{ for all } i \neq j \qquad (7.1f)$$

The data pertaining to this model are summarized in a covariance matrix, the relevant part of which is shown in Table 7.2. The deriviatons from model

(7.2) and from any other model can be made by taking the expectations of products of variables, since we know that for variables expressed in deviation form these products represent the covariances and variances of the variables of the model:

$$\sigma_{y_i x_j} = E(y_i^d x_j^d)$$

$$\sigma_{y_i y_i} = E(y_i^d y_i^d)$$

By substituting the structural equations in these forms, and using the algebra of expectations to simplify the expressions, the relationships are derived.

Let us do this for the example formulated in equation (7.2). With respect to the variances and covariances of the predetermined variables, nothing has to be done since they are not explained in the model. So the variances and covariances from the data should be equal to the variances and covariances specified in the model, which leads to:

$$\sigma_{x_1 x_1} = E(x_1^d x_1^d) = \phi_{11} \qquad (7.2.1)$$
$$\sigma_{x_2 x_1} = E(x_2^d x_1^d) = \phi_{21} \qquad (7.2.2)$$
$$\sigma_{x_2 x_2} = E(x_2^d x_2^d) = \phi_{22} \qquad (7.2.3)$$

The covariance between y_1 and x_1 can be expressed as the expectation of the product of these two variables in deviation form:

$$\sigma_{y_1 x_1} = E(y_1^d x_1^d)$$

Substitution of equation (7.2a) gives

$$\sigma_{y_1 x_1} = E[(\gamma_{11} x_1^d + \gamma_{12} x_2^d + \zeta_1)(x_1^d)]$$

This can be rewritten as

$$\sigma_{y_1 x_1} = E(\gamma_{11} x_1^d x_1^d + \gamma_{12} x_2^d x_1^d + \zeta_1 x_1^d)$$

Since the expectation of a sum is equal to the sum of the expectations, we get

$$\sigma_{y_1 x_1} = E(\gamma_{11} x_1^d x_1^d) + E(\gamma_{12} x_2^d x_1^d) + E(\zeta_1 x_1^d)$$

Since the expectation of the product of a constant and a random variable is equal to the product of the constant and the expectation of the random variable, it follows that

$$\sigma_{y_1 x_1} = \gamma_{11} E(x_1^d x_1^d) + \gamma_{12} E(x_2^d x_1^d) + E(\zeta_1 x_1^d)$$

But from (7.2.1) it is known that $E(x_1^d x_1^d) = \phi_{11}$, and according to (7.2e) $E(\zeta_1 x_1^d) = 0$. Also $E(x_2^d x_1^d) = \sigma_{x_2 x_1}$, which is equal to ϕ_{21} according to (7.2.2). Therefore it follows that

$$\sigma_{y_1 x_1} = \gamma_{11} \phi_{11} + \gamma_{12} \phi_{21} \qquad (7.2.4)$$

Though this procedure takes much longer than the intuitive approach, the obvious advantage is that in the formal procedure each step we take is certainly correct. Consequently the derived result is also certainly true, if the model is true. Although this result seems to differ from the result in equation (7.1.2) of the last section, the results are nevertheless in agreement as will be shown in the next section.

The derivation of the other variances and covariances can be carried out in exactly the same way. Therefore we will go through the derivations a little bit faster, starting with the covariance between y_1 and x_2:

$$\sigma_{y_1 x_2} = E(y_1^d x_2^d) = E[(\gamma_{11} x_1^d + \gamma_{12} x_2^d + \zeta_1)(x_2^d)]$$
$$= \gamma_{11} E(x_1^d x_2^d) + \gamma_{12} E(x_2^d x_2^d) + E(\zeta_1 x_2^d)$$

since $E(x_1^d x_2^d) = E(x_2^d x_1^d) = \phi_{21}$, $E(x_2^d x_2^d) = \phi_{22}$ and $E(\zeta_1 x_2^d) = 0$ it follows that

$$\sigma_{y_1 x_2} = \gamma_{11} \phi_{21} + \gamma_{12} \phi_{22} \qquad (7.2.5)$$

In the same way the covariance between y_2 and x_1 can be decomposed:

$$\sigma_{y_2 x_1} = E(y_2^d x_1^d) = E[(\beta_{21} y_1^d + \gamma_{21} x_1^d + \gamma_{22} x_2^d + \zeta_2)(x_1^d)]$$
$$= \beta_{21} E(y_1^d x_1^d) + \gamma_{21} E(x_1^d x_1^d) + \gamma_{22} E(x_2^d x_1^d) + E(\zeta_2 x_1^d)$$

since $E(x_1^d x_1^d) = \phi_{11}$, $E(x_2^d x_1^d) = \phi_{21}$, $E(\zeta_2 x_1^d) = 0$ and $E(y_1^d x_1^d) = \sigma_{y_1 x_1}$

$$\sigma_{y_2 x_1} = \beta_{21} \sigma_{y_1 x_1} + \gamma_{21} \phi_{11} + \gamma_{22} \phi_{21} \qquad (7.2.6)$$

The term $\sigma_{y_1 x_1}$ can be substituted by equation (7.2.4) if one wants to.

The covariance between y_2 and x_2 is equal to

$$\sigma_{y_2 x_2} = E(y_2^d x_2^d) = E[(\beta_{21} y_1^d + \gamma_{21} x_1^d + \gamma_{22} x_2^d + \zeta_2)(x_2^d)]$$
$$= \beta_{21} E(y_1^d x_2^d) + \gamma_{21} E(x_1^d x_2^d) + \gamma_{22} E(x_2^d x_2^d) + E(\zeta_2 x_2^d)$$

since $E(x_1^d x_2^d) = \phi_{21}$, $E(x_2^d x_2^d) = \phi_{22}$, $E(\zeta_2 x_2^d) = 0$ and $E(y_1^d x_2^d) = \sigma_{y_1 x_2}$

$$\sigma_{y_2 x_2} = \beta_{21} \sigma_{y_1 x_2} + \gamma_{21} \phi_{21} + \gamma_{22} \phi_{22} \qquad (7.2.7)$$

In this form $\sigma_{y_1 x_2}$ can be substituted by equation (7.2.5).

Finally the covariance between y_2 and y_1 can be derived:

$$\sigma_{y_2 y_1} = E(y_2^d y_1^d) = E[(\beta_{21} y_1^d + \gamma_{21} x_1^d + \gamma_{22} x_2^d + \zeta_2)(y_1^d)]$$
$$= \beta_{21} E(y_1^d y_1^d) + \gamma_{21} E(y_1^d x_1^d) + \gamma_{22} E(y_1^d x_2^d) + E(\zeta_2 y_1^d)$$

Since $E(y_1^d y_1^d) = \sigma_{y_1 y_1}$, $E(y_1^d x_1^d) = \sigma_{y_1 x_1}$, $E(y_1^d x_2^d) = \sigma_{y_1 x_2}$

and $E(\zeta_2 y_1^d) = E[(\gamma_{11} x_1^d + \gamma_{12} x_2^d + \zeta_1)(\zeta_2)] = 0$ it follows that

$$\sigma_{y_2 y_1} = \beta_{21} \sigma_{y_1 y_1} + \gamma_{21} \sigma_{y_1 x_1} + \gamma_{22} \sigma_{y_1 x_2} \qquad (7.2.8)$$

The terms $\sigma_{y_1 x_1}$ and $\sigma_{y_1 x_2}$ are already known and could be substituted, but the term $\sigma_{y_1 y_1}$ has not been derived yet. This variance will now be derived.

This is done in a similar way:

$$\sigma_{y_1y_1} = E(y_1^d y_1^d) = E[(\gamma_{11}x_1^d + \gamma_{12}x_2^d + \zeta_1)(y_1^d)]$$
$$= \gamma_{11}E(y_1^d x_1^d) + \gamma_{12}E(y_1^d x_2^d) + E(\zeta_1 y_1^d)$$

Since $E(y_1^d x_1^d) = \sigma_{y_1x_1}$, $E(y_1^d x_2^d) = \sigma_{y_1x_2}$

and $E(\zeta_1 y_1^d) = E[(\gamma_{11}x_1^d + \gamma_{12}x_2^d + \zeta_1)(\zeta_1)] = \psi_{11}$ it follows that

$$\sigma_{y_1y_1} = \gamma_{11}\sigma_{y_1x_1} + \gamma_{12}\sigma_{y_1x_2} + \psi_{11} \qquad (7.2.9)$$

where all terms are again known and could thus be substituted. The last variance which has to be derived is $\sigma_{y_2y_2}$:

$$\sigma_{y_2y_2} = E(y_2^d y_2^d) = E[(\beta_{21}y_1^d + \gamma_{21}x_1^d + \gamma_{22}x_2^d + \zeta_2)(y_2^d)]$$
$$= \beta_{21}E(y_2^d y_1^d) + \gamma_{21}E(y_2^d x_1^d) + \gamma_{22}E(y_2^d x_2^d) + E(\zeta_2 y_2^d)$$

since $E(y_2^d y_1^d) = \sigma_{y_2y_1}$, $E(y_2^d x_1^d) = \sigma_{y_2x_1}$, $E(y_2^d x_2^d) = \sigma_{y_2x_2}$ and $E(\zeta_2 y_2^d) = E[(\beta_{21}y_1^d + \gamma_{21}x_1^d + \gamma_{22}x_2^d + \zeta_2)(\zeta_2)] = \psi_{22}$ it follows that

$$\sigma_{y_2y_2} = \beta_{21}\sigma_{y_2y_1} + \gamma_{21}\sigma_{y_2x_1} + \gamma_{22}\sigma_{y_2x_2} + \psi_{22} \qquad (7.2.10)$$

Having derived the relationship between the variances and the covariances on the one hand and on the other hand the structural parameters of the formal model presented in equations (7.2a) to (7.2f), the derivations are also made for all models which are formally identical to this model.

It should be noted that the procedure presented here can be applied to any kind of model in order to derive the relationships between the variances and covariances obtainable from the data and the parameters of the structural model. Obviously, the outcome of this procedure depends on the characteristics of the model. If the model is changed, the relationships are also changed.

* The Formal Derivation for the Standardized Parameters

After the formal derivation of the relationships between the variances/covariances and the unstandardized parameters of the model we do not have to do very much more in this section. As it was indicated in chapter 6 the correlation is equal to the expectation of the product of standardized variables. This means that we have to do exactly the same in this section as in the last section but now for standardized variables. However if we keep in mind that the equations for variables in deviation form and in standardized form are exactly the same, the only difference being that all variables and coefficients are standardized, we should expect exactly the same result here, except that all parameters and variables are standardized. An advantage of the standardized variables is that even further simplifications can be introduced since we know that the covariance between two standardized variables is equal to the correlation coefficient, and the variances of standardized variables are equal to one.

If we apply these simplifications to equations (7.2.1) to (7.2.10) the following results can be obtained: Equations (7.2.1) to (7.2.3) remain the same except for standardization:

$$\rho_{x_1 x_1} = E(x_1^s x_1^s) = 1 = \phi_{11}^s \qquad (7.3.1)$$

$$\rho_{x_2 x_1} = E(x_2^s x_1^s) = \phi_{21}^s \qquad (7.3.2)$$

$$\rho_{x_2 x_2} = E(x_2^s x_2^s) = 1 = \phi_{22}^s \qquad (7.3.3)$$

Equations (7.2.4) to (7.2.10) change as follows:

$$\rho_{y_1 x_1} = E(y_1^s x_1^s) = \gamma_{11}^s + \gamma_{12}^s \phi_{21}^s \qquad (7.3.4)$$

$$\rho_{y_1 x_2} = E(y_1^s x_2^s) = \gamma_{11}^s \phi_{21}^s + \gamma_{12}^s \qquad (7.3.5)$$

$$\rho_{y_2 x_1} = E(y_2^s x_1^s) = \beta_{21}^s \rho_{y_1 x_1} + \gamma_{21}^s + \gamma_{22}^s \phi_{21}^s \qquad (7.3.6)$$

$$\rho_{y_2 x_2} = E(y_2^s x_2^s) = \beta_{21}^s \rho_{y_1 x_2} + \gamma_{21}^s \phi_{21}^s + \gamma_{22}^s \qquad (7.3.7)$$

$$\rho_{y_2 y_1} = E(y_2^s y_1^s) = \beta_{21}^s + \gamma_{21}^s \rho_{y_1 x_1} + \gamma_{22}^s \rho_{y_1 x_2} \qquad (7.3.8)$$

$$\rho_{y_1 y_1} = E(y_1^s y_1^s) = 1 = \gamma_{11}^s \rho_{y_1 x_1} + \gamma_{12}^s \rho_{y_1 x_2} + \psi_{11}' \qquad (7.3.9)$$

$$\rho_{y_2 y_2} = E(y_2^s y_2^s) = 1 = \beta_{21}^s \rho_{y_2 y_1} + \gamma_{21}^s \rho_{y_2 x_1} + \gamma_{22}^s \rho_{y_2 x_2} + \psi_{22}' \qquad (7.3.10)$$

These results are obtained by substituting the appropriate correlation coefficient for each covariance coefficient, and deleting the variances since these are identical to one and can therefore be ignored.

The correlation coefficients in the right-hand side of some of these equations can be substituted by the appropriate forms of earlier equations. For example $\rho_{y_1 x_1}$ in the right-hand side of equation (7.3.6) can be substituted by equation (7.3.4). If this is done, the set of equations turns out to be identical to the equations derived by using the decomposition rules in the first section of this chapter. Thus this derivation shows that the intuitive approach was correct. The advantage of the approach given here is that it can be applied to any model, even when the intuitive approach fails. A general approach to the derivations can be provided using matrix algebra which holds for all linear structural equation models. That approach is in fact exactly the same as the procedure specified in the last two sections.

Some Concluding Remarks

In this chapter it was shown that, for a specific example, the variances and covariances or the correlations could be expressed in the parameters of the model. The approach used can be applied to any kind of linear structural equation model. Therefore, in principle one can derive for any kind of linear structural equation model the relationships between the variances and covariances or correlations on the one hand and the parameters of the model on the other hand. This means that for each combination of variables (let us say i and j) the variances and the covariances or correlations (σ_{ij} or ρ_{ij}) can be expressed as a specific function (f_{ij}) of the parameters (p) of the model. In general the following relationships can be derived for each specific model:

$$\sigma_{ij} = f_{ij}(p) \text{ for all } i,j \qquad (7.4.a)$$

or

$$\rho_{ij} = f_{ij}(p^s) \text{ for all } i,j \qquad (7.4.b)$$

It should be clear that the relationships depend on the model which is specified. If the model is changed then the relationships of equation (7.4) are also changed. Some examples are given in the next chapter.

A final point is that the covariances, variances and correlations are complex functions of the parameters and therefore very sensitive to changes in the parameters. If one of the parameters changes, many derived coefficients change as well, while the same change in the structural parameters does not have an effect on the other unstandardized structural parameters in the model because of their unmixed character. For this reason the unstandardized structural parameters of the model are much more interesting than the coefficients which can be derived from these unstandardized structural coefficients.

However the research practice is different. It is very easy to obtain estimates of the variances, covariances and correlations from the data, but in order to obtain estimates of the structural parameters some further steps should be taken. The discussion of these steps will begin in the next chapter.

Further Reading

The relationship between measures of covariation and causal effect parameters is a major topic in the literature on path analysis. The ideas of path analysis were originally formulated by the geneticist Sewall Wright (1934). In 1954 Simon's famous article entitled "Spurious correlation: a causal interpretation" was published. After this, a proliferation of these ideas followed in the social sciences: see Blalock (1962 and 1964), Boudon (1965 and 1968), Duncan (1966) and Land (1969). Most of the earlier articles make no distinction between population and sample data and consequently the algebra of expectations is not used as it is employed here. More recently, some textbooks have appeared in which this distinction is made more clearly. Far and away the best on this topic is O.D. Duncan's (1975) "Introduction to Structural Equation Models", especially chapters 3 and 4. Other related texts include Heise (1975), who uses flow diagrams to explain the same issues; Asher (1976) and Birnbaum (1981) who introduce causal modelling as an extension of the regression model,

Kenny (1979) whose approach is similar to ours but more advanced; Opp and Schmidt (1976) who wrote a text in German in which they did not use expectations ; and Boudon (1967) who wrote about the same topic in French.

A large number of the papers mentioned above have been brought together in a reader edited by Blalock (1971), "Causal Models in the Social Sciences", which remains a worthwhile source.

Exercises

7.1 Below the causal diagram is given for the action example (exercise 2.2).

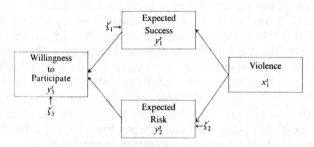

(a)Present this theory in a structural equation model, assuming linearity and additivity and using standardized variables.

(b)How many correlations are there between these variables?

(c)Express the correlations in the parameters of the model.

(d)Indicate for each term what it represents.

(e)What can we say about the variances of the standardized variables?

(f)Express also the variance of y_3^s, y_2^s and y_1^s in the parameters of the model.

7.2 It is not impossible that the violence judgment affects directly the willingness to participate. Assuming that this is so, how will it change the answers on the questions (a) to (f) in the previous exercise?

7.3 How many equations are there in these two cases which indicate a relationship between correlations and parameters and how many parameters are unknown and have to be estimated?

*7.4 If the model for y_1 is $y_1 = \gamma_{11}x_1 + \zeta_1$,
$$E(\zeta_1) = 0, E(y_1) = 0, E(x_1) = 0, E(x_1\zeta_1) = 0$$

(a)What is $E(y_1x_1)$?

(b)Express $\sigma_{y_1x_1}$ in parameters of the model.

(c)Express $\rho_{y_1x_1}$ in parameters of the model.

*7.5 Prove that the relationships derived in exercises (7.1c) and (7.2c) are correct.

Chapter 8
Introduction to Identification

It was said before that the variances and covariances or correlation coefficients, can easily be obtained by research, but that one is more interested in the values of the structural parameters since these are more fundamental to the causal process. Therefore we try to solve the structural parameters from the information supplied by the data. In doing so, the relationships between the two kinds of coefficients which have been derived in the preceding chapter play an important role. But while the variances and covariances can always be derived from the values of the structural parameters, a unique solution for the values of the structural parameters can not always be obtained from the values of the variances and covariances or correlations. The study of the conditions for the uniqueness of the solution of the parameters has been called the study of *identification* of the models. Much can be said about this topic but we will only give a brief introduction here. Simple tests for identification will be discussed in chapter 13.

An issue which is closely related to the problem of identification is the possibility of tests of structural equation models. This chapter will also indicate under what conditions models can be tested. But we start with the discussion of identification.

Necessary Conditions for Identification

The issue of identification of models is discussed in relation to four specific models which are presented in Figures 8.1 to 8.4. The first model, in Figure 8.1, has been discussed before and is identical to the simplified school career model. The equations (8.1.1) to (8.1.10) are identical to equations (7.1.1) to (7.1.10) derived from the simplified school career model. Notice, that from equation (8.1.6) onwards, we use the information implied by the previous equations to obtain a more efficient way of writing the set of equations (the reader may want to verify the claim that (8.1.1.) − (8.1.10) is identical to (7.1.1) − (7.1.10) as an exercise). The second model is a special case of the first model in that two more restrictions are added, i.e. $\beta_{21}^s = 0$ and $\gamma_{22}^s = 0$.

The third model and the fourth model also represent variations of the first model. They illustrate what happens when an important variable in the model

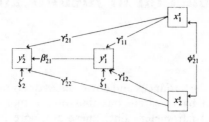

$$\rho_{x_1x_1} = \phi^s_{11} = 1 \qquad (8.1.1)$$
$$\rho_{x_2x_1} = \phi^s_{21} \qquad (8.1.2)$$
$$\rho_{x_2x_2} = \phi^s_{22} = 1 \qquad (8.1.3)$$
$$\rho_{y_1x_1} = \gamma^s_{11} + \gamma^s_{12}\phi^s_{21} \qquad (8.1.4)$$
$$\rho_{y_1x_2} = \gamma^s_{11}\phi^s_{21} + \gamma^s_{12} \qquad (8.1.5)$$

$$\rho_{y_2x_1} = \beta^s_{21}\rho_{y_1x_1} + \gamma^s_{21} + \gamma^s_{22}\phi^s_{21} \qquad (8.1.6)$$
$$\rho_{y_2x_2} = \beta^s_{21}\rho_{y_1x_1} + \gamma^s_{21}\phi^s_{21} + \gamma^s_{22} \qquad (8.1.7)$$
$$\rho_{y_2y_1} = \beta^s_{21} + \gamma^s_{21}\rho_{y_1x_1} + \gamma^s_{22}\rho_{y_1x_2} \qquad (8.1.8)$$
$$\rho_{y_1y_1} = \gamma^s_{11}\rho_{y_1x_1} + \gamma^s_{12}\rho_{y_1x_2} + \psi_{11}' \qquad (8.1.8)$$
$$\rho_{y_2y_2} = \beta^s_{21}\rho_{y_2y_1} + \gamma^s_{21}\rho_{y_2x_1} + \gamma^s_{22}\rho_{y_2x_2} + \psi_{22}' \qquad (8.1.10)$$

Figure 8.1   Model 1 with Correlations expressed in Parameters of the Model
(the model is identical to model 3 of Chapter 6)

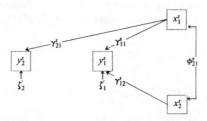

$$\rho_{x_1x_1} = \phi^s_{11} = 1 \qquad (8.2.1)$$
$$\rho_{x_2x_1} = \phi^s_{21} \qquad (8.2.2)$$
$$\rho_{x_2x_2} = \phi^s_{22} = 1 \qquad (8.2.3)$$
$$\rho_{y_1x_1} = \gamma^s_{11} + \gamma^s_{12}\phi^s_{21} \qquad (8.2.4)$$
$$\rho_{y_1x_2} = \gamma^s_{11}\phi^s_{21} + \gamma^s_{12} \qquad (8.2.5)$$

$$\rho_{y_2x_1} = \gamma^s_{21} \qquad (8.2.6)$$
$$\rho_{y_2x_2} = \gamma^s_{21}\phi^s_{21} \qquad (8.2.7)$$
$$\rho_{y_2y_1} = \gamma^s_{21}\rho_{y_1x_1} \qquad (8.2.8)$$
$$\rho_{y_1y_1} = \gamma^s_{11}\rho_{y_1x_1} + \gamma^s_{12}\rho_{y_1x_2} + \psi_{11}' \qquad (8.2.9)$$
$$\rho_{y_2y_2} = \gamma^s_{21}\rho_{y_2x_1} + \psi_{22}' \qquad (8.1.10)$$

Figure 8.2   Model 2 with Correlations expressed in Parameters of the Model
(the model is obtained from model 1 by imposing two restrictions, $\beta^s_{21} = 0$ and $\gamma^s_{22} = 0$)

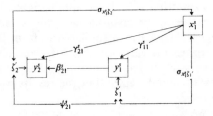

$$\rho_{x_1x_1} = \phi_{11}^s = 1 \qquad (8.3.1)$$
$$\rho_{y_1x_1} = \gamma_{11}^s + \sigma_{\zeta_1x_1} \qquad (8.3.2)$$
$$\rho_{y_2x_1} = \beta_{21}^s\rho_{y_1x_1} + \gamma_{21}^s + \sigma_{\zeta_2x_1} \qquad (8.3.3)$$

$$\rho_{y_2y_1} = \beta_{21}^s + \gamma_{21}^s\rho_{y_1x_1} + \gamma_{11}^s\sigma_{\zeta_2x_1} + \psi_{21}' \qquad (8.3.4)$$
$$\rho_{y_1y_1} = \gamma_{11}^s\rho_{y_1x_1} + \gamma_{11}^s\sigma_{\zeta_1x_1} + \psi_{11}' \qquad (8.3.5)$$
$$\rho_{y_2y_2} = \beta_{21}^s\rho_{y_2y_1} + \gamma_{21}^s\rho_{y_2x_1} + \gamma_{21}^s\sigma_{\zeta_2x_1}$$
$$+ \beta_{21}^s(\gamma_{11}^s\sigma_{\zeta_2x_1} + \psi_{21}') + \psi_{22}' \qquad (8.3.6)$$

Figure 8.3   Model 3 with Expressions for Correlations in Parameters of the Model (the model is derived from model 1 by omitting x_2^s, but recognizing this variable in the disturbance term)

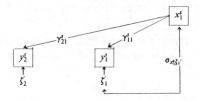

$$\rho_{x_1x_1} = \phi_{11}^s = 1 \qquad (8.4.1)$$
$$\rho_{y_1x_1} = \gamma_{11}^s + \sigma_{\zeta_1x_1} \qquad (8.4.2)$$
$$\rho_{y_2x_1} = \gamma_{21}^s \qquad (8.4.3)$$

$$\rho_{y_2y_1} = \gamma_{21}^s\rho_{y_1x_1} \qquad (8.4.4)$$
$$\rho_{y_1y_1} = \gamma_{11}^s\rho_{y_1x_1} + \gamma_{11}^s\sigma_{\zeta_1x_1} + \psi_{11}' \qquad (8.4.5)$$
$$\rho_{y_2y_2} = \gamma_{21}^s\rho_{y_2x_1} + \psi_{22}' \qquad (8.4.6)$$

Figure 8.4   Model 4 with Expressions for Correlations in Parameters of the Model (the model is derived from model 2 by omitting x_2^s, but recognizing this variable in the disturbance term)

is omitted. This variable will become a part of the disturbance term, and therefore cause correlations between some disturbance terms and between the disturbance terms and the predetermined variables. The third model is derived from the first model by omitting x_2^s as a separate variable, but by recognizing the presence of this variable in the disturbance terms of the endogenous variables. The final model is derived in a similar way from the second model. The equations which express the variances and correlations of the variables in the parameters of the various models are also presented in the figures. In the examples the variables are standardized, but the results would be similar for unstandardized variables.

The problem which we want to study for these models is whether the structural parameters can be uniquely determined on the basis of information about the values of the variances and covariances of the observed variables. This is the identification problem. We have seen in chapter 7 that 4 observed variables result in 10 distinct equations concerning the relationships between variances and covariances on the one hand, and the structural parameters on the other hand. For three observed variables the number of equations is six, which is $\frac{1}{2}3(3 + 1)$. If there are n variables the number of equations is equal to $\frac{1}{2}n(n + 1)$.

A general rule in algebra is that a *necessary condition* for solving unknowns in equations is that the number of unknowns should be equal to or less than the number of distinct equations. The unknowns in our cases are the structural parameters. The difference between the number of equations, which equals the number of different variances and covariances (or correlations) of observed variables, and the number of structural parameters which have to be found, is called the number of *degrees of freedom*, and is symbolized by *df*. With this notation the necessary condition can be formulated as follows:

A necessary condition for the identification of structural equation models is that the degrees of freedom should be equal to or larger than zero, that is, df ⩾ 0.

We will apply this rule to the four models in Figure 8.1 to 8.4. For the first model there are ten equations with ten parameters that have to be solved, i.e. ϕ_{11}^s, ϕ_{21}^s, ϕ_{22}^s, γ_{11}^s, γ_{12}^s, γ_{21}^s, γ_{22}^s, β_{21}^s, ψ_{11}', ψ_{22}'. Thus, $df = 0$, implying that the necessary condition is fulfilled. For the second model there are also ten equations, since the number of variables is equal to that in the first model, but this time only eight parameters have to be solved, since β_{21}^s and γ_{22}^s have fixed (zero) values. For this model $df = 2$, and the necessary condition is once more fulfilled. For the third model there are only six equations (since the model consists of only three variables), while there are nine parameters that have to be estimated: ϕ_{11}^s, γ_{11}^s, γ_{21}^s, β_{21}^s, ψ_{11}', ψ_{22}', ψ_{21}', $\sigma_{\zeta_1'x_1^s}$, $\sigma_{\zeta_2'x_3^s}$. For this third model $df = -3$, meaning that the necessary condition is not fulfilled at all. So the *"counting rule"* warns that a unique solution of the structural parameters can not be obtained for the third model; there are too many unknowns in relation to known facts. Finally, for the fourth model there are once again six equations, but now only six parameters have to be estimated: ϕ_{11}^s, γ_{11}^s, γ_{21}^s, ψ_{11}', ψ_{22}', $\sigma_{\zeta_1'x_1^s}$. Thus $df = 0$, and the necessary condition for identification is met for this model.

The determination of the number of equations should be clear by now; it is $\frac{1}{2}n(n + 1)$, where n is the sum of the number of x and y variables. Counting the numbers of the unknowns may not yet be completely obvious. In general one has to count the number of β, γ, ϕ and ψ parameters that are unknown if one is working with variables expressed as deviations from their mean. The number of β and γ parameters can be determined directly from the equations or diagrams. The number of ϕ parameters is equal to $\frac{1}{2}q(q + 1)$, where q is the number of x variables. The number of ψ parameters is at least p, which is the number of variances of the disturbance terms (ψ_{ii}). This number should be increased by the number of non-zero ψ_{ij} elements, which represent covariances between the disturbance terms.

In general the total so obtained will be equal to the total number of parameters which is unknown. Sometimes, as in models 3 and 4 above, $\sigma_{\zeta_i x_j}$ coefficients are also parameters of the model and should be added to the number of unknowns. However, we will see later that these coefficients should normally be avoided, since they only provide us with unsolvable problems. Therefore, working only with variables expressed as deviations from their mean one generally only has to count the number of β, γ, ϕ and ψ parameters to obtain the number of unknowns.

So far we have ignored the α coefficients since the rule was specified for models with variables expressed in deviations from their means. In such cases the α's can be ignored because the means of the variables are zero. If the raw scores have been used, one can also estimate the means and from them one can always obtain the α coefficients if necessary. How this can be done is discussed in chapter 10.

In this text we usually work with standardized variables or with variables in deviation form. So normally one has only to count the number of β, γ, ϕ and ψ coefficients which have to be estimated to determine the number of unknowns and the degrees of freedom.

Sufficient Conditions for Identification

With the first necessary condition test for identification it was shown that only three out of four models might yield unique solutions for the parameters. The third model turned out to be not identified. However, models which pass the necessary condition test may still be unidentified. The reason is that it is not necessarily true that the *sufficient conditions* for identification are fulfilled if the necessary conditions have been satisfied. There are also rules for sufficient conditions for identification, but the formulation of them is rather complex.

Therefore, we shall only illustrate the problem by trying to find a solution for the parameters of the three models which can possibly be identified according to the necessary condition rule. We start with the first model.

Consulting the equations that accompany Figure 8.1, it is seen that the first three equations directly express model parameters in correlations, meaning that these parameters are clearly identified:

$$\phi_{11}^s = \rho_{x_1 x_1} \qquad (8.1a)$$
$$\phi_{21}^s = \rho_{x_2 x_1} \qquad (8.1b)$$
$$\phi_{22}^s = \rho_{x_2 x_2} \qquad (8.1c)$$

Next we try to find a solution for γ_{12}^s in known variances and correlations. Multiplying equation (8.1.4) by ϕ_{21}^s, we have

$$\rho_{y_1 x_1}\phi_{21}^s = \gamma_{11}^s \phi_{21}^s + \gamma_{12}^s \phi_2^s \phi_{21}^s$$

while equation (8.1.5) states

$$\rho_{y_1 x_2} = \gamma_{11}^s \phi_{21}^s + \gamma_{12}^s$$

Subtracting the second equation from the first it follows that

$$\rho_{y_1 x_1}\phi_{21}^s - \rho_{y_1 x_2} = \gamma_{12}^s \phi_{21}^s \phi_{21}^s - \gamma_{12}^s$$
$$= \gamma_{12}^s (\phi_{21}^s \phi_{21}^s - 1)$$

Consequently

$$\gamma_{12}^s = \frac{\rho_{y_1 x_1}\phi_{21}^s - \rho_{y_1 x_2}}{\phi_{21}^s \phi_{21}^s - 1} \qquad (8.1d)$$

Since all coefficients on the right-hand side of this equation are known when the variances and covariances of the observed variables are known, equation (8.1d) represents a solution for γ_{12}^s. Next equation (8.1.4) provides a solution for γ_{11}^s, i.e.

$$\gamma_{11}^s = \rho_{y_1 x_1} - \gamma_{12}^s \phi_{21}^s \qquad (8.1e)$$

In a derivation which is similar to the way in which we have obtained a solution for the two parameters γ_{11}^s and γ_{12}^s from equations (8.1.4) and (8.1.5), the three parameters β_{21}^s, γ_{21}^s and γ_{22}^s can be solved from the three equations (8.1.6), (8.1.7) and (8.1.8). The derivation is quite tedious and only the result is given:

$$\gamma_{22}^s = \frac{a - c}{b - d} \qquad (8.1f)$$
$$\gamma_{21}^s = a - \gamma_{22}^s b \qquad (8.1g)$$
$$\beta_{21}^s = \frac{\rho_{y_2 x_1} - \gamma_{21}^s + \gamma_{22}^s \phi_{21}^s}{\rho_{y_1 x_1}} \qquad (8.1h)$$

where

$$a = \frac{\rho_{y_2x_1}\rho_{y_1x_2} - \rho_{y_2x_2}\rho_{y_1x_1}}{\rho_{y_1y_2} - \phi^s_{21}\rho_{y_1x_1}} \qquad b = \frac{\phi^s_{21}\rho_{y_1x_2} - \rho_{y_1x_1}}{\rho_{y_1x_2} - \phi^s_{21}\rho_{y_1x_1}}$$

$$c = \frac{\rho_{y_2x_1}\rho_{y_1y_1} - \rho_{y_2y_1}\rho_{y_1x_1}}{1 - \rho_{y_1x_1}\rho_{y_1x_1}} \qquad d = \frac{\phi^s_{21}\rho_{y_1y_1} - \rho_{y_1x_2}\rho_{y_1x_1}}{1 - \rho_{y_1x_1}\rho_{y_1x_1}}$$

Since all the coefficients on the right-hand side are known from the variances and covariances of the observed variables, the coefficients β^s_{21}, γ^s_{21} and γ^s_{22} have been solved.

Finally the coefficients ψ_{11}' and ψ_{22}' can be solved from equations (8.1.9) and (8.1.10):

$$\psi_{11}' = \rho_{y_1y_1} - (\gamma^s_{11}\rho_{y_1x_1} + \gamma^s_{12}\rho_{y_1x_2}) \qquad (8.1i)$$

$$\psi_{22}' = \rho_{y_2y_2} - (\beta^s_{21}\rho_{y_2y_1} + \gamma^s_{21}\rho_{y_2x_1} + \gamma^s_{22}\rho_{y_2x_2}) \qquad (8.1j)$$

This analysis shows that each parameter of the first model can indeed be solved, that is, expressed in the variances and covariances of the observed variables. Thus, this model is identified.

Let us now try to do the same for the fourth model. From equation (8.4.1) it follows that

$$\phi^s_{11} = \rho_{x_1x_1} = 1 \qquad (8.4a)$$

From equation (8.4.2) follows

$$\sigma_{x_1\zeta_1'} = \rho_{y_1x_1} - \gamma^s_{11} \qquad (8.4b)$$

but γ^s_{11} is not solved yet. So we have to find another equation which can be used to solve γ^s_{11}. The only possible candidate for a solution of γ^s_{11} is equation (8.4.5), since the other equations do not contain the term γ^s_{11}. But in equation (8.4.5) a new parameter—ψ_{11}'—appears which is not present in any other equation, and therefore has to be solved from (8.4.5). Therefore we are forced to the conclusion that no unique solution for $\sigma_{x_1\zeta_1'}$ and γ^s_{11} can be found. If one of them is given an arbitrary value, the value of the other parameter can be solved immediately from equation (8.4b). But there is no way of knowing the value for one of these two parameters, so the number of solutions is infinite. Thus, in this case not all of the model parameters can be uniquely determined. This means that the sufficient condition for identification of this model is not fulfilled, even though the necessary condition was met. This does not mean that none of the parameters can be determined. From equation (8.4.3) parameter γ^s_{21} can be solved, with equation (8.4.6) ψ_{22}' can be solved. Only γ^s_{11}, $\sigma_{x_1\zeta_1'}$ and ψ_{11}' can not be identified. Since these three parameters can not be uniquely determined, this model is called unidentified, or perhaps more appropriately, *unidentifiable*.

We now move to the second model and evaluate the identification status of the model. Here the inferences for the first model can be used since the same information is available for this model as for the first model, while the only difference between these two models is that two more parameters have been fixed at zero in the second model. Since the first model was identified, it follows that the second model should be identified too. This can also be derived from the equations. From equation (8.2.1) to (8.2.5) the coefficients ϕ_{11}^s, ϕ_{21}^s, ϕ_{22}^s, γ_{11}^s and γ_{12}^s can be solved in the same way as for the first model. In addition there are three equations available—equations (8.2.6), (8.2.7) and (8.2.8)—to solve γ_{21}^s. Finally, from equations (8.2.9) and (8.2.10) the coefficients ψ_{11}' and ψ_{22}' can be obtained. Thus it is shown that this model is identified. In this case there are even two equations which are not needed for identification, that is $df = 2$ as we have seen before. Such models are called *overidentified*, meaning that they contain fewer unknown parameters than distinct items of information. We shall see later that this is an important advantage.

Having discussed for four models how the identification can be checked, we can now provide a few general conclusions, which can be useful to determine the identification status of models in practice:

(1)   Single equation models with $\sigma_{\zeta_i x_j} = 0$ are always identified. Such models are known as *"regression models"* in the literature.

(2)   Simultaneous equation models without reciprocal causal effects and with the standard assumptions that $\sigma_{\zeta_i x_j} = 0$ for all i,j and $\sigma_{\zeta_i \zeta_j} = 0$ for all $i \neq j$, are always identified. These kinds of models are referred to as *"recursive models"*.

(3)   Single or simultaneous equation models with effects of x_i on y_j and with $\sigma_{\zeta_i x_j} \neq 0$ are definitely not identified.

(4)   Simultaneous equation models with reciprocal causal effects (*"nonrecursive models"*) are definitely not identified if the same endogenous variables are affected by the same set of causal variables.

The first two conclusions can be summarized by saying that all recursive structural equation models are identified when all important variables have been incorporated. The last point assures that $\sigma_{\zeta_i x_j} = 0$, and that $\sigma_{\zeta_i \zeta_j} = 0$, thus satisfying the assumptions.

The third conclusion indicates the importance of the assumption that predetermined variables and the disturbance terms should be unrelated to each other, which is assured when all important common causes have been introduced in the model. If this is not true, there are two possibilities: (1) one ignores the covariation between the predetermined variables and the disturbance terms, but then the estimates of the γ coefficients will be wrong, or

(2) one specifies such covariations in the model. But this option will lead to unidentified models, meaning that no unique solution for the parameters can be obtained. Thus the incorporation of all important common causes is really very important.

The fourth conclusion specifies only one condition under which models with reciprocal causation are not identified. The identification of such models which have been called "nonrecursive" should always be checked with the procedures which will be discussed in chapter 13 or by other rules given in the literature.

Theory Adjustment for Identification

Before one starts to collect data in order to estimate the structural parameters and to test the causal theory, one should check the identifiability of the structural equation model, since it is a waste of time to collect data which can not produce a unique solution of the parameters. Thus, before the data collection is started one should be as sure as possible that the model which is formulated is identified. When an identification test indicates that the model is not identified, one has to adjust the causal theory in order to obtain an identified model. In this section this adjustment is discussed.

In the preceding section it was shown that the identification of models without reciprocal causation, i.e. of recursive models, is assured when all important common causes are introduced. If this is done, recursive models are always identified, as can be inferred from conclusion (2) of the previous section.

With respect to *nonrecursive* models, the situation is more complicated. Even if one has introduced all common causes the model can still be unidentified. Without going into details, the problem often lies in the fact that the variables which affect the endogenous variables do not vary from one equation to the other. Therefore the solution should be sought by introducing more variables which affect only specific variables and not others. In Figure 8.5, a typical

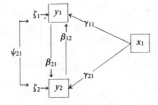

Figure 8.5   Example of a Model which is Unidentified

example of an unidentified model is presented. Introduction of the two new variables x_2 and x_3, the first affecting only y_1 and the second affecting only the other endogenous variable (y_2), will assure identification of the model. The adjusted model is presented in Figure 8.6.

The search for such predetermined variables is not always easy, but without such variables there is no hope of obtaining identified nonrecursive models. With more endogenous variables, the situation is more or less the same and thus the same adjustments to the theories make the models identified, although it is possible that one does not need specific causal variables for each endogenous variable. However it does no harm to formulate the theory in such a way that the model is overidentified. This can protect the researcher against unexpected results like zero effects which could endanger the identification if the model was *"exactly identified"*.

This section suggests that adjustment of theories should be made by the *introduction* of new predetermined variables which affect only one or a few endogenous variables in order to assure identification. In order to obtain identification, one should never adjust the theory by *omitting* effects which were specified as important in the model, since this will produce biased values for the other parameters (if these effects are really important).

Overidentification and the Test of Models

In discussing the identification of the model (Figure 8.2) it turned out that there were two more equations than there were unknown parameters $(df = 2)$. In this case one speaks of overidentification.

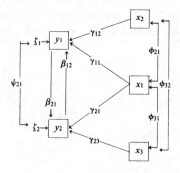

Figure 8.6   Adjusted Version of Model of Figure 8.5, such that it is identified

For the solution of the parameters as many equations are necessary as there are parameters to be solved. Therefore, if there are more equations than parameters, the extra equations can be used for a test of the model. Such a test is not possible if the model is exactly identified ($df = 0$), since in that case all equations are necessary to obtain the values of the parameters and no equations are left for the test.

In order to show why a test is possible in case of an overidentified model, a new symbol has to be introduced. The obtained values of the coefficients are indicated with their usual symbol with a hat above it . Thus $\hat{\gamma}_{21}$ indicates the derived value of the parameter γ_{21}. With these values of the coefficients, the population variances and covariances (correlations) can be computed using the relationships between these coefficients and the parameters of the model as discussed before. But since these relationships differ for each different model (see Figures 8.1 to 8.4) it follows that the values of the reproduced variances and covariances (or correlations) which are computed depend on the model specified. If the model is correct the coefficients obtained will be exactly the same as the real population covariances and variances. However if the model is wrong, the two sets of values for the same variances and covariances can differ and these differences give an indication of the correctness of the model.

For example, if the parameters of the first model represented in Figure 8.1 are computed, there is only one solution since the model is exactly identified ($df = 0$). If for this model the population correlation matrix is computed from the values of the parameters, this matrix will be exactly the same as the real population matrix. On the other hand, if the parameters of the model of Figure 8.2 would have been computed from equations (8.2.1) to (8.2.6) and (8.2.9) and (8.2.10), two equations are left for a test: (8.2.7) and (8.2.8). According to these two equations the following two identities should hold if the model is correct:

$$\hat{\rho}_{y_2x_2} - \rho_{y_2x_2} = 0 \text{ or } (\hat{\gamma}_{21}^s \hat{\phi}_{21}^s) - \rho_{y_2x_2} = 0 \qquad (8.5)$$

and

$$\hat{\rho}_{y_2y_1} - \rho_{y_2y_1} = 0 \text{ or } (\hat{\gamma}_{21}^s \hat{\rho}_{y_1x_1}) - \rho_{y_2y_1} = 0 \qquad (8.6)$$

This model assumes that β_{21}^s and γ_{22}^s are zero, and therefore the equalities (8.5) and (8.6) should only hold if these two assumptions are really true. If not, the equalities had to be according to equations (8.1.7) and (8.1.8) of model 1:

$$\hat{\rho}_{y_2x_2} - \rho_{y_2x_2} = 0 \text{ or } (\hat{\beta}_{21}^s \hat{\rho}_{y_1x_2} + \hat{\gamma}_{21}^s \hat{\phi}_{21}^s + \hat{\gamma}_{22}^s) - \rho_{y_2x_2} = 0 \qquad (8.7)$$

and

$$\hat{\rho}_{y_2y_1} - \rho_{y_2y_1} = 0 \text{ or } (\hat{\beta}_{21}^s + \hat{\gamma}_{21}^s \hat{\rho}_{y_1x_1} + \hat{\gamma}_{22}^s \hat{\rho}_{y_1x_2}) - \rho_{y_2y_1} = 0 \qquad (8.8)$$

It can be seen that these two equations (8.7) and (8.8) reduce only to (8.4) and (8.5) if β_{21}^s and γ_{22}^s are zero.

In this way the difference between the real population covariances and variances and the reproduced covariances and variances given the model, can be used to test the model. Clearly these tests are only possible if $df > 0$, i.e. for overidentified models. If $df \leq 0$ there are no equations left for the test and the fit of the models will in general be perfect.

Some Limitations

So far we have indicated how the model parameters can be solved from equations relating parameters and variances and covariances (or correlations). We have also shown that tests of models are possible if $df > 0$. There are however some limitations to the approach sketched here:(1)The solutions have to be derived for each model separately. This can lead to mistakes. Sometimes the solutions may not even be found at all for complex models. A more general approach which can do this job routinely is preferable.(2)If $df > 0$, several solutions are possible for the parameters and these solutions may differ. In such cases it is unclear which one to choose or how to combine the different solutions. It would be better if only one solution could be obtained which in some way was an optimal solution for the parameters.(3)The *"residuals"* can indeed be used as an indication if the models fit to the data, but it is unclear how large the residuals have to be before one decides to reject the model. A formal criterion for such a decision would be attractive.(4)In this section we have assumed perfect information about the population variances and covariances but information is almost never available for a whole population. In general one has only information for one specific sample. This means that the information can differ by chance from population data. Such chance deviations will also appear in the parameters and the residuals which are obtained from these sample variances and covariances. Therefore one should have a procedure which can take into account such random fluctuations as well.

This review indicates that the discussion up till now has been considerably simplified. We have restricted ourselves to relatively simple models and to population data. In the next chapter the sampling problem will be introduced. In later chapters more practical procedures for sample data and for more complex models will be discussed which can overcome the problems which have been mentioned here. However, we will see that the procedure which will be suggested is still based on the same derived relationships between the parameters and the variances and covariances, but the estimation procedure and testing procedure is far more efficient.

Further Reading

The way in which we have introduced the identification problem in this chapter differs from the usual approach. Only Duncan (1975) and Kenny (1979) use an approach more or less similar to ours. The usual approach is to present the identification problem and its solution quite generally so that it can be applied to any kind of model. A difficulty of this more general aproach is that it requires a technical discussion which goes far beyond the level of this text.

In general the identification problem has been presented in the way in which it is treated by econometricians for these types of models. The classic paper on this topic of Koopmans is reprinted in the reader of Blalock (1971). The reader interested in this econometric approach can refer to introductions of the problems by Wonnacott and Wonnacott (1980) and Blalock (1969a), and a more elaborate discussion by Christ (1966).

With respect to testing we postpone the discussion until chapter 11, where the testing procedure of LISREL is treated in more detail.

Exercises

8.1 In exercise (7.1) the relationship between the correlations and the parameters of a model have been derived.
(a)Check whether in that case the necessary condition for identification is fulfilled.
(b)Can you say without solving the equations whether the sufficient condition for identification is fulfilled in this case?
(c)Check by solving the equations that also the sufficient conditions are fulfilled.
(d)How many ways are there to solve the parameters?
8.2 In exercise (7.2) the relationship between the correlations and the parameters of an extended model are derived.
(a)Check whether in that case the necessary condition for identification is fulfilled.
(b)Can you say without solving the equations whether the sufficient condition for identification is fulfilled in this case?
(c)How many ways are there to solve the parameters?
8.3 Below we have presented a hypothetical correlation matrix for the example of exercises (8.1) and (8.2):

	y_1	y_2	y_3	x_1
y_1	1.00			
y_2	.72	1.00		
y_3	$-.24$	$-.44$	1.00	
x_1	.80	.90	$-.43$	1.00

Compute the parameters according to the model of exercise (8.1).

8.4 In exercise (8.1d) and (8.2c) it was indicated that the parameters could be computed in different ways.

(a)Do these different procedures lead to the same results?

(b)The answer to (a) indicates a limitation of the approach discussed so far. Are there other limitations?

8.5 Returning to the problem for secondary analysis which you are working on, ask yourself the following questions:

(a)Is the model of the author identified according to the simple rules or not, or is it not directly possible to evaluate? (If the identification status is unclear this should be checked later with the program.)

(b)If the model is not identifiable, make the model identifiable.

(c)Is the model also restrictive enough to be testable?

(d)If the model is exactly identified, do you think all coefficients are really necessary in the theory to explain the data?

Chapter 9

Introduction to Sampling and Sample Data

In chapter 8 we saw that the values of the parameters can be obtained from the population covariances or correlations, provided that the model is identified. In practice however, the study of entire populations is generally too expensive and time consuming. Therefore investigators usually have to rely on studies of subsets of cases from the populations, which are called samples. For these samples statistical measures such as the mean, standard deviation, variance, covariance and correlation can be computed, but these measures need not to be the same as the population measures. They only represent estimates of population measures. Whether these estimates are "good" depends on the way the sample is drawn and on the amount of nonresponse, i.e. the amount of cooperation one encounters in the study. Both points are discussed in this chapter.

Even if everything proceeds according to one's expectations, sampling introduces an element of uncertainty into the research. The sample covariances are estimates of the population covariances and will differ by chance from the true values of the population covariances, due to sampling fluctuations. Therefore the distribution of the sample covariances given the population measures will also be discussed. The effects of the random fluctuations on the results of the analyses will be the topic of the last section.

Population and Sample

It is important to emphasize that the word *"population"* as we use it here, is a statistical concept. It covers not only populations of people or living organisms, but also of other types of units. For example, all public speeches of the presidents can be units of a research project. In this case one is dealing with a population of speeches. From this population, a smaller number can be drawn to reduce the amount of work. This smaller number of speeches which is selected, is called the *sample*. Similarly, all cities or communities of a country can be defined as a population. Out of these populations samples can be drawn.

A research decision which has to be taken at some point is a delineation of the population to which the researcher wants to generalize the findings of the study. This decision is determined partially by the theory which is specified.

In the theory one should indicate the population to which one thinks the theory applies. The choice of the population is determined in part by practical considerations such as cost limitations or limitations of the sampling frame. In addition, the data collection in most research is restricted to units from the country of the researcher and restricted in time. Clearly, this mixture of well-considered, pragmatic and arbitrary choices somewhat restricts the possibilities for generalization. If particular restrictions apply, it is not possible to draw conclusions which go beyond the country, the present time, the people for which one has the names, and so on. It is not even always clear whether conclusions can be generalized to the restricted population. This depends on the way in which the units have been selected. This brings us to the next topic.

Sampling Procedures

A problem with selection of units from a population is that the researcher can select those cases for which the theory holds and ignore the ones for which the theory does not hold. In order to avoid criticism of that kind, impartial selection procedures should be used. This purpose is well satisfied by procedures based on a chance or random mechanism. Samples which are drawn using chance mechanisms to select units are called probability samples; more precisely, each element of the population must have a known probability of being selected as part of the sample.

There are several ways in which a probability sample can be drawn. It is not our intention to discuss the various procedures in detail, since this quickly becomes a specialized subject which is treated in other texts. Here we discuss only the general principles in relation to estimation and testing of structural equation models.

The sampling procedure which is most useful for our purposes is the so-called simple random sample, in which each element of the population has an equal probability of being chosen. The principle of the simple random sample can be illustrated in the following way. Each unit of the population is represented by a card. Then the cards are shuffled and one of them is taken at random for the sample. Then a second card is chosen and so on. This process continues up until the total sample size has been reached. At that point a simple random sample has been drawn.

In the case of a large population which cannot be written on cards or for which the cards cannot be shuffled, other aids are available. One of these is a table with random numbers. Suppose, one wants to draw a sample of 100 cases out of a population of 150,000 cases which are numbered from 1 to 150,000. Then one may read the first 100 numbers of six digits from a table with random numbers, starting at an arbitrary point and deleting all numbers which are higher than 150,000. In this way a simple random sample can be obtained.

One can think of yet other procedures to choose units randomly from a large population in order to obtain a simple random sample from that population. The important thing with such procedures is that the researchers are not allowed to influence the choices. An unfortunate consequence of the use of random samples is that one does not always obtain the same result, as we will see in the next sections. An advantage is that the variation in the selected units is not influenced by the researcher, but is merely due to the fluctuations arising from a chance mechanism. In the next chapters we will see that the aspect of random fluctuations can be taken into account in the analysis. By using random sampling we are therefore able to derive conclusions from the sample with respect to the causal theory in the population.

A more practical procedure, which nevertheless leads to a sample which has approximately the same characteristics as the simple random sample, is the systematic sampling procedure. If all units are listed on cards and the cards are systematically stored (for example in drawers), one cannot shuffle the cards. Nevertheless one can approximate the random sample by selecting every k^{th} card, starting with a randomly selected unit among the first k cards. Suppose we want to draw a sample of 500 out of 15,000 cases in the population. Then we have to select every 30th card and we have to start with a randomly selected card out of the first 30 cards. If the total sample size is large, this systematic sampling procedure leads to samples which have approximately the same characteristics as random samples. In other words generalization of the results of the data analysis from such samples to the population is permitted.

In contrast to these two sampling procedures, there are also procedures which can lead to samples which have quite different characteristics from simple random samples. Examples of these are stratified samples and cluster samples. In a stratified sample the population is first divided into a number of strata, and from each of these strata a simple random or systematic sample is drawn. For example, in opinion research often some low frequency categories of respondents are disproportionally chosen in the sample in order to get a clear idea of the opinion of this group. In cluster sampling the units themselves are not sampled, but clusters of units. Within each cluster one may or may not go on to draw a random sample. For a typical example, one can draw a sample of city blocks and interview all or a selection of the people in the sampled blocks. The samples which result in such cases can be quite different from a simple random sample and will usually involve systematic deviations from the simple random sample.

For univariate statistics such as the percentage in a particular category, the mean of a distribution and the standard deviation or variance, computational adjustments are available in the literature to correct for the difference between simple random samples and more complicated sample designs. These latter designs can lead to more precise estimates for the univariate population statistics and at the same time reduce the costs of data collection considerably.

For bivariate statistics, such as the covariance and the correlation coefficient, however, it is harder to utilize advantages of the complicated sample design. Also, correction procedures are not readily available. As we have seen, we need the covariance and correlation coefficients to estimate the structural parameters and to test the causal theories. So the conclusion has to be that one should be careful with the use of other kinds of sampling procedures than simple random sampling, at least if one wants to generalize the estimates and test the causal hypotheses from the specific sample to the population for which the theory was developed.

Bias in the Sample

In research practice one should always be aware of the possibilities of bias in the composition of a sample. It may not be easy to obtain a complete list of names of the population from which a random sample can be drawn. If so, one has to find solutions which approximate such lists as well as possible (for example, a telephone directory), thereby keeping the risk of bias in mind (only richer people have a telephone). Other sources of *bias* can be found in the process of carrying out the sampling instructions, from the first list to the final choice of respondents by interviewers. All these practical steps can lead to errors in the sample.

There is another important source of sampling error: *nonresponse*. Nonresponse refers to the failure to obtain information for some of the units in the sample. There are various types of nonresponse, depending on the survey situation. In survey research it may be impossible to locate certain respondents (for example because they have moved), respondents may not be found at home during the first or second visit, they may not be able to participate due to sickness or other circumstances and they may refuse to cooperate in the research. Lack of data occurs not only in survey research; in other kinds of study this may also occur. For instance, in studies of government documents access to certain documents may not be allowed.

At first sight it may not be clear how nonresponse influences the generalizability of the sample results to the population. If the refusals have nothing to do with the topic of the study, the effect can be considered to be random and will not harm the representativeness of the sample in relation to the population. On the other hand if people refuse to cooperate on the basis of their ideas about the topic of study, nonresponse can have a systematic effect on the sample and generalization to the population is dangerous.

General rules on this point are difficult to formulate. An example may illustrate what is meant. In the school career study 50% of the heads of the elementary schools did not answer the questionnaires. The question is whether these refusals harm the representativeness of the sample. If the reason for their refusal is that they never answer questionnaires and that this has nothing to do with the kind of school or the results of the children in the school, the effect on the sample will be random and it will not harm the representativeness of the sample. On the other hand, if in particular the heads of elementary schools with bad results refuse to answer, the relationship with the research topic is very clear and generalization is dangerous in this case.

Thus, nonresponse will never improve the quality of the data and it may very well be a source of bias. The best strategy is therefore to reduce the amount of nonresponse as much as possible. Sometimes incentives can be given to respondents to cooperate (a present or an amount of money, especially in panel studies which require prolonged participation). Another procedure is to ask respondents who have refused cooperation to at least answer the one or two central questions of the survey. It is also important to collect information on the reasons why people refuse to cooperate, if they do. Such information can be helpful for the evaluation of the sample. For example, if we know that 90% of the refusals in the school career study is caused by the fact that people always refuse to cooperate in such research, we can decide that the sample is not necessarily very biased in this case and continue the research. On the other hand, if this is only true for a small percentage we have to know more.

What can be done once the data have been collected and nonresponse seems a problem? A practice which is very common is to evaluate the distribution of the sample data with what is known from the population. For example, for all schools in the Netherlands it is known how many children go to the different kinds of secondary schools. The distribution of these children across the regions and their scores on the school test is also known. So one can compare the information from the sample with the available information on the population. If the deviations are too large, one can improve the similarity by unequal weighting of the units. In the sample data for the school career model the various types of secondary school were not represented in quite the same way as they were in the population of the Netherlands in that year. Therefore weights were attached to the pupils to correct for the discrepancy. (In fact we also carried out some analyses starting with the raw, unweighted data and came out in much the same way, indicating only minor distortions).

Apart from *total nonresponse* there is usually also the problem of missing values on some of the variables under investigation. Later in this chapter two methods are discussed of dealing with this *partial nonresponse*. One of these methods, called listwise deletion, in fact transfers partial nonresponse to the total nonresponse category.

Sample Statistics

About the sample statistics like the mean, variance, standard deviation, covariance and correlation we can be very brief because the definition and computation does not differ very much from what we have said before about the same measures for the populations. An important difference is that for the sample statistics latin symbols will be used.

Starting with the mean we can state as before that the mean of the variable y for the sample is defined as the sum of all values divided by the total number of cases. The mean of the variable y is denoted by $\bar{y}$. In a formula this is

$$\bar{y} = \frac{1}{n} \sum y \qquad (9.1)$$

summing over all values of y, where n is the total number of cases in the sample.

For population data the variance was defined as the mean squared deviation from the mean. Following the definition, one has to compute all deviations from the mean, square them, add these and divide the result by n. In general the sample variance is denoted by s_{yy} and is computed as follows:

$$s_{yy} = \frac{1}{n-1} \sum (y - \bar{y})^2 \qquad (9.2)$$

summing over all values of y.

In the literature it is shown that a division by $n - 1$ instead of n, leads to a better estimate of the population variance (σ_{yy}).

The standard deviation of a variable is defined in the same way as for the population, that is as the square root of the variance

$$s_y = \sqrt{s_{yy}} \qquad (9.3)$$

For the covariance the same change in the divisor is introduced and for the same reason as in the case of the variance. Thus the sample covariance of the variables x and y is equal to the sum of the product of the deviations from their means, divided by $n - 1$, or

$$s_{yx} = \frac{1}{n-1} \sum (y - \bar{y})(x - \bar{x}) \qquad (9.4)$$

summing over all units.

Finally the correlation denoted by r_{yx}, is defined as before, that is, as the covariance of the two variables divided by the product of their standard deviations:

$$r_{yx} = \frac{s_{yx}}{s_y s_x} \qquad (9.5)$$

Table 9.1 The Computation of the Sample Mean $(\bar{y}_5)$, the Variance $(s_{y_5y_5})$ and the Standard Deviation (s_{y_5}) for the Variable y_5 of the School Career Theory

Respondent	y_5 ~	$y_5 - \bar{y}_5$	$(y_5 - \bar{y}_5)^2$
1	6	3.85	14.82
2	ˎ 7	4.85	23.52
3	7	4.85	23.52
4	3	.85	.72
.	.	.	.
.	.	.	.
.	.	.	.
447	4	1.85	3.42

$$\sum y_5 = 961 \qquad \sum (y_5 - \bar{y}_5)^2 = 1739.72$$
$$\bar{y}_5 = \frac{961}{447} = 2.15 \qquad s_{y_5y_5} = \frac{1739.72}{446} = 3.892$$
$$s_{y_5} = \sqrt{s_{y_5y_5}} = 1.973$$

Table 9.2 The Computation of the Sample Covariance $(s_{y_5y_3})$ and the Correlation $(r_{y_5y_3})$, given that $\bar{y}_5 = 2.15$ and $\bar{y}_3 = 2.18$, $s_{y_5} = 1.973$ and $s_{y_3} = 1.969$

Respondent	y_5	y_3	$y_5 - \bar{y}_5$	$y_3 - \bar{y}_3$	$(y_5 - \bar{y}_5)(y_3 - \bar{y}_3)$
1	6	6	3.85	3.82	14.71
2	7	7	4.85	4.82	23.38
3	7	7	4.85	4.82	23.38
4	3	3	.85	.82	.70
.	.	.	.	.	.
.	.	.	.	.	.
.	.	.	.	.	.

$$\sum (y_5 - \bar{y}_5)(y_3 - \bar{y}_3) = 1700.84$$
$$s_{y_5y_3} = \frac{1700.84}{446} = 3.805$$
$$r_{y_5y_3} = \frac{3.805}{1.973 \times 1.969} = .979$$

For an example of the computations of all these measures we refer to Tables 9.1 and 9.2. In practice, it is preferable to do such computations by computer in order to prevent errors and to obtain faster results. For the estimation and testing of causal theories the covariance or correlation matrix, pertaining to all the variables in the theory, is used. We therefore begin to discuss the way in which these matrices can be computed by the computer.

Table 9.3   A Possible LISREL Input for the Computation of the Sample
                 Correlation Matrix for the School Career Study

```
COMPUTATION OF THE CORRELATION MATRIX
DATA     NI=7 NO=447
LABELS
*
'     Y 1'  '     Y 2'  '     Y 3'  '     Y 4'  '     Y 5'
'     X 1'  '     X 2'
RAW     XM=0 MV=1
 70 6 6 80 6 74 6
 80 6 7 90 7 74 6
          ETC.
OUTPUT   ND=7
```

Computation of Covariance and Correlation Matrices with LISREL

For the estimation and testing of causal theories and for various measures that
help in the final interpretation of these theories the computer program LISREL
will be used throughout this book. In the coming chapters separate parts of
the output of the LISREL program are presented and discussed. Readers who
have access to a computer in which LISREL has been installed will find it ad-
vantageous to become familiar with the program as we go along. The minimal
starting point for an analysis is a correlation matrix or a covariance matrix.
This type of data input can be obtained from LISREL and other computer
programs, such as given in the next section. We begin to illustrate how a
correlation matrix can be computed from the raw data with LISREL.

As an example we show the computation of the correlation matrix for the
variables of the school career theory. In Table 5.2 part of the raw data matrix
for this model was given. In order to compute the correlation matrix for the
seven relevant variables, the LISREL input cards of Table 9.3 can be used.
Each line of this input represents a separate card or record or instruction. The
first card must be a title which will be printed as the heading on the output
pages. The second and several of the other cards begin with keywords. They
may be abbreviated to their first two letters: **DATA (DA), LABELS (LA), RAW
(RA), OUTPUT (OU)**. The second card gives the instruction that the Number of
Input variables **(NI)** equals 7 and that the Number of Observations **(NO)** equals
447. The third to fifth card is one set of instructions: the keyword **LABELS** is
followed by an "*" to indicate free format reading and by two cards in which
labels are assigned to the input variables (in the example short symbols like
"Y1" are presented, but the program can retain variable names of up to eight
characters). Subsequently **RAW** data are introduced. It is indicated that there
are missing values:**MV=1,** and that that the real number **0.** is to be treated
as a missing value: **XM=0.**. Without missing values in the data the keyword
RAW is sufficient. Next 447 lines follow with the scores on seven variables.
Finally, as **OUTPUT** we instruct the program to print seven numbers after the

Table 9.4   The LISREL Output for the Job Presented in Table 9.3

	Y 1	Y 2	Y 3	Y 4	Y 5	X 1	X 2
Y 1	1.00000000						
Y 2	.81133063	1.00000000					
Y 3	.78578892	.85341767	1.00000000				
Y 4	.80717385	.76244374	.75865101	1.00000000			
Y 5	.79214354	.86046091	.98786946	.77258788	1.00000000		
X 1	.23069253	.15257013	.24162263	.43222029	.24522466	1.00000000	
X 2	.19625111	.28210791	.29686456	.23791096	.29659488	.16516328	1.00000000

Table 9.5   A Possible SPSS Input for the Computation of the Sample Correlation Matrix for the the School Career Study

```
RUN NAME          COMPUTATION OF THE CORRELATION MATRIX
VARIABLE LIST     Y1,Y2,Y3,Y4,Y5,X1,X2
INPUT FORMAT      FIXED(F3.0,2F2.0,F3.0,F2.0,F3.0,F2.0)
N OF CASES        447
MISSING VALUES    Y1 TO X2(BLANK)
PEARSON CORR      Y1 TO X2
OPTIONS           2,5
STATISTICS        1
READ INPUT DATA
  70 6 6 80 6 74 6
  80 6 7 90 7 74 6
          ETC.
FINISH
```

decimal point (**ND=7**) in the output. The default is **ND=3** and will be used for all parameter estimates, but for the correlations we prefer more digits.

The output of these instructions is presented in Table 9.4. There are a number of alternatives to obtain this output. For these alternatives we refer to the LISREL user's guide.

Computation of Covariance and Correlation Matrices with SPSS

In this section it is indicated briefly how a sample covariance or correlation matrix can be obtained with the SPSS computer program. There are many other programs which can do the same thing. The set-up for SPSS is illustrated since this package is used very frequently in the social sciences. We again do not give a complete overview, but merely illustrate the procedure for the special case of the school career data. Still, this example shows a common situation and is instructive for the intended type of analysis. The SPSS instruction cards to obtain a correlation matrix are presented in Table 9.5. Each line of this input represents a separate card. The keywords such as **RUN NAME** etc. start in the first column, the specific information starts always in the 16th column. The first card indicates the name of the job. The second card gives the names of the variables as they will be read from the data matrix. The third card indicates how the computer should read the data. Here it is indicated that the first variable is punched in three columns, the second and the third variable in two columns, the fourth again in three columns, and so on. There is no digit after the point. The **F** in these statements always stands for "format". In the fourth card the number of cases is specified, which indicates to the computer that the data matrix contains 447 cards. The fifth card indicates when the computer should read the information obtained as a missing value. In our example missing values for all variables are indicated by blanks; this could have been done in another way, for example, by -1 or 99.

On the sixth card it is indicated that we want the correlations for the variables y_1 to x_2. This list does not have to be exactly the same as the variable list: the variable list can be much longer. The seventh card shows what **OPTIONS** are chosen in the computation of the correlation matrix. The "5" merely indicates that some standard output has to be suppressed and is not very important. More essential is **OPTION 2**, which indicates that we want to completely ignore cases for which missing data occur in one of the seven variables (this is called *listwise deletion*). This is a rigorous solution to the missing values problem and the result may be that one is left with only very few cases. An alternative is to compute each correlation between two variables on the basis of all known cases for those two variables (*pairwise deletion*). This happens when one leaves out the "2" on the **OPTIONS** card. With this option each correlation may be based on a different set of cases. This may cause problems because the variables can become perfectly related to each other. For such a matrix LISREL cannot run some analyses and will mention that the input matrix is **"NOT POSITIVE DEFINITE"**. In such cases a solution is to use listwise deletion.

Listwise deletion of cases is a clear solution to the missing value problem. Disadvantages are the possibly large reduction in sample size, and the possibility that the partial nonresponse is correlated with the variable of interest. If so, listwise deletion may be a source of bias in the sample. Pairwise deletion on the other hand, has the advantage that the correlations will be based on more cases and will therefore be closer to the true value. Here a problem is what the sample size has to be in a subsequent analysis of the correlation matrix since the sample size differs from correlation to correlation. In such situations one generally uses the number of cases of the correlation computed on the lowest number of cases. In fact this choice is quite arbitrary. Overall, we suggest that the listwise deletion option should be preferred, at least if this does not reduce the number of cases too much. On the eighth card it is

Table 9.6   The Output produced by SPSS for the Job outlined in Table 9.5 (The upper half of the table gives the means and standard deviations, while in the matrix the correlations between the variables are presented)

VARIABLE	CASES	MEAN	STD DEV
Y1	383	53.7128	22.5069
Y2	383	3.0470	1.7835
Y3	383	3.3003	1.7845
Y4	383	50.4595	27.8085
Y5	383	3.2637	1.7830
X1	383	50.9491	28.0352
X2	383	3.2480	1.4700

- - - - - - - - - - P E A R S O N   C O R R E L A T I O N   C O E F F I C I E N T S

	Y1	Y2	Y3	Y4	Y5	X1	X2
Y1	1.0000	.8113	.7858	.8109	.7921	.2763	.1963
Y2	.8113	1.0000	.8534	.7641	.8605	.1905	.2821
Y3	.7858	.8534	1.0000	.7611	.9879	.2799	.2969
Y4	.8109	.7641	.7611	1.0000	.7747	.4664	.2435
Y5	.7921	.8605	.9879	.7747	1.0000	.2827	.2966
X1	.2763	.1905	.2799	.4664	.2827	1.0000	.1399
X2	.1963	.2821	.2969	.2435	.2966	.1399	1.0000

indicated by the "**1**" that one wants the correlations to be computed. If one wants the covariances one should specify on this card a "**2**" instead of the "**1**". The next card indicates that now the computer has to start to read the data which are presented next according to the afore-mentioned format. And the whole input is finished off with the card "**FINISH**". There are many more ways to do the same job. For example, one may want to read the data from another file, or write the results on another file and so on. For a complete set of instructions we refer to the SPSS manual and its updates, where all possible options are indicated.

The result of this particular job is that the computer provides us with the means and standard deviations of the variables and with the correlations between the variables. Table 9.6 gives the output of the program for this particular job. It can be seen that the number of cases is 383 for all variables as a result of the listwise deletion option. Comparing Tables 9.4 and 9.6 we see that only minor differences are obtained. These are due to a different handling of missing values. LISREL used pairwise deletion and in SPSS we used listwise deletion. The analyses done in this text are based on the correlation matrix presented in Table 9.6, because we think that the listwise deletion procedure is better than the pairwise procedure provided by LISREL.

The Relationship between S and Σ

Having discussed the sampling procedures and the computation of the sample statistics we can now also say something about the relationship between the sample covariance matrix S (or correlation matrix R) and the population covariance matrix Σ (or the correlation matrix Σˢ). It will be clear by now that the sample measures are not necessarily identical to the population measures. In fact there is only one population covariance or correlation matrix while many different sample matrices may be obtained. In general a different matrix is obtained for each new sample from the same population.

Although it might seem from the last sentence that everything becomes uncertain by sampling, this uncertainty turns out to have its limits.

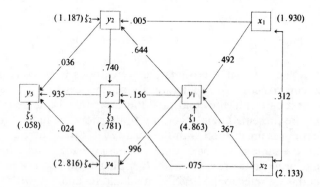

Figure 9.1   The Causal Model for the School Theory with the Values of the Parameters as they have been chosen for the Experiment

Table 9.7   The Covariance Matrix Obtained from the Model in Figure 9.1

	y_1	y_2	y_3	y_4	y_5	x_1	x_2
y_1	5.731						
y_2	3.698	3.573					
y_3	3.710	3.272	3.844				
y_4	5.708	3.663	3.695	8.501			
y_5	3.736	3.274	3.798	3.788	3.815		
x_1	1.064	.695	.705	1.059	.709	1.930	
x_2	.937	.605	.756	.934	.751	.312	2.133

The simplest way to discuss this point is to give the results of an experiment in which we draw samples from a completely known population. In that way we can demonstrate what the consequences are of sampling. This illustration with an experiment substitutes a formal derivation of the relationship which is too complicated for this text.

Imagine that the causal effects governing the school career process are exactly known for the population and are represented by the values of Figure 9.1. On the basis of these parameter values the covariance matrix for the population (Σ) can be computed and turns out to be equal to the matrix presented in Table 9.7. The derivation can be done using the relationships between the parameters of the model and the covariances between the variables, such as discussed in Chapter 7. The next step is that we draw 400 simple random samples of 500 cases and 400 samples of 50 cases from a very large population with the covariance matrix presented in Table 9.7. For each sample the covariance matrix (s_i) is computed where i indicates the number of the sample. After these steps the distributions of the sample covariances can be studied by presenting them in histograms and by computing the means and standard deviations over the 400 sample covariance estimates.

For the covariance between the variables y_5 and y_4 the results of this experiment are presented in Figures 9.2 and 9.3. In Figure 9.2 the result for the 400 small samples is summarized. In the population the covariance between these two variables was equal to 3.788, as can be verified in Table 9.7. The experiment shows that the mean of the estimates in the 400 samples is approximately identical to this value. The result is true for the small samples as well as the large samples. Both results suggest that the distribution of the sample covariances is centered around the true value of this coefficient in the population. The reader should realize that only the mean of the sample covariances is approximately equal to the true value of that parameter and not each sample estimate separately. Figures 9.2 and 9.3 clearly indicate that the individual sample values may differ from the true value. In case of large samples this distribution seems to be symmetric and to look like the normal distribution, while for small samples the distribution is not symmetric anymore and therefore not a normal distribution. More importantly, we see that in the large sample experiment the dispersion (measured by the standard deviation)

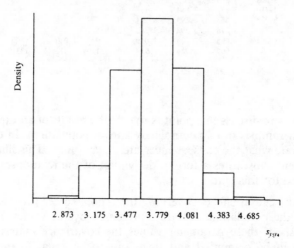

Figure 9.2   The Histogram for $s_{y_5y_4}$ obtained from 400 Samples of 500 Cases. The Mean Value is 3.779, the Standard Deviation is .302.

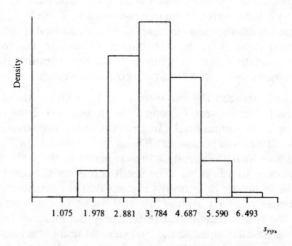

Figure 9.3   The Histogram for $s_{y_5y_4}$ obtained from 400 Samples of 50 Cases. The Mean Value is 3.784, the Standard Deviation is .903.

is much smaller than in the small sample experiment. For the large sample experiment, the standard deviation is .302, while in the small sample experiment the standard deviation is .903. This indicates that the larger the sample, the more precise the information becomes. In the large sample experiment we see that approximately 95% of all sample values lie within the range of 3.184 (= 3.788 − 2 × .302) to 4.392 (= 3.788 + 2 × .302). In the small sample experiment approximately 95% of the sample values lie within the range of .982 (= 3.788 − 2 × .903) to 5.594 (= 3.788 + 2 × .903). This indicates very clearly that the uncertainty caused by sampling can be considerably reduced by increasing the sample size. In that way the sample covariances will lie closer to the true values of the parameters in the population.

The results which we have presented here as results of a sampling experiment can also formally be derived in case the variables in the population have a multivariate normal distribution. In that case it can be proven that

(1) The large sample distribution for each sample covariance (s_{ij}) is the normal distribution with the mean equal to σ_{ij} and with a standard deviation which depends on the size of the sample n (see Figure 9.2 for an illustration).

(2) For small samples the distribution of s_{ij} is not the normal distribution anymore (see Figure 9.3), but it still is exactly known. The mean of the distribution is again the population value (σ_{ij}), at least if the denumerator in equations (9.2) and (9.4) is taken to be $n - 1$ instead of n. The standard deviation also varies with the sample size.

(3) Even the joint distribution or joint density function of all elements of S is exactly known. This distribution also depends on the population covariance matrix Σ and the sample size n.

Therefore this density function is often denoted with $f(S \mid \Sigma, n)$, i.e. it is a function of S, given that Σ and n have certain values. For the precise form of this function, we refer to the more advanced literature, since this function is too complicated to be discussed in this introductory text.

If the variables in the population do not have a multivariate normal distribution, much less is known about the relationship between the sample and the population measures. A problem is that one can get very bad estimates of the covariance or correlation matrix on the basis of one sample estimate if the distribution of the variables deviates too much from a normal distribution. Therefore "robust" estimates have been suggested in the literature which are more stable estimates from sample to sample. A very simple procedure for obtaining robust estimates is that in the computation one leaves out the values of a certain percentage of cases with the most extreme scores since outliers can affect the estimates considerably. For more information on this point, the reader should refer to the literature. However, it should be clear from this discussion that it is good practice to check the distribution of the variables before a covariance or correlation matrix is computed. If an SPSS file has been made for data modifications, this is easily done with the procedure **SCATTERGRAM**. This presents plots in which it is easy to detect outliers which seem unreasonable. Such outliers are sometimes the result of errors and can be corrected by returning to the questionnaire forms. Quality controls of the data are very important in general.

Finally a remark should be made concerning situations where crude categorical variables have been used for what are in principle continuous variables. In such cases the covariances and correlations which are obtained from the sample data might be very bad estimates of the population covariances and correlations. This is especially true for variables for which the distributions are skewed in opposite directions by the categorization. In such cases the differences between the true covariances and the sample covariances can become so large that the analysis of such data can lead to different models from the models which have generated the population data. In such cases one can either try to improve the measurement of the variables before one starts the analysis of such data, or use a correlation measure other than the Pearson correlation coefficient to summarize the association between such categorical variables. LISREL offers some alternative measures which may be used as input for further analysis. These are discussed in the next section.

* Estimation of Correlations for Categorical Variables

When analyzing ordinal variables, a common practice is to assign integer values to the various categories. For example 1,2,3 are assigned to the various categories of an opinion question ranging from "disagree" to "agree". In fact these numbers could be changed, as long as their order is preserved. When correlation coefficients are estimated on the basis of such scores, the results may be very bad, as we have suggested above. In order to obtain better estimates, there exist two possible options. The first possibility is to derive better estimates from assumptions concerning the distribution of the variables. The second is to derive better estimates from assumptions concerning the relationships between the variables. It is clear that nothing can be done without assumptions because we lack the necessary information.

Following the first approach, it is assumed that the two variables have a bivariate normal distribution which does not show in the data because of crude measurement. This situation is illustrated in Figure 9.4, where y and x are dichotomized variables. Assuming bivariate normality, the values of the thresholds y_0 and x_0 can be determined and the correlation between the assumed continuous variables can be estimated. For this purpose the *polychoric correlation coefficient* has been suggested in the literature.

Table 9.8   Types of Correlation Coefficients for Various Measurement
Levels

first variable	second variable	
	Ordinal	Interval/ratio
Ordinal	Polychoric	Polyserial
Interval/ratio	Polyserial	Product Moment

Similar ideas lead to the estimation of a correlation between an ordinal variable and a continuous variable, using the *polyserial correlation coefficient*. The various procedures to estimate the correlation are summarized in Table 9.8. In Table 9.9 a LISREL instruction file is presented leading to the computation of the various correlation coefficients. Following the title and description of the data, it is indicated that the real number 0 is to be treated as a missing value and that the Maximum number of distinct Values (**MV**) of the categorical variables is seven. Variables having from 2 to 7 categories are now treated as ordinal variables. The last card specifies again that we want an output with seven digits after the point. We will show one portion of the output from the school career data. The first endogenous variable was "scholastic achievement" and was measured as an interval variable. The second endogenous variable was "teacher's recommendation" and was measured with seven categories. With the instruction of Table 9.9 the output of Table 9.10 was obtained.

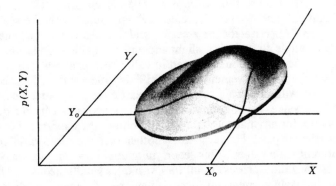

Figure 9.4   The Effect of Crude Categorical Measurement in Case of a
Bivariate Normal Distribution

Table 9.9   The LISREL Instruction File to Analyze Categorical Data

```
COMPUTATION OF CORRELATIONS WITH DISCRETE VARIABLES
DATA      NI=7 NO=447
RAW       XM=0 MV=7
  70 6 6 80 6 74 6
  80 6 7 90 7 74 6
      ETC.
OUTPUT  ND=7
```

The polyserial correlation turned out to be .843. In the same way all other correlations between the variables can be estimated. It should be mentioned that it might occur that by use of this procedure a "not positive definite" correlation matrix will be obtained. In such cases some procedures to estimate the parameters are not possible as we will see in the next chapters.

We want to discuss briefly the second procedure, which makes use of the assumption of linear relationships between the variables. Given this assumption the category values can be determined which maximize the correlation between the variables. In this way also the best estimate of the correlation between the variables, assuming a linear relationship, is obtained. The correlations which are computed in this way can be used in a subsequent analysis.

From the school career variables four variables have in fact an ordinal measurement level: "teacher's recommendation", "parents' preference" and "school choice". They are all coded in seven categories of school types which are ordered in terms of difficulty but not necessarily with equal intervals. The variable "socio-economic status" is also a categorical variable and has six categories, which are also not necessarily equally spaced. We used the program HOMALS (Homogeneity Analysis by Alternating Least Squares) to compute the scale values of these four variables. The correlation between "teacher's recommendation" and "parents' preference" computed with the scale values 1 to 7 was .8534. With the new set of scale values it has become .8637. So, in this example there was a slight increment in this correlation. On the other hand, some correlations dropped in value. For example, the correlation between "scholastic achievement" and "SES" is .1963 with 1, 2, 3 scores and becomes .1945 with new scale values. The reason for this is that we computed one set of scale values for all four variables simultaneously. One can determine the scale values for any pair of variables and obtain the maximized correlation for that particular pair. However, for another pair the same variables might obtain different scale values. This seems quite unnatural, and we therefore applied the optimization process to all four variables simultaneously. Overall, it turned out that eight correlations increased and eight correlations dropped, but in both directions the deviations were very small. The largest difference was a drop from .7921 to .7749 for the correlation between "scholastic achievement" and "school choice".

Table 9.10 A Part of the LISREL Output From the Input Instruction of Table 9.9

```
COMPUTING CORRELATION BETWEEN VARIABLES    VAR 2 AND    VAR 1

VARIABLE    VAR 2 HAS   7 VALUES AND IS TREATED AS A DISCRETE VARIABLE

NUMBER OF MISSING VALUES ( CODE =   0.0000 )        2

MARGINAL FREQUENCES FOR VARIABLE    VAR 2
   CATEGORY      1      2      3      4      5      6      7
   FREQUENCY   140     32    123     47     47     44     12

ESTIMATED THRESHOLD VALUES FOR VARIABLE    VAR 2

  -.48    -.29    .42    .73    1.15    1.93


VARIABLE    VAR 1 HAS MORE THAN   7 VALUES AND IS TREATED AS A CONTINUOUS VARIABLE

NUMBER OF MISSING VALUES ( CODE =   0.0000 )      4

MEAN FOR VARIABLE    VAR 1            53.415

STANDARD DEVIATION FOR VARIABLE    VAR 1    22.617


TECHNICAL OUTPUT FROM MINIMIZATION

CORRELATION      FUNCTION           SLOPE

0.0000        .75846093E+03     -.33560857E+03
 .2900        .67148049E+03     -.27979156E+03
 .5800        .58995180E+03     -.28794057E+03
 .8700        .52979704E+03      .23365204E+03
 .8225        .52811964E+03     -.10208154E+03
 .8433        .52699067E+03      .15300404E+01
 .8431        .52699048E+03     -.25746196E-01
 .8431        .52699048E+03      .30818972E-04


   POLYSERIAL CORRELATION IS    .843
```

Given these small differences between the correlations obtained for the variables expressed in the original scores and the improved estimates obtained with the new scale values, we decided to use the 1, 2, 3 scores. In other applications however, it may be useful to improve the estimates of the correlations by one of the two suggested procedures.

Some Final Remarks

In Chapter 8 we have seen that the parameter values of a model can be computed as soon as we have information about the covariances or correlations between the variables, provided the model is identified. In this chapter we have seen that normally we do not have information about a population, but only about one sample. We have also seen that the sample information summarized in the covariance matrix S is not necessarily identical to the population information summarized in Σ. The matrix S can only be seen as an estimate of the matrix Σ. This means that we cannot simply calculate the values of the effect parameters from this sample information, but that we have to take into account the difference between S and Σ. In the next chapter we shall discuss in detail how the parameter values can be estimated in spite of the differences between sample and population.

Clearly, it may be anticipated that the difference between S and Σ also affects the estimates of the parameters. For each sample different estimates of the parameters can be expected, depending on the particular sample which has been used to estimate the parameters. But this chapter has suggested that the deviations from the true parameter values are predictable, at least if random sampling or systematic sampling is used and enough cooperation has been obtained so that the sample is not biased systematically by nonresponse, but is only affected by random sampling fluctuations.

Even under these conditions we cannot be completely sure of the results in the case when the distribution of the variables deviates considerably from a multivariate normal distribution. In that case the use of robust estimates for the covariances has been suggested in order to obtain better estimates of the population covariances.

In case of very crude categorization of the variables which has caused skewed distributions of the variables, we suggest not to continue the analysis but first to improve the measurement in order to avoid incorrect conclusions or to use other estimation procedures for the correlations between the variables. Suggestions for these alternatives are given in the last section.

Further Reading

The sampling procedures of this chapter are discussed in many statistics books, such as Jessen (1978), Raj (1968), Som (1973) and Yamane (1967). The exact nature of the relationship between the sample statistics and the population statistics is a very specialized and complex topic. It is discussed in advanced texts such as Cochran (1977), Hansen, Hurwitz and Madow (1953) and Kish

(1965). The nonresponse problem is addressed in Bethlehem and Kersten (1982) and Bethlehem and Keller (1983).

For the discussion of the advantages and computation of robust estimates there is a simple text in German by Arminger (1979) and there are more complete, but also more complex articles by Devlin et al. (1975) and Gnànadesikan and Kettering (1972).

The problem of crude categorization has been discussed by Olsson (1979a) in a study of another type of model, but where the same problem can arise. Another illustration of this point is given by Van Doorn et. al.(1983). Correlation measures for ordinal and dichotomous variables are described by Olsson (1979b) and Olsson, Drasgow and Dorans (1982).

The other suggested procedure for improved estimates of the correlation coefficients has been developed in France and is referred to as *correspondence analysis* (Benzecri 1973, Gifi 1981, Hill 1974).

A serious alternative to the suggested improved estimates for the correlation coefficients is improvement of the measurement itself, leading to continuous variables. Such procedures are suggested by Lodge et. al.(1976, 1979) and Lodge(1981), Hamblin (1974), Saris et. al.(1977). Van Doorn et. al.(1982) have shown that results of the analysis can considerably be improved by use of proper measurement instruments.

Exercises

9.1 In the Netherlands there were at the time of the school career research 3060 primary schools. From these schools 103 schools were randomly chosen for questioning.

(a)For what population is this sample representative?

(b)Only 45 schools gave replies to the questions. What kind of effect does this have on the generalizability of the results?

(c)The teachers were asked to give information about half of the children in the class: 50% was asked to give information about children of which the name started with letters A to K while the others were asked information about children with names starting with L to Z. Does this procedure affect negatively the representativeness of the sample ?

(d)The analyses are done, using the obtained 383 questionnaires from children from 45 schools as the sample. What is your overall idea of the representativeness of this sample for the population of Dutch children of the highest class of the primary school? Why?

(e)The researchers have made a comparison for a few variables with population information available at the Central Bureau of Statistics. It turned out that with respect to the teacher's recommendation and the final choice the distribution in the sample does not deviate considerably from the population information. Does this information help us very much in evaluating the representativeness of this sample?

(*f*)Could you suggest a better practical procedure for obtaining a random sample from the population of Dutch school children in the highest class of the elementary school?

9.2 In exercise (5.1) we asked you to evaluate 10 actions. These actions were randomly chosen from a list of 40 actions.

(*a*)Indicate at least two procedures to do this.

(*b*)How high is the probability for each action in the population to be chosen? one action without replacement? Is this a random sample?

The mean, standard deviation and correlations between the variables of exercise 1 of chapter 5 can be computed from the data matrix specified by you there.

(*c*)Write out the program cards for this job.

(*∗d*)Punch these cards and compute these statistics using the SPSS program.

(*e*)Check by drawing a few scattergrams whether there are serious outliers in your data.

(*f*)If so what should be done in this case?

9.3 In Table 9.6 the computed correlations between the seven variables of the school career example are given for 383 cases.

(*a*)Do you think that we would obtain the same results if we repeated the whole procedure in exactly the same way?

(*b*)There are at least two reasons why you should not expect the same result in (a). Do you have any idea what these reasons are?

(*c*)Given your answers on the questions (9.1d) and (9.1f), do you think that it makes sense to continue the analysis?

9.4 With respect to the secondary analysis:

(*a*)Check in the same way as we have done here whether the sample in the study is a random sample or not.

(*b*)To what kind of population can the results be generalized, if at all?

Chapter 10
Introduction to Estimation

In chapter 8 it was shown that the values of the parameters are obtainable from information on the variances and covariances (or correlations) of the variables, provided that the model is identified. However, in chapter 9 it became obvious that most of the time we only have information about a sample and not a population. It was shown that the sample variances, covariances and correlations are not necessarily identical to the population variances, covariances and correlations. Clearly one should take the differences between these two into account when formulating methods to estimate the structural parameters from information gathered from the sample.

In the literature many different methods have been discussed for estimating the parameters of the models considered here. We discuss three very general principles which can be used for a larger variety of models than those discussed in this volume. In the final chapter some other commonly used procedures are mentioned.

In this chapter the instructions for the LISREL program, which estimates the parameters, are also introduced. Furthermore, we begin to interpret the results of the analysis. Detailed interpretations follow in the subsequent chapters. Two more specialized issues are discussed at the end of this chapter. The topics of these two sections are: (1) the way to estimate intercepts with LISREL and (2) the iterative procedure which is used in LISREL to obtain estimates of the parameters. These sections are not necessary for the understanding of the subsequent chapters.

Least Squares Estimation

The sample covariance matrix S, which is an estimate of the population covariance matrix Σ, can be computed from the data. Instead of S, one can also compute the sample correlation matrix R, which is an estimate of the population covariance matrix of the standardized variables Σ^s. This population covariance matrix is equal to the correlation matrix for the same variables. In equations (7.4a) and (7.4b) of chapter 7 it was shown that all elements of the population covariance or correlation matrix can be written as functions of the parameters (p) of a particular structural equation model

$$\sigma_{ij} = f_{ij}(p) \text{ for all } i,j \qquad (10.1a)$$

Table 10.1   The Correlation Matrix R for Variables of the Simplified School
Career Theory (see Chapter 2); $N = 383$

	Scholastic Achievement y_1	Choice of Secondary School y_2	Quality of Elementary School x_1	Socio-Economic Status x_2
y_1	1.000			
y_2	.792	1.000		
x_1	.276	.283	1.000	
x_2	.196	.297	.140	1.000

or for standardized variables and standardized effects (p^s)

$$\rho_{ij} = f_{ij}(p^s) \text{ for all } i,j \qquad (10.1b)$$

We define the *residual* as the discrepancy between the observed sample
covariance (or correlation) and the population covariance (or correlation):
$(s_{ij} - \sigma_{ij})$ or $(r_{ij} - \rho_{ij})$. According to equation (10.1a) or (10.1b) the residual
for any element can also be defined as $(s_{ij} - f_{ij}(p))$ or $(r_{ij} - f_{ij}(p^s))$. If the

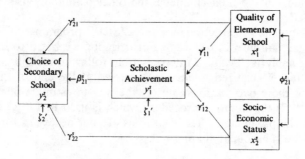

$$y_1^s = 0y_1^s + 0y_2^s + \gamma_{11}^s x_1^s + \gamma_{12}^s x_2^s + \zeta_1'$$
$$y_2^s = \beta_{21}^s y_1^s + 0y_2^s + \gamma_{21}^s x_1^s + \gamma_{22}^s x_2^s + \zeta_2'$$

where $\mu_{y_i^s} = \mu_{x_i^s} = \mu_{\zeta_i} = 0$ for all i
$$\text{Cov}(\zeta_i', x_j^s) = 0 \text{ for all } i,j$$
$$\text{Cov}(\zeta_i', \zeta_j') = 0 \text{ for all } i \neq j$$

Figure 10.1   The Simplified School Career Theory (Chapter 2), represented
Diagrammatically and by Equations

Table 10.2   The Derived Relationships between the Population Correlations and the Parameters of the Simplified School Career Model

$$\rho_{x_1x_1} = \phi^s_{11}$$

$$\rho_{x_2x_1} = \phi^s_{21}$$

$$\rho_{x_2x_2} = \phi^s_{22}$$

$$\rho_{y_1x_1} = \gamma^s_{11} + \gamma^s_{12}\phi^s_{21}$$

$$\rho_{y_1x_2} = \gamma^s_{11}\phi^s_{21} + \gamma^s_{12}$$

$$\rho_{y_2x_1} = \beta^s_{21}(\gamma^s_{11} + \gamma^s_{12}\phi^s_{21}) + \gamma^s_{21} + \gamma^s_{22}\phi^s_{21}$$

$$\rho_{y_2x_2} = \beta^s_{21}(\gamma^s_{11}\phi^s_{21} + \gamma^s_{12}) + \gamma^s_{21}\phi^s_{21} + \gamma^s_{22}$$

$$\rho_{y_2y_1} = \beta^s_{21} + \gamma^s_{21}(\gamma^s_{11} + \gamma^s_{12}\phi^s_{21}) + \gamma^s_{22}(\gamma^s_{11}\phi^s_{21} + \gamma^s_{12})$$

$$\rho_{y_1y_1} = \gamma^s_{11}(\gamma^s_{11} + \gamma^s_{12}\phi^s_{21}) + \gamma^s_{12}(\gamma^s_{11}\phi^s_{21} + \gamma^s_{12}) + \psi_{11}'$$

$$\rho_{y_2y_2} = \beta^s_{21}(\beta^s_{21} + \gamma^s_{21}(\gamma^s_{11} + \gamma^s_{12}\phi^s_{21}) + \gamma^s_{22}(\gamma^s_{11}\phi^s_{21} + \gamma^s_{12}))$$
$$+ \gamma^s_{21}(\beta^s_{21}(\gamma^s_{11} + \gamma^s_{12}\phi^s_{21}) + \gamma^s_{21} + \gamma^s_{22}\phi^s_{21})$$
$$+ \gamma^s_{22}(\beta^s_{21}(\gamma^s_{11}\phi^s_{21} + \gamma^s_{12}) + \gamma^s_{21}\phi^s_{21} + \gamma^s_{22}) + \psi_{22}'$$

model is correct, the residuals have to be very close to zero, since they would only be allowed to differ by chance. If the model is incorrect, the residuals will have larger values.

The first two estimation procedures that are discussed here are based on these residuals. The first principle is known as the *Unweighted Least Squares* (ULS) method. According to this method, one has to look for those values of the parameters which minimize the sum of the squared residuals i.e.:

$$\mathrm{Cr}_{ULS} = \sum_{ij} \left[s_{ij} - \sigma_{ij} \right]^2 \qquad (10.2a)$$

or, for standardized variables,

$$\mathrm{Cr}_{ULS^s} = \sum_{ij} \left[r_{ij} - \rho_{ij} \right]^2 \qquad (10.2b)$$

Since we know from equations (10.1a) and (10.1b) the relationship between the (co)variances and the parameters of the model, we can also write for the criterion functions,

$$\mathrm{Cr}_{ULS} = \sum_{ij} \left[s_{ij} - f_{ij}(p) \right]^2 \qquad (10.3a)$$

or, for standardized variables

$$\mathrm{Cr}_{ULS^s} = \sum_{ij} \left[r_{ij} - f_{ij}(p^s) \right]^2 \qquad (10.3b)$$

The parameter values for which one of these criterion functions obtains its minimum are called the Unweighted Least Squares (*ULS*) estimates.

The ULS principle can be illustrated with the simplified model of the school career theory. In Table 10.1 the sample correlation matrix for this model is presented. In Figure 10.1 the model is presented in a path diagram as well as by equations, and in Table 10.2 the derived relationships of the correlations and model parameters are presented again.

For this example, the criterion function of equation (10.3b) can now be specified by entering the available information for each term. In this instance $\mathrm{Cr}_{ULS^{\sigma}}$ becomes:

$$
\begin{aligned}
\mathrm{Cr}_{ULS^{\sigma}} = &\left[1.000 - \phi_{11}^{s}\right]^{2} \\
&+ \left[0.140 - \phi_{21}^{s}\right]^{2} + \left[1.000 - \phi_{22}^{s}\right]^{2} \\
&+ \left[0.276 - \left(\gamma_{11}^{s} + \gamma_{12}^{s}\phi_{21}^{s}\right)\right]^{2} + \left[0.196 - \left(\gamma_{11}^{s}\phi_{21}^{s} + \gamma_{12}^{s}\right)\right]^{2} \\
&+ \left[0.283 - \left(\beta_{21}^{s}\left(\gamma_{11}^{s} + \gamma_{12}^{s}\phi_{21}^{s}\right) + \gamma_{21}^{s} + \gamma_{22}^{s}\phi_{21}^{s}\right)\right]^{2} \\
&+ \left[0.297 - \left(\beta_{21}^{s}\left(\gamma_{11}^{s}\phi_{21}^{s} + \gamma_{12}^{s}\right) + \gamma_{21}^{s}\phi_{21}^{s} + \gamma_{22}^{s}\right)\right]^{2} \\
&+ \left[0.792 - \left(\beta_{21}^{s} + \gamma_{21}^{s}\left(\gamma_{11}^{s} + \gamma_{12}^{s}\phi_{21}^{s}\right) + \gamma_{22}^{s}\left(\gamma_{11}^{s}\phi_{21}^{s} + \gamma_{12}^{s}\right)\right)\right]^{2} \quad (10.4) \\
&+ \left[1.000 - \left(\gamma_{11}^{s}\left(\gamma_{11}^{s} + \gamma_{12}^{s}\phi_{21}^{s}\right) + \gamma_{12}^{s}\left(\gamma_{11}^{s}\phi_{21}^{s} + \gamma_{12}^{s}\right) + \psi_{11}'\right)\right]^{2} \\
&+ \left[1.000 - \left(\beta_{21}^{s}\left(\beta_{21}^{s} + \gamma_{21}^{s}\left(\gamma_{11}^{s} + \gamma_{12}^{s}\phi_{21}^{s}\right) + \gamma_{22}^{s}\left(\gamma_{11}^{s}\phi_{21}^{s} + \gamma_{12}^{s}\right)\right)\right.\right. \\
&\quad + \gamma_{21}^{s}\left(\beta_{21}^{s}\left(\gamma_{11}^{s} + \gamma_{12}^{s}\phi_{21}^{s}\right) + \gamma_{21}^{s} + \gamma_{22}^{s}\phi_{21}^{s}\right) \\
&\quad \left.\left. + \gamma_{22}^{s}\left(\beta_{21}^{s}\left(\gamma_{11}^{s}\phi_{21}^{s} + \gamma_{12}^{s}\right) + \gamma_{21}^{s}\phi_{21}^{s} + \gamma_{22}^{s}\right) + \psi_{22}'\right)\right]^{2}
\end{aligned}
$$

It is seen that the value of this criterion function depends upon the values of the model parameters. For example, if ϕ_{11}^{s} is chosen to be .5, the value of the function would be larger than when ϕ_{11}^{s} is chosen to be equal to 1. For the other parameters, various values can also be selected and in each case the value of the function can be evaluated. The ULS estimates are found if the parameter values have been obtained for which the function $\mathrm{Cr}_{ULS^{\sigma}}$ as small as possible, which in turn means that the residuals are as small as possible for the specified model. The exact procedure by which those parameter values can be found, is discussed in one of the next sections, after the two other estimation methods have been introduced. This procedure is the same for all three methods.

Here we have only illustrated the ULS criterion function for the standardized variables, but for the unstandardized variables the method is exactly the same. Since this is also true for the other estimation methods, we will from now on only discuss one of the two kinds of formulations.

The second estimation method is based on the *Generalized Least Squares* (GLS) principle and is a slight variation of the ULS principle. According to the ULS principle, each residual term is weighted equally. The Generalized Least Squares principle suggests to attach unequal weights to the various residuals. Why and in what way the weights are chosen is beyond the scope of this introductory text, but can be found in the literature. Nevertheless the criterion function for this weighted or Generalized Least Squares method can be given. The criterion function is denoted by Cr_{GLS}, and is defined as

$$Cr_{GLS} = \sum_{ij} w_{ij}(s_{ij} - \sigma_{ij})^2 \qquad (10.5)$$

or, after substitution of (10.1a),

$$Cr_{GLS} = \sum_{ij} w_{ij}(s_{ij} - f_{ij}(p))^2 \qquad (10.6)$$

The estimates of the parameters for which this function is minimized are called Generalized Least Squares (GLS) estimates. It can be inferred that the ULS estimates are obtained by choosing the weights for each residual as equal to unity. The ULS and GLS estimators only differ in these weights. Both are based on the minimization of the residuals.

Maximum Likelihood Estimation

There is a third general estimation principle which is completely different from these two principles and which is called the *Maximum Likelihood* (ML) principle. One of the estimation procedures available in the LISREL program has been derived using this principle. In this approach, one looks for the parameter values which have most likely produced the observed covariances or correlations. In order to derive the criterion function for this estimator, one has to know the probability density function of the sample covariances and variances. In the previous chapter we have denoted this function by $f(S \mid \Sigma, n)$ since the probability of obtaining certain kinds of sample covariance matrices depends upon the value of the population covariance matrix Σ and the size of the sample (n).

In order to illustrate this point once more, Figure 10.2 shows the probability density functions for two different values of a population covariance. It should be clear from this figure that for the distribution on the left hand side, values of $s_{ij} < -.2$ are quite likely, while these values are very unlikely for the other distribution. Similar remarks can be made for other values of s_{ij}.

In research we are confronted with the opposite situation: we do not know σ_{ij} but only one value of s_{ij}, and we want to find the value of σ_{ij} which has most likely led to the obtained value of s_{ij}. Obviously if we find $s_{ij} = -.2$ it would be better to choose $\sigma_{ij} = 0.0$ than $\sigma_{ij} = .25$.

Following this idea, the ML principle suggests that given the values of S we have to try to find the most likely population values of the matrix Σ. This means that we have to find the values of the elements of Σ which maximize the function $f(S \mid \Sigma, n)$. In this function we can substitute the values of S which we know from the sample, and the sample size n. Then this function only contains the elements of Σ as unknowns. It is usually called the *likelihood function* and is denoted by $L(\Sigma)$. Substitution of equation (10.1a) into this function, for all elements of Σ, gives the criterion function for the maximum likelihood method

$$\mathrm{Cr}_{ML} = L\{f_{ij}(p\,)\} \qquad (10.7)$$

The values of the parameters for which this function is maximized are called Maximum Likelihood (*ML*)estimates. The form of the criterion function depends on the distribution of the observed variables. In the LISREL approach it is assumed that the variables have a multivariate normal distribution. As a result of this assumption, the probability density function is known exactly as is the likelihood function. For this exact formulation and derivation we refer to the literature. At this point the specific form of the likelihood function is not important, but one should be aware that this approach assumes that the variables have a multivariate normal distribution. If this assumption deviates much from reality, one should consider this as a possible explanation for unexpected results.

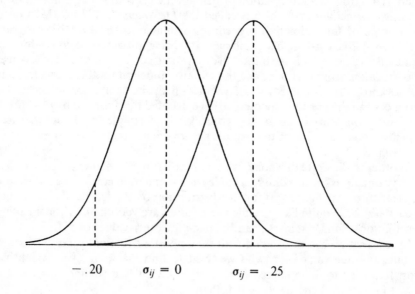

$$-.20 \qquad \sigma_{ij} = 0 \qquad \sigma_{ij} = .25$$

Figure 10.2 Two Density Functions for s_{ij}, one for $\sigma_{ij} = 0$ and one for $\sigma_{ij} = .25$

* Choice of an Estimation Method

Some of the advantages and disadvantages associated with each of the estimation methods are now briefly discussed. The argument is often put forward that the ML estimates should not be used because the assumptions underlying the derivation are not fulfilled. Although this argument is correct in principle, this point should not be exaggerated. It is possible that an estimator leads to good estimates of the parameters even though the assumptions underlying the derivation of the estimator are not fulfilled. It is therefore more useful to compare the performance of the different estimators than to decide the matter simply on the basis of a theoretical argument. As yet, not very much is known about the quality of the different estimators. However, some studies are available.

It is known that for large samples and a multivariate normal distribution of the variables, or slightly weaker conditions, the ML and the GLS estimators are equally good, while the ULS estimator is not as good as these other two. Furthermore, it is known that all three estimators tend to give similar, correct estimates with increasing sample sizes.

Relatively little is known about the properties of the GLS and the ULS estimators for small samples, but it is known that the ML estimator is quite accurate and useful in such cases. Overall, the ML estimates are probably at least as good as the other two kinds of estimates. This also justifies the use of this estimator and its implementation in the LISREL program.

An advantage of GLS and ML estimators compared to ULS estimators is that they are *"scale invariant"*. This property has to do with the scale in which the variables have been expressed. In chapters 3 and 4 it was shown that standardized as well as unstandardized variables can be used in data analysis. The difference between the two is a scale transformation. If an estimation procedure is "scale invariant", this means that the estimates obtained for standardized and unstandardized variables only differ by this scale transformation. In such instances the distinction between the two criterion functions (*a*) and (*b*), as they were specified in the previous section, is not essential, since one can compute the standardized solution from the unstandardized solution and vice versa. In general the ML and GLS estimators have this property, but the ULS estimators are not scale invariant. For them, a rather different solution can be obtained using standardized and unstandardized variables, and these different results can not be derived from each other by a simple transformation. It is often desirable to work with scale invariant procedures, especially when the scales are constructed quite arbitrarily, as it is common in the social sciences. Thus, there are good arguments to prefer the ML and the GLS estimators for this reason.

The ULS estimators have also an advantage in that they can be used in

Table 10.3 The LISREL Formulation of the Simplified School Career Theory presented in Figure 10.1

BETA	y_1	y_2
y_1	0	0
y_2	β_{21}	0

GAMMA	x_1	x_2
y_1	γ_{11}	γ_{12}
y_2	γ_{21}	γ_{22}

PSI	ζ_1	ζ_2
ζ_1	ψ_{11}	0
ζ_2	0	ψ_{22}

PHI	x_1	x_2
x_1	ϕ_{11}	
x_2	ϕ_{21}	ϕ_{22}

situations when the other two procedures fail to provide solutions. This happens when one of the variables in the data matrix is completely dependent upon one or more of the other variables in the matrix. In such cases the matrix is called *"not positive definite"*. Such correlation or covariance matrices can not be analyzed using GLS or ML estimators, but it is still possible to use the ULS principle to obtain estimates of the model parameters.

Summarizing the review of estimation procedures, it can be concluded that the Maximum Likelihood estimator seems a good choice. Only when one is dealing with an input matrix which is "not positive definite", should the ULS estimator be used.

Running the LISREL program

Before showing how parameter estimates can be obtained using the LISREL program, something has to be said about the notation used. In this program all models are formulated in a series of effect matrices and covariance or correlation matrices. To illustrate this Table 10.3 presents the simplified school career theory depicted in Figure 10.1 in matrices. All models discussed in this book can be formulated in these four matrices. The effect matrix BETA (BE) contains the effects of the endogenous variables (y) on each other. In this specific case only β_{21} has to be estimated. The values of the other three parameters are fixed at zero and are therefore called *fixed parameters* while β_{21} is a so called *free parameter* since this parameter has no fixed value but the value has to be estimated. In the LISREL program the parameter β_{21} is denoted by BE(2,1).

Table 10.4   The Input for the LISREL Program to obtain Estimates for the Simplified School Career Model by analyzing the Correlation Matrix

```
DATA ANALYSIS WITH THE SIMPLIFIED SCHOOL CAREER MODEL
DATA      NI=7 NO=383 MA=KM
KM
*
1.0000000
 .8113306 1.0000000
 .7857889  .8534177 1.0000000
 .8108940  .7641449  .7610636 1.0000000
 .7921435  .8604609  .9878695  .7747339 1.0000000
 .2763330  .1905062  .2799446  .4663920  .2827473 1.0000000
 .1962511  .2821079  .2968646  .2435010  .2965949  .1398519 1.0000000
LABELS
(7A8)
 ACHIEVE  RECOMM  PREFER   TEST  CHOICE QUALITY      SES
SELECT
 1 5 6 7/
MODEL     NY=2 NX=2 BE=FU,FI GA=FU,FR PS=DI,FR
FREE      BE(2,1)
OUTPUT    MR TV MI
```

The GAMMA (**GA**) matrix contains the effects of the predetermined variables (x) on the endogenous variables (y). In this specific case all parameters in the matrix have to be estimated. We can also say that all parameters of GAMMA are free parameters. In the program these parameters are denoted as **GA(1,1)**, **GA(2,1)**, **GA(1,2)** and **GA(2,2)**.

The covariance matrix of the disturbance terms PSI (**PS**) contains two free parameters: ψ_{11} and ψ_{22} or in the program's notation **PS(1,1)** and **PS(2,2)**. The other elements ψ_{21} and ψ_{12} are assumed to be zero. Such a matrix, with zeros in all cells except the diagonal, is called a diagonal matrix. In large models it can be useful to indicate that a matrix is diagonal since it reduces the computational work.

The matrix PHI (**PH**) is the covariance matrix for the x variables. This is a symmetric matrix like all covariance matrices; for all elements $\phi_{ij} = \phi_{ji}$. In principle all the parameters of this matrix have to be estimated. However in the first section of this chapter it was indicated that the best estimate for each ϕ_{ij} is $s_{x_i x_j}$ (for standardized variables the best estimate is $r_{x_i x_j}$). Such a relationship always holds for the elements of the matrix PHI and the elements of the matrix S (R for standardized variables), since no explanation is given for the x variables. Therefore, the parameters of the matrix PHI do not have to be estimated for the models discussed in this book. These parameters are automatically set equal to their best estimates which are the sample estimates $s_{x_i x_j}$

Having indicated the notation of the LISREL program the estimation of the parameters by the program can be introduced. The way in which the input of the program can be organized is illustrated for the simplified school career theory presented in Figure 10.1, and in matrix notation in Table 10.3 while the estimation is done on the basis of the correlation matrix provided in Table 9.6. One possible input for the LISREL program is presented in Table 10.4. For alternatives we refer to the LISREL User's Guide (Jöreskog and Sörbom,1983).

The first line gives the title of the task. The next fifteen lines specify the information obtained from the sample. First it is stated that the number of input variables (**NI**) is equal to 7, the number of observations (**NO**) is equal to 383, and that the matrix to be analyzed (**MA**) is the correlation matrix (**KM**). Next it is specified how the correlation matrix will be presented to the computer program. There are several options, but we have chosen the simplest one: "**KM**" indicates that the correlation matrix is read in as input matrix. The "*****" on the next line indicates that the matrix is read in *free format*. This means that the matrix can be introduced in any form the researcher wants. The only restriction is that the numbers have to be separated by blanks or commas. Subsequently, the correlation matrix is entered. Thereafter the labels of the variables are indicated. For each variable a name of at most 8 letters is specified. In order to indicate to the computer how the names should be read it is mentioned on the next line that 7 names follow, each taking 8 columns. Finally, the four variables which are needed in the analysis are selected. The program understands that the first variable mentioned will be y_1, the second y_2, the third x_1 and the last x_2. The y variables should always be mentioned first, starting with y_1 through the last y variable, followed by the x variables.

Having specified the information about the data, one indicates what the model, that has to be analyzed, looks like and what parameters have to be estimated. First of all there is a statement with the keyword "**MODEL**", in which one has to indicate how many y variables and x variables (**NY** and **NX**) there are. Furthermore the free and fixed parameters have to be specified. This is done in two steps: first something is said about the matrices and next about the individual parameters in the matrices, if that is still necessary.

In this example it is indicated that BETA is a full matrix (**FU**) which only contains fixed parameters (**FI**). This is not completely correct because β_{21} is a free parameter. Therefore this element is mentioned in the next line as a free parameter by simply writing "**FREE   BE(2,1)**". Alternatively one could have written:

```
MODEL    BETA=FU,FR
FIXED    BE(1,1) BE(1,2) BE(2,2)
```

In this input the BETA matrix is specified to be "full and free" first, but next three coefficients are fixed (at zero, if nothing else is indicated).

For GAMMA it is specified that it is a full matrix (**FU**) with only free parameters (FR). This specification does not need any correction. For PSI the simplest solution is to say that PSI is diagonal (DI) and that all parameters on the diagonal are free (FR). By specifying the free parameters in these three matrices the whole model is specified for the program except the matrix PHI. But the coefficients of this matrix are automatically made identical to the corresponding elements of S (or R) by the program because the best estimates for the ϕ coefficients are identical to the elements of this matrix.

In the last line the output of the program is requested. Using the given line, one generally gets a little bit too much information; later, when the different output options are explained, the reader can choose for him-/herself between the different options.

Three more remarks need to be made about this input. The first is that we have not mentioned anything about the values of the fixed parameters. This was not necessary because all fixed parameters had to have the value zero. This value is given to the parameters by default. Any other value has to be specified. This can be done in the following way:

START   k   BE(1,1) BE(1,2) BE(2,2)

In this line the symbol **k** stands for any arbitrary number. If **k=0** the statement is not necessary . For any other value the statement should be of this form and should be placed after the specification of the free parameters. The second remark is that it was not specified whether we wanted to obtain the unstandardized or the standardized parameters. However, the general rule holds for the models in this book that if the correlation matrix is analyzed, the values of the standardized parameters are obtained. If the covariance matrix is analyzed, the unstandardized parameters are estimated and on request one can also obtain the values of the standardized coefficients.

A final remark is that the estimation procedure was not mentioned in the input of Table 10.4. This is not necessary if one wants the Maximum Likelihood estimates. This is the default option in LISREL. There are in fact in LISREL VI five different estimation procedures available: the three we have discussed before and Two Stage Least Squares and Instrumental Variables. If one wants to use another estimation procedure than the ML procedure, one has to add a message to the output card. The abbreviations for the different procedures are **UL** for ULS, **GL** for GLS, **TS** for Two Stage Least Squares and **IV** for Instrumental Variables. For further details on this topic we refer to the User's Guide. In this example it makes no difference if another procedure is used since the model is exactly identified ($df = 0$), which means that there is only one solution for the parameters of the model.

The part of the output which gives the estimates of the parameters of the model is presented in Table 10.5. From this table, Figure 10.3 can be derived as well as equations (10.8) and (10.9).

Table 10.5   A Part of the LISREL Output Obtained with the Input Given in Table 10.4

```
LISREL ESTIMATES (MAXIMUM LIKELIHOOD)

      BETA

              ACHIEVE      CHOICE
ACHIEVE         0.000       0.000
CHOICE           .749       0.000

      GAMMA

              QUALITY        SES
ACHIEVE          .254       .161
CHOICE           .056       .142

      PHI

              QUALITY        SES
QUALITY        1.000
    SES          .140      1.000

      PSI

              ACHIEVE      CHOICE
                 .898        .349

      SQUARED MULTIPLE CORRELATIONS FOR STRUCTURAL EQUATIONS

              ACHIEVE      CHOICE
                 .102        .651
```

$$y_1^s = .254x_1^s + .161x_2^s + \zeta_1' \qquad (10.8)$$
$$y_2^s = .749y_1^s + .056x_1^s + .142x_2^s + \zeta_2' \qquad (10.9)$$

The matrix representation and the representation in equations is always possible. The presentation of results in a diagram is only possible for simple models. All three forms of presentation give the same information (the reader should check this point). In the diagram the variances of the disturbance terms are given within parentheses in order to emphasize that these numbers do not represent the disturbance terms themselves. These disturbance terms are different for all students and will not be estimated. Only the variances of the disturbance terms will be estimated and presented.

Since the correlation matrix is analyzed the parameters are standardized and their values can therefore be compared. We see that the effects of the two predetermined variables on scholastic achievement are about the same, but the magnitude of these effects is rather small. The proportion of unexplained variance of variable y_1^s is thus rather large ($\psi_{11}' = .898$). The two predetermined variables have even less effect on the choice of the secondary school (y_2^s), but scholastic achievement (y_1^s) has a large effect on this variable, as had been anticipated. Therefore, the proportion of unexplained variance is much less than that for scholastic achievement ($\psi_{22}' = .349$). Since many researchers prefer to use the proportion of explained variance, the program also prints the squared multiple correlation for each structural equation. Since the total amount of variance is 1 for standardized variables, the amount of explained variance is $1 - .898 = .102$ for the first equation and $1 - .349 = .651$ for the second equation.

Estimation of the Full School Career Model

This example was relatively simple. In order to illustrate a more complex example, Table 10.6 gives the input for the computation of the LISREL estimates of the full school career model, discussed in the earlier chapters (see, for example, the discussion of the model in chapter 4). Table 10.6 shows that the input for such a complex model is not very much more complicated than for a simple model. The only difference is that a larger number of free parameters has to be specified. The selection is omitted because all variables are used in this case and they are already placed in the proper order: first the y variables from y_1 to y_5, and then the x variables.

The ML estimates computed by LISREL for the full school career theory are presented in Table 10.7 and Figure 10.4. The reader may again verify how the first representation relates to the second.

Compared to the earlier analysis of the simplified model, the interpretation of the effects on variable y_1^s is exactly the same, while the explanation of "choice of secondary school" has become quite different in this model. Here "teacher's recommendation", "parents' preferences" and the "school test score" are introduced as explanatory variables, while "scholastic achievement" and the two

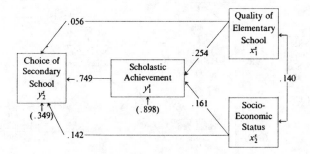

Figure 10.3 The Result of the Analysis presented in Table 10.5 Assembled in a Path Diagram

Table 10.6   The Input for the LISREL Program to Obtain Estimates for the
                   Full School Career Model by Analyzing the Correlation Matrix

```
DATA ANALYSIS WITH THE FULL SCHOOL CAREER MODEL
DATA    NI=7 NO=383 MA=KM
KM
*
1.0000000
 .8113306 1.0000000
 .7857889  .8534177 1.0000000
 .8108940  .7641449  .7610636 1.0000000
 .7921435  .8604609  .9878695  .7747339 1.0000000
 .2763330  .1905062  .2799446  .4663920  .2827473 1.0000000
 .1962511  .2821079  .2968646  .2435010  .2965949  .1398519 1.0000000
LABELS
*
'     Y 1' '     Y 2' '     Y 3' '     Y 4' '     Y 5'
'     X 1' '     X 2'
MODEL   NY=5 NX=2 BE=FU,FI GA=FU,FI PS=DI,FR
FREE    BE(2,1) BE(3,1) BE(4,1) BE(3,2) BE(5,2) BE(5,3) BE(5,4)
FREE    GA(1,1) GA(1,2) GA(2,1) GA(3,2)
OUTPUT  MR TV MI SS
```

predetermined variables can only have indirect effects. It is clear from the estimates obtained that the preferences of the parents have the largest effect (.916), while the direct effects of "teacher's recommendation" and "school test score" are very small. Note, that the direct effects are explicitly mentioned here. The reason is that the picture is quite different for the indirect effects. We can see that "teacher's recommendation" has a strong effect on "parents' preferences" and thus this variable has a rather strong indirect effect, apart

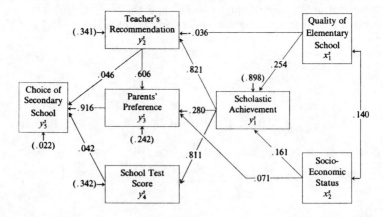

Figure 10.4   The Results of Table 10.7 Assembled in a Path Diagram

Table 10.7 A Part of the LISREL output obtained with the Input given in Table 10.6

LISREL ESTIMATES (MAXIMUM LIKELIHOOD)

BETA

	Y 1	Y 2	Y 3	Y 4	Y 5
Y 1	0.000	0.000	0.000	0.000	0.000
Y 2	.821	0.000	0.000	0.000	0.000
Y 3	.280	.606	0.000	0.000	0.000
Y 4	.811	0.000	0.000	0.000	0.000
Y 5	0.000	.046	.916	.042	0.000

GAMMA

	X 1	X 2
Y 1	.254	.161
Y 2	-.036	0.000
Y 3	0.000	.071
Y 4	0.000	0.000
Y 5	0.000	0.000

PHI

	X 1	X 2
X 1	1.000	
X 2	.140	1.000

PSI

Y 1	Y 2	Y 3	Y 4	Y 5
.898	.341	.242	.342	.022

SQUARED MULTIPLE CORRELATIONS FOR STRUCTURAL EQUATIONS

Y 1	Y 2	Y 3	Y 4	Y 5
.102	.659	.756	.658	.977

from the direct effect which turned out to be small. In the same way the results indicate that the direct effect of "scholastic achievement" on "choice of secondary school" is assumed here to be zero, but the indirect effects are quite large, since this variable has quite strong effects on the three intervening variables (y_2^s, y_3^s and y_4^s). On the other hand, it seems that the quality of the elementary school and the socio-economic status of the parents do not play an important role in the choice process except for the fact that they have some effect on the achievement of the students. Finally, the results indicate that the variable "choice of secondary school" is very well explained, since there is only 2.2% unexplained variance left. For the intervening variables the amount of unexplained variance is also relatively small, but the variable y_1^s is still not adequately explained by this theory. However, as we have mentioned in chapter 4, the explanation of this variable was not the purpose of this study in the first place. The explanation of this variable requires the incorporation of different causal variables, such as "intelligence", which have been left out. Therefore, the variance of the disturbance term which contains omitted variables like "intelligence" is also rather large (.898).

We have now given a preliminary interpretation of the results produced by the program, but results are not always and automatically correct. There are several issues that should be critically considered in evaluating the results. First of all, before continuing the interpretations, one should take into account that the model might not be correct in view of the data and has to be rejected. This possibility will be discussed extensively in the next chapter, which deals with the test of models. Obviously, it is only useful to interpret solutions in full detail after it has been shown that the model fits the data.

A second problem which we have to take into account is that the results obtained are specific for only one sample, and do not necessarily represent the correct estimates of the parameters for the population of interest. In chapter 13 we return to this issue. There, this point is discussed more fully and it is shown that intervals can be constructed which, with a certain probability, contain the true population values of the parameters.

A third and final problem which may sometimes be encountered is that the optimal solution for the set of parameters has not been obtained. In LISREL the estimation procedure begins with a set of initial estimates of the parameters which are improved step by step by the program. These initial estimates will lead to a satisfactory final result most of the time. Incidentally, the optimal estimates might not be obtained. One can then decide to check this point and specify other start values for some parameters. If the program comes up with other and better estimates, the value of the criterion function for the new solution will be smaller than for the first run of the program. Starting values are specified using the keyword START, for example:

START   .5 BE(5,2) BE(5,3) BE(5,4)

This statement assigns the start value .5 to three parameters. It should be added after the model specification cards. The reader may want to add this or a similar statement to the input of Table 10.6 and check whether it has any effect on the estimates.

Comparison of estimates

So far we have estimated only the standardized coefficients using the correlation matrix as the matrix to be analyzed. If the covariance matrix is analyzed, both the unstandardized and the standardized coefficients can be obtained simultaneously. The input for this task is given in Table 10.8. This table

Table 10.8 The Input for the LISREL Program to Obtain Estimates for the Full School Career Model by Analyzing the Covariance Matrix

```
DATA ANALYSIS WITH THE FULL SCHOOL CAREER MODEL
DATA    NI=7 NO=383 MA=CM
KM
*
1.0000000
 .8113306 1.0000000
 .7857889  .8534177 1.0000000
 .8108940  .7641449  .7610636 1.0000000
 .7921435  .8604609  .9878695  .7747339 1.0000000
 .2763330  .1905062  .2799446  .4663920  .2827473 1.0000000
 .1962511  .2821079  .2968646  .2435010  .2965949  .1398519 1.0000000
SD
*
  22.5069    1.7835    1.7845   27.8085    1.7830   28.0352    1.4700
LABELS
*
'      Y 1' '     Y 2' '     Y 3' '     Y 4' '     Y 5'
'      X 1' '     X 2'
MODEL   NY=5 NX=2 BE=FU,FI GA=FU,FI PS=DI,FR
FREE    BE(2,1) BE(3,1) BE(4,1) BE(3,2) BE(5,2) BE(5,3) BE(5,4)
FREE    GA(1,1) GA(1,2) GA(2,1) GA(3,2)
OUTPUT  MR TV MI SS
```

shows that the input is only changed on three points compared with the earlier analysis (Table 10.6). First, it is indicated that the matrix to be analyzed (**MA**) is the covariance matrix (**CM**). Secondly, we see that in addition to the correlation matrix another series of numbers is introduced which represents the standard deviations of the variables (**SD**). These standard deviations are given to the program in the same way and in the same order as the correlations. Alternatively, we could have provided the covariance matrix to the program immediately. But the input in Table 10.8 was constructed most easily from the input specified in Table 10.6. From these standard deviations and correlations the program can compute the variances and covariances as was shown in chapter 9. In the case where the covariance matrix is analyzed instead of the correlation matrix, the unstandardized coefficients are obtained automatically. These estimates of the unstandardized coefficients will be given by the LISREL program under the heading "**LISREL ESTIMATES**". The standardized coefficients can also be obtained in the same run if one adds **SS** to the output specification; **SS** stands for "standardized solution". The estimates of these standardized coefficients are presented by LISREL under the heading **STANDARDIZED SOLUTION**.

Since the same matrix representation is used as before, we present the output of the job specified in Table 10.8 directly in a table. Table 10.9 presents both the unstandardized and standardized coefficients. Two different sets of standardized coefficients are provided because one can estimate these coeffi-

Table 10.9   The Estimates of the Standardized and Unstandardized Parameters of the Full School Career Model

Parameter	ML estimates			ULS estimates		
	Unstandardized	Standardized Direct	Standardized Derived	Unstandardized	Standardized Direct	Standardized Derived
β_{21}	.065	.821	.821	.080	.992	.992
β_{31}	.022	.280	.282	.038	.441	.462
β_{41}	1.002	.811	.811	1.262	.955	.938
β_{32}	.607	.606	.610	.441	.470	.465
β_{52}	.046	.046	.047	-.142	.033	-.142
β_{53}	.916	.916	.921	1.494	.925	1.422
β_{54}	.003	.042	.042	-.018	.047	-.276
γ_{11}	.204	.254	.254	.291	.353	.375
γ_{21}	-.002	-.036	-.036	-.013	-.179	-.199
γ_{12}	2.461	.161	.161	2.627	.204	.187
γ_{32}	.086	.071	.071	.094	.081	.082
ϕ_{11}	785.972	1.000	1.000	785.972	1.000	1.000
ϕ_{22}	2.161	1.000	1.000	2.161	1.000	1.000
ϕ_{21}	5.764	.140	.140	5.764	.140	.140
ψ_{11}	455.046	.898	.898	336.517	.702	.788
ψ_{22}	1.083	.341	.341	.848	.237	.265
ψ_{33}	.769	.242	.244	.490	.226	.170
ψ_{44}	264.825	.342	.342	92.882	.190	.120
ψ_{55}	.071	.022	.023	-.595	.022	-.187

cients directly from the correlation matrix as was done in the last section, or one can derive them indirectly from the unstandardized coefficients, obtained by analyzing the covariance matrix. The last procedure is illustrated in this section.

The interpretation of the unstandardized solution will be postponed until more certainty is obtained about the correctness of the model. Here we concentrate on the differences between the results obtained with the two estimation procedures. With respect to these differences the following remarks can be made.

First of all, Table 10.9 shows very clearly that the ML and ULS estimates do not necessarily agree with each other. In this case the ULS estimates are even not acceptable: $\psi_{55} < 0$, which is impossible since ψ_{55} is the variance of ζ_5 and should always be a positive number.

The two solutions will be identical only if the model is exactly identified ($df = 0$). In this example, the differences in the estimates are sometimes very large, up to the point that the conclusions will depend on the procedure being used. For example y_2 and y_4 seem completely determined by y_1 in the ULS solution, while the ML solution suggests that some other variables may be influential as well (this may be checked by comparing the estimates of β_{21} and β_{41}).

Secondly the two standardized solutions obtained with the ML procedure are the same except for rounding errors, while the two standardized solutions obtained with the ULS procedure are not the same. Clearly, it makes a difference for the ULS procedure whether the covariance matrix or the correlation matrix is analyzed. In general, the ULS estimates depend upon the scale in which the variables are expressed. For the ML estimation procedure it does not matter what scale is used; we can simply compute one solution from the other; only deviations due to rounding errors will occur. Therefore the ML estimator is called 'scale invariant'. This is a very desirable property since the scales in social science research are often arbitrary. For the ULS estimator this means that a different solution is obtained each time that the scale is changed. For this and other reasons which were discussed in the section concerned with the choice of an estimation procedure, we generally recommend the use of the ML estimation procedure. Only if the data differ considerably from a multivariate normal distribution or if the matrix to be analyzed is 'not positive definite', should the ULS estimator be used.

Finally the equality of the two standardized solutions for the ML procedure can also be used to check whether the optimal estimates are obtained in the unstandardized solution. If this is not so, the two standardized solutions will differ from each other. If such a problem arises one has to repeat the estimation using different starting values. This point is discussed in more detail in the section on computation of estimates.

So far we have not discussed the estimation of the intercepts in the equations. This point was left out on purpose because most researchers are only interested in the effects of variables on each other. For special purposes the intercepts may be useful. The computation of these coefficients is illustrated in the next section. Readers who are not interested in the values of the intercepts in the equations but only in the effects of the variables on each other can proceed to the next section.

* Estimation of the intercepts

The LISREL program has been developed with the idea of estimating the effects of the variables on each other without taking into account the intercepts in the equations. However, the intercepts can also be estimated but this procedure is more complicated than the normal one. In this section we show

Table 10.10   The Input for the LISREL Program to Obtain Estimates for the
Full School Career Model Including Intercepts by Analyzing
the Moment Matrix

```
DATA ANALYSIS WITH THE FULL MODEL INCLUDING INTERCEPTS
DATA    NI=8 NO=383 MA=MM
KM
*
1.0000000
 .8113306 1.0000000
 .7857889  .8534177 1.0000000
 .8108940  .7641449  .7610636 1.0000000
 .7921435  .8604609  .9878695  .7747339 1.0000000
 .2763330  .1905062  .2799446  .4663920  .2827473 1.0000000
 .1962511  .2821079  .2968646  .2435010  .2965949  .1398519 1.0000000
 .0        .0        .0        .0        .0        .0        .0        .0
SD
*
   22.5069    1.7835    1.7845   27.8085    1.7830   28.0352    1.4700 0
ME
*
   53.7128    3.0470    3.3003   50.4595    3.2637   50.9491    3.2480 1
LABELS
*
'      Y 1' '     Y 2' '     Y 3' '     Y 4' '     Y 5'
'      X 1' '     X 2' '     X 3'
MODEL   NY=5 NX=3 BE=FU,FI GA=FU,FI PS=DI,FR
FREE    BE(2,1) BE(3,1) BE(4,1) BE(3,2) BE(5,2) BE(5,3) BE(5,4) C
        GA(1,1) GA(1,2) GA(2,1) GA(3,2) C
        GA(1,3) GA(2,3) GA(3,3) GA(4,3) GA(5,3)
OUTPUT  MR SS TV MI
```

how these estimates can be obtained, but for the explanation we largely refer
to the literature.

In order to explain the procedure we start by rewriting the equations. For
example, in the school career theory the equation for y_1 was
$$y_1 = \gamma_{11}x_1 + \gamma_{12}x_2 + \alpha_1 + \zeta_1$$
This equation can also be written as follows:
$$y_1 = \gamma_{11}x_1 + \gamma_{12}x_2 + \gamma_{13}x_3 + \zeta_1 \qquad (10.10)$$
where $x_3 = 1$ for all cases. In this formulation x_3 looks like a variable but it
is actually a constant: x_3 always has the value 1. Therefore x_3 could also be
ignored and γ_{13} really represents the intercept. In the notation of this equation
the effect of the "variable" x_3 represents the intercept.

In chapter 6 it was shown how one can take the expectation of a product
of two variables. This is done here for y_1 and x_3:
$$E(y_1x_3) = E(y_1) = \gamma_{11}E(x_1) + \gamma_{12}E(x_2) + \gamma_{13} + 0 \qquad (10.11)$$
From this form γ_{13} can be obtained if one has information about $E(y_1)$, $E(x_1)$,
$E(x_2)$, and γ_{11} and γ_{12}. Informally one could say that γ_{11} and γ_{12} can be estimated in the usual way. Information about the sample means of the variables
should be added to the input in order to estimate γ_{13}. This is exactly what
is done as can be seen in the input for LISREL presented in Table 10.10.
By comparing this input with the input presented in Table 10.8, the following

Table 10.11   A Part of the LISREL Output Obtained with the Input given in Table 10.10

```
        LISREL ESTIMATES (MAXIMUM LIKELIHOOD)

            BETA

                    Y 1         Y 2         Y 3         Y 4         Y 5
            Y 1     0.000       0.000       0.000       0.000       0.000
            Y 2      .065       0.000       0.000       0.000       0.000
            Y 3     ^.022        .607       0.000       0.000       0.000
            Y 4     1.002       0.000       0.000       0.000       0.000
            Y 5     0.000        .046        .916        .003       0.000

            GAMMA

                    X 1         X 2         X 3
            Y 1      .204       2.461      35.336
            Y 2     -.002       0.000       -.331
            Y 3     0.000        .086       -.020
            Y 4     0.000       0.000      -3.356
            Y 5     0.000       0.000       -.035

            PHI

                    X 1         X 2         X 3
            X 1   3379.731
            X 2    171.231      12.705
            X 3     50.949       3.248       1.000

            PSI

                    Y 1         Y 2         Y 3         Y 4         Y 5
                  453.858       1.080        .767      264.130        .071
```

differences can be observed. First of all, the number of input variables has increased to 8 due to x_3. Secondly, it is not the covariance matrix which is analyzed, but the *moment matrix*, indicated by **MM**. This is denoted writing **MA=MM** in the second line. The elements of this matrix are computed in the same way as the covariances and variances but, instead of the deviation from the mean, the deviation from zero is used. This means that the sums of squares and the sums of cross-products are analyzed. Equation (10.10) clarifies this point. It is beyond the scope of this introductory text to justify this point. For further information the literature should be consulted. Thirdly, the means are added as information to the data. This point has been mentioned before. The fourth difference is that in the input matrix a row has to be added for the "variable" x_3, but as this "variable" is a constant, all the elements in the row have to be zeros. Finally, the coefficients which represent the constants in the equations are added to the model specification as free parameters. Given these changes in the specification of the input, all the parameters in the model including the constants can be estimated by the LISREL program.

The maximum likelihood estimates for the parameters of the model are presented in Table 10.11. The elements γ_{13}, γ_{23}, γ_{33}, γ_{43} and γ_{53} represent the constants for the different equations of the model. This table shows that the values of the unstandardized parameters are the same as those obtained when we analyzed the covariance matrix. Only constants are added to the previous results. We will not discuss this result here, but postpone this interpretation until we are more certain that the correct model has been found.

A warning has to be given here in order to prevent mistakes. On request the LISREL program also computes a "standardized solution" in this case. However the results of this computation are not correct and do not represent the standardized solution. This can easily be checked by comparing these results with those presented in Table 10.9. The reason for the deviations is that here the variables are not expressed in deviations from their means and so the standardization is done on the wrong type of variables. If one needs the standardized solution one should not analyse the moment matrix, as we have done here, but the correlation matrix or the covariance matrix.

* Computation of the Estimates

Three different estimation methods have been discussed which, in some sense, all lead to optimal estimates of the parameters. A general procedure is discussed here to compute these optimal solutions. For each estimation method the maximum or minimum of a complicated function of parameters has to be found. The way to find such a maximum or minimum is most easily explained if the problem is first reduced to one with only one parameter. Figure 10.5 shows an arbitrary relationship between various parameter values and values of the criterion function. In addition, the tangent to the function has been drawn, for various values of the parameter p. It can be seen that if the tangent at some point has a positive slope, this indicates that the function is increasing and that the parameter value has to be increased in order to arrive at the maximum of the function. If the tangent has a negative slope this indicates a decreasing function, and the parameter value has to be decreased in order to arrive at the maximum of the function. It is typical for the maximum of the function that the tangent neither indicates an increasing nor a decreasing function, but rather is parallel to the horizontal axis of the graph. In Figure 10.6 the graph of a different function has been drawn for which the minimum has to be determined. It will be clear from the figure that a similar argument can be presented to locate the parameter value which corresponds to a minimum value of the criterion function.   These observations suggest that the

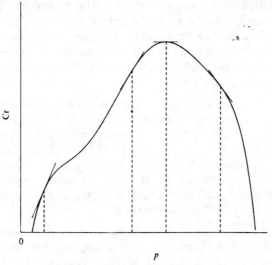

Figure 10.5   The Relationship between p and Cr, and the Tangents to the Function

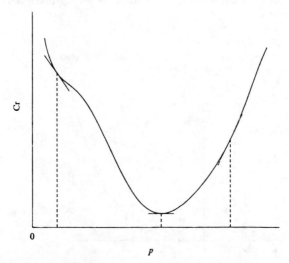

Figure 10.6   The Relationship between p and Cr, and the Tangents to the Function

optimal value of a function can be found by starting with some arbitrary value of the parameter, and subsequently changing the value of this parameter on the basis of information concerning the tangent. This process can be stopped as soon as the tangent is parallel to the horizontal axis. It is indeed exactly this procedure which is used in the LISREL program to find an optimal set of parameter values. The procedure is more complicated, since the functions are usually functions of many different parameters. But this only means that the procedure has to be generalized.

What has just been shown for one parameter can also be done for this parameter while keeping all other parameters constant. The simple situations of Figures 10.5 and 10.6 still pertain. This procedure can be followed for all parameters. In this way it becomes evident in which direction the parameter values have to be changed. Subsequently, a change can be made in these parameter values, and the tangents for all these new parameter values can be computed in the next step, and so on, until changing any of the parameters, does not bring about any further improvement.

Usually this procedure leads to a solution. It does not mean, however, that the solution obtained is always the optimal solution that one is seeking. This point can easily be clarified using another example of a function of one parameter. The example is provided in Figure 10.7. Suppose the search for the minimum of this particular function is begun with a parameter value between a and b. The program will then find, as an optimal estimate, the

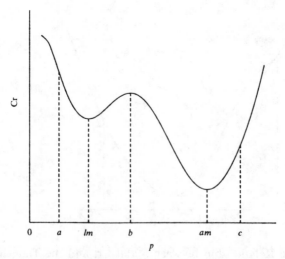

Figure 10.7   The Relationship between p and Cr with a Local and an Absolute Minimum

parameter value indicated by *lm*. If, on the other hand, the program starts with a value for the parameter between *b* and *c*, the value indicated with *am* will be obtained as the best or optimal estimate. Figure 10.7 clearly indicates that the value *am* indeed represents the *absolute minimum* of the function, while the value *lm* merely represents a *local minimum*. This can always happen with a searching procedure as indicated here, especially when one starts with values of the parameters which are very far removed from the actual, true values. It is therefore important to start with as good a set of initial estimates as possible. Of course this can also save computing time. Fortunately the LISREL program automatically computes quite good initial estimates, so the users of this program do not have to concern themselves about this point too much.

Another related point is that the LISREL program always produces a solution, even if the model is not identified. For an unidentified model, the solution that is given depends on the starting values. If one begins with various starting values, exactly the same value for the criterion function Cr can be obtained, but the estimated parameter values can vary considerably, since in this instance many different parameter values can fit the data just as well. If this happens the model is clearly not identified. Fortunately, the program generally provides a warning in such cases.

Some General Remarks

In this chapter it has been shown that there are several procedures available to estimate the parameters of the models discussed in this book. Here we discussed three general principles that are readily available in the LISREL program. The results obtained with these procedures do not necessarily agree with each other. But for several reasons which have been mentioned in the section on 'Choice of an estimation method', we recommend the use of the ML estimates as long as the data do not deviate too far from a multivariate normal distribution and the covariance matrix is "positive definite". There are many more procedures to estimate the parameters and some are even more often used than the procedures introduced here.

We presented the LISREL approach to estimation because of its usefulness in a variety of models for which the other procedures can not be used. Also the availability of the LISREL program was an important advantage which led to this decision. We will return to this point in the epilogue where we discuss alternative approaches.

In this chapter a start was also made with the interpretation of the results but, in general, the interpretation should be delayed until one is quite certain that the model is in acceptable agreement with the data. This brings us to the next topic: the test of the models.

Further Reading

The general estimation methods discussed in this chapter are explained in most statistics books. Elementary texts about estimation have been written by Wonnacott and Wonnacott (1972) and Wallpole (1974), while a somewhat more advanced text is that of Hoel (1971).

The application of these estimation principles to the type of models discussed here, is given by Jöreskog (1969, 1973), Jöreskog and Goldberger (1972), Lawley and Maxwell (1971), Browne (1975 and 1982), Bentler(1983) and Shapiro(1983). But all of these texts are rather technical. There is no simple introduction to this topic. Therefore we have tried to present a very elementary sketch.

The actual computation algorithms in LISREL are treated most elaborately in an article by Gruvaeus and Jöreskog (1970) and in an appendix of Lawley and Maxwell (1971), but neither one of these texts is simple. These two texts indicate references for further reading on this topic, but these do not include a simple text. Considerable knowledge of matrix algebra and iterative procedures is required in order to read this literature.

In the last section of the epilogue some references are given to alternative estimation procedures for the models discussed in this book.

Exercises

10.1 In the exercises of the first chapters we discussed the arms race model. For the USA we formulated the model presented below.

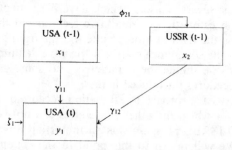

With respect of the deployment of ICBM's, the correlation matrix, means and standard deviations are presented in the next table (Hamblin et al., 1980). There is only one solution for the parameters in this model which can easily be calculated manually.

(a)How large are the coefficients? (Note: assume for a moment that $\rho_{ij} = r_{ij}$.)

	USA(t)	USSR(t)	USA(t-1)	USSR(t-1)
USA(t)	1.000			
USSR(t)	.720	1.000		
USA(t-1)	.972	.789	1.000	
USSR(t-1)	.669	.990	.738	1.000
means	1420.647	1259.824	1323.000	1121.529
sd.	507.143	929.826	599.372	926.688

(b)Is it possible that we get different results if we use the ULS estimator? (Note: This can be checked by writing out the criterion function and showing that the solution obtained in (a) is the optimal solution.)

(c)Is the obtained result in agreement with the theory?

(d)Fixing the effect of x_2^s on y_1^s at zero leads to a situation where several solutions are possible. How many?

(* e)Compute, using the LISREL program, the optimal estimates according to the ML estimation procedure.

10.2 For the three variables mentioned in exercise 10.1 the standard deviations are also known. Given this information the unstandardized coefficients can be computed.

(a)Compute the unstandardized coefficients manually.

(* b)Check with the LISREL program that the program will give the same results.

(c)Indicate two ways to compute the standardized solution with each estimation procedure.

(d)Are all four solutions the same except for rounding errors?

10.3 By substituting the variable USSR(t) for y_1 in the model, the same analysis can be repeated for the USSR's deployment.

(a)Calculate again the parameters γ_{11} and γ_{12} using the correlations presented above.

(b)Does the conclusion once again arise that γ_{12} can be omitted?

(c)Are the conclusions, drawn here, necessarily correct or do we have to wait with these conclusions? Why?

* **10.4** The two models can also be analyzed simultaneously.

(a)Formulate the model for this analysis.

The correlation matrix is also known and presented in the table above.

(b)Compute, using the program, the parameters of this model,

—using the correlation matrix;

—using the covariance matrix (ULS and ML estimates);

—using the moment matrix (ULS and ML estimates).

(c)Compare the results and comment on them.

(d)Prove that the standardized solution obtained from the moment matrix is incorrect.

10.5 With respect to the secondary analysis:

(a)Specify the LISREL instructions to estimate the effect parameters for the study of interest using the model of the author and your own model.

(b)Check if the program provides you with unexpected results, i.e. wrong signs of effects, or very small or very large effects where you do not expect them.

(c)If such effects occur, think of reasons why this can happen and introduce corrections in the model which seem to be appropriate.

Chapter 11
Introduction to Testing

One of the most neglected topics in the social science literature of the last decade has been the testing of causal models. The emphasis during this period has been predominantly on the estimation of effects. In our view this development has been very unfortunate. To restore the balance we have at several points focussed the attention on aspects which are related to the testing of causal models. In this way it was indicated that one has to be prepared for the testing stage as early as the theory formulation stage, by introducing all common causes of the major cause and effect variables. It was also shown that the covariances between the variables are functions of the effect parameters of the model, and, in chapter 8, that models can be tested if more of such equations are available than are strictly needed for estimation of the parameters, i.e. if the number of degrees of freedom is greater than zero. In chapter 9 the data were discussed against which the model has to be tested, and in chapter 10 the estimation of the parameters was discussed. In this chapter the procedures for testing models are explained.

In order to do so some comparisons are made between observed correlation matrices and the reproduced correlation matrices calculated for different models. Then the test statistics are introduced and the effect that sampling has on the values of these statistics is specified. Next we indicate how this information can be used to formulate a test. The power of the test is introduced and the usual testing procedures are reconsidered. Finally, we mention how the tests can be adjusted and under what conditions one can rely on the tests specified in this chapter.

The Estimated Population Covariance or Correlation Matrix

In chapter 7 it was shown that the covariances and correlations between the variables can be expressed as functions of the parameters:

$$\sigma_{ij} = f_{ij}(p) \text{ for all } i,j \qquad (11.1a)$$

or

$$\rho_{ij} = f_{ij}(p^s) \text{ for all } i,j \qquad (11.1b)$$

This also means that an estimate of the population covariance matrix (and correlation matrix) can be derived if the parameters have been estimated. If

Table 11.1   The Sample Correlation Matrix for the Variables of the Simplified School Career Model

CORRELATION MATRIX TO BE ANALYZED

	ACHIEVE	CHOICE	QUALITY	SES
ACHIEVE	1.000			
CHOICE	.792	1.000		
QUALITY	.276	.283	1.000	
SES	.196	.297	.140	1.000

Table 11.2   The Estimated Population Correlation Matrix Derived from Figure 11.1

FITTED MOMENTS

	ACHIEVE	CHOICE	QUALITY	SES
ACHIEVE	1.000			
CHOICE	.792	1.000		
QUALITY	.276	.283	1.000	
SES	.196	.297	.140	1.000

these estimates are denoted by $\hat{\sigma}_{ij}$ (and $\hat{\rho}_{ij}$), it follows that

$$\hat{\sigma}_{ij} = f_{ij}(\hat{p}) \text{ for all } i,j \tag{11.2a}$$

or

$$\hat{\rho}_{ij} = f_{ij}(\hat{p}^s) \text{ for all } i,j \tag{11.2b}$$

In Figure 11.1 the path diagram for the simplified school career model, with the parameter estimates obtained from the correlations in Table 11.1, have been presented. In chapter 7 we discussed how this information can be used to compute the correlations between the variables, using equations such as equations (11.2). For example, $\rho_{y_1 x_1}$ is equal to the direct effect γ_{11}^s (.254) plus the joint effect of x_1^s and x_2^s $\gamma_{12}^s \phi_{21}^s$ (.161 × .140), which is is .276. In the same way all correlations can be computed. The LISREL program provides this information on request. The results of these computations for this example are presented in Table 11.2. Comparison of the two correlation matrices in Tables 11.1 and 11.2 indicates that they are exactly identical.

In this instance the equality of these two matrices is not incidental. It can be verified in Figure 11.1 that the model is a *"saturated recursive model"*. This means that all effects which are possible in a model without reciprocal effects have been introduced. For such models the number of degrees of freedom is equal to zero, which means that the number of correlations is equal to the number of parameters which have to be estimated. In chapter 8 it was argued that in such exactly identified models only one solution can be found, that this solution will perfectly fit the data and that as a result of this, the estimated

Table 11.3 The Estimated Population Correlation Matrix for the Model of Figure 11.1, with $\gamma_{21}^s = 0$

FITTED MOMENTS

	ACHIEVE	CHOICE	QUALITY	SES
ACHIEVE	1.000			
CHOICE	.792	1.000		
QUALITY	.276	.231	1.000	
SES	.196	.297	.140	1.000

population correlations (called **FITTED MOMENTS** in the LISREL output) have to be identical to the sample correlations. This result can generally be found for any type of model with zero degrees of freedom (exceptions to this rule exist and pertain to models in which some of the parameters can not be identified).

If $df > 0$ the similarity of these two matrices depends upon the correctness of the extra or overidentifying restrictions. This point can be illustrated by estimating two alternative models for the simplified school career theory. In Table 11.3 the estimate of the population correlation matrix is given for the model of Figure 11.1, with the extra restrictions that the effect of x_1^s on y_2^s is

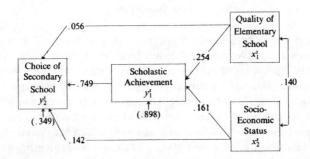

Figure 11.1 The Path Diagram with the Estimated Values for the Standardized Parameters of the Simplified School Career Model

Table 11.4   The Estimated Population Correlation Matrix for the Model of Figure 11.1, with $\beta_{21}^s = 0$

FITTED MOMENTS

	ACHIEVE	CHOICE	QUALITY	SES
ACHIEVE	1.000			
CHOICE	.119	1.000		
QUALITY	.276	.283	1.000	
SES	.196	.297	.140	1.000

zero ($\gamma_{21}^s = 0$). In this new model there is one parameter less to be estimated. Consequently $df = 1$, and a test is possible. Of course, the estimation was based on the same correlation matrix (Table 11.1). Comparison of Tables 11.1 and 11.3 indicates that $r_{y_2x_1} = .283$, but $\hat{\rho}_{y_2x_1} = .231$. This relatively small deviation has been produced by fixing γ_{21}^s at zero.

The size of such deviations depends on the magnitude of the error that exists in the model. This can be illustrated by fixing another parameter at zero, i.e. β_{21}^s instead of γ_{21}^s. In the original analysis reported in Figure 11.1, γ_{21}^s was .056 and β_{21}^s was .749. It is evident that a model with $\beta_{21}^s = 0$ will deviate further from the true model than the model with $\gamma_{21}^s = 0$. The model with $\beta_{21}^s = 0$ was estimated and the population correlation matrix estimated, resulting in the figures of Table 11.4. Comparison of this result with Table 11.2 indicates that $r_{y_2y_1} = .792$, but that $\hat{\rho}_{y_2y_1} = .119$. This deviation is indeed considerable, and much larger than when tables 11.2 and 11.3 were compared.

Test Statistics

Although the above presented comparison of the observed and reproduced correlation matrices gives an indication of the fit of the models to the data, it is desirable to have a more precise test. This is especially so because random fluctuations due to sampling can always be expected. Therefore a procedure is required which can help to decide whether the deviations are just sampling fluctuations or consequences of misspecifications in the model.

For this purpose statistical measures are used which are called *test statistics*. In case the distribution of a test statistic is known—indicating for a correct model the fluctuation of the measure due to sampling—a comparison can be made between the observed value and the expected range of values if the model is correct and so one can determine whether the model is correct or not.

As an extension of the three different estimation procedures specified three different test statistics can also be formulated. The best candidate for the ULS estimator is the sum of the squared residuals which have been defined before as the differences between the observed and the reproduced correlation or covariance coefficients. This statistic, denoted by T_{ULS} is defined in (11.3):

$$T_{ULS} = \sum_{ij} \left(s_{ij} - \hat{\sigma}_{ij} \right)^2 \qquad (11.3a)$$

or

$$T_{ULS} = \sum_{ij} \left(r_{ij} - \hat{\rho}_{ij} \right)^2 \qquad (11.3b)$$

It will be clear from these formulas that this statistic becomes larger if the deviations between the observed and reproduced coefficients increase. It is easy to compute this statistic but unfortunately it is not very helpful to do so since the distribution of this statistic is unknown so far. This means that there is no test available as yet for the models estimated with the ULS procedure.

For the other two estimation procedures, test statistics can be formulated for which the distributions are known. For both procedures only one formulation is given since these statistics are scale invariant. If the GLS estimator is used the following test statistic T_{GLS} can be used:

$$T_{GLS} = \frac{1}{2}(N - 1) \sum_{ij} \left(w_{ij}(s_{ij} - \hat{\sigma}_{ij})^2 \right) \qquad (11.4)$$

The value of this statistic also depends on the size of the residuals. It has a large value if the residuals are large and a small value if the differences between the observed and reproduced correlations are small. This statistic differs from the measure specified in equation (11.3) in two aspects: the residuals are weighted in the same way as in the estimation procedure and an adjustment factor is introduced: $\frac{1}{2}(N - 1)$.

The test statistic used for Maximum Likelihood estimation is quite different from those ones mentioned before. In order to explain this measure we start with a model with $df = 0$. Such a model, if exactly identified, will perfectly fit to the data. Therefore the likelihood function $L(\hat{p})$ will reach a value which can not be improved upon by any other model with the same variables. Thus, if the values of the likelihood functions for more restricted models are computed and compared with the value of the model which fits perfectly, an indication can be obtained of how far the other models (M_a) deviate from the model that fits perfectly (M_p). The comparison is carried out by computing the ratio of the likelihood function for the model of interest and the model that fits perfectly: $L(\hat{p}_{M_a})/L(\hat{p}_{M_p})$. But since the distribution of this ratio is not known, the following measure is used as the test statistic for maximum likelihood estimation:

$$T_{ML} = -2\ln[L(\hat{p}_{M_a})/L(\hat{p}_{M_p})] \qquad (11.5)$$

Just like before, the larger the value of this statistic is, the further the model is from having a perfect fit and the statistic will approach zero when the model approaches a perfect fit.

In this section it was shown that useful test statistics can be specified for two estimation procedures, while this is not possible at the moment for the ULS estimator. This is another noteworthy advantage of the GLS and ML estimators. The distribution of the two statistics is discussed next.

The Distributions of the GLS and ML Test Statistics

An important property of the two statistics discussed in the previous section is that their distribution due to sampling fluctuation is known, given that the model is correct. Under certain conditions which we will discuss later, the distributions of both statistics approach the χ^2-distribution (which is written in full as the "chi square distribution") if the model is correct. Originally the χ^2-distribution was derived as part of the study of the normal distribution. The sum of k squared independent normally distributed variables, with means of zero and variances equal to one, has a distribution which has been called the χ^2-*distribution*. The form of this distribution depends on the number of variables in the sum, i.e. it depends on k. Three examples of such distributions are presented in Figure 11.2. These distributions are exactly known and tables have been constructed for them just as has been done for the normal distribution. The χ^2-table is presented in Appendix B.

The χ^2-distribution has turned out to be useful in a large variety of situations. One of them is the goodness of fit test of linear structural equation models. Here knowledge about the χ^2-distribution can be used as follows. Under certain conditions, which we will discuss later, the test statistics for a correct model will be distributed approximately as χ^2 distributed variables, with the value of k identical to the degrees of freedom of the model. For example, for $df = 10$, this means that the probability of finding a test statistic close to zero is very small (see Figure 11.2). It is much more likely that a value will be obtained of between 5 and 15, while values larger than 20 are again very unlikely.

Since the χ^2 distribution is exactly known for any number of degrees of freedom, even more precise statements can be made. For instance, it is known that on the average one may expect that the test statistics for a good model will be equal to the degrees of freedom. The χ^2 table can also be used to find that, for a correct model with $df = 10$, in 95% of the samples the test statistics may be expected to be smaller than 18.3, and, for $df = 1$, smaller than 3.84, and so on (see Appendix B).

This discussion indicates that the relationship between the test statistics and the χ^2 distribution is very helpful in indicating what deviations from zero can be anticipated as a consequence of sampling fluctuations. In turn, this information is very useful in formulating a test which (1) indicates how good the theoretical model fits the empirical data, and (2) takes into account the sampling variations that normally characterize the data.

A Model Test

Since the probability distribution of the test statistics for correct models is now known, a model test can be formulated. The χ^2 table gives information on how large a test statistic might be in 95% of the samples, provided the model is correct. If, in a paricular sample, a value is found which is smaller than this *"critical value"*, the model is not rejected, since the value could be produced by sampling fluctuations. If a value of the statistic is obtained which is larger than this critical value, we know that the deviation has only a 5% probability of being produced by sampling fluctuations, assuming that the model is the right one. Therefore, the hypothesis that the model is correct is rejected in such

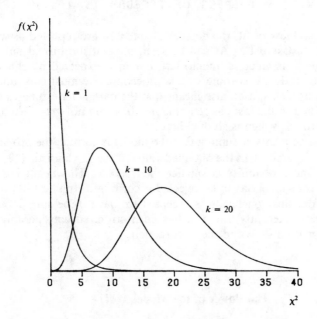

Figure 11.2   The Density Function of Three Different χ^2 Distributed Variables

cases. In this instance it is more likely that the deviation is due to specification errors in the model than to random fluctuations in the data.

The reader should be aware of the fact that conclusions concerning the model can be wrong, since any value of a test statistic can be produced by sampling fluctuations. In the procedure described the probability of a wrong conclusion, i.e. that the theory is rejected while the theory is in fact correct, is 5%. One can reduce this error by testing on the .01 level instead of the .05 level. In that case the probability of arriving at a wrong conclusion of the same kind will be reduced to 1%. In general the 5% risk is seen as acceptable in social science research. This risk level is called the α or *significance level* of the test.

Let us now look at how this works using the full school career model discussed in this text, and estimated with the Maximum Likelihood method. This model has 9 degrees of freedom. From the χ^2 table it follows that, with a probability of 95%, the test statistic should be smaller than 16.9. In the LISREL program the test statistic is computed which is derived from the Likelihood Ratio measure. The program gives the results of this test as follows:

MEASURES OF GOODNESS OF FIT FOR THE WHOLE MODEL:
CHI-SQUARE WITH 9 DEGREES OF FREEDOM IS 173.50 (PROB. LEVEL=0.000)

In this test of goodness of fit, the degrees of freedom are reported as well as the value of the test statistic. As can be seen, the statistic turned out to be equal to 173.50. This value is (much) larger than is expected by chance, in 95% of the cases, and so according to this procedure, we must conclude that the model is wrong. This result also means that the parameter estimates which have been obtained in the last chapter (Figure 10.4) are not very informative for the causal process which is studied here.

The program also prints, assuming that the model is correct, the probability that the χ^2 value is larger than the obtained value of the test statistic (173.50). For this model the probability is smaller then .0005. This result indicates once more that the model has to be rejected according to this test.

However, before this conclusion is accepted we have to be sure about the quality of the test. Recently, this test has been criticized considerably, and with reason, as will be shown in the next section.

The Power of the Model Test

So far we have used only the information about the distribution of the test statistic when the model is correct. However, it is not possible to evaluate the

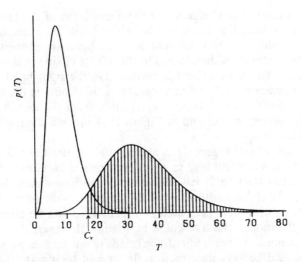

Figure 11.3 The Distribution of the Test Statistic for a Correct Model (Left) and an Incorrect Model (Right) which differs considerably. T is the Test Statistic; C_v is the Critical Value. The Shaded Area denotes the Probability of rejecting the Model if the Model is Incorrect

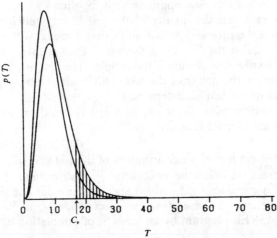

Figure 11.4 The Distribution of the Test Statistic for a Correct Model (Left) and an Incorrect Model (Right) which differ little. T is the Test Statistic; C_v is the Critical Value. The Shaded Area denotes the Probability of rejecting the Model if the Model is Incorrect

quality of a test without knowledge about the distribution of the test statistic if the model is incorrect. This point can be clarified with an example.

In Figure 11.3 and 11.4 two different test situations are presented, both for a model with 7 degrees of freedom. On the left hand side is the distribution of the test statistic if the model is correct. On the right hand side two distributions are presented for the test statistic if the model is incorrect. In Figure 11.3 this distribution deviates considerably from the distribution associated with the correct model and in Figure 11.4 the two distributions are approximately the same.

If the right hand side of Figure 11.3 applies and we use the test specified in the last section, the test will lead to rejection with nearly all samples. This is so because the test statistic T will almost always be larger than the critical value for the .05 level test; with $df = 9$ this is 16.9. When the difference between the two distributions presented in Figure 11.3 can be attributed to a large error in the model, the test would be useful. However, if the error is very small (for example a standardized coefficient is not zero as assumed but .001) this test would be very unattractive. In case of such a small error we do not want to reject the model.

If Figure 11.4 applies, the opposite problem arises. When the specification error is very small, the test used is acceptable. But if the error is large (for example a standardized coefficient is not zero as assumed but .3) this test is not acceptable because it would not detect serious specification errors. This test would reject incorrect models approximately as often as a correct model.

Both cases illustrate that the quality of the test is very much determined by knowledge about the probability that an incorrect model will be rejected. This probability is called the *"power of the test"*. Thus it turns out that the test procedure of the previous section is too simple. The test procedure should include information on the power of the test. Obviously the next question is: how can the power of the test be determined?

The procedure to determine the power of a test is based on an important result which has been derived recently:

> For an incorrect model the distribution of the test statistic approaches in most practical cases the noncentral χ^2 distribution of which the *noncentrality parameter* (λ)—which specifies how far the distribution shifts to the right in case of an incorrect model—can be computed with the LISREL program by an analysis of population data.

The noncentral χ^2 distribution is described completely in tables such as the one in Appendix C. The probability that the statistic is larger than a certain value is therefore also exactly known and can be obtained from these tables for the noncentral χ^2 distribution if one knows the degrees of freedom and the value of the noncentrality parameter (λ) for a test. Examples of such distributions are given in Figures 11.3 and 11.4. In Figure 11.3 the value of λ is equal to 25, in Figure 11.4 the value is equal to 2. The two examples also illustrate how the value of λ affects the distribution and consequently the power of the test, which is the probability that an incorrect model is rejected.

The values of the noncentrality parameter (λ) can be determined in a procedure which is divided in three steps:

(1)   One has to determine an alternative model as well as the values of the additional parameters for which one wants to detect that the model is incorrect. We suggest choosing .1 as a reasonable value for a standardized parameter. An effect of .1 represents an effect of some importance, which one does not want to overlook.

(2)   Next the population covariance or correlation matrix is computed with the values of the parameters of the original model and the values of the additional parameters. This can be done with the LISREL program or manually, using the relationships which can be specified between the covariances (correlations) and the parameters of the model.

(3)   The matrix obtained is then analyzed using the original model while the sample size is specified as equal to the sample size one is going to use or has used in the study. This analysis provides a value of the test statistic which is a good approximation of the noncentrality parameter (λ).

Given the value of λ, the degrees of freedom and the probability level of the test chosen, the power of the test can be determined using the tables for the noncentral χ^2 distribution. Appendix C provides the required information for the test with an α level of .05. For tests at other α levels, one is referred to the statistical literature.

The description of the procedure so far, indicates that it is not very difficult to determine the power of a model test. However, it is clear that the procedure requires prior knowledge about the model with respect to the values of the parameters, the willingness of the researcher to specify an alternative model and the willingness to choose the specific values for which the power of the test is evaluated. These choices which have to be made also indicate that the power of the test depends on the alternative model chosen and the values of the parameters added. These points will be illustrated below.

Table 11.5   The Input for LISREL in order to compute the Correlation
              Matrix with $\gamma^s_{22} = .10$ for the Evaluation of the Power of the
              .05-Test

```
RUN TO DETERMINE THE POWER OF THE TEST FOR THE SCHOOL DATA
DATA    NI=7 NO=383 MA=KM
KM
*
1.0000000
 .8113306 1.0000000
 .7857889  .8534177 1.0000000
 .8108940  .7641449  .7610636 1.0000000
 .7921435  .8604609  .9878695  .7747339 1.0000000
 .2763330  .1905062  .2799446  .4663920  .2827473 1.0000000
 .1962511  .2821079  .2968646  .2435010  .2965949  .1398519 1.0000000
LABELS
*
'     Y 1' '     Y 2' '     Y 3' '     Y 4' '     Y 5'
'     X 1' '     X 2'
MODEL   NY=5 NX=2 BE=FU,FI GA=FU,FI PS=DI,FI
START    .821 BE(2,1)
START    .280 BE(3,1)
START    .811 BE(4,1)
START    .606 BE(3,2)
START    .046 BE(5,2)
START    .916 BE(5,3)
START    .042 BE(5,4)
START    .254 GA(1,1)
START    .161 GA(1,2)
START   -.036 GA(2,1)
START    .100 GA(2,2)
START    .071 GA(3,2)
START    .898 PS(1,1)
START    .341 PS(2,2)
START    .242 PS(3,3)
START    .342 PS(4,4)
START    .022 PS(5,5)
OUTPUT  MR
```

Table 11.6   The Computed Matrix given the Parameters Specified in Table
              11.5

FITTED MOMENTS

	Y 1	Y 2	Y 3	Y 4	Y 5	X 1	X 2
Y 1	1.000						
Y 2	.831	1.041					
Y 3	.797	.882	1.020				
Y 4	.811	.674	.647	1.000			
Y 5	.803	.884	1.002	.665	1.008		
X 1	.277	.205	.212	.224	.213	1.000	
X 2	.197	.256	.281	.159	.276	.140	1.000

Evaluation of a .05 Level Test

In order to illustrate the above specified procedure the different steps for the full school career model are discussed, starting with step 1.

Step 1: in this case we choose as an alternative model the full school career model of Figure 10.4, extended with the interesting effect of "SES" (x_2^s) on the "teacher's recommendation" (y_2^s). This hypothesis represents the common idea that lower class children are discriminated against in the school system. So far it was hypothesized that this effect (γ_{22}^s) is zero. Clearly, we like the probability of rejection of the original model to be quite high (a power close to .8) if the effect (γ_{22}^s) is larger than .1. We think that such an effect is important enough to be detected.

Step 2: with the estimated parameter values obtained in the last chapter (see Figure 10.4) and the hypothetical value of $\gamma_{22}^s = .1$, the correlation matrix for this model can be computed using the LISREL program. Table 11.5 presents the input for this computation. There are no parameters estimated in this run. The program merely computes the correlation matrix associated with the given set of parameters values. Therefore all parameters are specified to be fixed on the **MODEL** card. This means that they do not have to be estimated. The values of the parameters which are not equal to zero are specified in the lines beginning with the word **START**. The reader should verify that all parameter values are the same as in Figure 10.4 with exception of one parameter, γ_{22}^s. This parameter has obtained the value .1 as explained before.

The results of this run are presented in Table 11.6. There are some difficulties with this output: along the diagonal it can be seen that some of the variances of the standardized variables are supposed to be larger than one, and one of the correlations is larger than one as well. Such undesired consequences can be expected because the amount of unexplained variance of variable y_2^s is increased by the introduction of the effect of x_2^s and therefore the value of ψ_{22}' should have been adjusted. In Table 11.6 we see the consequence of the failure to adjust for this fact. The values on the diagonal are not equal to one as they should be. For example ψ_{22}' has to be .041 smaller. In the next run with the input of Table 11.5, we change the value of ψ_{22}' accordingly and inspect the output again. Now the value of ρ_{y2y2} will be one but it might be that ρ_{y3y3} and ρ_{y4y4} are still not equal to 1. Therefore, the parameters ψ_{33}', ψ_{44}' and ψ_{55}' are adjusted subsequently in the same way, each run correcting the ψ' parameter which comes next in the causal ordering of the model. In this way we finally end up with the correct correlation matrix for the chosen set of parameter values. In the next step the computed correlation matrix for the given set of parameter values is analyzed once more with the original model of chapter 4. We know in advance that this model does not agree with the computed correlation matrix because γ_{22}^s is assumed to be zero while the

Table 11.7   The Input to LISREL for obtaining the Value of the
Noncentrality Parameter for a .05-level Test of the School
Career Model

```
RUN TO DETERMINE THE POWER OF THE TEST FOR THE SCHOOL DATA
DATA    NI=7 NO=383 MA=KM
KM
*
1.000
 .831 1.000
 .797  .857 1.000
 .811  .674  .647 1.000
 .803  .859  .983  .665 1.000
 .277  .205  .212  .224  .213 1.000
 .197  .256  .281  .159  .276  .140 1.000
MODEL   NY=5 NX=2 BE=FU,FI GA=FU,FI PS=DI,FR
FREE    BE(2,1) BE(3,1) BE(4,1) BE(3,2) BE(5,2) BE(5,3) BE(5,4) C
        GA(1,1) GA(2,1) GA(1,2) GA(3,2)
OUTPUT  MR
```

Table 11.8   The Power of the .05 Level Test for the School Career Model
against Several Alternative Models with different Sizes of Errors

Error in γ_{22}	Power of the .05 test	Error in ψ_{31}	Power of the .05 test
.02	.064	.02	.051
.04	.116	.04	.057
.06	.230	.06	.071
.08	.423	.08	.102
.10	.660	.10	.183
.12	.856	.12	.445
.14	.961	.14	1.000
.16	.994	.16	1.000
.18	1.000	.18	1.000

* These values have been computed with the program 'Power' developed by
J. den Ronden and A. Satorra

correlation matrix is computed with $\gamma_{22}^s = .1$. Therefore the value of the test
statistic will deviate from zero. Now it gives an indication of the shift which
will occur in the distribution of the test statistic due to this misspecification
in the model.

The input for LISREL in order to perform this step is presented in Table
11.7. One can check that the input is exactly the same as the input used
to estimate the original model (see Table 10.6), except for the correlation
matrix which is taken from step 2. The number of observations specified is
383 and the number of degrees of freedom is 9. The result of the analysis
is that the value of the test statistic is 11.99. Given this value of the non-

Table 11.9 Four Different Decision Situations with respect to the Fit of Models to the Data

| Value of the Test | Power | |
Statistic T	Low	High
> critical value	1. reject	2. ?
< critical value	3. ?	4. accept

centrality parameter λ, the power of the test can be determined with the table in Appendix C, taking into account that the test is done at the .05 level. According to the Appendix the power of the .05 level test is approximately equal to .66. This is quite acceptable. It means that in approximately 66% of the samples a misspecification for γ_{22}^s, in which this parameter is assumed to be zero while it is in fact .1, will be detected with a .05 level test.

The power of the test has also been computed for other values of γ_{22}^s. The results are summarized in Table 11.8. This table shows that small deviations from zero for γ_{22}^s will probably not be detected by the .05 level test because the power is rather low, while deviations larger than .1 have a very high probability of being detected.

In the same way the power of the test against other models can be evaluated. For example, what is the power of the test against the alternative which assumes that $\psi_{31}' \neq 0$?. If $\psi_{31}' = .1$, we find that the power of the .05 level test is only .18, which is rather low (see Table 11.8). But for $\psi_{31}' = .12$ the power is already equal to .44 and for $\psi_{31}' = .14$ the power is 1.0. This means that the test specified in the previous section is very sensitive as regards the variables omitted in the equations for the variables y_3^s and y_1^s, at least if the covariance resulting from these omitted variables is larger than .12. Having discussed how the power can be determined we can now reconsider the procedure of testing the models.

The Testing Procedure Reconsidered

In Table 11.9 four different test situations are distinguished which may all be encountered in practice. The distinction is made on the basis of the value of the test statistic and the power of the test. The first situation is characterized by the fact that the test statistic T is larger than the critical values for the .05 level test and that the power of the test is relatively low. Here 'relatively low' means that even very small, substantively uninteresting deviations from the true model would lead to rejection of the model under investigation. This is of course a relative matter. In a rather crude state of theory formulation, a deviation of .01 would probably be uninteresting while in a later stage it might be interesting and might have to lead to rejection of a model. As a guideline we propose that a deviation of .1 should be detected with rather high power (.8), while smaller deviations are not so important. Therefore, we speak of a 'relatively high' power if deviations smaller than .1 also have a high (.8) power of being detected.

Returning to the first decision situation, we are faced with relatively low power. This means that models with small errors will not be rejected. So if one is dealing with a study for which the test statistic is nevertheless larger than the critical value, it is most likely due to large misspecifications in the model. Therefore the model has to be rejected.

In the second situation, the test statistic is also larger than the critical value, but in this case the power is relatively high. This time it is not clear whether the model contains large specification errors or small ones, because any kind of small specification error leads to a high value for the test statistic. Therefore, it is not clear in this situation what the decision should be. Given this second type of situation, one has to adjust the test in order to reach a more decisive position. How these adjustments can be made is the topic of the next section.

In the third situation the value of the test statistic is smaller than the critical value, but the power of the test is relatively low. This means that even substantively large deviations have a low probability of being detected. In such a situation it is not clear what the decision should be. Therefore, one also has to adjust the test with this type of result.

In the fourth situation there is little doubt about the decision to be taken. In this situation the test statistic is smaller than the critical value of the .05 level test, but this time the power is high. Substantial deviation will thus most likely be detected. Therefore, if we obtain a test statistic which is smaller than the critical value, the most likely situation is that the model does not deviate considerably from the specified model.

From this overview we see that the decision to reject or accept a model is more complex than was specified originally. One has to take into account the power of the test. Having done that, we see that there are two situations where the decision is clear, while in the other two the test has to be adjusted before one can make a clear decision. How these adjustments can be made is the topic of the next section. Because of the complexity of the topic this seciton can be omitted.

* Adjustment of the Testing Procedure

For adjustments of the testing procedure there are two possibilities. The first is the adjustment of the α level of the test and the second is the adjustment of the sample size on which the test is based. Both adjustments are discussed below. We begin with the adjustment of the α level.

In Figure 11.5 we have once more presented the distribution of the test statistic T for both a correct and an incorrect model. In this figure it can be seen that changing the α level of the test will change the critical value and so also the power of the test. For instance, if the power is relatively low (situation 3 of Table 11.9), one can increase the power by increasing the α level of the test. In doing so, the critical value of the test moves to the left, which means that the power will increase. On the other hand, when the power is relatively high (situation 2 of Table 11.9), for example due to a very large sample, the power can be reduced by decreasing the α level of the test. By doing so the critical value for which the model will be rejected moves to the right and the power will become smaller. It seems reasonable to choose a test in such a way that the α level is approximately equal to $1 -$ the power of the test. This would mean that the probability of an erroneous rejection of a correct model is equal to the probability of erroneously accepting a wrong theory. However, if one wants to attach unequal values to the different types of error, one may

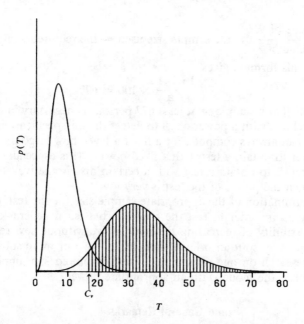

Figure 11.5   The Distribution of the Test Statistic T if the Model is correct (left) and if the Model is incorrect (right)

equally well adjust the test accordingly. If the two types of error become very small, the standard tables can not provide the appropriate information and one has to rely on special programs to choose the proper test or on approximations of the noncentral χ^2 distribution. For these topics we refer to the literature.

The second type of adjustment is explained most easily with an example. Suppose one is faced with the following situation in a model with $df = 10$ and a sample size of 100: for a deviation of .1 in one parameter, the noncentrality parameter of a .05 level test is equal to 2.4. In this case the power is very low (.138). If one obtains an insignificant value of the test statistic, the judgment would be indecisive, such as described for situation 3 in Table 11.9. In such a position it is desirable to have a test with more power. This is possible by carrying out the following steps: First of all, one has to consult the tables of the noncentral χ^2 in Appendix D to find out the value of the noncentrality parameter in order to have a power of .8. For this example with 10 degrees of freedom, the noncentrality parameter has to be equal to 16.241. However, one is dealing with a test based on 100 cases, for which the noncentrality parameter is only 2.4. Since the values of the noncentrality parameter are a linear function of the sample size, it follows that the necessary sample size can be determined in the following way:

$$\frac{\text{the required value of } \lambda}{\text{the obtained value of } \lambda} \times \text{the sample size used} = \text{the required sample size}$$

In our example this formula gives

$$\frac{16.241}{2.4} \times 100 = 677$$

This result means that a sample of at least 677 persons is necessary in order to obtain a .05 level test with a power of .8 to detect the misspecification of .1. In this way one can always compute, for a fixed α level, how large the sample has to be in order to obtain a test with a fixed power. It is especially fruitful to use this approach to obtain a test with a certain discriminative power for situations in which the power of the test is very low.

After the determination of the appropriate sample size for the test, one has to collect new data in order to test the model. That is, in general one will not have the possibility of increasing the sample size without new research. Alternatively, one may split an original sample into two or more subsamples and begin the research on one subsample. The unexplored subsamples may later be used to test the model with an appropriate power.

Some General Remarks

Having specified how we think that causal models should be tested, two more general remarks can be made. The first remark has to do with the arguments about testing in the literature (see the references). Recently, this topic has been discussed very frequently, particularly the problem of large sample sizes. Various solutions to this problem have been suggested, none of which is dealing explicitly with the power of the test. However, we feel that establishing the power of the tests is crucial to the testing procedure and we have therefore bypassed some of the other proposed solutions suggested in the literature.

A second point is that in the presentation of the power of the test, alternative models have been discussed which differed from the original model with respect to only one parameter. But the same approach can also be applied if the models differ on more points. Sometimes such evaluations are extremely useful, because it could happen that deviations from the model at various places might compensate each other and in this way lead to a very low power of the test. This would mean that such models, which might differ considerably from each other for different parameters, would be hard to distinguish by the usual testing procedure and would therefore lead to wrong conclusions, if one does not take the power of the test into account.

* Conditions for the Use of the Test Procedure

So far it has not been indicated under what conditions the χ^2 distribution is a good approximation for the distributions of the test statistics. In this section the available knowledge on this point is summarized.

If the observed variables have a multivariate normal distribution and samples larger than 100 are used, the distribution of the test statistic T_{ML} approaches the χ^2 distribution very well. Under these conditions the test discussed in this chapter can be used without hesitation.

When one is dealing with multivariate normally distributed observed variables, combined with samples smaller than 100, more caution is necessary. The study of Boomsma (1983), which is the largest study of this problem so far, shows that the distribution of the test statistic derived for the likelihood ratio measure might deviate from the χ^2 distribution. With small samples the values of the test statistics are frequently too large, which leads to a too frequent rejection of correct models for small sample sizes. Boomsma's work also provides information about the quality of the approximation of the χ^2 distribution for the distribution of this test statistic in case of non-normal distributions and categorical variables. Categorization of the variables does not have much effect on the quality of the approximation but the skewness of the distributions of the observed variables has a considerable effect. If the median absolute skewness of the variables is larger than 1.25, one might expect that the models are rejected too often. In such cases the deviations are so large that one can not really use the χ^2 distribution as an approximation for the distribution of the test statistic T_{ML}. Although he studied only large samples, it seems evident that the same is true for small samples.

With respect to the approximation of the χ^2 distribution for the test statistic T_{GLS}, not much is known. But on theoretical grounds one might expect that the approximation is acceptable, even under mild deviations from normality.

Satorra and Saris(1983) have studied the quality of the approximation of the non-central χ^2 distribution for the distribution of the test statistic T_{ML} under the condition of a multivariate normal distribution of the variables. Under this condition this approximation was very good even for very small samples ($n = 25$). Their conclusion was that this approximation is good enough for all practical cases studied so far. Whether this conclusion also holds for non-normal distributions is not known as yet.

Our general conclusion is that one can rely on the test procedure which has been presented unless the samples become very small and/or the variables have very skewed distributions. If one is faced with such conditions one should not rely too heavily on the test procedure discussed in this chapter.

Further Reading

Elementary ideas about testing causal models have been presented by Simon (1954), Blalock (1962) and Goldberg (1966). These papers are reprinted in the reader of Blalock "Causal Models in the Social Sciences" (1971).

Overall measures of goodness of fit are discussed in more technical literature, such as Lawley and Maxwell (1971), Jöreskog (1973) and Browne (1975). Specht (1975) obtained approximately the same results in a way which is probably more closely related to the social science tradition. Birnbaum (1981) argues for a goodness of fit test of causal models in the framework of the regression approach to causal modelling. The first three references do not require basic knowledge of matrix algebra and knowledge of statistics, but the others do.

With respect to the approximation of the distribution of the test statistcs by the χ^2 distributions, we can refer to the above mentioned literature for large sample characteristics. For small sample studies, one uses "Monte Carlo" experiments. A large Monte Carlo study has been done by Boomsma (1983), and a small study by Geweke and Singleton (1980). In a study of population data Olsson (1979b) also indicated that there are problems with skewed variables.

Alternative procedures for the test discussed in this chapter have been discussed by Bentler and Bonnett (1980), Hoelter (1983) and Wheaton et. al. (1977). The last paper is cited very frequently alhough it does not present any arguments for the alternative proposed. We believe that the alternatives developed lack the statistical foundation which is provided in the approach using the power of the test. The importance of this concept in testing has been discussed in a simple way by Lehman (1978) and by Kruskal (1978).

The procedure for the testing of causal models which is specified here is more fully explained in Saris and Satorra (1985). Several examples can be found in Saris, Den Ronden and Satorra (1984). The derivation of the specified procedure has been discussed in Satorra and Saris (1985) and an evaluation of the procedure can be found in Satorra and Saris (1982).

If the noncentrality parameter is too large, approximations of the noncentral χ^2 distribution by the normal distribution can be used. These approximations can be found in Johnson and Kotz (1970). An illustration of this approach is given in Saris, Den Ronden and Satorra (1984).

Excercises

11.1 In the exercises of chapter 10 it was expected that x_2^s had a positive effect on y_1^s but this was not always found. The effect $\gamma_{12}^s = -.069$ for the United States. This effect, having a wrong sign and being small, was in a next run of the program fixed at zero which suggests that the armament level of the USA is not affected by the armament level of the USSR. Analyzing both data sets in this way the following values of the parameters have been obtained:

$$\gamma_{11}^s = .912 \quad \gamma_{11}^s = .789$$
$$\phi_{21}^s = .738 \quad \phi_{21}^s = .738$$

(a)How large are the correlations between the variables in these two cases if this model is assumed to be correct?

(b)How large are the residuals?

(c)The test statistics for these two data sets are respectively 1.85 for the USA and 64.88 for the USSR. What conclusion can we draw from these results?

11.2 In order to evaluate the power of the test we have to carry out several steps which are specified below as exercises.

(a)Choose a value of γ_{21}^s which you think should be detected.

(b)Use the chosen values from a and the obtained values from exercise 1 to compute the correlation matrix for the alternative model.

(c)Specify the program to analyze the new matrix. (The number of observations is 25.)

(*d)Analyze the data and use the value of the test statistic to determine the power of the test.

(e)In case γ_{21}^s is chosen as equal to .1, the value of the test statistics are 4.25 for the USA and .42 for the USSR. What is the power of the test in both cases?

(f)Given the result of e and of 1.c, what conclusions can be drawn with respect to these two data sets?

11.3 The analysis in exercise 2.e showed that the power was rather low in one case.

(a)Can the power of the test be increased in this case by adjustment of the α level? If so, how?

(b)Is there another way to increase the power of the test? If so, how?

(c)Is this last solution possible in this case?

11.4 With respect to the secondary analysis:

(a)Specify reasonable alternative models for the formulated models.

(b)Determine the power of the test for the different models.

(c)Evaluate what conclusion can be drawn from this evaluations and the obtained test statistic for the data.

Chapter 12
Correction of Rejected Theories

Using the test of chapter 11 theories are often rejected, especially in less developed sciences such as the social sciences. The question then becomes where the model is incorrect or how the model should be changed. In this chapter some procedures are introduced to detect such *specification errors* in structural equation models.

In general,improvement of a model requires extensions of the original model by adding effects or covariances. Thus, each correction makes the original model more complicated. Therefore a procedure is needed which can be used to verify whether the corrections introduced are really worthwhile, in that they improve considerably the fit of the model to the data. Therefore this chapter is concerned with fitting of models to data and not with testing of models as in the previous chapter.

Specification Errors and Residuals

The problem of this chapter is introduced by once more considering the school career study. In chapter 10 the parameters for the full model were estimated from the sample data. The model with the parameter estimates is reprinted in Figure 12.1. On the basis of the parameter values, the model has been tested in chapter 11. It turned out that this model had to be rejected, given the value of the test statistic and the power of the test. Therefore the conclusion can be drawn that the parameter values for this model, as they are shown in Figure 12.1, can not produce an estimate of the population correlation matrix which looks very much like the correlation matrix obtained from the data. This can be illustrated by computing estimates of the residual correlations, which are defined as $(s_{ij} - \sigma_{ij})$. Table 12.1 presents the computed residuals for the estimated model. The table indicates that for this model, there exist considerable deviations between the obtained sample correlations and the estimated population correlations.

The largest residual of .242 is obtained for the variables y_4^s and x_1^s. According to the model and the obtained estimates, this correlation has to be identical to the indirect effect of x_1^s via y_1^s ($.254 \times .811$) plus the joint effect of x_1^s and x_2^s via y_1^s ($.140 \times .161 \times .811$). The sum of these two terms is equal to .224. But the obtained sample correlation was equal to .466 (see Table 9.6),

Table 12.1   The Residuals for the Full School Career Theory if the Variables
are Standardized

FITTED RESIDUALS

	Y 1	Y 2	Y 3	Y 4	Y 5	X 1	X 2
Y 1	-.000						
Y 2	.000	-.000					
Y 3	.000	-.009	.011				
Y 4	-.000	.106	.124	.000			
Y 5	.000	.013	.016	.118	.020		
X 1	-.000	.000	.077	.242	.079	0.000	
X 2	-.000	.126	.076	.084	.081	0.000	0.000

which means that the specified model could not reproduce this correlation.
The residual is $.466 - .224 = .242$. Similar computations can be made for
the other residuals.

The question is then how the original model can be changed to improve
the goodness of fit, or how to reduce the size of the residuals. Evidently, the
fixation of additional effects to zero can not improve the fit of the model. This
would mean that the parameter values which are now found to be different
from zero, are subsequently fixed at zero. But this can only raise the value

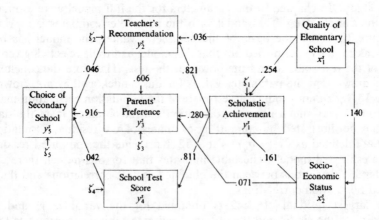

Figure 12.1   A Causal Diagram of the Full School Career Theory with
Estimates of the Parameters

of the test statistic, and never decrease it. So if one wants to improve the fit of the model, the number of restrictions has to be reduced. Very occasionally can the introduction of restrictions lead to acceptable models; this case is not discussed here but references are given for the relevant literature.

Our attention should then shift to which restrictions should be relaxed. This question is not easily answered. In the example discussed before, the residual associated with the correlation between variables y_4^s and x_1^s could be reduced by extending the model with a direct effect between these two variables, that is, by entering a free parameter γ_{41}^s. If γ_{41}^s is not equal to zero, this direct effect should be added to the relationship indicated before ($\beta_{41}^s \gamma_{11}^s + \beta_{41}^s \gamma_{12}^s \phi_{21}^s$, which may then increase the estimated value of the population correlation between the two variables, thereby reducing the residuals at the same time. But a reduction of this residual can also be brought about by entering the causal effect β_{43}^s, or the effect β_{42}^s, because these effects create new indirect effects between x_1^s and y_4^s which will also result in increments of the population correlation.

There is still another option. Consider the possibility that an important causal variable of y_4^s has been omitted, which is correlated with x_1^s. This means that $\sigma_{x_1 \zeta_4} \neq 0$, which in turn implies that this covariance should be added to the existing relationship, and this also increases the reproduced correlation between these two variables.

In a similar way, a large variety of solutions for the various residuals in the matrix with the residuals can be suggested. This discussion indicates that the matrix with residuals, which the program LISREL prints on request, gives information on the variables between which the largest residual has been found, but it does not in any way indicate what parameter has to be introduced to alleviate the problem of poor fit.

The choice of a correction of the model is of course a theoretical problem and should be treated as such. One should only introduce corrections which are theoretically acceptable. For example, we have suggested that reduction of the residual association between the variables y_4^s and x_1^s can possibly be obtained by introduction of the effects γ_{41}^s, β_{43}^s, β_{42}^s or the covariance $\sigma_{x_1 \zeta_4}$. Which of these four possibilities has to be chosen should be decided on theoretical grounds. This means that corrections require the same kind of reasoning as is necessary for the formulation of the model. The residuals can be helpful in locating variables between which the largest problems exist but they can not indicate which correction should be introduced.

Even with respect to the detection of the variables between which the largest residual exists, one has to be careful. So far we have analyzed the correlation matrix, which means that all variables are standardized. Therefore a difference in the size of the variances of the variables, all of which are equal to 1, can not influence the relative size of the residuals. However if the covariance

Table 12.2   The Normalized Residuals for the Full School Career Theory

NORMALIZED RESIDUALS

	Y 1	Y 2	Y 3	Y 4	Y 5	X 1	X 2
Y 1	-.000						
Y 2	.000	-.000					
Y 3	.000	.134	.151				
Y 4	-.000	1.735	2.050	.000			
Y 5	.007	.189	.219	1.949	.279		
X 1	-.000	.000	1.486	4.621	1.522	0.000	
X 2	-.000	2.433	1.466	1.628	1.555	0.000	0.000

matrix is analyzed, this approach can be very misleading because the sizes of the residuals depend also on the scales in which the variables are expressed. Variables with a very large variance are in such cases more likely to have large residuals as well. In order to avoid this problem, it is in general better to inspect the table with the *"normalized residuals"* to detect the largest residual. In Table 12.2 the normalized residuals are presented. The normalized residuals presented in this table are the same residuals as in Table 12.1 but corrected in some way in order to make them comparable. For details on the corrections we refer to the literature.

Comparing the order of the coefficients in Table 12.1 and 12.2, one can discover that, for the largest residuals at least, the order has remained the same. In this case this is due to the fact that the correlation matrix was analyzed. This is not necessarily so when the covariance matrix is analyzed. Therefore the normalized residuals should be used for determination of the largest residual. On the other hand, the normalization of the residuals prevents the decomposition of the coefficients in terms of effects specified in the model. For that purpose the original residuals can better be used.

Detection of Specification Errors

If a model is rejected, there are usually several residuals which are not equal to zero. For each of the nonzero residuals at least three corrections can be contemplated, as we have seen: (1) one may want to introduce a direct effect between the variables for which a nonzero residual has been found, (2) one can introduce a direct effect elsewhere in the model in positions which create indirect or spurious relationships between the variables for which nonzero residuals have been found, and (3) it can be hypothesized that an important variable has been omitted in both equations, which means that a covariance $\sigma_{x_i \xi_j}$ or ψ_{ij}' has to be recognized.

This review indicates that there are several ways to correct a rejected model and it has already been emphasized that the alteration is a theoretical matter and should be treated as such. Still, this does not mean that one should ignore information that one can obtain from programs such as LISREL. The so called *"modification indices"* which the LISREL program prints on request provide such an informative tool, which is discussed in this section.

In general, one strives to add as few corrections as possible to the original model in order to stay as close as possible to the original theory, which one still believes to be correct for the largest part. This means that a procedure is wanted which detects the correction that will produce the largest reduction in the test statistic.

The modification indices which can be computed by LISREL can provide information about the decrease in the value of the test statistic which might be expected on average if a single constraint is relaxed and all estimated parameters are held fixed at their estimated value. Comparison of these values can of course indicate the parameter for which the largest improvement in value of the test statistic can be obtained. However one should realize that this suggestion is, according to this procedure, carried out under the condition that all other parameters will remain the same as they have been estimated. We will return to this condition below, but it means that one can not rely completely on the values obtained from the program with respect to the reduction in value of the test statistic. Nevertheless, this procedure certainly provides useful information about parameters which might be considered for introduction in the model. However, this procedure should never be a substitute for theoretical arguments and therefore should not be used automatically.

In Table 12.3 the modification indices for the school career theory are presented as they were obtained for the rejected model of Figure 12.1. It can be verified that the modification index associated with γ^s_{41} is the largest of all (70.91). This result suggests that γ^s_{41}, which was fixed at zero, may have caused a considerable error, and that relaxation of this restriction may lead to a reduction in value of the test statistic of around 71 points. This would of course be a considerable improvement in the fit of the model.

Before we introduce this correction, first we have to ask ourselves whether the introduction of this parameter is theoretically justifiable. This means that we have to find an argument for this direct effect of x^s_1 on y^s_4. This effect should be independent of the variable "school achievement" because otherwise it should be an indirect effect. We can think of only one reason for this direct effect: the schools which try to prepare their pupils for the better secondary schools not only try to teach them better but also train the pupils in filling in tests like those which are used. If these schools indeed train their pupils for these tests, one can expect a direct effect of x^s_1 on y^s_4. Since we first thought this effect to be unlikely, we left it out when formulating the original theory

Table 12.3   The Modification Indices computed by the LISREL Program
for the School Career Model

```
MODIFICATION INDICES

     BETA

              Y 1        Y 2        Y 3        Y 4        Y 5
     Y 1     0.000     18.680     22.434     68.820     19.685
     Y 2     0.000      0.000     27.383     43.385     18.734
     Y 3     0.000      0.000      0.000     13.211      2.551
     Y 4     0.000     36.843     46.048      0.000     45.907
     Y 5      .019      0.000      0.000      0.000      0.000

     GAMMA

              X 1        X 2
     Y 1     0.000      0.000
     Y 2     0.000     18.680
     Y 3    10.315      0.000
     Y 4    70.913      8.257
     Y 5      .083       .029

     PSI

              Y 1        Y 2        Y 3        Y 4        Y 5
             0.000      0.000      0.000      0.000      0.000

     MAXIMUM MODIFICATION INDEX IS    70.91 FOR ELEMENT ( 4, 1) OF GAMMA
```

but we have to admit that such a process is not completely impossible.

Now that we have also found a theoretical argument for the parameter which the program suggested, it is reasonable to introduce this parameter into the model and to estimate the parameters again in order to see whether this effect is large and whether this change in the model indeed reduces the value of the test statistic in the expected way. This means that in the next run of the program the original model extended with the parameter γ_{41}^s is estimated. The likelihood ratio test statistic was indeed considerably reduced. The value drops from 173.50 for the original model to 95.06 for the new model, which has only one degree of freedom less. This means that the reduction of the value of the test statistic is even larger than the expected value. The estimate of γ_{41}^s is also considerably different from zero (.262). Both results indicate that this correction was indeed a good choice.

Although this procedure turned out to work well in this case, this does not have to be so all the time. Continuing the corrections can illustrate this point. In the last analysis mentioned, where γ_{41}^s was introduced as a new parameter, the modification index for the parameter ψ_{42}' is found to be the largest. This suggests a correction which we consider not very likely. In our opinion, we have introduced all important explanatory variables for y_4^s in the model. Nevertheless, the LISREL program indicates that probably the largest specification error in the new model is that an important causal variable of y_4^s and y_2^s has been omitted in the equations. Normally we would not introduce this correction into the model since we do not have a theoretical argument for it but, for the sake of this illustration, we continued this analysis introducing ψ_{42}' as a free parameter. For this new model a test statistic is obtained of 37.68 which is again a considerable reduction compared with the last model. In the output for this model β_{13}^s has the largest modification index. This would suggest an even more unacceptable correction than the last one. It suggests that the "parents' preferences" (y_3^s) are affecting the "scholastic achievement" of the children (y_1^s). But the parent's preferences are expressed after the school results are obtained. Therefore this correction is theoretically impossible and should not be introduced at all, although it has been suggested by the program.

This example illustrates that one should not follow these suggestions automatically, since they might lead to a-theoretical models. One should in advance consider where corrections to the model are reasonable and where they are not. In this specific case we tend to expect mainly specification errors in the GAMMA matrix. In this matrix some parameters have been set at zero because we thought they represented only minor effects. We are much more reluctant to adopt corrections in the matrices BETA and PSI. The argument here is that we are more certain that we have not omitted important variables. We also think that we have introduced all important effects between the y^s variables. The omitted effects will thus be rather small or completely zero. Therefore we will later try to see how far we can correct this model by only introducing the effects of the exogenous variables on the endogenous variables (elements of GAMMA).

But before we proceed with this application, we want to make some more comments to this approach of model correction. In the next section we deal with the question when to stop with model corrections. In the remaining part of this section some remarks are made on the detection procedure for specification errors.

First of all we have seen that there are situations where the suggestion obtained from the modification indices is unacceptable on theoretical grounds. In such cases one should of course not follow this suggestion and stick to the theoretical ideas and look for other corrections.

A second point which has to be mentioned is that this procedure does not always lead to optimal corrections with respect to reduction in the value of the test statistic. The introduction of a parameter with a lower value for the modification index can produce a larger reduction in the test statistic. One of the reasons for this phenomenon is that the procedure does not take into account that the various specification errors in a model may be related to each other. For example, restricting γ_{41}^s to zero while this parameter is actually different from zero, means not only that $\rho_{y_4x_1}$ will be too small, but also that $\rho_{y_4y_2}$, $\rho_{y_4y_3}$, $\rho_{y_4x_2}$ and $\rho_{y_5x_1}$ will be too small (check that there are even more coefficients which will be too small). This shows that relaxing this restriction will improve the fit in various parts of the model. If these dependencies are taken into account, simpler models can often be derived. Unfortunately however, a procedure which can do this is not readily available.

Both points mentioned indicate that the use of the modification indices does not always lead to optimal results. Therefore one is advised to use these modification indices in addition to theoretical considerations and not as an alternative.

How Many Corrections?

In the last section it was shown that correction for important specification errors will improve the fit of the model to the data. The amount of improvement can be evaluated as the reduction in value of the test statistic or as the reduction in the size of the residuals, which represent the differences between the observed correlations and the expected correlations according to the specified model.

In this section the question of when the correction of the model can be stopped will be raised. The criterion for stopping is obviously that a sufficiently good fit is obtained but the question remains how we can determine when this point is reached. One possibility is to use the *proportion of improvement in fit* which is obtained by changing the model. Crucial in this approach is the choice of the starting model. For this purpose we suggest using the model which was expected to be correct but has been shown to need improvement. The purpose of the whole set of steps which are carried out next is to reduce the value of the test statistic so far that we can be quite sure that all serious specification errors have been found. The starting model is called the null model. If the difference between the test statistics of the null model and the alternative model is divided by the value of the test statistic for the null model, the investigator gets an impression of where he or she stands: whether much is already explained or whether there is still a long way to go. The measure to be used is symbolized by delta (Δ), and is formulated as

$$\Delta = \frac{T_0 - T_a}{T_0} \qquad (12.1)$$

where T_0 is the value of the test statistic for the null model and T_a is the value of the test statistic for the alternative model. The value of Δ lies between 0 and 1. If a full recursive model or a perfectly fitting model is specified as the alternative model, then $T_a = 0$, and $\Delta = 1$, while if no improvement is made compared with the null model, $T_a = T_0$ and so $\Delta = 0$. If one relaxes the parameters step by step, one gets an indication of how much improvement is made in each step and where one stands. The decision to stop can be made for various reasons. One possibility is that one stops when Δ becomes larger than a certain value. In the literature .9 has been proposed for this purpose. Another possibility is that one stops when the improvement levels off.

We think that both criteria can be used, as will be shown later, but we would also like to suggest that one should not only look at these numerical indicators, but also at the plausibility of the obtained results and the extent of the changes in parameter estimates from run to run. Since we concentrate, in this text, on detection and testing of the causal structure, the changes in the parameter values by corrections to the model are of utmost importance for the investigator. If the changes at some point are so minimal that they do not change the interpretation of the coefficients, and Δ is already rather high (.9) so that no radical changes can be expected anymore, one may as well stop adding the corrections. On the other hand, when considerable improvement is still possible or the parameter estimates change considerably by reasonable changes to the model, then it makes sense to continue adding corrections. In order to clarify the discussion, the procedure will be illustrated for the school career data.

An Example

According to the substantive arguments given before, corrections are only expected in the matrix with the γ parameters. We do not see any strong theoretical reasons for changes of other model parameters at the moment. We also want to introduce as few corrections as possible and for this purpose the modification indices are used to guide the corrections. In each step the improvement in fit is evaluated. With these three points in mind, further exploration of the school career data is carried out to improve the original model.

The results of these analyses are summarized in Table 12.4. In the analysis of the null model, the parameter γ_{41}^s turned out to have the largest modification index. As the introduction of this parameter into the model as a new effect seemed reasonable, this parameter is added to the model and the first alternative model is analyzed. In this run of the program the test statistic was reduced from 173.5 to 95.06, which is considerable. In percentages of the original value of the test statistic, this is a reduction of 45.2%. But this also means that there is still 55% improvement possible. So we try to find other corrections which make sense.

Table 12.4   Exploratory Analysis of the School Career Data

Model	Description	Df	T	Δ	RMR*	GFI*	AGFI*
1	null model	9	173.50	—	.073	.892	.665
2	model 1 + γ_{41}	8	95.06	45.2%	.056	.934	.770
3	model 2 + γ_{22}	7	75.90	56.3%	.046	.950	.799
4	model 3 + γ_{31}	6	65.41	62.3%	.038	.957	.799
5	model 4 + γ_{42}	5	59.87	65.5%	.033	.960	.777
6	model 5 +						
	γ_{51} and γ_{52}	3	59.72	65.6%	.033	.960	.629
7	model 5 + β_{42}	4	7.38	95.7%	.008	.995	.962
8	model 7 + β_{43}	3	.16	99.9%	.000	1.000	.999

* The measures of fit will be discussed in the next section.

In the analysis of the first alternative model, the parameter ψ_{42}' turned out to have the largest modification index. However we do not think that we have omitted any important variable in the model. We therefore rejected this suggestion. There were also β coefficients with rather large values for the modification indices. But also for these parameters we thought that they were not very likely. Therefore we restrict the corrections only to the GAMMA matrix. In the GAMMA matrix the largest modification index was found for the parameter γ_2^s. This is the effect of socio-economic status on the teacher's recommendation. This effect was omitted in the null model mainly because we did not want to make the model too complex. We were not absolutely certain that this effect was zero, we only thought it to be relatively small. In order to improve the fit of the model we think that it is reasonable to check this possibility. Therefore this parameter is introduced in the second alternative model. Analyzing this second model, we see that the test statistic becomes 75.90 with 7 degrees of freedom as now two more parameters have been introduced. The total improvement in fit of these two parameters is $(173.50 - 75.9)/173.5 = .563$ which means that these two corrections have improved the fit by 56.3%. That means that the second parameter also considerably improves the fit of the model, although less so than the first parameter. The improvement is still not 90% so we decide again to continue with the corrections, still restricting them to the GAMMA matrix. The γ^s parameter with the largest modification index in the last model was γ_{31}^s. This parameter would represent an effect of the quality of the school (x_1^s) on the parents' preferences (y_3^s). Although this effect was ignored in the past it is not impossible if we imagine that it could represent the effect that the parents of each school might have on each other. This parameter is introduced in the third alternative model and the data are again analyzed with this new model.

In this case the test statistic is equal to 65.41, which means that now a

62.3% improvement of fit is obtained. This indicates that the improvements become smaller and smaller even though we still have not reached the 90% improvement level. In the last run the modification index for γ^s_{42} was the largest of all γ^s coefficients, which were still not introduced as a parameter in the model. This parameter would represent the effect of the socio-economic status of the child (x^s_2) on its score on the school test (y^s_4). This effect is unlikely, unless we are willing to accept the idea that higher status families also train their children to perform well on such school tests. As this effect is not completely impossible, even though it is unlikely that the effect would be large, we have introduced this parameter in the fifth alternative model.

The result of the analysis with the fifth model is that the test statistic becomes 59.87, which means that an improvement of 65.5% is obtained. This improvement is indeed not very large compared with the last one and the coefficient is also rather small, which is somewhat reassuring in this case. But it also means that we have not progressed much farther with respect to the improvement of the model in this way. In the GAMMA matrix only two corrections are still possible, namely the introduction of γ^s_{51} and γ^s_{52}. For both parameters the modification indices are rather small: .105 and .030 respectively. This means that one can not expect much improvement with these two corrections. For illustrative purposes we have nevertheless introduced these two parameters.

It turned out that the improvement was very limited as can be seen in Table 12.4. Therefore we rejected these two corrections. But this led to the situation where we had introduced all the parameters which we thought to be plausible but the model still did not fit the data very well. The question now arises whether we were really correct in restricting the corrections to the model to the GAMMA matrix. At least this analysis indicates that the corrections to this matrix are not sufficient to obtain an acceptable model. This result put some doubt on our starting point. In principle there are two directions in which we can go. The first is to forget the previous restriction. The second possibility is to look for completely different conclusions. In the rest of this section we will follow the first approach. In a later chapter the alternative approach will be followed because it will turn out that the first approach does not lead to a satisfactory result.

In all analyses it was clear that large modification indices were present for β^s_{42}, β^s_{43} and ψ_{43}' and ψ_{42}'. The last two parameters suggest that important variables are omitted. We are still not willing to accept this alternative. The first two parameters suggest that effects have been omitted on the variable y^s_4. So far these effects have been ignored, since we anticipated two small effects which might cancel each other out: first of all one can expect a negative effect as a consequence of the fact that the students become nervous due to the high expectations; at the same time , one may argue that students will try to do their best if they know that much is expected from them. It could be possible that one of these effects is larger than the other and consequently that there is a significant effect of y_2^s or y_3^s on y_4^s. However we still expect that this effect, if it exists, will be rather small.

Since the modification index for β_{42}^s was the largest in the fifth model, we have introduced this parameter first.

The result of the analysis of the data with this new model is that the test statistic acquires the very low value of 7.38, which represents an improvement of fit of 95.7% compared with the null model. This one correction leads to a fit of the model which is acceptable according to the 90% criterion. But, for this model as well, the modification index of γ_{43}^s is still large and one also wonders why β_{42}^s should be included and not β_{43}^s. This seems inconsistent. Therefore we also explored this extra possibility.

In this last model estimated, the test statistic became .16 which represents an approximately perfect fit. But what is more important, in this last step it turned out that the values of the parameters changed considerably compared with model 7. In particular, β_{41}^s and β_{42}^s changed by about .1, which is of substantive importance. And since we are of the opinion that β_{41}^s and β_{42}^s are just as plausible or implausible, we think that both or none of the two need to be introduced into the model. Given the changes in the values of the parameters, we decide that it is necessary to continue adding the corrections even though model 7 had already obtained the proportion of improvement of 90%.

Although the final model fits the data according to the previously mentioned criteria and all introduced parameters can be defended on theoretical grounds, this does not mean that the final model also represents the true mechanism which produced the observed data. In fact we are suspicious about certain parts of the final model. We see it as unrealistic that β_{42}^s and β_{43}^s, the effects of "teacher's recommendation" and "parents' preferences" on the test score are .245 and .138 respectively. In our opinion these values are much too high. Therefore we are not completely satisfied with the model obtained, although it can not be denied that it might be a reasonable description of the causal process. However, in this case we are still prepared to reject this model if we can find an even simpler and or more plausible model which also fits the data. In chapter 15 it will be shown that such a model exists but for the time being we stick to the model obtained here.

* Some Alternative Measures

Although the proportional improvement in the value of the test statistic seems to be a useful tool for determining whether to continue or to stop adding the corrections, a number of alternative *measures of fit* of models which are also available in LISREL have recently been developed. These measures will be discussed briefly in this section.

The first measure which we want to discuss is called the *root mean squared residual* (*RMR*). This measure is directly based on the residuals which we have discussed before and is defined as follows:

$$RMR = \sqrt{\frac{1}{k} \sum_{ij} (s_{ij} - \sigma_{ij})^2} \qquad (12.2)$$

where the sum is taken over all distinct elements of Σ and k is the total number of distinct elements.

It will be clear that this measure is close to zero if all residuals become close to zero. This means that this measure can indicate when the fit of the model to the data becomes better when comparing models for the same data set. On the other hand, it is unclear how large this measure has to be to speak of a bad fit of the model to the data. This means that this measure is mainly useful for comparison of different models which are fitted to the same data, because the values of the measures can only be compared under that condition.

In order to avoid the problem of the interpretation of such measures, one can normalize them so that the value will lie between 0 and 1. This is done for the measures which are called *goodness of fit indices* (*GFI*). They are also available in LISREL . These measures are defined as follows:

$$GFI = 1 - \frac{T_i}{\text{Max}(T_i)} \qquad (12.3)$$

where T_i is the value of the test statistic and $\text{Max}(T_i)$ is in some sense the maximum value which T_i can obtain. The i is added because this measure can be obtained for the ULS estimating procedure as well as the GLS estimator. In case of an ML estimation, the same *GFI* estimator will be computed as would have been done for the GLS estimator.

It will be clear that one advantage of this measure of fit is that its value is easier to interpret than the RMR. If *GFI* is zero the fit is bad, if *GFI* is close to 1 the fit is good. This measure can be used to compare models for the same data set but one can even compare models for different data sets. A problem now with these measures is that we have little experience with them so it is unclear when one can speak of an acceptable fit, and of a good fit, etc.

Another problem with this measure is that the number of parameters used in order to obtain a good fit is not taken into account. It is of course in general possible to obtain a better fit with more parameters . Therefore it makes sense to have a measure which also takes into account the number of parameters used or, equivalently, the number of degrees of freedom left.

In LISREL there is also a measure of fit which takes into account the number of degrees of freedom. The measure is called the *adjusted goodness of fit index* (*AGFI*) and is defined as:

$$AGFI = 1 - (k/df)(1 - GFI) \qquad (12.4)$$

where k is equal to the number of distinct elements in Σ and df is of course the number of degrees of freedom. This measure also lies in principle between 0 and 1 where 0 indicates a very bad fit and 1 a very good fit. Also in this case it is still unclear when one can speak of a good fit, etc.

In order to give some idea of the relationship between the quality of the model and the values of the fit indices, we have presented in Table 12.4 the values obtained for the different models. This table indicates that it is quite difficult to give simple rules for the interpretation of these indices. More experience with these measures is required in order to say more about this point.

Having discussed the different goodness of fit measures available in LISREL, we want to say a little bit more about them by comparing them with the test statistic discussed before and the measure for the proportional improvement which we have discussed in the last section.

Comparing these measures with the test statistics, it is clear that they have the advantage that their values do not depend on the sample size. This is also true for the measure Δ of the last section but not for the test statistics. This is also why test statistics are very sensitive to small errors in the case of a large sample and much less sensitive in the case of a small sample. The measures of fit discussed do not have this problem due to the fact that they are independent of the sample size. On the other hand one should be aware of the fact that these measures are also affected by other characteristics of the model just as the test statistics are. This means that these measures are very sensitive to some errors for some models and not for other models. Controlling the sensitivity would require the evaluation of the power of these procedures. However it is not feasible to evaluate the power of the test each time for every correction which one would like to introduce. We will return to this problem later.

If we compare the measures of this section with the measure Δ discussed in the last section, it will be clear that these measures are quite different in nature. The measures in this section provide in some sense an absolute level of fit of the model to the data while the measure of the last section can only provide a relative judgement. This becomes clear if one realizes that a comparison always is made with the fit of the null-model which is in fact an arbitrary choice. In the literature also other suggestions than we have chosen, have been made for the null model.

On the other hand the measure Δ can very easily be interpreted as the proportional improvement in fit of the new model compared with the null model. Such a simple interpretation is not available for the measures of this section. In our opinion the measure of the proportional improvement is a very handy tool in the process of evaluating different steps in the search for a model that fits. Whether the other measures can do as well will depend on the possibility of obtaining an easy interpretation of these measures.

Some General Remarks

In this chapter we have seen that the normalized residuals can indicate between which variables the largest errors in the model exist. We have also shown that these residuals do not indicate what kind of correction has to be made because several corrections for the same residual are possible.

Next we have discussed the use of the modification indices as procedures to obtain hints for adding corrections to the model. But we have indicated that these hints should not be used as substitutes for theoretical arguments because they can lead to completely unrealistic models.

The next topic was the criterion for stopping with the corrections. In this respect we have suggested using the measure for the proportional improvement of the model combined with an evaluation of the consequences for the estimates of the parameters if further parameters are added to the model. This approach has also been illustrated by the school career example. For this example we have shown that an approximately perfectly fitting model can be obtained.

Although it will be possible in general to find a final model which nearly perfectly fits the data, this does not mean that this model represents also the true mechanism which produced the observed data. It may be unique for this data set. The reason for this remark is that the formulation of the theory in this model correction phase is largely based on data exploration. As a consequence of *capitalizing on chance*, the theory developed might provide a good description of the data set used but a very bad description of any other data set.

In order to avoid such problems, one should introduce in this exploration phase only those corrections for which one can make a reasonable argument for different data sets. In doing so one can not completely avoid the above mentioned problems but one is more protected against them. However, even if only those corrections are introduced for which a theoretical argument is available, one still has to test this new theory on new data in order to test whether this theory also holds for fresh data.

When one has a very large sample to begin with, it is possible to split the sample into two random parts: one which is used for the data exploration and one which is used for the testing of the final model. If one has too few cases for this approach, one has to collect new data. How the test can be done will be discussed in the next chapter.

A final remark we have to make, deals with the point that so far only parameters have been added to the model. This is done in order to improve the fit of the model. However it is possible that the final model is not the simplest model which fits the data. It is possible that in the original model parameters were available which could have been omitted. Furthermore it is possible that parameters have been added to the model in an earlier step in order to improve the fit, while these parameters turn out to be not necessary in a later phase. The topic of the next chapter is to determine which parameters are necessary and which are not. This is done in order to obtain a model which fits the data and is as simple as possible.

Further Reading

The approach using modification indices to detect specification errors has recently been introduced in the literature. Some remarks about this topic can be found in the LISREL User's Guide (Jöreskog and Sörbom, 1983). The same problem of detection of specification errors has been dealt with by Costner (1969) , Costner and Schoenberg (1973) and Sörbom (1975). Saris, De Pijper and Zegwaart (1979) have suggested a procedure which also takes into account the correlations between the estimates, but unfortunately this approach is too expensive to use with contemporary computers.

The use of the proportional improvement of fit has been introduced in the literature by Bentler and Bonnett (1980). They suggested taking another model as the null model. Their paper is also interesting to read for some other suggestions related to fitting of models which have been left out here because of their complexity. This does not mean that their suggestions are not useful. The reader can find out for him/herself, after some experience has been obtained with the analysis of data in the way described here (see also exercises 12.2 and 12.3).

A completely different approach to the detection of specification errors makes use of the residuals in each separate equation. A good discussion of this approach is given by Draper and Smith, in their book "Applied Regression Analysis" (1966, chapter 3).

Exercises

12.1 Figure 12.1 presents the estimates for the Full School Career Model. This model has been found by relaxing the restrictions in GAMMA and BETA. One restriction which is not relaxed is $\beta_{51}^s = 0$. This effect is a priori impossible as the "scholastic achievement" was not known by the committee which made the decision.

(a) If the residual between y_5^s and y_1^s is large what kind of explanation would you suggest for this error?

(b) Would there be any reason to introduce β_{51}^s?

(c) Some people suggest to start with a full recursive model and to introduce restrictions only if an effect turns out to be very small. Do you agree with this approach? Why not?

(d) If the model fits with $\beta_{51}^s = 0$ what conclusion can be drawn?

12.2 By introduction of new effects a fitting model can always be obtained for recursive models.

(a) Why?

(b) Should we always proceed till a fitting model has been found?

(c) For nonrecursive models it is not always possible to obtain a fitting model. Why?

(d) Is it possible that the value of the test statistic decreases if new restrictions are introduced?

(e) Is it possible that the probability connected with the test statistic increases if new restrictions are introduced?

12.3 We have suggested the use of your own theory as the null model for computation of Δ.

(a) What would be the effect if one uses as null model a model with all β^s and γ^s parameters equal to zero?

(b) A measure like Δ is independent of the sample size. Why do people want fit measures to have this property?

(c) Does this property prevents the rejection of theories in case of very small and uninteresting effects ?

(d) Why should we not only rely on statistical measures in order to find a fitting model?

12.4 With respect to the secondary analysis:

(a) Try to improve the model if it did not fit the data. Do not forget that the model should be as plausible as possible. Do not introduce parameters which are not necessary in general.

Chapter 13
Confidence Intervals
and Simplification of Models

In chapter 9 it was discussed how sample data were often used as a (well considered) substitute for information on the total research population. It was also shown that numerous samples can be drawn from one and the same population, and that these may result in sample covariance matrices S which differ from the single population covariance matrix Σ. Consequently, estimates of the model parameters which are based on these different sample covariance matrices will also differ from the true, population values of the parameters. In this chapter, the univariate frequency distribution of the parameter estimates is discussed. The distributions give insight into the quality of the single set of parameter estimates that one usually obtains in actual, substantive research.

More specifically, the distributions tell us how to construct intervals within which the true parameter values can be found with a certain probability. Furthermore, it is shown how one can test whether a particular parameter does not differ significantly from zero. This test procedure can also be used to simplify models, by deleting parameters which do not differ from zero in a significant way.

The Distribution of Parameter Estimates in Large Samples

Since the sample covariance matrices differ from each other by chance, the parameter estimates obtained from these different matrices will also vary from sample to sample. The variation in values of the parameter estimates as a result of sampling can be studied. We start with the case where large samples have been used. In chapter 9 an experiment was discussed where, for given values of the parameters in the population, 400 random samples of 500 cases each, were drawn. In this chapter we indicate what happens when these data matrices are analyzed with the program LISREL, in order to obtain the estimates of the parameters in the structural equation model. Figures 13.1 and 13.2 give the distributions of the estimates for parameters β_{53} and γ_{21}, which were .935 and .005 in the population. Figures 13.1 and 13.2 indicate how the distributions of the LISREL estimates appear in this case. It turns out that these distributions do not differ systematically from normal distributions. Furthermore, the means of the distributions were .935 and .009 respectively, which are approximately identical to the true values of the parameters. The standard deviations of the estimates were .011 and .039. The figures indicate that only very few parameter values are found at a distance of more than two standard deviations from the mean; this is what one expects for a normal distribution.

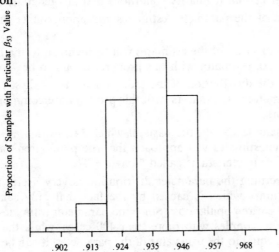

Figure 13.1   The Distribution of Parameter β_{53} in 400 Samples, Each with $n = 500$. The Mean is .935, the Standard Deviation (*sd*) .011

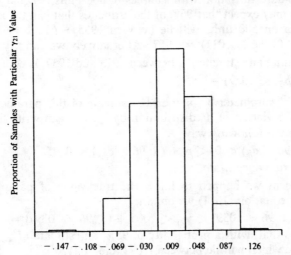

Figure 13.2   The Distribution of Parameter γ_{21} in 400 Samples, Each with $n = 500$. The Mean is .009, the Standard Deviation (*sd*) .039

These results can be generalized, at least for large samples. It can be proven that ML estimates (for the other estimators we refer to chapter 10) have the following properties, when one is dealing with multivariate normally distributed variables and under certain regularity conditions that are generally fulfilled:

(1)The distribution of the parameter estimates will approximate the normal distribution.

(2)The expectation or mean of the estimates will be identical to the true value of the parameters. An estimator with this property is said to be *"unbiased"*.

(3)The variance of the distribution of the estimator is the smallest of all possible unbiased estimators. Estimators with this property are commonly called *"efficient"* estimators.

(4)The larger the sample size on the basis of which ML estimates are calculated, the closer the estimates will approach the true population values. An estimator with this characteristic is called *"consistent"*.

Knowledge concerning the parameter distribution is very useful in that it reduces the uncertainty which is caused by the fact that only samples can be studied and not entire populations. Since the parameter estimates are normally distributed for samples with more than 400 cases, while the mean of their distribution is equal to the true value of the parameter, it can be expected that 95% of the parameter estimates will lie within 1.96 standard deviations from the true value of the parameter. In our example, β_{53} has a true value of .935 and the standard deviation with samples of 500 units is equal to .011. Consequently we may expect that 95% of the estimates that can be computed from sample data on 500 units will lie between .935 − (1.96 × .011) = .913 and .935 + (1.96 × .011) = .957. Alternatively we can say that the probability of finding an estimate $\hat{\beta}_{53}$ between .913 and .957, is equal to .95, i.e. $\mathrm{Pr}(.913 < \hat{\beta}_{53} < .957) = .95$.

Denoting the ith parameter by p_i, the ML estimate of this parameter by $\hat{p}_i$ and the standard deviation of its distribution by $\sigma_{\hat{p}_i}$, one can write the result more generally in the following way

$$\mathrm{Pr}\big(p_i - (1.96 \times \sigma_{\hat{p}_i}) < \hat{p}_i < p_i + (1.96 \times \sigma_{\hat{p}_i})\big) = 0.95 \qquad (13.1)$$

Let us apply this rule once more.

In our experiment we happen to know the true value of parameter γ_{21} (.005). Applying equation (13.1) we obtain:

$$\mathrm{Pr}\big(.005 - (1.96 \times .039) < \hat{\gamma}_{21} < .005 + (1.96 \times .039)\big) = .95$$

The equation says that, with a probability of 95%, an estimate of γ_{21} will be found in a sample which will lie between -.071 and .081.

This discussion indicates that knowledge of the distributional properties of an estimator reduces the uncertainty about the parameter estimates considerably.

The Distribution of Parameter Estimates in Small Samples

For small samples there is less information about the properties of the ML estimators available than for large samples. The reason is that such properties have not been derived yet. Only a few studies have tackled this problem.

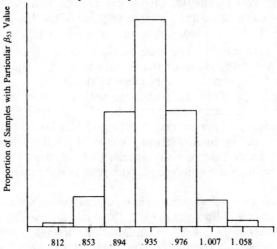

Figure 13.3 Distribution of Parameter β_{53} in 400 Samples, Each with $n =$ 50. The Mean is .935, the Standard Deviation (sd) .041

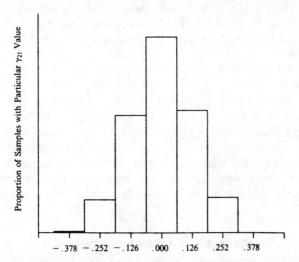

Figure 13.4 Distribution of Parameter γ_{21} in 400 Samples, Each with $n =$ 50. The Mean is .000, the Standard Deviation (sd) .126

Essentially these studies use the same approach as we have chosen before: from a population with known parameter values a large number of samples is drawn and subsequently analyzed. The results of these analyses give an indication of what one might expect for similar models. In Figures 13.3 and 13.4 the results for two parameters of our experiment with samples of 50 cases are presented. The model in this example is based on the school career theory. Figures 13.3 and 13.4 indicate again that the distributions look very much like normal distributions. The mean of the distribution of $\hat{\beta}_{53}$ is again identical to .935, while the mean of the $\hat{\gamma}_{21}$ distribution is equal to .000. Again we see that these means are very close to the true values of the two parameters. Comparison of these distributions with the distributions of the same parameters for large samples indicates that the standard deviations are now considerably larger (.041 compared to .011 and .126 compared to .039). Although the spread of the distribution in the case of small samples is larger compared to large samples, the rule still applies that only very few outcomes of the parameter estimates are removed at more than two standard deviations from the true value.

The obtained results are not very different from those other researchers have reported on small samples. Boomsma (1982, 1983) has carried out the largest study of this problem so far. For unstandardized parameters he generally found only slight deviations from normality, even in the case of very small sample sizes ($n = 25$). The result was somewhat less favorable for standardized coefficients. In general, the means of the unstandardized estimates were very close to the true values of the parameters, which indicates that the estimator is approximately unbiased. Furthermore, since the shapes of the distributions were quite symmetrical, the standard deviation could be used to indicate the spread.

In order to emphasize that the result is only an approximation, we will not write "probability = .95", but "probability ≈ .95" which means that the probability approximates .95. Equation (13.1) then becomes

$$\Pr\left(p_i - (1.96 \times \sigma_{\hat{p}_i}) < \hat{p}_i < p_i + (1.96 \times \sigma_{\hat{p}_i})\right) \approx .95 \qquad (13.2)$$

According to the studies available, equation (13.1) can be used if the sample size is larger than 400, while equation (13.2) should be preferred if the sample size is smaller than 400. The studies have indicated that one should be careful in the case of very small samples, such as 25 cases with standardized coefficients, since considerable errors can occur in the parameter estimates.

Construction of Confidence Intervals

Up to this point it was assumed that we know the true values of the parameters. The question was what to expect of the ML estimates over a large number of samples. In practice the situation is quite different. Information is available for only one sample and from this information one set of estimates for the parameters can be obtained. Then the question is what these estimates tell us about the values of the parameters in the population.

First of all we could obtain the true values of the parameters if the research could be repeated, since the mean of the estimates is approximately the same as the true value of the parameter. Secondly, it was indicated previously that the calculated parameter value will give a better estimate of the true parameter value, the larger the sample is, since ML estimators are consistent. A third point, which we discuss more extensively in this section, is that we can try to find intervals which have a certain probability of containing the true value of the parameter of interest.

These intervals can be derived easily from equations (13.1) and (13.2). Some algebraic manipulations lead to the following result:

$$\Pr\left(\hat{p}_i - (1.96 \times \sigma_{\hat{p}_i}) < p_i < \hat{p}_i + (1.96 \times \sigma_{\hat{p}_i})\right) = .95 \qquad (13.3)$$

This form says that the probability that the interval $\hat{p}_i - 1.96 \times \sigma_{\hat{p}_i}$ to $\hat{p}_i + 1.96 \times \sigma_{\hat{p}_i}$ contains p_i is approximately .95. So if $\hat{p}_i$ and $\sigma_{\hat{p}_i}$ are available from a sample, such an interval can be constructed, and we know that in 95 out of a hundred cases this interval contains the true value of the parameter. Such a constructed interval is called the *"confidence interval"*. It is clear that the size of the interval depends on the chosen probability level, but normally 95% is used.

Intuitively the obtained result is easily understood if one looks at the sampling distribution of a specific parameter. In Figure 13.5 the sampling distribution of β_{53} has been drawn, with a true value of .935 and a standard deviation of .011. Consequently 95% of the estimates on the basis of the various samples will lie within a distance of $1.96 \times .011 = .022$ from the true value. The interval within which 95% of the parameter estimates will be found is indicated in Figure 13.5; its boundaries are a and b. Let us now introduce two arbitrary estimates of this parameter, one within the interval from a to b and one outside this interval. We also know that the standard deviation in both cases is .011. Formula (13.3) suggests that we should construct an interval by subtracting and adding a value of $1.96 \times .011 = .022$ to the value of the estimates. If we do that for both estimates, then it turns out that for the estimate within the interval from a to b, the true value will be within the constructed interval, while for the estimate outside the a-b interval, the true value will fall outside the constructed interval. We know that 95% of the sample estimates will lie between a and b, while only 5% will lie outside this interval. Consequently also 95% of the constructed intervals around the estimates will contain the true parameter. This is exactly what equation (13.3) says.

The only point that has not been discussed so far is how the standard deviation of the sampling distribution can be obtained if one has only access to the data of one sample. This point is very complicated and is beyond the scope of this introduction. For the moment it is sufficient to know that an estimate of the standard deviation is indeed obtainable from the information about one sample, and that this estimate is generally referred to as the *"standard error"*. The estimate of the standard deviation $\sigma_{\hat{p}_i}$ will be denoted with $\hat{\sigma}_{\hat{p}_i}$, in order to make a distinction between standard deviation and the standard error.

The standard errors of the estimates are computed by the LISREL program if they are requested. It should be added that this is only true if the model is identified. Otherwise the program prints a message to the effect that it can not compute the standard errors; this indicates that the model is most probably not identified. The standard errors are presented in the same way as the estimates of the parameters. In Tables 13.1 and 13.2 the output of the program for the fitting model of the school career data is given, and Table 13.3 indicates how this information can be used to compute the confidence intervals for the various effect parameters. Table 13.2 shows that the standard errors for this

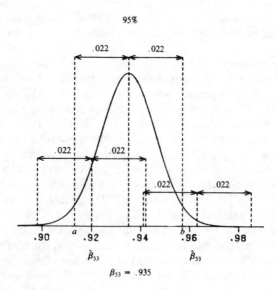

Figure 13.5 The Construction of Two Confidence Intervals for Two Estimates of β_{53}, where $\sigma_{\hat{\beta}_{53}} = .011$ and the True Value of the Parameter is .935

Table 13.1 The LISREL Estimates of the Fitting School Career Model

LISREL ESTIMATES (MAXIMUM LIKELIHOOD)

BETA

	Y 1	Y 2	Y 3	Y 4	Y 5
Y 1	0.000	0.000	0.000	0.000	0.000
Y 2	.799	0.000	0.000	0.000	0.000
Y 3	.249	.618	0.000	0.000	0.000
Y 4	.429	.245	.138	0.000	0.000
Y 5	0.000	.046	.916	.042	0.000

GAMMA

	X 1	X 2
Y 1	.254	.161
Y 2	-.049	.132
Y 3	.085	.062
Y 4	.261	.013
Y 5	0.000	0.000

PHI

	X 1	X 2
X 1	1.000	
X 2	.140	1.000

PSI

Y 1	Y 2	Y 3	Y 4	Y 5
.898	.324	.235	.235	.022

SQUARED MULTIPLE CORRELATIONS FOR STRUCTURAL EQUATIONS

Y 1	Y 2	Y 3	Y 4	Y 5
.102	.676	.765	.765	.978

sample of 383 respondents are rather small. Therefore the constructed 95% confidence intervals in Table 13.3 are also rather small. Thus, on the basis of the different parameters, we can obtain quite precise information about the sizes of the different parameters.

Table 13.3 also shows that, even if we account for the uncertainty produced by the sampling fluctuations, our preliminary interpretation of the theory still holds. For example, β^s_{53} may lie between .885 and .947, but this parameter is clearly much larger than β^s_{52} (which is most likely between .015 and .077) and β^s_{54} (which is probably between .017 and .067). Which one of these last two effects is the strongest is not clear yet, since the intervals overlap considerably. The interpretation shows once more that the direct effect of "parents' preferences" (y^s_3) on "choice of secondary school" (y^s_5) is far more important than the direct effect of the "teacher's recommendation" (y^s_2) and the "test score" (y^s_4). In a similar way the other parameters can be compared.

Table 13.2   The Standard Errors Computed by LISREL for the Fitting
School Career Model

STANDARD ERRORS

BETA

	Y 1	Y 2	Y 3	Y 4	Y 5
Y 1	0.000	0.000	0.000	0.000	0.000
Y 2	.031	0.000	0.000	0.000	0.000
Y 3	.044	.044	0.000	0.000	0.000
Y 4	.046	.054	.051	0.000	0.000
Y 5	0.000	.016	.016	.013	0.000

GAMMA

	X 1	X 2
Y 1	.049	.049
Y 2	.031	.030
Y 3	.026	.026
Y 4	.026	.026
Y 5	0.000	0.000

PHI

	X 1	X 2
X 1	0.000	
X 2	0.000	0.000

PSI

Y 1	Y 2	Y 3	Y 4	Y 5
.065	.023	.017	.017	.002

Table 13.3   Construction of the 95% Confidence Intervals for the Effect
Parameters of the Fitting Model for the School Career Data,
Computed from Tables 13.1 and 13.2

Parameter	Parameter Estimate	Standard Error	Confidence Interval from	to
γ_{11}	.254	.049	.158	.350
γ_{12}	.161	.049	.065	.257
β_{21}	.799	.031	.738	.860
γ_{21}	-.049	.031	-.109	.011
γ_{22}	.132	.030	.073	.191
β_{31}	.249	.044	.163	.335
β_{32}	.618	.044	.532	.704
γ_{31}	.085	.026	.034	.136
γ_{32}	.062	.026	.011	.113
β_{41}	.429	.046	.339	.519
β_{42}	.245	.054	.139	.351
β_{43}	.138	.051	.038	.238
γ_{41}	.261	.026	.210	.312
γ_{42}	.013	.026	-.038	.064
β_{52}	.046	.016	.015	.077
β_{53}	.916	.016	.885	.947
β_{54}	.042	.013	.017	.067

We return to this point in the next chapter.

To conclude this section it should be emphasized that in the case of small samples, the calculations do not give a result which is as precise as in this case. There are two reasons for this lack of precision. The first is that equation (13.3) only holds approximately in that case. The second reason is that all standard errors will be much larger, so that the uncertainty will be much larger. However, in principle the procedure is exactly the same when one is dealing with small samples. But the reader should be warned that occasionally the estimates of the standard deviations and the estimates of the parameters can be inaccurate for very small samples.

Significance Tests of Individual Parameters

After the discussion of confidence intervals, the step to tests of hypotheses concerning individual parameters is not very difficult. The most interesting test for individual parameters is whether or not an effect is zero. If the true value of a parameter is zero ($p_i = 0$) and the standard deviation is known, the distribution of the estimates which one may expect can be drawn. For example, with a sample size of 50, the standard deviation of parameter γ_{21} was .126. With this information we know that approximately 95% of the estimates will lie within a distance of $1.96 \times .126 = .247$ from zero. It can also be derived with the Z-table that 99% of the estimates should lie within a distance of $3 \times .126 = .378$ from zero. If in a sample an estimate for the same parameter is obtained of .8, most people will conclude that this result is very unlikely if $p_i = 0$, since the deviation from zero is larger than one may expect if the deviation is due to random fluctuations in the sample. In general the conclusion is then that the hypothesis $p_i = 0$ has to be rejected. It should be clear, however that the deviation could have occurred by chance; thus one runs the risk of drawing the wrong conclusion. But in this example the conclusion seems obvious.

If an estimate $\hat{p}_i = .07$ is obtained, the situation is not so clear, since there is a difference from zero, but the discrepancy is not larger than what may be expected by chance, given that one chooses for instance the 95% confidence interval. Normally, the conclusion in such a case is that the hypothesis $p_i = 0$ should not be rejected, since the obtained value lies within the 95% confidence interval, indicating the values that might be expected if the hypothesis is true. So the obtained discrepancy can indeed be attributed to random fluctuations. This conclusion however, can also be wrong. This point is illustrated in Figure 13.6. The figure shows two distributions; one with $p_i = 0$ and one with $p_i = .25$, but both with the same standard deviation. From this figure it seems clear that samples from both populations could have given a sample estimate of $p_i = .07$. If $p_i = .25$ is true, and we conclude on the basis of the test that the hypothesis $p_i = 0$ can not be rejected (that is, should be accepted), the conclusion is obviously wrong.

The figure also illustrates the other type of error. If $p_i = 0$, the probability that we find an estimate which differs more than $.247$ from zero is approximately 5%. In such cases we would conclude that the hypothesis has to be rejected, but this would be erroneous. The probability that we make such an error is 5%.

This discussion shows that we can always make two kinds of mistakes as we have seen before : we run the risk of rejecting a correct hypothesis (α-error) and we run the risk of accepting a wrong hypothesis (β-error). Normally the following test procedure is used to control the different possible errors. The probability of an α-error is chosen to be not larger than 5%, which is called the "significance level". The consequence of this choice is that one has to use the 95% confidence intervals around the hypothesized parameter values. If the parameter estimate is within this confidence interval, the hypothesis

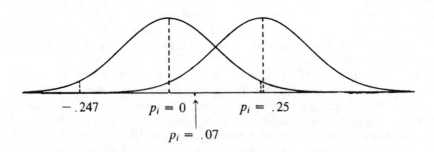

Figure 13.6   Two Distributions for p_i, One with $p_i = 0$ and the Other with $p_i = .25$, but Both with the Same Standard Deviation ($.126$), for Samples of 50 Units

is not rejected; if the value is outside the confidence interval, the hypothesis is rejected. Another formulation of the same issue is that the hypothesis is rejected, if the obtained estimate differs more than $1.96 \times \hat{\sigma}_{\hat{p}_i}$ from zero. From a practical point of view this is an easier way of checking the correctness of the hypothesis.

But so far the β-error has been ignored. It will be clear that in case of small samples the test can be quite indecisive if the standard errors and, consequently, also the confidence intervals are very large. In order to improve what is called the power of the test, which is identical to reducing the risk of accepting a wrong hypothesis (β-error), one can increase the sample size. This point is illustrated in Figure 13.7 where the same competing hypotheses of Figure 13.6 have been given. By increasing the sample size from 50 to 500 as we also did in our experiment, the standard deviation reduces approximately by a factor $\sqrt{50/500}$, and becomes .039. Therefore both distributions become less spread out, and therefore we see that the test in this case leads to the conclusion that $p_i = 0$, and the risk involved in making this conclusion is not

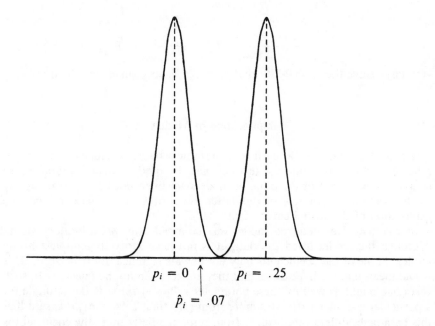

Figure 13.7 Two Distributions for p_i, One with $p_i = 0$ and the Other with $p_i = .25$, but Both with the Same Standard Deviation (.039) for Samples of 500 Units

Table 13.4   The T-Values Computed by LISREL for the Fitting School Career Model

T-VALUES

BETA

	Y 1	Y 2	Y 3	Y 4	Y 5
Y 1	0.000	0.000	0.000	0.000	0.000
Y 2	25.936	0.000	0.000	0.000	0.000
Y 3	5.701	14.138	0.000	0.000	0.000
Y 4	9.432	4.533	2.693	0.000	0.000
Y 5	0.000	2.967	58.928	3.325	0.000

GAMMA

	X 1	X 2
Y 1	5.170	3.274
Y 2	-1.597	4.420
Y 3	3.253	2.369
Y 4	9.862	.485
Y 5	0.000	0.000

PHI

	X 1	X 2
X 1	0.000	
X 2	0.000	0.000

PSI

Y 1	Y 2	Y 3	Y 4	Y 5
13.784	13.784	13.784	13.784	13.784

very large since the probability that $p_i = .25$ is very small (less than .05).

Simplification of Models

The preceding test can be used to determine whether coefficients differ significantly from zero. But the test can also be used in data exploration, to simplify models that fit the data, or modelswhichcan not be improved upon. In this section an example of this latter use is presented; this continues the exploration of the school career data.

In chapter 12 a preferred model was obtained after 8 exploratory steps. Although the model fitted the data, it is not necessarily the simplest fitting model. Some of the coefficients may not deviate significantly from zero. This would mean that the hypothesis that they are zero can not be rejected. In such cases one might as well fix these parameter values at zero. If the estimate for a particular parameter deviates more from zero than $1.96 \times \sigma_{\hat{p}_i}$, it is said that this parameter differs significantly from zero, or briefly that "the coefficient is *significant*". Alternatively one can say that a coefficient is significant if

$$t_i = \left| \frac{\hat{p}_i}{\hat{\sigma}_{\hat{p}_i}} \right| > 1.96$$

In Table 13.4 the t-values for all parameters are given. They are computed by LISREL using the information from Tables 13.1 and 13.2. It should be clear that the program divided each $\hat{p}_i$ of Table 13.1 by the estimate of the standard error for that parameter in Table 13.2, in order to obtain the t-value listed in Table 13.4. Inspection of Table 13.4 shows that all parameters are significant, except for γ_{21}^s and γ_{42}^s. For these two parameters, the deviation from zero is so small that it might have been generated by random fluctuations in the data. Thus, from the point of developing a structural theory, these two parameters might as well be equal to zero. If this correction of the model is introduced, this presents a correction in the opposite direction of what was done in the previous chapter.

If several parameters are not significant, the problem arises whether all parameters should be deleted simultaneously, or step by step. We recommend doing it stepwise, since nonsignificant coefficients may become significant as soon as other parameters are left out. We return to this point later. But if this is the preferred approach, the order in which the different parameters have to be left out of the model becomes a problem. The only way to solve this problem is to use theoretical ideas to specify the order. In our example we decide first of all, to delete γ_{42}^s, since this parameter was not incorporated in the original theory, i.e. it was not expected to differ significantly from zero, while γ_{21}^s was indeed expected to be significant.

The fixing of γ_{42}^s at zero leads to a test statistic of .40 for a model with 4 degrees of freedom. The difference in fit with the model of Table 13.1 is only .24, for one degree of freedom, which means that the increase in the statistic is not too much. Thus, we decide that this coefficient can indeed be fixed at zero without harming the fit of the resulting model.

The output for this new model indicates that the t-value associated with the γ_{21}^s parameter is still smaller than 1.96. Therefore we decide to fix γ_{21}^s at zero as well, in order to further simplify the obtained model. Introducing this simplification does not harm the fit of the model either; the test statistic is now 2.95, which means an increase compared with the previous run of 2.55 for one degree of freedom. Thus this increase is again very small and we can decide that this simplification is also acceptable. For this last model all parameters differ significantly from zero, and the fit of the model is also acceptable. Consequently, we can now conclude that we have possibly found the most parsimonious model which fits the school career data. This "preferred" model is also quite acceptable on theoretical grounds, as is indicated in the next chapter dealing with the interpretation.

Some Final Remarks

This chapter concludes with a few more comments. First of all, the fit of the model does not uniquely establish a particular model as *the* correct model. In fact, it is shown in chapter 15 that another model fits the school career data just as well as the preferred model which was selected here.

A second point is that a parameter which led to a significant improvement may sometimes again be considered for elimination at a later point. During the development of the school career model, this happened with γ_{42}^s, which was introduced in chapter 12, but has been eliminated again in this chapter. Such a sequence of findings is possible because the results of the tests are always conditional on the model that has been fitted to the data. In Figure 12.1 the diagram of the original school career model was presented. If there is a nonzero residual between variables y_4^s and x_2^s, this residual can be reduced by introducing a direct effect between these variables (γ_{42}^s), as we have seen in step 5 of the series of corrections in chapter 12. This correction was significant at that moment. Later, parameter β_{43}^s was also introduced for other reasons. But this parameter can also reduce the residual between variables y_4^s and x_2^s, since it creates an additional indirect effect and some spurious relationships (check this). Consequently it is possible that after introduction of β_{43}^s, the effect γ_{42}^s is not significant anymore and can therefore be left out. This is exactly what happened in this analysis.

The finding that a parameter which is significant in one model is not significant in another model is a general one and should be taken into account when one is exploring the data. It is for this reason that we have to begin with the correction of a model. The simplification should be performed after the selection of a model which fits the data.

The investigator should also be aware of the fact that, according to the same argument, a nonsignificant parameter in an earlier stage of the data exploration does not mean that this effect can be ignored at all stages. This is a mistake frequently made in actual research. Scholars often think that a relationship between variables for which the correlation is zero can be ignored in their further research. However, in Figure 13.8 we have shown an example from which it becomes clear that the correlation between two variables (y_1 and y_2) may be zero, but where the effects will turn out to be nonzero if the

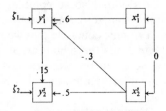

Figure 13.8   A Path Diagram of a Model with a Correlation between y_1 and y_2 of Zero, while y_1 has nevertheless an Effect on y_2

correct model is found. This example shows once more how important theory is for effective analysis and that different results can be obtained for individual parameters, depending on the model being estimated.

Further Reading

The distribution of estimates and the construction of confidence intervals is a standard topic in introductory statistics text books. See for example the text of Wonnacott and Wonnacott (1972) and Wallpole (1974).

A more complete discussion of the distribution of the LISREL estimates and their confidence intervals can be found in the work of Boomsma (1982 and 1983). The ULS and GLS estimators are only discussed in technical texts such as Browne (1975), Jöreskog and Goldberger (1972) and Sik-Jum Lee and Bentler (1980). In chapter 10 this literature is summarized and it is shown how this information can be used to make a choice between the different estimation procedures.

The use of t-values is common practice in the regression and econometric literature. For example, see Johnston (1972) and Christ (1966). In this literature it is shown that the ratio $\hat{p}_i / \hat{\sigma}_{\hat{p}_i}$ is distributed according to a well-known statistical distribution (Student's t). Boomsma (1982 and 1983) has shown that the t-values obtained from the LISREL program do not have this characteristic, since the estimates of p_i and the standard error are often highly correlated. We nevertheless continue to use the term t-value, because this is the common way of speaking about these ratios. In this text we have assumed that the distribution of the t-values obtained approximates the normal distribution.

Exercises

13.1 We expect that in a population a parameter (p_i) is equal to 0 while $\sigma_{\hat{p}_i} = .05$ for samples of 600 units while $\sigma_{\hat{p}_i} = .10$ for samples of 300 units.
(*a*)Between what values will the estimates lie in 95% of the samples of 600 units ?
(*b*)Between what values will the estimates lie in 95% of the samples of 300 units ?
If we find in a study that $\hat{p}_i = .12$:
(*c*)Do we have to reject the original hypothesis that $p_i = 0$ if the sample size $n = 600$?
(*d*)Do we have to reject the original hypothesis that $p_i = 0$ if the sample size is $n = 300$?

(e)Is it possible that we make an error in both cases? Why?

13.2 In the arms race example the following results are obtained for the different coefficients

Parameters	USA		USSR	
	Estimates	Standard Errors	Estimates	Standard Errors
γ_{11}	1.05	.08	.128	.04
γ_{21}	-.106	.08	.895	.04

(a)Determine, for all coefficients, the .95 confidence intervals,

(b)Given these intervals, what is your conclusion with respect to the significance of the coefficients?

(c)Draw the same conclusions using the t-values.

(d)Are these conclusions necessarily correct?

(e)Is it acceptable to fix the value of γ_{21}^s to zero in both cases as has been done before?

13.3 With respect to the secondary analysis:

(a)Can you also simplify the model which you have found?

(b)If so, simplify the model step by step until the model has to be rejected or that the correction is not acceptable anymore on theoretical grounds.

Chapter 14
The Interpretation of the Results

We have now gone through all the steps mentioned in the introduction—see the flow chart in Figure 1 of the introductory chapter—and a model has been obtained which fits to the sample correlation matrix. At this point it is useful to concentrate once more on the substantive interpretation of the results. One reason for doing this is that the model which was finally preferred differs in certain respects from the model which was developed in the original theory. It is instructive to bring out these differences. As a second point of interest, the results which have been obtained are far more precise than the model with which the study started. In this chapter it is shown how this more refined information can be used in the formulation of a more advanced theory.

The interpretation of the unstandardized solution has not been discussed yet. Therefore we start with the presentation of the unstandardized solution for the final model. Subsequently the standardized solution is discussed, allowing the comparison of the different effects. Finally the concept of total effect, which is the sum of the direct and indirect effects, is introduced and the use of these concepts is illustrated.

Interpretation of the Unstandardized Solution

In the interpretation of the unstandardized solution, the scales in which the various variables are expressed play an important role. In the school career model the variables x_1, y_1, and y_4 are all measured on a similar scale. For example, "scholastic achievement" (y_1) is measured on a 100-point scale expressed in percentage scores, covering the range from the best 1 percent to the worst one percent of all students in The Netherlands. The 7-point scales of the variables y_2, y_3 and y_5 are all expressed on a scale for school levels. Finally, "socio-economic status" is expressed in (six) status points. These dimensions or units of measurement are referred to again in the subsequent discussion.

Table 14.1 presents the unstandardized solution for the final model. Using this table, the equations for all endogenous variables can be formulated. In this section all variables are expressed in deviation scores in order to describe the unstandardized solution . Therefore we have to add a "d" to the names of the variables. We start with the equation presenting the explanation for

Table 14.1   LISREL Output, Showing the Unstandardized Solution of the Preferred School Career Model

```
LISREL ESTIMATES (MAXIMUM LIKELIHOOD)

    BETA
```

	Y 1	Y 2	Y 3	Y 4	Y 5
Y 1	0.000	0.000	0.000	0.000	0.000
Y 2	.062	0.000	0.000	0.000	0.000
Y 3	.020	.618	0.000	0.000	0.000
Y 4	.527	3.859	2.200	0.000	0.000
Y 5	0.000	.046	.916	.003	0.000

```
    GAMMA
```

	X 1	X 2
Y 1	.204	2.461
Y 2	0.000	.155
Y 3	.005	.075
Y 4	.260	0.000
Y 5	0.000	0.000

```
    PHI
```

	X 1	X 2
X 1	785.972	
X 2	5.764	2.161

```
    PSI
```

Y 1	Y 2	Y 3	Y 4	Y 5
455.046	1.037	.748	181.911	.071

```
SQUARED MULTIPLE CORRELATIONS FOR STRUCTURAL EQUATIONS
```

Y 1	Y 2	Y 3	Y 4	Y 5
.102	.674	.766	.767	.978

```
TOTAL COEFFICIENT OF DETERMINATION FOR STRUCTURAL EQUATIONS IS .351
```

"scholastic achievement" y_1^d. The equation for this variable is

$$y_1^d = .204x_1^d + 2.46lx_2^d + \zeta_1 \qquad (14.1a)$$

The variance of the disturbance term turned out to be 455.0, while the variance of the variable y_1^d is 506.6. This means that $(455.0/506.6) \times 100\% = 89.8\%$ of the variance in the achievement variable remained unexplained, and only 10.2% was explained by the variables introduced in this study. Clearly this result is not very good; some important variables have certainly been ignored in the model (for example, "intelligence"). But in this study the interest was not centered on the explanation of "scholastic achievement". Therefore the list of causal variables has been limited. It may be noted that the two variables which have been introduced have both significant effects. This result indicates that the hypothesis that "attending better schools and coming from higher status families leads to better achievements at the end of elementary school", probably as a result of better training, is in agreement with the data.

With respect to the effects of the different institutions, it is difficult to make a comparison because of the different units of measurement of the two variables. The result says that if one could increase the "level of the elementary school" (x_1^d) with one grade point, without affecting the "status of the family" (x_2^d), the effect of this increment would on average be an increase of .204 grade points in the "scholastic achievement" of students. If one could increase the "status of the family" (x_2^d) with one status point, without changing the "quality of the elementary school" (x_1^d), the effect on "achievement" would be an increase of on average 2.46 grade points. Another way of saying this is that for an increase of a pupil's school achievement by 10 points, an increase of approximately 50 points is required on the elementary school quality scale, or an increase of roughly 4 points in the social class level. Both these changes are quite large, which means that the effects are relatively small.

Let us now consider the second endogenous variable. It is indicated in Table 14.1 that the following equation could be specified:

$$y_2^d = .062y_1^d + .155x_2^d + \zeta_2 \qquad (14.1b)$$

The variance of the disturbance term in this equation was 1.037, while the variable y_2^d had a variance of 3.181. This means that for this variable the unexplained variance is 32.6% and the explained variance is 67.4%. Obviously this result is considerably better than that obtained for the first equation. However, substantively the result is unanticipated at certain points.

In chapter 4 it was argued that the "teacher's recommendation" (y_2^d) would depend on the "scholastic achievement" (y_1^d) of the student and on the "quality of the elementary school" (x_1^d). However, the analysis revealed that the last variable does not have a significant effect, while the influence of "parents' social class" (x_2^d) had to be introduced in order to obtain a fitting model. This suggests that the mechanism which leads to recommendation of the teacher differs from what was anticipated in chapter 4. The maximum status difference of 5 status points will on average not even lead to a difference in recommendation of one school level point (.155 × 5 = .775). The effect of "scholastic achievement" is potentially much larger: on average the difference of 90 grade points between the lowest and the highest achievement level creates a difference of almost 6 grade points in recommendation (.062 × 90), making up the whole range in the recommendation variable. Thus it seems that the "teacher's recommendation" is mainly determined by the "scholastic achievement" and that, in addition, students from higher status families obtain a somewhat higher recommendation than the students from lower status families.

For the third endogenous variable the following equation has been obtained:

$$y_3^d = .020y_1^d + .618y_2^d + .005x_1^d + .075x_2^d + \zeta_3 \qquad (14.1c)$$

The amount of explained variance in this case is again large. The variance of the disturbance term turned out to be .748 while the total variance of y_3^d was 3.184. Therefore the unexplained variance was 23.4% of the total variance and the amount of explained variance 76.6%. Although this result is quite acceptable, the school career theory of chapter 4 has to be readjusted once more, given equation (14.1c). In chapter 4 the effect of the "quality of the elementary school" on the "parents' preferences" was not expected. But in the analysis of the data this effect was necessary to obtain a model which fitted. In chapter 4 it was hypothesized that the preferences of the parents were a weighted average of the "opinion of the teacher" (y_2^d), the "opinion of the parents themselves" (thought to be proportional to the scholastic achievement of their child, measured by y_1^d) and the "opinion of the people of their own status level" (x_2^d). The simplest correction of this "preference formation" hypothesis is that the list is extended to include the opinions of the parents of children in the same school. With a higher elementary school standard, the preference of parents moves to higher levels of secondary schooling for their children. And since parents (who as a result of their children's education are linked to an elementary school) will have contact with each other on school affairs, one may argue that such parents also affect each other's opinions. Although it is again not easy to compare the effects of the different variables, it is at least clear that the parents' preferences are mainly determined by the "recommendations of the teacher" (y_2^d) although the parents also take into account their own ideas. The other two variables have somewhat smaller effects.

With respect to the explanation of the test score, the largest changes in the theory have occurred. The following equation has been found in the preferred model:

$$y_4^d = .527y_1^d + 3.859y_2^d + 2.200y_3^d + .260x_1^d + \zeta_4 \qquad (14.1d)$$

The variance of the disturbance term is 181.9 which is rather small compared to the total variance of y_4^d which is 780.7. The unexplained variance is 23.3% and the explained variance is 76.7%. In chapter 4 we expected that the test score would only be affected by the "achievement of the student" (y_1^d). In the analysis it turned out that a model had to include several additional effects in this equation in order to fit the data. The quite large effect of x_1^d seems to indicate that the better schools not only train their students to achieve better results scholastically, but that they also train the students in handling the exam forms used in the school tests. Moreover, the effects of "preferences of the parents" (y_3^d) and of the "teacher's recommendation" (y_2^d) seem to indicate that the students who are expected to perform well also obtain better results. One possible explanation would be that they are more motivated to do well during the tests. It should be clear that this result deviates considerably from the norms with respect to tests. Normally one expects them to measure only school achievement and nothing else. Therefore this result would indicate that the school test which is used is not a very valid test. For a valid test only β_{41} had to be very large, approximately 1, and all the other effects very small. In this analysis we have found that other variables have considerable effects on the test score as well. We will return to this point later because we still think that this result is unacceptable.

Finally, we discuss the equation which has been obtained for the last endogenous variable, "choice of secondary school", i.e.

$$y_5^d = .046y_2^d + .916y_3^d + .003y_4^d + \zeta_5 \qquad (14.1e)$$

In this case the variance of the disturbance term is really very small (.071), while the total variance of y_5^d is 3.178. This means that the unexplained variance is only 2.2% and the explained variance is 97.8%. This is a very good result which indicates that the right variables have indeed been introduced in the equation and it is probable that no important variables have been omitted. That is, all effects of the exogenous variables and the variable "scholastic achievement" are mediated by the intervening variables y_2^d, y_3^d and y_4^d. The empirical evidence indicates that this set is complete, which clarifies the mechanism by which these exogenous variables and achievement affect the secondary school choice.

The equation is also clear with respect to the relative importance of the different items of information used by the committee which finally determines the choice of secondary school. The result indicates that the committee normally follows the preferences of the parents, and that the effect of the recommendation of the teacher and the test score on this decision is only very minimal. This represents an interesting refinement of the original school career theory, in which the size of the various effects was unknown. Finally it should be noted that the last equation is so precise that, if we know the score of a student on y_2^d, y_3^d and y_4^d, we can almost exactly predict the type of school which the student attends. This is less true for predictions of the scores on the variables y_2^d, y_3^d and y_4^d by means of equations (14.1b), (14.1c) and (14.1d), because the variance of the disturbance term in these equations is larger. The prediction of the scholastic achievement score will even be very bad when equation (14.1a) is used.

Interpretation of the Standardized Solution

Most of the conclusions provided above could have been drawn from the standardized solution. The advantage of the unstandardized solution is that one can indicate the effects of different variables in the original measurement units, and that predictions for the endogenous variables can be computed (taking into account the value of the intercept). The disadvantage of the use of the unstandardized solution is that it is difficult to compare the sizes of the coefficients when they are computed for variables which have been expressed in different measurement units. If one wants to make such comparisons, the standardized solution has clear advantages, since all variables are expressed in the same units (standard deviations), and the effects indicate the change in the effect variable, expressed in standard deviations, caused by a change of one standard deviation in the causal variable, thereby keeping all the other variables in the equation constant. On the basis of this interpretation, the coefficients may be compared.

For the school career model the path diagram with standardized coefficients is presented in Figure 14.1. If the model is relatively simple, such diagrams are often given in the literature. Such path diagrams are very useful because one can see immediately what variables have the largest direct effect on the endogenous variable by comparing the values which are attached to all arrows coming in for the endogenous variable of interest. If we start with the variable "scholastic achievement" it is clear that the omitted variables (or disturbance term) have the largest effects. This means, as we already have seen, that this variable is not very well explained by the variables in the model. The two predetermined variables which have been introduced have approximately the same effect. Concerning the "teacher's recommendations" it is clear that

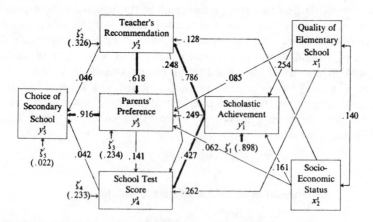

Figure 14.1 The Path Diagram of the Preferred School Career Model with Standardized Parameters as Estimated by LISREL

"scholastic achievement" has the largest direct effect while the "socio-economic status" of the parents contributes only very little to the explanation. The "preferences of the parents" are affected by many variables but the major direct effect comes from the "teachers' recommendation" and in addition only "scholastic achievement" has a moderately large direct effect. The situation for the "school test score" is unclear, since many variables affect this variable. At least we can say that the direct effect of "scholastic achievement" is the largest one, followed by the "quality of the elementary school" while the "parents' preferences" and the "teacher's recommendation" also have a moderate effect on this variable. Finally, if the direct effects on the "choice of a secondary school" are compared, there is no doubt that the "parents' preferences" have the largest effect, while the other two effects are very small.

The results of this comparison are shown in Figure 14.1 by presenting the largest direct effects for each endogenous variable by a thick arrow. In doing so the process which we have studied becomes very clear. The main stream of the process is that "scholastic achievement" affects the "teacher's recommendation", this variable then affects the "parents' preferences" and this variable affects the "choice of the secondary school". This result is far more precise than the original school career theory of the fourth chapter, where it was impossible to indicate which variable would be the most influential in each equation.

Direct, Indirect and Total Effects

Figure 14.1 underlines that one should not only concentrate on the direct effects between variables when one interprets a path diagram. For example, the variable "scholastic achievement" does not have a direct effect on the "choice of secondary school". This does not mean that this variable has no effect at all. In fact, "scholastic achievement" has a very important contribution in the process in an indirect way ,via the variables "teacher's recommendation" and "parents' preferences". This shows that if one is interested in the overall effect of different variables on each other, the discussion should not be restricted to the direct effects but should include indirect effects as well. The sum of these direct and indirect effects gives a better impression of what is called the *total effect* of a variable.

In some cases the computation of the total effects is rather easy and can be done directly from the path diagram. For example, the total effect of y_4^s on y_5^s is equal to the direct effect between the two (.042) since there is no indirect effect. The total effect of y_3^s on y_5^s is equal to a direct effect (.916) and an indirect effect via y_4^s (.141 $\times$ .042), which leads to a total effect of .92. Determination of the total effect of y_2^s on y_5^s becomes more complicated.

It is equal to the sum of the direct effect ($.046$), the indirect effect via y_3^s ($.618 \times .916$), the indirect effect via y_3^s and y_4^s ($.618 \times .141 \times .042$) and the indirect effect via y_4^s alone ($.248 \times .042$). In total this is $.627$. The computation of the total effect from y_1^s on y_5^s is even more complicated and it even becomes risky to compute the effect from the diagram, since there are so many different paths that one can easily forget one. Therefore a more formal procedure is needed for these complicated cases.

In order to explain the formal procedure the equations obtained from the data are once more repeated, but now for the standardized variables.

$$y_1^s = .254x_1^s + .161x_2^s + \zeta_1' \qquad (14.2a)$$
$$y_2^s = .786y_1^s + .128x_2^s + \zeta_2' \qquad (14.2b)$$
$$y_3^s = .249y_1^s + .618y_2^s + .085x_1^s + .062x_2^s + \zeta_3' \qquad (14.2c)$$
$$y_4^s = .427y_1^s + .248y_2^s + .141y_3^s + .262x_1^s + \zeta_4' \qquad (14.2d)$$
$$y_5^s = .046y_2^s + .916y_3^s + .042y_4^s + \zeta_5' \qquad (14.2e)$$

Given this set of equations the total effects can be derived for all variables in a systematic way. The procedure is illustrated for the total effect of the variable y_1^s on all the other y^s-variables.

If we start with the total effect on y_2^s the solution is very simple. Equation ($14.2b$) indicates that the effect is $.786$, since there is no indirect effect in this case from y_1^s. If we now move to the total effect of y_1^s on y_3^s, an indirect effect can be expected. This can also be seen in the equation because variable y_2^s is present in the equation for y_3^s and we know from equation ($14.2b$) that y_2^s is influenced by y_1^s. In order to derive the total effect we substitute equation ($14.2b$) in equation ($14.2c$), which leads to:

$$y_3^s = .249y_1^s + .618(.786y_1^s + .128x_2^s + \zeta_2') + .085x_1^s + .062x_2^s + \zeta_3'$$

After some reordering we get:

$$y_3^s = (.249 + .618 \times .786)y_1^s + .085x_1^s + (.062 + .618 \times .128)x_2^s + .618\zeta_2' + \zeta_3'$$
$$(14.3)$$

In this equation it is seen that the total effect of y_1^s on y_3^s is equal to $.249 + .618 \times .786$, which is also what we expect following the path diagram, since it is identical to the direct effect plus the indirect effect via y_2^s.

In the same way the total effect of y_1^s on y_4^s can be derived by substitution of ($14.2b$) and (14.3) in equation ($14.2d$). The equations ($14.2b$) and (14.3) have to be introduced because in the equation for y_4^s the variables y_2^s and y_3^s are present and they are at least partially influenced by y_1^s. We do not use equation ($14.2c$), because in ($14.2c$) y_2^s is mentioned and we would be forced to do the same substitution which we have already done before, and which has led to equation (14.3). In this case the result is:

$$y_4^s = .427y_1^s + .248(.786y_1^s + .128x_2^s + \zeta_2')$$
$$+ .141[(.249 + .618 \times .786)y_1^s + .085x_1^s$$
$$+ (.062 + .618 \times .128)x_2^s + .618\zeta_2' + \zeta_3']$$
$$+ .262x_1^s + \zeta_4'$$

After the reordering of terms we get:
$$
\begin{aligned}
y_4^s = (&.427 + .248 \times .786 + .141 \times .249 \\
&+ .141 \times .618 \times .786)y_1^s \\
&+ (.262 + .141 \times .085)x_1^s + \\
&+ (.248 \times .128 + .141 \times .062 \\
&+ .141 \times .618 \times .128)x_2^s \\
&+ (.248 + .141 \times .618)\zeta_2' \\
&+ .141\zeta_3' + \zeta_4'
\end{aligned}
\tag{14.4}
$$

Equation (14.4) shows that the total effect of y_1^s on y_4^s is rather complicated. It is equal to the direct effect .427 plus the indirect effect via y_2^s alone (.248 $\times$ .786) plus the indirect effect via y_3^s alone (.141 $\times$ .249) plus the indirect effect via both variables (.141 $\times$ .618 $\times$ .786). In total the effect is .725, which is a quite large effect and much larger than the direct effect alone, i.e. .427.

Finally, the total effect of y_1^s on y_5^s is derived by substitution of equations (14.2b), (14.3) and (14.4) in equation (14.2e) since the variables y_2^s, y_3^s and y_4^s all appear in equation (14.2e), which in turn are all influenced by y_1^s. The result is:
$$
\begin{aligned}
y_5^s = &.046(.786y_1^s + .128x_2^s + \zeta_2') \\
&+ .916[(.249 + .618 \times .786)y_1^s + .085x_1^s \\
&+ (.062 + .618 \times .128)x_2^s + .618\zeta_2' + \zeta_3'] \\
&+ .042[(.427 + .248 \times .786 + .141 \times .249 \\
&+ .141 \times .618 \times .786)y_1^s \\
&+ (.262 + .141 \times .085)x_1^s \\
&+ (.248 \times .128 + .141 \times .062 \\
&+ .141 \times .618 \times .128)x_2^s \\
&+ (.248 + .141 \times .618)\zeta_2' \\
&+ .141\zeta_3' + \zeta_4'] + \zeta_5'
\end{aligned}
$$

Reordering these terms as before leads to the following equation
$$
y_5^s = .740y_1^s + .089x_1^s + .137x_2^s + f(\zeta')
\tag{14.5}
$$
where $f(\zeta')$ is a function of all the disturbance terms. The result in equation (14.5) indicates that y_1^s has a quite large effect on y_5^s although the direct effect of this variable is equal to zero. This illustrates that one should not conclude on the basis of the size of the direct effect whether or not a variable has an effect on another variable; one has to use the total effect for this purpose. In this case the difference is very large because y_1^s has so many indirect effects as can be seen in Figure 14.1.

Equation (14.5) also indicates that, compared to the variable "school achievement", "quality of the school" and "socio-economic status" do not have very much effect on the final "choice of secondary school". This can be considered as a fortunate outcome, since one would like the choice of school to be based mainly on the "capacities" of the student. According to the results this is indeed true.

However one should not forget that the two predetermined variables both

Table 14.2   The Direct, Indirect and Total Effects of the Variables of the School Career Theory on Choice of Secondary School

Causal Variable	Direct Effect on y_5	Indirect Effect on y_5	Total Effect on y_5
School Test Score (y_4)	.042	.000	.042
Parents' Preference (y_3)	.916	.006	.922
Teacher's Recommendation (y_2)	.046	.581	.627
School Achievement (y_1)	.000	.740	.740
Quality of Elementary School (x_1)	.000	.277	.277
Socio-Economic Status (x_2)	.000	.256	.256

affect "scholastic achievement". If, therefore, one would like to determine the total effect of these two variables on y_5^s, one has to go one step further and substitute equation (14.2a) for y_1^s in equation (14.5), in order to get the total effect of x_1^s and x_2^s on y_5^s. If this is done one gets:

$$y_5^s = .740(.254x_1^s + .161x_2^s + \zeta_1') + .089x_1^s + .137x_2^s + f(\zeta')$$

and after some reordering and multiplications:

$$y_5^s = .277x_1^s + .256x_2^s + u_5 \qquad (14.6)$$

where $u_5 = f(\zeta') + .74\zeta_1'$

In this way it is apparent that both variables have an effect on the "choice of secondary school" and that the effects are about equally strong.

By now we have computed the total effects of all endogenous variables. In the same way the effects of all the other variables on each other can be computed. The next step is the comparison of the sizes of the different total effects. Obviously, this can only be done for the standardized coefficients because for unstandardized coefficients the measurement units are different and this would complicate the comparison. Therefore the standardized coefficients have been used here. In Table 14.2 all direct, indirect and total effects are presented. Table 14.2 shows that the largest change in the "choice of secondary school" can be obtained if we are able to change the "parents' preferences". In this case the direct and the total effect have approximately the same magnitude. With respect to the other variables, there is quite a difference between these two types of effects. According to the computed total effects, it is also very effective to try to raise the "teacher's recommendation" or to give the students extra training to increase their "scholastic achievement", since these two variables have also a quite large effect on the "choice of secondary

Table 14.3   The Total Effects of All Variables on All Endogenous Variables

TOTAL EFFECTS

TOTAL EFFECTS OF X ON Y

	X 1	X 2
Y 1	.254	.161
Y 2	.200	.254
Y 3	.271	.259
Y 4	.458	.168
Y 5	.277	.256

TOTAL EFFECTS OF Y ON Y

	Y 1	Y 2	Y 3	Y 4	Y 5
Y 1	0.000	0.000	0.000	0.000	0.000
Y 2	.786	0.000	0.000	0.000	0.000
Y 3	.735	.618	0.000	0.000	0.000
Y 4	.725	.335	.141	0.000	0.000
Y 5	.740	.627	.922	.042	0.000

school". Inspection of their direct effect does not suggest these possibilities. The exogenous variables have also some effect but much less than the other variables mentioned so far. These results suggest that only a slight effect can be expected from putting the student in a better school. If one really wants to improve a student's chances, one should manipulate the other variables. Finally, it is also clear from Table 14.2 that it does not help very much to train the students in filling in the test forms because the test score has only a very small effect on the whole process.

This example shows that the computation of the total effect is very useful and that one has to be careful with one's conclusions concerning the overall effects of variables up until one has computed the total effects. The difference between the direct and total effects can indeed be very considerable, as in the example discussed. Therefore it is important to compute the total effects before drawing conclusions about the overall effects of variables on other variables.

The LISREL program can be instructed to compute the total effects of all the variables on the endogenous variables. For the school career data the result is presented in Table 14.3. In the first matrix the estimated values for the total effects are presented. From this matrix a set of equations can be constructed in which the relationships are indicated between the endogenous variables and the exogenous variables, similar to equation (14.6) which we have derived before. In our example this set of equations is:

$$y_1^s = .254x_1^s + .161x_2^s + u_1 \qquad (14.7a)$$
$$y_2^s = .200x_1^s + .254x_2^s + u_2 \qquad (14.7b)$$
$$y_3^s = .274x_1^s + .259x_2^s + u_3 \qquad (14.7c)$$
$$y_4^s = .458x_1^s + .168x_2^s + u_4 \qquad (14.7d)$$
$$y_5^s = .277x_1^s + .256x_2^s + u_5 \qquad (14.7e)$$

It can be confirmed that equation (14.7e) is the same as equation (14.6) which we had derived. In the econometric literature this set of equations is called the *"reduced form"* and contrasts with the "structural form" discussed so far. Since the disturbances (or residuals) in these equations are functions of all the disturbances in the model, the disturbances in the reduced form are not independent of each other. In the second matrix of Table 14.3 the total effects of the endogenous variables on each other are given. The total effects of the different variables on y_5^s which we have derived above (Table 14.2) are presented in the fifth row as can be verified. The LISREL program computes the effects of all the other variables on each other as well. In this case effects different from zero are only found below the diagonal due to the fact that the model is recursive. In the case of nonrecursive models a full matrix can be obtained.

Some General Remarks

After a preferred model has been selected it is important to return to the interpretation of the causal mechanism which has produced the data in order to check whether the changes in the causal mechanism, as it was specified originally, make sense. In fact one should think about this point continuously while one is changing the model in order to improve the fit. In this example it was shown that the specified mechanism is not completely unrealistic, but in the next chapter it is shown that there is another simple model which corresponds more closely to the original theory.

It was also shown that the unstandardized solution has the advantage that the effects can be described in the original measurement units. This facilitates the computation of predictions for the endogenous variables in the original measurement units, given the values on the causal variables. On the other hand the standardized solution has the advantage that it allows comparison of different effects.

In the last section the total effects of variables were introduced and it was shown that one should use these coefficients to evaluate the overall effects of different variables. The direct effects should not be used alone, since they ignore the indirect effects of the variables. It should also be noted that the correlation coefficients should not be used to assess the overall effect of a variable, since they include the spurious and joint effects. An illustration of the errors that can be made with the use of the correlation coefficient for this purpose is the correlation between the "test score" (y_4^s) and the "choice of secondary school" (y_5^s), which is .775, while the total effect of variable y_4^s on y_5^s is only .042. This means that a very large part (.733) of the correlation is due to spurious relationships. This example shows very clearly that the use of the correlation coefficient to indicate the relative importance of effects can also lead to completely incorrect conclusions.

So the only right choice for the evaluation of overall effects of variables is the estimate of the total effect, which is also intuitively clear since it is the sum of the possible direct and indirect effects.

Further Reading

For the interpretation of the results one should consult the literature listed in chapters 2 and 3. The evaluation of the total effect of variables has been mainly studied by sociologists using path analysis. A clear discussion of this point is given by Duncan (1975), while the same topic is also discussed in papers of Finney (1972), Alwin and Hauser (1975) and Lewis-Beck (1974). Duncan also gives an illustration for nonrecursive models but for such models one needs matrix algebra. These models have therefore not been discussed here. Schmidt (1979) has given these derivations in terms of matrix algebra.

In all econometric text books which we have mentioned in chapters 10 and 11, the distinction between the structural form and the reduced form is discussed. However, the interpretation is not given in terms of total effects of the endogenous variables, as we have done in this text.

Exercises

14.1 Equation 14.1b indicates the effects of "scholastic achievement" (y_1^d) and "SES" (x_2^d) on the "teacher's recommendation" (y_2^d). This equation was

$$y_2^d = .062y_1^d + .155x_2^d + \zeta_2$$

(a)The effect of x_2^d seems much larger than the effect of y_1^d. Why is this not true?

(b)How much should y_1^d increase in order to obtain a "teachers recommendation" which is one level higher?

(c)How can one realize such a change in y_1^d?

(d)How much should x_2^d increase in order to obtain a "teacher's recommendation" which is one level higher?

(e)Is this change in x_2^d realistic?

(f)Is it also possible to say something about the absolute level of the variable y_2^d if we know the score on y_1^d and x_2^d for a student?

14.2 In Table 14.2 the direct and indirect effects on variable y_5^s are presented.

(a)Using Table 14.3 make a similar table for the variable y_3^s.

(b)Which variable has the largest total effect on y_3^s?

(c)Is this effect mainly due to the direct or indirect effects?

(d)If we want to change the "parents' preferences" which variable should be chosen to obtain an effect which is as large as possible?

(e)The choice of y_2^s in question 14.2d could be recommended because of the largest direct effect. Why is this choice nevertheless incorrect?

(f)Some people use the sizes of the correlation coefficients to determine which variable has the largest effect on another variable. Why is this approach also incorrect?

14.3 With respect to the secondary analysis:

(a)Give the interpretation of the final model in verbal form as we did in this chapter, comparing the model with the original model of the author.

(b)Indicate the most important direct and total effects.

(c)Draw conclusions with respect to possible changes in the variables if this was the purpose of the study.

Chapter 15
Has the Causal Mechanism been Revealed?

In earlier chapters it has been shown how models can be formulated, tested, corrected and simplified. The final question which has to be answered is: when can it be said that the causal mechanism for a certain process has been found? The mere fact that a model which fits the data has been obtained does not imply that this model is correct. It is always possible to propose various models which all fit a particular set of data. Therefore additional criteria are called for to determine whether the correct model has been obtained.

In this chapter three such criteria are discussed. Plausibility of the fitting model is the first. Secondly, the proportion of explained variance of the endogenous variables in the model should be sufficiently high. If the proportion of explained variance is low, it can mean either that (1) large measurement errors are ignored, or (2) important variables are missing or (3) the functional form of the relationships is different from the hypothesized form. Such specification errors in the models can generate serious biases in the parameter estimates and lead to wrong conclusions with respect to the causal mechanism. The third criterion is replicability of the results. The causal effects should be the same in different samples and at different points in time. If this is not so, the causal mechanism has not been discovered.

The Fit of the Model is not the Only Criterion

The mere fact that a model fits the data does not imply that this model is indeed the correct causal model. It can easily be shown that many models can perfectly fit the same set of data. In the first place, it is known that all full recursive models, i.e. models without reciprocal causation in which all possible effects are introduced, fit the data. This means that a model which fits can be found for any causal ordering of the variables. If there are 7 variables, as in our example, $7 \times 6 \times 5 \times 4 \times 3 \times 2 \times 1 = 5040$ causal orderings are feasible. Therefore there are certainly 5040 full recursive models which perfectly fit the same data for these seven variables. It can be expected, moreover, that these models can be simplified by omitting non-significant coefficients. This will lead to many more models that fit. But other kinds of models can be looked for as well. We may specify many nonrecursive models which will fit.

In sum, it is clear that many different models can be constructed which fit any set of data. Consequently the fit of a model can never "prove" the correctness of a model. Other criteria are necessary to choose a model out of all possible models that fit. Three will be discussed. The first criterion is the plausibility of the model.

The Plausibility as a Criterion

The *plausibility* of a model refers to a judgement made about the theoretical argument underlying the specified model. We suggest that the choice of a model as the correct causal model is partially made on theoretical grounds. In this text this criterion was used at the outset. In the second chapter it was suggested that the first thing to do is to specify the causal order of the variables. If the causal order is well-grounded in the theory or research design, a large number of models can be ruled out immediately. This consequence is very attractive but it has to be remembered that this decision is made on theoretical grounds and that therefore the conclusions are valid only if the decision is made on the basis of plausible arguments.

In our example, we believe that the assumptions made about the causal ordering of the variables can not be questioned since the ordering of the variables was based on the chronological sequence of events in the school career of a student. Therefore no variation on this point was introduced and no test of the causal ordering was made. This means that in this case $5040 - 1$ (that is, minus the one sequence of variables which we used throughout this text) models have been ruled out from the start, merely on the basis of the plausibility of the specific causal ordering of the variables.

The plausibility of a particular causal ordering is not always so strong. In such cases, empirical tests are necessary. For example, if for two endogenous variables the causal ordering is unclear, one can hypothesize reciprocal causation and test using the t-values whether both effects or only one of them, are significantly different from zero. Such a result will clarify the causal ordering of the variables. It should be clear, however, that one can not test all possible effects, allowing for all possible causal orderings. This is not possible because a model with reciprocal causation between all variables is not identified (the reader should check this). The causal ordering implied by the distinction between predetermined and endogenous variables is a minimal requirement in order to obtain an identifiable model. Given this partial ordering of the variables, the causal ordering of a few variables can be studied, but it will be clear that the possibilities are limited. In general the causal order is established in advance, by making assumptions, and is not tested by empirical evidence.

This means that a large number of models will be excluded completely on the basis of the plausibility of the theoretical argument.

But not only will models with different causal orderings of the variables be excluded on the basis of the plausibility criterion. The theory can also suggest in what parts of the model the specification is complete and where one might expect specification errors. In our example, it was argued on theoretical grounds in chapter 12 that specification errors are most likely to occur in the GAMMA matrix. We ruled out the possibility of errors in the PSI matrix (that is, we ruled out correlated disturbance terms). Although we did not expect specification errors in the BETA matrix, this possiblity could be considered if necessary. Given these restrictions, we looked in chapter 12 for a model that fits the data. It can be confirmed that the model which fits the data for the chosen restrictions is the only one which does so. This means that this would be the only plausible model which fits according to our theory. However it should be clear that other models which fit can be found if one allows other corrections to be made. For example, the reader can check whether other models which fit can be constructed, allowing for correlations between the disturbance terms. We ruled out these models since we did not expect to have omitted important variables in several equations at the same time.

This example illustrates that the plausibility criterion also helps to rule out certain models within the restrictions determined by the chosen causal ordering. These models are ruled out since they seem to be unrealistic on theoretical grounds. Using this approach three possible situations can result:

(1)It might be impossible to find a model which fits. In that case one has to conclude that the theory must be wrong.

(2)One model which fits is found. In this case the model can be accepted for the time being as the most likely candidate for the correct causal model.

(3)Several models which fit are found. In that case, one has to think of other tests to rule out some of these models as possible candidates.

In our example it appears that we ended up in the second situation, since only one model which fits has been found. However, this model also contains β coefficients, which we did not expect. It turned out that these effects were relatively large. The effect of "teacher's recommendation" on the "test score" was .248 and the effect of the "parents' preferences" on the "test score" was .241. Since we did not expect these effects to be so large, we still have serious doubts about the correctness of the model obtained. On the other hand, if this model is not correct one might wonder how one can ever find a model which fits within the restrictions we have specified with respect to the causal order and the plausible effects.

One possible mistake up to this point is that we have assumed that all variables are measured perfectly, that is without measurement error. It is possible that the residuals, which were found when the model of chapter 4 was tested, are due to measurement error. Although measurement problems require a much fuller treatment than is possible here, we will provide a brief illustration of their importance. The example illustrates very nicely how the use of the plausibility criterion can lead to very useful results.

Modelling Measurement Errors

In order to illustrate the possible impact of measurement errors, we begin once again with the model from chapter 4, which is shown in Figure 15.1. Most of the variables in this model are directly observable and were probably measured without serious errors. The one exception is the variable "scholastic achievement". This variable is measured by the teacher's prediction of the child's score on the test. This variable is certainly not the same as scholastic achievement. It is a judgement of the teacher about the achievement of the student, which is not necessarily the same as the achievement itself. Furthermore, the teacher's judgement is asked in a very special way. Therefore it is reasonable to make a distinction between the variable of interest and its indicator, the prediction score. This is done in Figure 15.2. In this new model these two variables are presented separately. The variable "scholastic achievement" is presented in a circle instead of a quadrangle in order to emphasize that this is not an observed variable like the rest, but an unobserved variable. This variable is assumed to exist and to have the place specified in the theory. The variable "teacher's prediction" is added and is a directly observed variable (it is the old variable 'scholastic achievement'). In this way

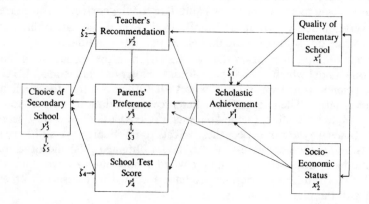

Figure 15.1   The Causal Diagram for the Full School Career Theory of Chapter 4

a distinction has been made between the "teacher's prediction" (of the test score) and the variable "scholastic achievement". The explanation of "teacher's prediction" of the test score is assumed to be the same as the explanation of the variable "teacher's recommendation".

If the theory of Figure 15.2 is correct, the effects of "scholastic achievement" on the other variables and the effects on "scholastic achievement" must have been underestimated in the earlier analysis since the wrong variable has been used for "scholastic achievement". Consequently many correlations between the y^s-variables and the y^s and x^s-variables must have been underestimated as well. Since this is exactly what we have seen in the analysis carried out so far, this new theory seems attractive as an alternative.

This is not the place to explain how the parameters of a model with unmeasured variables can be estimated and how such a model can be tested. However, the principle is no different from what we have done so far. The covariances and variances of the observed variables can be expressed in the parameters of the model and from these equations the parameters can be es-

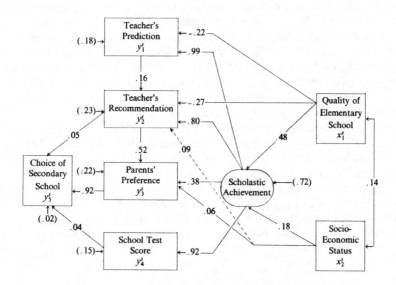

Figure 15.2 The Causal Diagram for the Adjusted School Career Theory, Making a Distinction between School Achievement and Teacher's Prediction of the Test Score. (The dashed line indicates an effect which is added later in order to obtain a model which fits)

timated if the model is identified. If $df > 0$ the model can even be tested.

If the same data as used before with the model depicted in Figure 15.2 are analyzed the result of the analysis with LISREL is a T value of 13.35 with 6 degrees of freedom (Pr = .04). If we compare this result with the fit of the model of chapter 4, which had a T value of 173.50 with 9 degrees of freedom, it is clear that the new model fits the data much better. The values obtained for the parameters are presented in Figure 15.2. If the effect of "socio-economic status" (SES) on "teacher's recommendation" is added to the model, the T value reduces to 2.52 with 5 degrees of freedom (Pr = .77). This model obviously fits the data. The parameter values change only minimally by this additional effect, while the effect itself is also very small (.09), but it is significantly different from zero.

These results lead to the interesting conclusion that the model of chapter 4 is rejected if it is tested against the data, assuming that the variable "prediction of the test score" is identical to "scholastic achievement". If it is assumed that these two variables differ, their correlation turns out to be .88, which differs considerably from 1, while the same model of chapter 4 with only one minor correction fits the data immediately. The parameter estimates are also in agreement with the expectations. All effects of "scholastic achievement" and all effects on "scholastic achievement" become larger. Consequently, all correlations between the y^s-variables become larger, as do the correlations between the y^s and x^s-variables. For this reason a model which fits better has been found and fewer corrections to the model are necessary than in earlier analyses. (The reader might wonder why two effects of the "quality of the elementary school" are negative, but this is not surprising if one looks at the argument for equation (4.2d) in chapter 4).

Having found this model which fits the data and which deviates only minimally from the suggested model in chapter 4, Blok and Saris (1979) drew the conclusion that this model is much more plausible than the earlier model which fits the data as well. For the time being they accepted the model of Figure 15.2, including the effect of "socio-economic status" on "teacher's recommendation", as the most likely candidate for the causal model.

These results show the importance of the plausibility criterion on the research process. It also shows that measurement procedures can play a very important role. For more information on this point we refer to the literature.

The Proportion of Explained Variance as a Criterion

Even if a plausible model which fits the data is found, this does not imply that the correct causal model has been found. One obvious point of criticism might be that the variables do not explain enough of the variance of the endogenous variables. In general, this means that specification errors are present in the model and that therefore the estimates of the parameters are not very informative. Given this consequence, there is good reason to use the proportion of explained variance as a criterion for the decision whether or not to accept the model as correct. If the explained variance is too low, one should not accept the model as correct.

Of course this argument leads immediately to the question of how large the proportion of explained variance has to be in order to accept a model as a possible candidate for the correct causal model. In order to answer this question, a distinction has to be made between the situation in which variables are measured perfectly and the situation in which some variables contain measurement error. For good quality data an R^2 of approximately .90 should be required. This target is much higher than one finds in most empirical studies in the social sciences. However a high threshold is necessary in order to avoid unjustified causal inferences. If the explained variance is lower, it becomes more likely that important variables have been omitted. If these variables are also related with the causal variables, spurious relationships are ignored which can lead to biased estimates of the effects. Only if the unexplained variance is rather small ($<$ 10%), one can trust the estimates of the causal effects. It is our experience that this threshold can be reached if good data are available and much attention is paid to the theory formulation.

If the data contain measurement error, the explained variance will in general be much lower. Elsewhere it is indicated how one can correct for measurement error. Taking these corrections into account, we think that one has to insist that the proportion of explained variance should be approximately .90 before one can decide to accept a model as a candidate for the correct causal model.

The second question to be dealt with is what one must do if the required proportion of explained variance is not obtained. Apart from the possibility of measurement error, which should first be taken into account, there are two other possibilities. The first is that important causal variables have been omitted. The second is that the form of the relationships between the variables is incorrectly specified. In both cases one has to go back to the theory to see which variables might have been omitted or at what point the specification of the relationships might have been incorrect. In fact, this means that the empirical cycle (Figure I.1) is started all over again. In order to make the discussion more concrete, these points are illustrated once more with the school career example.

The Form of the Relationships Reconsidered

In Figure 15.2 the school career model is presented which we have accepted as a possible candidate for the correct causal model, since the model fits the data

and was also plausible according to our theoretical hypotheses. In the diagram
the estimates of all parameters are also indicated. If we compute the explained

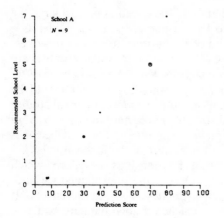
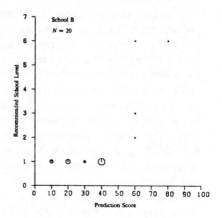
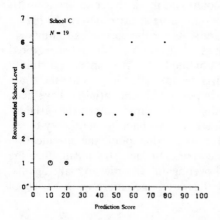

Figure 15.3   The Relationships between the Variables "Prediction Score" and
"Teacher's Recommendation" for Three Schools. The Sizes of
the Octagons indicate the Frequencies with which the Points
occur.

variance, which is identical to 1 minus the variance of the disturbance term, we see that the choice of the secondary school and the test score are explained approximately at the required level (.98 and .85 respectively). The proportion of explained variance of the other variables is not high enough according to the previously established criterion. This means that we have to look for the misspecifications in the model which caused this lack of explained variance. It would take too long to discuss all the variables again here. Therefore we will concentrate on the variable "teacher's recommendation" since this variable plays an important role in the model and has the lowest proportion of explained variance.

The possibility of omitted variables was explored first. In chapter 4 it was suggested that the levels of the secondary schools in the surroundings of the elementary school might play a role in the recommendations by the teacher. However, the test of this hypothesis only led to an improvement of explained variance of one percent, which is insufficient (see Saris and Blok, 1982). Since no other omitted variables could be discovered, we continued to explore the possibility that the form of the relationship was wrongly specified. After much exploration it was discovered that teachers in different schools use different strategies in translating the prediction of the test score into a recommendation for a secondary school. In Figure 15.3 the relationships between these two variables are presented for three different schools. This figure illustrates that the school teachers are rather systematic in their judgements. In all three cases there is a very systematic relationship. However, it is clear that the relationships differ from school to school. It seems that each teacher has his/her own system to split up the continuum of the 'prediction score' variable into 'achievement' categories for which different recommendations are made. In school A a recommendation for school type 2 or higher is given if the prediction score is 30 or higher (although one pupil with a prediction score of 30 is recommended for the lowest type of secondary school). In school B this is done if the prediction score is higher than 50, etc. These data illustrate that the relationship between the predicted school achievement and the recommendation differs from school to school. This means that so far we have obtained an average relationship which is possibly not applicable to any of the schools. The fact that this complication in this relationship was ignored might have been the reason that the proportion of explained variance for the variable "teacher's recommendation" is too low.

In order to see whether the proportion of explained variance can be increased if the differences between the schools are taken into account, a new variable was created, called "school potential". This variable has as many categories as the variable "teacher's recommendation", i.e. 7. For each school a student's potential is simply determined as the highest recommended school type within his or her predicted achievement group. The coding scheme is illustrated by means of Figure 15.4. In school D 6 students received a predicted achievement score of 6; the highest recommended school type within this group of students is 3. Therefore all of these six students obtain the score 3 on the "school potential" variable. The elementary school teacher seems to think that school type 3 is feasible for these students, although sometimes a lower score is given. In the same way the students with prediction score 7 were given the 'potential score' 5, which is the highest recommendation in this category for school D. Following this procedure a potential score is given to each student, using the relationship between the predicted achievement and the type of school recommended by his or her own teacher. In this way the 'school potential' is a teacher specific classification of the students according to the teacher's subjective evaluation of the relationship between the prediction score and the possible recommendations.

This is an example of an ad hoc procedure which typically involves making use of the empirical distributions. Nevertheless, it is interesting to

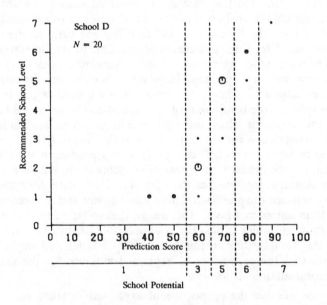

Figure 15.4   The Determination of the Scores for the New Variable "School Potential" Using the Information about the Relationship between the "Prediction Score" and the "Teacher's Recommendation" in School D

see whether more can be explained concerning the recommendation variable if the fact that each school teacher specifies his or her own relationship between the predicted achievement. This hypothesis can be tested by exploring the relationship between the "teacher's recommendation" and the new variable "school potential". It turns out that for these two variables the explained variance is .90. This means that an increase of 21% in the proportion of explained variance has been obtained. One has to be careful with drawing conclusions from this fact. The result merely suggests that instead of having omitted important variables, the form of the relationship between the prediciton score and the teacher's recommendation is school specific. It has been shown that, by taking this condition into account, the required threshold for explained variance is reached.

In relation to the general discussion in this chapter, this example illustrates that it makes sense to use the proportion of explained variance as a criterion for the decision whether or not one accepts a model as correct. In this example we have seen that rejection of a model which does not explain enough variance can lead to considerable improvements in the specification of the model and therefore to more insight into the causal process itself. Our impression is that, in general, social science researchers are too easily satisfied with the results obtained in an analysis. If the proportion of explained variance is as low as .40 we do not think that one can have faith in the correctness of the specified causal model. In such cases there is a very high risk of drawing wrong conclusions from the results obtained, since they are most likely in error.

Replicability of Results as a Criterion

If a model with an acceptable fit has been found, which is plausible from a theoretical point of view and explains enough of the variance of the endogenous variables, we can still not be certain that the correct causal model has been found. The possibility exists that the accepted model only fits the set of data for which the model has been developed. One ought to be aware of this possibility, especially if the model has been improved using the same data set over and over again. The danger of modelling the features which are peculiar to a specific sample and data set, is called "capitalization on chance". Therefore, a question which should be raised after the data exploration is whether the introduced corrections in the model are really necessary ? This means that we want to test whether the subset of parameters which are making up the difference between two models are so important that they have to be included in the model. This question is a special case of the question whether a subset of parameters of a model is significantly different from zero and therefore should be included.

A formal test can be specified for such questions if:
(1) the two models which are compared are hierarchically ordered
(2) the less restrictive model fits the data.

With *hierarchical ordering of models* is meant that the more restrictive model can be obtained from the less restrictive model by introducing restrictions on a number of parameters. If two models are not hierarchically ordered there can always be found a third model of which both models are specific cases. In such a case the overidentifying restrictions towards that third model can be tested. In the other case the overidentifying restrictions going from the less restricted to the more restricted can be tested.

Why the second condition was stated is difficult to explain yet but this condition will become evident if the testing procedure is explained.

The significance test which will be discussed next is based on the following argument: Suppose that the more restrictive model has df_0 degrees of freedom and has a value for the test statistic of T_0 while the alternative, less restrictive model, has df_a degrees of freedom and a value of the test statistic of T_a for the same data. The fact that the models are hierarchical means that the more restricted model is a special case of the other model and can be obtained by introduction of $df_0 - df_a$ additional restrictions. If these restrictions are correct, we expect that the difference d which is equal to $T_0 - T_a$, will be relatively small. If the restrictions are not correct we expect that the statistic d will be rather large because the fit of the restricted model will be much less than the fit of the alternative model which does not contain the incorrect restrictions.

A test of significance for the statistic d can be formulated for hierarchical models. This test is based on the following general result which holds under the same conditions which have been discussed in the chapter on testing:

> The statistic d is approximately distributed as a χ^2 variable if the restrictions are correct and as a noncentral χ^2 variable if the restrictions are incorrect. The number of degrees of freedom for this test are equal to the difference in degrees of freedom between the two models.

Given this result it will be clear that the same approach can be used as in chapter 11 to formulate a test. For a given significance level and degrees of freedom the critical value of the test can be determined. Furthermore alternative models can be formulated for which the power of the specified test can be evaluated. If the power is too low or too high the test can be adjusted as we have shown in that chapter.

An even stronger test is that, for any set of data, changes in the causal variables should lead to the same changes in the endogenous variables. If this can be shown, one can be more certain that the causal mechanism has been established and that the coefficients are the structural parameters. If not, the causal mechanism has not been found yet and one has to look for the variable(s) which do change the coefficients from one to another set of data.

Is there a formal procedure by which the hypothesis that the coefficients remain the same from data set to data set can be tested? Obviously, the parameter estimates can be obtained for each sample separately, by maximizing the criterion function Cr_{ML}, as we have indicated in chapter 10, where

$$\text{Cr}_{ML} = L_k \{ f_{ij}(p_k) \} \text{ for the } k^{\text{th}} \text{ sample} \qquad (15.1)$$

But in using the approach it is difficult to test whether the sets of parameters from the different samples are the same. In LISREL a more efficient alternative procedure is available, called multi-sample analysis. In the alternative procedure all parameters are estimated simultaneously by maximizing a criterion function which is the product of the forms in (15.1)

$$\text{Cr}_{ML} = L_1 \{ f_{ij}(p_1) \} L_2 \{ f_{ij}(p_2) \} \ldots L_k \{ f_{ij}(p_m) \} \qquad (15.2)$$

under the condition that

$$p_1 = p_2 = \ldots = p_m = p \qquad (15.3)$$

This criterion function is identical to the likelihood function for m nonoverlapping samples if the variables are multivariate normally distributed. If so, this estimation procedure leads once again to maximum likelihood estimators. The test of the hypothesis in equation (15.3) is performed against a model which fits perfectly for each set of data. It can be formulated with the likelihood ratio statistic

$$\frac{\text{Cr}_{ML}(\hat{p}_{Ma})}{\text{Cr}_{ML}(\hat{p}_{Mp})} \qquad (15.4)$$

In this form $\hat{p}_{Ma}$ represents the set of parameter values which have been estimated under the assumption of a model in which the parameters for all data sets are equal to each other, while $\hat{p}_{Mp}$ represents the set of parameter values which leads to a perfect fit to all data sets. The χ^2 distribution can be used once more for this test, because -2 times the logarithm of the likelihood ratio statistic is χ^2 distributed, at least for large samples. The number of degrees of freedom is equal to the total number of distinct elements in all covariance matrices together minus the total number of parameters which has to be estimated.

In practice the procedure is only slightly more complex than the analysis of one sample at a time. The problem with this test is more at the substantive level, since it is often very difficult to find appropriate sets of data for purposes of comparison. These points can be illustrated with an example.

Multi-Sample Analysis with LISREL

Up to this point the school career model has been tested with data which were collected in 1977 and which were representative for the population of

Dutch school children who were on the point of going from the elementary to the secondary school. In order to test whether the obtained results are replicable with other data, it was necessary to find another set of data for the same population at a different point in time. The most complete data set which could be found was collected in 1966 with a sample of 1738 students. However in this data set, data for only 6 of the 7 variables were collected. The variable "parents' preferences" was not measured in 1966. Furthermore, some variables were defined somewhat differently in that other categories were used.

For these two sets of data, the categories of all available variables were made as identical as possible, while the changes in the categories of the 1977 study have been restricted to a minimum in order to keep the results as comparable as possible. The consequence for the analysis of the 1977 data is that the differences in the correlation and covariance matrices are indeed very small (at most .006) and can be ignored.

We also had to check what would happen if the variable "Parents' Preferences" was omitted, in order to see whether it would later be possible to compare the earlier results with the new results. This would not be the

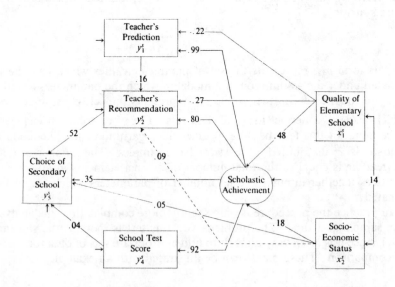

Figure 15.5   The Causal Diagram for the Simplified School Career Theory derived from Figure 15.2 by Omitting the Variable "Parents' Preferences" (y_3^s) with the Expected Values for the Parameters

case if completely different results were obtained in an analysis of the reduced data set. The result which we expected, based on our analyses in the earlier stage, is summarized in Figure 15.5. This result is derived from Figure 15.2 by leaving out the variable "parents' preferences". The consequences of this simplification are that some indirect effects become direct effects while some direct effects become larger. The derivation is made using the procedure explained in the previous chapter to compute total effects (the reader should check this).

In analyzing the reduced correlation matrix from 1977, using the model of Figure 15.5, a problem arose. The problem was that no solution was obtained if the effects of "teacher's recommendation", "scholastic achievement" and "school test score" on the "choice of secondary school" were all three introduced into the model. The problem probably arose because of the very high correlations between these three variables. For this reason it was decided to fix the effect of the 'school test score', which was expected to be only .04, at zero. Having introduced this minor specification error, the program could compute a solution and an acceptable fit for this model was obtained ($T = 3.55$, Pr $= .17$). More importantly, all parameter estimates for this analysis were very close to the expected values presented in Figure 15.5. The largest deviation was 0.08, which might well be due to the small error which had been introduced. Since this result is in such close agreement with the earlier result, further comparisons with other data sets make sense, using the model of Figure 15.5 instead of the model in Figure 15.2.

The basic information for the two sets of data is summarized in Tables 15.1 and 15.2. Some differences are immediately apparent when we compare these two tables. First we see that the means of all variables have increased in the period from 1966 to 1977, while the standard deviations (with the exception of x_2^5) have decreased during the same period. This is indicative of a trend in Dutch society to give better and more equal chances to all pupils in the education system (de Jong et al., 1982).

In the correlation matrices, the most striking difference is the decrease of the correlations with the variable "quality of the elementary school". The reason for these large differences is that in 1966 special groups were set up for children who had been chosen to receive different types of secondary education. They were also trained differently. This system was abolished between 1966 and 1977. This difference represents a structural change in the process and therefore one can expect deviations in the parameters. Nevertheless, for illustrative purposes, we begin with the assumption that all parameters remained the same from 1966 to 1977.

Due to the fact that our model is more complex than the models without unmeasured variables, we can not explain the analysis here. For this topic we refer to the LISREL Users Guide. The result of the analysis is that the

Table 15.1   The Summary Statistics for the 1966 Data of the School Career
Study

	y_1	y_2	y_3	y_4	x_1	x_2
y_1	1.000					
y_2	.725	1.000				
y_3	.791	.699	1.000			
y_4	.650	.755	.648	1.000		
x_1	.682	.472	.651	.486	1.000	
x_2	.283	.298	.274	.308	.282	1.000
mean	43.23	2.30	43.19	2.45	46.95	2.86
s.d.	28.08	2.10	28.63	2.03	28.72	1.10

Table 15.2   The Summary Statistics for the 1977 Data of the School Career
Study

	y_1	y_2	y_3	y_4	x_1	x_2
y_1	1.000					
y_2	.811	1.000				
y_3	.811	.764	1.000			
y_4	.792	.861	.775	1.000		
x_1	.276	.191	.466	.283	1.000	
x_2	.196	.282	.244	.297	.140	1.000
mean	53.71	3.05	50.46	3.26	50.95	3.25
s.d.	22.51	1.78	27.81	1.78	28.04	1.47

same parameter values are obtained for both sets of data and that the test
statistic is computed for the hypothesis specified in equation (15.3), i.e. that
all parameters remain the same. The value of the test statistic was 346.39
with 20 degrees of freedom. This means that this hypothesis has to be rejected
as we expected. So we must conclude that not all coefficients remain the same
through time.

In order to shorten the discussion we have next tested the hypothesis that
only the effects of 'quality of the elementary school' on the other variables
were different. However this was not sufficient to obtain an acceptable fit.
Next the assumption that the variances of the disturbance terms are identical
through time was relaxed. In this case an acceptable fit was obtained (T =
16.78, df = 12 and Pr = .16). Table 15.3 presents the result.

The result suggests that the same model could be fitted to both sets of data
and that the effect parameters in these two sets of data remained the same,
apart from the effect parameters relating to the variable "quality of elementary
school". This is a remarkable result because it shows that, with the exception of three effect parameters, replicable results have been obtained for all
effect parameters in the model. This provides a basis for confidence in the
correctness of the causal model formulated in this study.

After this illustration some general remarks should be made about such com-

Table 15.3   The Parameter Values of the School Career Theory estimated simultaneously with LISREL

Effect on	Effect from	Estimated Parameter Value in	
		1966	1977
Achievement	School Quality	.618	.439
Achievement	Socio-Economic Status	2.856	2.856
Achievement	Disturbance	320.904	479.636
Predicted Test	School Quality	.114	-.170
Predicted Test	Achievement	.852	.852
Predicted Test	Disturbance	184.201	102.327
Recommendation	School Quality	-.013	-.017
Recommendation	Socio-Economic Status	.131	.131
Recommendation	Achievement	.050	.050
Recommendation	Predicted Test	.020	.020
Recommendation	Disturbance	1.658	.766
Test Score	Achievement	1.000*	1.000*
Test Score	Disturbance	143.177	106.478
School Choice	Socio-Economic Status	.093	.093
School Choice	Achievement	.026	.026
School Choice	Recommendation	.487	.487
School Choice	Disturbance	1.575	.669

* This coefficient has been fixed to 1 for reasons of identification.

parative studies. In the first place, much effort should be devoted to making the scales of observed variables comparable and to correct for possible deviations in the sampling procedure between the different samples. Otherwise the procedures described here might lead to misleading results and erroneous conclusions. Secondly, something has to be said about standardization. Where the scales for all variables are made identical between the different samples, the coefficients are directly comparable from sample to sample even when the variances of the variables differ considerably between the samples. There is therefore no reason to standardize the variables. This means that in this case one should analyze the covariance matrix instead of the correlation matrix. If the correlation matrices are analyzed, one does not test whether the unstandardized effects remain the same across the samples but whether the standardized coefficients do. These are the unstandardized effects multiplied by the ratio of the standard deviations of the causal and endogenous variables. But this is quite a different test from the one we want to perform and the results can also be quite different. This test with standardized variables would also require the equality of the ratio of the standard deviations or some process by which the differences which occur are compensated for.

This kind of comparative replication has been neglected too much in the social sciences. But we hope here to have indicated that a test of the replicability of the results on new data is a necessary requirement in the process of determining whether the correct causal model has been found.

What Next?

Having gone through all these steps, the reader may wonder what the next step is. Obviously, the answer depends on the results obtained in the different stages. If a plausible fitting model is found which has sufficient explanatory power and can be replicated on any new set of data, the research process is completed and there is a reasonable probability that the correct causal model has been found. In such cases one can also have confidence in the conclusions derived from these results, which means that the results can be applied in practice.

This satisfactory stituation is, however, reached in only a very few cases in the social sciences. In many fields, models still do not fit the data at all well. Often this is not even detected by reseachers developing the models since they did not test them rigorously enough. In such cases the procedures described in chapters 11, 12 and 13 of this text need to be followed.

Another very common situation in the social sciences is that very little of the variance in the endogenous variables is explained. This is probably often due to the use of very unreliable or invalid measurement instruments. Further study of measurement errors is the necessary step in such cases. It seems that many social scientists are easily satisfied with their results. An explained variance of 40% is commonly accepted as a good result. We think that in such cases there is good reason to start all over again with the model, because it will certainly contain serious specification errors.

If one is in the situation where the results of a study can not be replicated with new data, one has to think of variables which might have caused the differences in the parameter values. Such exercises can provide completely new insight into the causal mechanism or into the conditions under which the specified model will hold true.

Finally, the key to good results is the time spent on developing a plausible model. Our impression is that not enough time is spent on this phase of research in the social sciences. Often models are developed by model fitting which makes them vulnerable to chance capitalization. It also leads to trial-and-error models which are rejected with the same ease as they have been formulated. This procedure does not seem to be very fruitful. If the researcher takes the effort to spend a lot of time in formulating a plausible explanation for each variable, it is also more likely that the explained variance will be higher and that replication of the results is possible. Such a time consuming activity can not be undertaken for very large models. In such cases the work tends to become superficial. We suggest that one reduces the problems to manageable proportions in order to obtain results.

The school career study provides a good example. The problem was made manageable by ignoring the explanation of the scholastic achievement scores. Such an explanation would require a different study. Then a lot of time was invested in developing a reasonable model for each equation (chapter 4), until the researchers had confidence in the formulation. Having done this they stuck to this theory, even though the model was first rejected and they found other models which could fit the data in the process. These models were rejected because they believed that it was possible to find a model to fit the data which was closer to the original theory. We have also seen that this effort paid off, because it turned out that the theory specified in chapter 4 fitted the data, if the measurement errors in one variable were taken into account. This final result was also much more plausible than the easily obtainable results derived in the earlier chapters by a series of model correction steps without correction for measurement error.

The considerable time spent on the development of the theory also paid off in the sense that relatively high proportions of explained variances were obtained and that the results could by and large be replicated. Nevertheless, we do consider that in this example the correct description of the causal mechanism has not yet been found. An illustration of this point was given in the section where we showed that, by formulating a conditional relationship for the "teacher's recommendation" variable, the proportion of explained variance could be increased from .68 to .90. It is likely that similar results can also be obtained for the variable "parents' preferences". New studies in this field should concentrate on this point and on the replication of the result for the variable "teacher's recommendation" which we have presented in this chapter.

This discussion indicates that one has to decide what has to be done next depending on the state of the results. In some cases one has to start all over again. In other cases detailed studies are required. If the results already appear satisfactory, replications must be carried out. The whole series of studies can be terminated when a plausible model has been found which explains enough of the variance of the endogenous variables and which fits different sets of data simultaneously. It will be clear that these requirements are fulfilled in only a few research fields. Nevertheless our point of view is that these requirements should be fulfilled before one can have confidence in inferences drawn from the results of causal modelling.

Further Reading

The topics discussed in this chapter have so far received little attention in the literature. There are several books discussing the formulation of causal models, for example Blalock (1964, 1969b), but these set the discussion in a different context from that presented here.

The requirement of high proportions of explained variance has been debated for some time, see for example Duncan (1975). In this topic we have clearly chosen for the "hard" line because the consequence of another position is the possibility of specification errors and biased estimators in the models preferred. This issue is discussed extensively in the econometric literature which we have already mentioned before.

The testing of subsets of parameters has been discussed by Satorra and Saris (1985) and an example of such a test on the same data used here is given by Saris, Den Ronde and Satorra (1984).

The simultaneous analysis of several data sets is only discussed in technical texts such as Jöreskog (1969), Lawley and Maxwell (1971) and Sörbom (1975). The topic of whether to standardize or not has been discussed very clearly by Kim and Ferree (1981), where references to the whole discussion on the merits of standardization can be found.

Exercises

15.1 In this chapter it was indicated that one of the arguments used to defend a model as the causal model is its plausibility. In this exercise we will try to criticize the school career model on this point.

(a) Is there any other causal ordering of the variables possible given the sequence of events presented in chapter 2?

(b) Can you think of variables affecting more than one variable in the model which have been omitted?

(c) Can you give a good argument for the large effects of y_2^s and y_3^s on y_4^s which have been found?

(d) Is the argument acceptable to you that "scholastic achievement" is not well measured?

(e) What is your overall idea of the plausibility of the model?

15.2 The second criterion is explained variance. We have given three reasons for low explained variance.

(a) Why can measurement error lead to low explained variance?

(b) Why can omitted variables lead to low explained variance?

(c) Why can wrong model specifications lead to low explained variance?

(d) Give for all three cases an argument as to why they might lead to bad estimates of the parameters and wrong conclusions (specify models to illustrate this point).

15.3 The third criterion is replicability

(a)Some people split their sample in two parts. On one part they try to find a fitting model. The second part is used for a test. Is this a proper replication study?

(b)It is also possible to test the same model in different subgroups at the same point in time. Is this a proper replication study?

(c)If the test of the hypothesis specified in equation (15.3) indicates that the effects are different, what does this mean?

15.4 With respect to the secondary analysis.

(a)Check what the state of the art is on the three criteria for the topic you have studied.

(b)Decide what should be done next:

(c)Having gone through all the steps necessary to write the paper, you can now finish it off by preparing a paper on the basis of the answers to the different questions. Normally a paper consists of the following sections:

Introduction

Theory (of the writer, critic, your own theory)

Data (the measurement procedures, reliability, validity; and the sampling procedure and quality of the sample)

Methodology (procedures for estimation, testing, correction and simplification)

Results (test of the model of the author, of your own model, possible corrections and simplifications and the final interpretation)

Discussion (indicate the state of the research and what has to be done next).

Epilogue

In the introduction it was mentioned that several approaches have been developed to test and analyze causal theories for nonexperimental data. In this epiloque a comparison is made between the different approaches in order to give the reader some idea of the position of the LISREL approach in the full gamut of possibilities.

The different approaches are more or less discussed in the historical sequence in which they appeared in the literature. The first approach which is discussed is the analysis of cross-tables used in the matching procedure and continued in loglinear modelling. Secondly the correlational approach is presented. Subsequently the path analysis is discussed as well as the econometric approach. Finally, the LISREL approach is placed in this context.

Cross-Table Analysis

Cross-table analysis is especially useful for data which are not metric of nature. For such data it is possible to form groups of respondents with the same score on several variables. Within such groups the relationship between two other variables can be studied. For example in Table E.1 the relation between the variables "quality of elementary school" (x_1), "socio-economic status" (x_2), "scholastic achievement" (y_1) and "choice of secondary school" (y_2) is presented in an adjusted way. Within the eight groups that have been formed, the scores of the respondents on three variables are approximately the same. The word 'approximately' is used because the scores on the original variables have been categorized in only two classes. A contrast is made between pupils which have a score above and below the mean. This recoding of the data is made in order to simplify the presentation. We will return to this point later.

If the data are summarized in this form the effects of the variables on each other can be studied. For example, the difference between group 1 and 2 with respect to their "choice of a secondary school" can only be caused by the variable y_1 which is the variable "scholastic achievement" since the pupils have the same score on the other variables x_1 and x_2. If the variables presented are the only important variables, the comparison of groups 1 and 2 indicates whether the variable y_1 has an effect on the variable y_2 for these specific groups. Comparison of group 3 with group 4, 5 with 6 and 7 with 8 provides similar information for the relationship between the variables y_1 and y_2, but each time

286

Table E.1 The Cross-Table of the Variables of the Simplified School Career Model

Group Number	x_1	x_2	y_1	Absolute Number with $y_2 = 1$	Percentage with $y_2 = 1$	Total Number of Respondents
1	0	0	0	2	2.9	69 = 100%
2	0	0	1	29	60.4	48 = 100%
3	0	1	0	1	2.9	35 = 100%
4	0	1	1	31	86.1	36 = 100%
5	1	0	0	1	2.1	47 = 100%
6	1	0	1	29	46.8	62 = 100%
7	1	1	0	1	6.7	15 = 100%
8	1	1	1	38	53.5	71 = 100%
Total				132	34.5%	383 = 100%

for different sub-groups. In this case we see that the difference between groups 1 and 2 in "choice of secondary school" is 57.5%. For groups 3 and 4, 5 and 6 and 7 and 8 we find respectively 83.2%, 44.7% and 46.8%. For all subgroups there seems to be a considerable effect of the variable "scholastic achievement" on the "choice of the secondary school".

A similar analysis can be done in order to determine whether the effect of x_1 on y_2 exists. This can be done by comparison of group 1 with 5, 2 with 6, 3 with 7 and 4 with 8. In this case the the differences are respectively -0.8 The effect does not seem to be very large. Only the last comparison shows a considerable difference. For the subgroup with a high social economic status ($x_2 = 1$) and good scholastic achievement ($y_1 = 1$), the quality of the elementary school (x_1) makes a difference in secondary school choice.

Finally we can also analyze the effect of x_2 on y_2 by comparison of group 1 with 3, 2 with 4, 5 with 7 and 6 with 8. In these cases the differences are respectively 0%, 25.7%, 4.6% and 6.7%. From these results we see that in fact for only one subgroup the effect exists, namely for the group which is at a school below average ($x_1 = 0$), and which has a scholastic achievement above average ($y_1 = 1$).

Although the causal hypotheses can be tested in this way, a major problem with this approach is that the comparisons are often made on the basis of very few cases. This is in the given example not so clear because the variables were recoded. But if the original variables would have been used with respectively

10, 6 and 10 classes for x_1, x_2 and y_1 the total number of groups would have become $10 \times 6 \times 10 = 600$. In such a situation one needs very large samples in order to obtain reasonable numbers of cases in the different groups for the comparisons. If there are even more variables as is the case in this study the situation becomes nearly impossible unless one has samples up to 30.000 cases. Only census bureau's can afford to draw such samples occasionally. This means that the comparison of specific groups is only possible in case of a study of variables with a limited number of categories. In general this leads to a recoding of the variables. This reduces of course the precision of the measurement and as a consequence not all respondents in the different groups can be seen as having the same score anymore. This means that one has not completely ruled out the possibility that the differences between the various groups on the effect variables can be attributed to the differences between the respondents on other variables than the causal variables of interest.

Recently a more efficient approach has been developed which is known as *loglinear modelling*. The procedure is very similar to the approach which has been discussed here for metric variables. This similarity can be seen very clearly by comparison of Figure I.1 and Figure E.1. Figure E.1 indicates that the only difference is the kind of model which is specified and the kind of data which is used to estimate the parameters and to test the model. The model parameters do not describe the covariances between the variables but the frequencies which can be expected in the cells of a table like the one we presented in Table E.1. These parameters can be estimated from the data summarized in the table. Next a test of the model can be done by comparing the reproduced frequencies given the values of the parameters with the observed frequencies. For this test the maximum likelihood ratio test can be used and the reasoning in the model estimation, testing and fitting is the same as the one we discussed for the LISREL approach.

This procedure for the analysis of cross-tables with loglinear models is more efficient than the earlier approaches like matching and elaboration because the parameters are estimated using all information available in the table at once. In the earlier approaches the effects were estimated for each pair of groups separately. This does not mean that the problem of the sample size is completely unimportant in this case. Even in this more efficient approach one needs a very large number of cases if one wants to detect very specific effects.

An important advantage of the loglinear approach compared with the LISREL approach is that no assumptions are necessary with respect to linearity and additivity. It is possible to detect conditional relationships very easily by this approach and these loglinear models with conditional relationships can be estimated and tested just as easily. This point can be illustrated with the example given in Table E.1. Here one can see that the effects of the different variables are not identical for the different groups. For example,

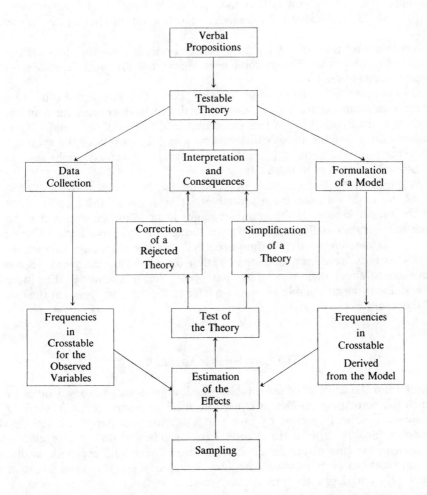

Figure E.1   A Flow Chart for the Testing of Causal Hypotheses for Categorical Variables

the effect of y_1 on y_2 is for the first two groups 57.5% while the same effect is equal to 83.2% for the third and fourth group. A test on the differences of the effects can be performed routinely and parameters can be introduced in the model. The LISREL models do not take these interaction effects into account. The assumption is that they are not present or at least not very important. Otherwise a LISREL model has to be reformulated (see chapter 4).

Another advantage of the loglinear procedure is that the variables are not assumed to be metric. The example even shows that the procedure does not require ordinal variables.

On the other hand, the example has also shown that in practice often very crude measurements have to be used in order to have enough cases in the various cells of the table. In fact this might lead to loss of very much information. Such simplifications will somehow affect the quality of the analysis. Depending on the nature of the data, this lack of precision might lead to considerable mistakes in the analysis.

In general this approach based on cross-tabulations is especially of interest if one has to do with non-metric variables. In such cases LISREL would not be the proper choice. If the variables might in principle be expected to be approximately normally distributed even though this does not seem to be so due to the measurement procedure used, one can use alternative procedures which recently have been developed within the LISREL framework. Some information about these procedures has been given in chapter 9. For more details about the cross-table analysis we refer to the literature given at the end of this chapter.

The Correlational Approach

Apart from the analysis of cross-tables, the literature shows many studies in which the correlation coefficient is used in order to evaluate causal theories. However, it should be clear by now that this statistical measure is not appropriate for this purpose. In chapter 7 it was indicated that the correlation is equal to the sum of the direct effect, indirect effects and correlations due to combinations of other variables (joint and spurious). This means that in general the correlation (at least the zero-order correlation coefficient) is not a good estimate of the effect of one variable on another. This measure therefore cannot be used to test causal models.

A correct procedure using the correlation coefficient makes use of the *partial correlation coefficient*. A partial correlation coefficient represents the correlation between two variables controlling for some other variables. For example $\rho_{y_1 x_1 . x_2}$ is a coefficient which represents the correlation between y_1 and x_1 after

x_2 has explained all it can of these two variables. This means that all the correlation between y_1 and x_1 which is due to x_2 has been taken out. This coefficient is also called the *first order partial correlation coefficient*. In the same way $\rho_{y_2y_1 \cdot x_1x_2}$ is the *second order partial correlation coefficient* between y_2 and y_1 controlling for x_1 and x_2. These partial correlation coefficients can easily be computed from the zero order correlation coefficients in the following way:

$$\rho_{y_1x_1 \cdot x_2} = \frac{\rho_{y_1x_1} - (\rho_{y_1x_2}\rho_{x_1x_2})}{\sqrt{(1 - \rho_{y_1x_2})(1 - \rho_{x_1x_2})}} \qquad (E.1)$$

and

$$\rho_{y_2y_1 \cdot x_1x_2} = \frac{\rho_{y_2y_1 \cdot x_1} - (\rho_{y_2x_2 \cdot x_1}\rho_{y_1x_2 \cdot x_1})}{\sqrt{(1 - \rho_{y_2x_2 \cdot x_1})(1 - \rho_{y_1x_2 \cdot x_1})}} \qquad (E.2)$$

In the same way higher order partial correlation coefficients can be formulated. From these formulas it is clear that from the zero order correlation coefficients the first order partial correlation coefficients can be computed and from these the second order partial correlation coefficients and so on.

These measures can be used for the testing of causal models. This can be seen quite easily. Whenever the direct effect between two variables in a theory is assumed to be zero, the partial correlation coefficient between these two variables controlling for all variables which have a direct effect on the last

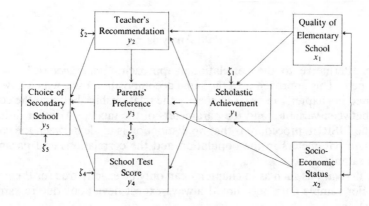

Figure E.2   A Reprint of the School Career Theory of Chapter 4

variable in the causal order ought to be zero. For the school career model of chapter 4—presented again in Figure E.2—this means that the following coefficients have to be zero if the theory is correct: $\rho_{y_2x_2 \cdot y_1x_1}$, $\rho_{y_3x_1 \cdot y_2y_1x_2}$, $\rho_{y_4x_1 \cdot y_1}$, $\rho_{y_4x_2 \cdot y_1}$, $\rho_{y_4y_2 \cdot y_1}$, $\rho_{y_4y_3 \cdot y_1}$, $\rho_{y_5x_1 \cdot y_2y_3y_4}$, $\rho_{y_5x_2 \cdot y_2y_3y_4}$ and $\rho_{y_5y_1 \cdot y_2y_3y_4}$.

These hypotheses can also be tested because sample estimates of these partial correlation coefficients can be computed from the data. This means that the testing procedure of the correlational approach is comparable with the testing process in LISREL. Instead of the covariances the partial correlation coefficients are used to test these hypotheses. Especially for very simple examples and standardized variables it can be shown that these two approaches should give the same results. (The reader may want to check this for three variables).

A disadvantage of the procedure using partial correlations is that various hypotheses are tested separately and not the model as a whole. As a consequence one does not know what decision one has to make if, for example, 6 hypotheses hold and one is rejected. Should the whole model be rejected or not?

Another disadvantage of this correlational approach is that one does not get an estimate of the causal effects themselves. In order to obtain an estimate of these effects one has to make further calculations. Due to these disadvantages one can say that this procedure is more or less made obsolete by more efficient methods, although the approach itself is correct. One of the methods which made this procedure obsolete was the LISREL program because it can perform the same test more efficiently and it provides estimates of the effects at the same time.

Path Analysis

As an alternative to the correlational approach, *"path analysis"* has been developed. This approach uses the same decomposition rules which have been discussed in chapter 7 in order to specify the relationships between the correlations between variables and the parameters of the model. A major difference with the LISREL procedure is that no distinction is made between the correlations and parameters in the population and the correlations and parameters in the sample.

The derivations such as in chapter 7 can only be exactly true for the population. For sample data one should always expect deviations due to sampling fluctuations.

Another difference is that the parameters of the path models used to be estimated by solving the equations, which are obtained by the decomposition rules, by hand. This is of course not only very inefficient but it also leads to a lot of mistakes and to complications. If $df > 0$, there are in general different ways to solve the equations (see chapter 8). In such a situation it is unclear what solution should be chosen. In the literature on path analysis it is said that these differences only occur if the model is incorrect for the data. It has therefore been suggested that differences in the solutions can be used as a test of the model. However, it is very difficult to build a formal test on this approach apart from the fact that it requires a lot of work.

Given these complications it will be clear that path analysis has been left aside by most researchers as soon as a more efficient approach was found. LISREL is one of them, but in the history of this field another tradition has also been influential. This tradition will be called the econometric approach and is discussed in the next section.

But before we discuss the econometric approach we first want to discuss one more issue related to path analysis, which was very important in the global development of the field. We want to mention here the discovery that models with unmeasured variables could also be analyzed using the same approach. The first discussion of this point was published in 1969 for the model presented in Figure E.3. In this model there are two variables denoted by ξ^s (ksi) and η^s (eta) of which the first is the causal variable and the second the effect variable. The disturbance term is ζ' as usual. Furthermore it is assumed that ξ^s influences x_1^s, x_2^s and x_3^s, while η^s affects three other variables: y_1^s, y_2^s and y_3^s.

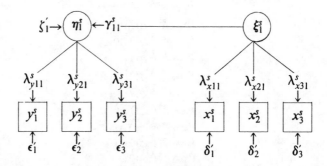

Figure E.3   A Causal Model with Two Unobserved Variables ξ^s and η^s and Six Observed Variables x_1^s, x_2^s, x_3 and y_1^s, y_2^s, y_3

The disturbance terms are denoted by δ'_1, δ'_2 and δ'_3 for the x-variables and by ϵ'_1, ϵ'_2 and ϵ'_3 for the y-variables. In this model different symbols have been used from before because it is assumed that ξ^s and η^s are not measured directly but that x_1^s, x_2^s and x_3^s are the indicators for the ξ^s variable and y_1^s, y_2^s and y_3^s are the indicators for the η^s variable. In general the interest is centered on the effect of the theoretical variables on each other and not on the relationships between the indicators. Nevertheless, the correlations between the indicators represent the only information obtainable from the data. The correlation between the variables of interest or the effect of these variables on each other is not available.

The important discovery in path analysis was that this last effect can be estimated from the correlations between the observed variables. The way in which this effect can be estimated was derived in exactly the same way as before:

(1)First the correlations between the observed variables are expressed in the parameters of the model by the decomposition rules, and next

(2)the parameters are solved using the information with respect to the correlations.

Since this possibility is of great importance the procedure is illustrated below. For the model specified the following set of equations for the correlations between the observed variables can be derived:

$$\rho_{y_2 y_1} = \lambda_{y21}^s \lambda_{y11}^s \qquad (E.3a)$$

$$\rho_{y_3 y_1} = \lambda_{y31}^s \lambda_{y11}^s \qquad (E.3b)$$

$$\rho_{x_1 y_1} = \lambda_{x11}^s \gamma_{11}^s \lambda_{y11}^s \qquad (E.3c)$$

$$\rho_{x_2 y_1} = \lambda_{x21}^s \gamma_{11}^s \lambda_{y11}^s \qquad (E.3d)$$

$$\rho_{x_3 y_1} = \lambda_{x31}^s \gamma_{11}^s \lambda_{y11}^s \qquad (E.3e)$$

$$\rho_{y_3 y_2} = \lambda_{y31}^s \lambda_{y21}^s \qquad (E.3f)$$

$$\rho_{x_1 y_2} = \lambda_{x11}^s \gamma_{11}^s \lambda_{y21}^s \qquad (E.3g)$$

$$\rho_{x_2 y_2} = \lambda_{x21}^s \gamma_{11}^s \lambda_{y21}^s \qquad (E.3h)$$

$$\rho_{x_3 y_2} = \lambda_{x31}^s \gamma_{11}^s \lambda_{y21}^s \qquad (E.3i)$$

$$\rho_{x_1 y_3} = \lambda_{x11}^s \gamma_{11}^s \lambda_{y31}^s \qquad (E.3j)$$

$$\rho_{x_2 y_3} = \lambda_{x21}^s \gamma_{11}^s \lambda_{y31}^s \qquad (E.3k)$$

$$\rho_{x_3 y_3} = \lambda_{x31}^s \gamma_{11}^s \lambda_{y31}^s \qquad (E.3l)$$

$$\rho_{x_2 x_1} = \lambda_{x21}^s \lambda_{x11}^s \qquad (E.3m)$$

$$\rho_{x_3 x_1} = \lambda_{x31}^s \lambda_{x11}^s \qquad (E.3n)$$

$$\rho_{x_3 x_2} = \lambda_{x31}^s \lambda_{x21}^s \qquad (E.3o)$$

Furthermore six equations can be specified which decompose the variances of the observed variables in the explained and unexplained variances. But we will not discuss these equations any further because we want to concentrate on the effect of ξ^s on η^s, which is γ_{11}^s.

In sum, there are above 15 equations specified with 7 unknown parameters.

This would suggest that the necessary condition for identification is fulfilled. We can also show that the sufficient condition is fulfilled. From the data we can get information about all correlations mentioned and from equations (E.3a), (E.3b) and (E.3f) the coefficients λ^s_{y11}, λ^s_{y21} and λ^s_{y31} can be solved. If we take the ratio of $\rho_{y_2y_1}$ and $\rho_{y_3y_1}$ we get:

$$\frac{\rho_{y_2y_1}}{\rho_{y_3y_1}} = \frac{\lambda^s_{y21}}{\lambda^s_{y31}} \text{ or } \lambda^s_{y21} = \lambda^s_{y31}\frac{\rho_{y_2y_1}}{\rho_{y_3y_1}}$$

Substitution of this result in the equation (E.3f) gives the solution for λ^s_{y31} which is:

$$\lambda^s_{y31} = \sqrt{\frac{\rho_{y_3y_2}\rho_{y_3y_1}}{\rho_{y_2y_1}}}$$

Having found λ^s_{y31} the other coefficients can be obtained by substitution of this result in the equations used earlier:

$$\lambda^s_{y21} = \frac{\rho_{y_3x_2}}{\lambda^s_{y31}}$$

$$\lambda^s_{y11} = \frac{\rho_{y_3y_1}}{\lambda^s_{y31}}$$

In the same way the coefficients λ^s_{x11}, λ^s_{x21} and λ^s_{x31} can be solved from (E.3m) to (E.3o). This leaves 9 equations to solve the parameter γ^s_{11}. But it can be seen very easily that this parameter can be solved from each of the other equations once the different λ^s parameters mentioned above are obtained. This means that this parameter can certainly be solved from 9 different equations. For instance from (E.3c) we get

$$\gamma^s_{11} = \frac{\rho_{x_1y_1}}{\lambda^s_{x11}\lambda^s_{y11}}$$

This discussion illustrates that path analysis has taught us in a very simple way that the effect of two variables which are not directly observed can be estimated if one is willing to specify a model for the causal process as we have done above. It is even possible to test such theories because there are 8 degrees of freedom left as we have seen.

The discussion of models of this kind opened the eyes of many scientists in the social sciences for the fact that these models were similar to the model which had been discussed for a long time in psychology under the name of factor analysis. This discovery called for a unification of this field. This idea was especially coming up because the factor analysis was a well established approach with well developed estimation and testing procedures. In that period it seemed useful to use these tools for the path analysis problems, especially because solving equations by hand is not the most efficient approach. In fact the LISREL approach grew out of these more efficient factor analysis approaches. In this case the programme was extended in order to make it possible also to deal with the kind of models which have been presented in this paragraph. This means that the path analysis is also out of date. However, the formulation of the relationships between the covariances and the parameters of the model are still made in the same way and the discussion of the models in terms of path diagrams and in terms of direct and indirect effects and spurious relationships is still very useful and should not be ignored.

The Econometric Approach

Before we move on to the LISREL approach we have to mention first one other tradition which began some 50 years before the LISREL approach. This was the regression approach. When social scientists discussed the path analysis models and tried to solve them by hand, they discovered rather quickly that they were trying to solve problems which had been solved for some time by econometricians. The econometricians had both discussed the estimation of single linear equations as well as of sets of such linear equations. Futhermore the analysis of disturbance terms was discussed in order to detect specification errors in the equations.

The social scientists discovered that the same techniques as used by the econometricians could be used for their models without unobserved variables. This means that they discovered that the techniques of the econometricians could be used for estimation of all models discussed in this book except for the models in Figure E.3. Due to the fact that these techniques where available in the major statistical packages a large number of examples can be found in the literature in which the econometric approach is used to estimate the kind of models we have discussed here. Using these techniques each equation was estimated separately by a procedure which is called *Ordinary Least Squares (OLS)* or *Two Stage Least Squares (TSLS)* or a related estimation procedure. It would lead too far to discuss these approaches here. For their explanation we refer to the literature mentioned at the end of this chapter. What should be clear is that the social scientists had found in these procedures in some sense very efficient tools to estimate the parameters of their models.

But what has been neglected originally and is still neglected nowadays by the scholars who use this approach is that the models should not only be estimated but also be tested. Within the regression approach a problem is that one has to do a lot of work to carry out a test of the theories. The reason is that each equation is estimated separately and that the computer does not store the information of all the parameters of all equations to compute the reproduced correlation matrix and the matrix with the residuals. If one wants to perform such a test one has to do it by hand and this is done very seldom.

Due to this fact one can still find a lot of examples of models in the literature which are presented as final theories but which can easily be detected to be unacceptable if one analyzes the same data once again with LISREL, using the preferred model of the authors. Our guess from analyzing many of these sets of data is that more than 50% are rejected if the test discussed in chapter 12 is applied.

The major problem is that many parameters are omitted between the intervening variables. In general one is not so aware of such effects or one is not so interested in these effects. However omitting such effects while they are important might lead to quite different estimates of the parameters and therefore to wrong conclusions. In chapter 13 we have illustrated this point for the school career example in which several parameters were also omitted according to our ideas at that point in time. For a more elaborate discussion of this point we refer to the literature.

Here still another issue is discussed. Some scholars have been aware of the above mentioned problems and have suggested to analyze full recursive models. This meant that they only specified the causal order of the variables and drew all possible arrows between the variables, avoiding reciprocal causation. Then each equation was estimated separately and for each parameter the t-value was determined. If the t-value was larger than 2 the coefficient was left in the model. If the t-value of the coefficient was smaller than 2 the parameter was made equal to zero.

Although this method seems to be appropriate we would like to illustrate by our usual example that this is not so. If this method was applied to the school career data using the before specified causal order (see Figure E.2.), a direct effect between y_5^s and y_1^s would be specified which is impossible according to our prior knowledge. We know that the school committee has to make the decision (y_5^s) without information about the "scholastic achievement" (y_1^s) of the students. As a substitute it has available the "recommendation of the teacher" (y_2^s), "the preference of the parents" (y_3^s)) and the "school test score" (y_4^s) of the student. This means that a direct effect would be specified which is impossible. Such a priori knowledge is very attractive in causal models because it provides possibilities for testing the model. If no model can be obtained which fits the data without this effect, one knows that the model has to be incorrect.

With this knowledge let us now look at the proposed method. It can happen that the effect in a specific set of data is significantly different from zero . In such a case the parameter is left in the model and the error in the model will not be detected. This is according to us a major drawback of this method. Another problem of this method is that it is very vulnerable to capitalizing on chance because the choice of a model completely depends on the specific set of data which has been analyzed. But maybe the most important disadvantage in this method is of a psychological nature. It discourages people to think about their theories apart from the causal order of the variables. After the research is done one can always develop a "theory", i.e. why the parameters which are significant are significant But because of the fact that at least some of these coefficients are significant due to sampling fluctuations and not much investment in the theory is made, other researchers are not so convinced about such theories and they start all over again. Using the same approach they will probably come up with another ad hoc theory, because sampling fluctuations play again a role and the researcher did not think again. As a consequence very little cumulative knowledge will be obtained as can be seen in the literature.

Returning to the discussion of the econometric approach, we think that the fact that a researcher can not test the theories with this approach in a routine way, is a major disadvantage. This does not say anything negative about the procedures, but without a test one is never sure whether one is estimating the parameters for the proper model. The LISREL program has the advantage that it provides both an efficient estimation procedure and a test of the model at the same time. This is one of the major benefits of this approach. Another benefit is that one does not have to use a different estimation procedure for recursive and nonrecursive models as is recommended by the econometricians. The estimation procedure provided by LISREL can estimate both models just as well. This advantage is of course not so important but from a didactic point of view it is attractive because one does not have to teach a different estimation procedure for each model one is dealing with. We return to this point in the next section.

The LISREL Approach

The LISREL approach has been developed around 1970. A number of social scientists had discovered that they were studying similar problems under different names. The sociologists called it path analysis, the econometricians structural equation models, and psychometricians studied factor analysis. Then in 1970 a conference was held where the communalities were discussed and a general linear model was dicussed which consisted of a causal model as we have discussed in this book but for which the causal and effect variables were not directly observed. For each of the unobserved variables indicators were available. This is a very common situation in social science research. Often we are not interested in the relationships between the observed variables themselves because we know that they are only indicators of the variables which are really of interest. Such a situation is made explicit in the model of Figure E.3. The identification of a general model including unmeasured

variables was discussed at the 1970 conference by Wiley, and Jöreskog introduced the LISREL program for estimation and testing. The approach which
Jöreskog introduced has been discussed in this book for simpler models, i.e.
models without the unmeasured variables. But from these historical notes and
from the discussion of measurement errors in chapter 15, it will be clear that
the LISREL approach is much more general than has been suggested so far.
In fact the LISREL approach provides means of estimating and testing a very
large variety of linear models of which the one discussed here is only one of
the simplest examples. A major advantage of this approach is that for all these
models the same methodology can be used which has been discussed here and
which was already presented in Figure I.1 in the introduction.

One of the models which can be analyzed in this way is the model of Figure
E.3. This is a very important fact because the econometric approach which
is efficient in estimating the models of this book does not provide the tools
to estimate and test the models with unobserved variables. But these models
are very important in the social sciences. In order to illustrate this point one
can simply carry out some calculations and see what happens if one ignores
the measurement errors or unreliability which usually exist in the data. These
calculations are performed on a simpler model than the model of Figure E.3.
The model is presented in Figure E.4. There are again two

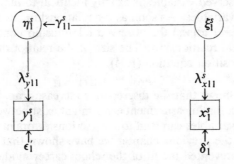

Figure E.4   A Causal Model with Two Unobserved Variables ξ^s and η^s and
Two Observed Variables x_1^s and y_1^s

Table E.2 The Effect of Measurement Errors on the Correlation between the Observed Variables in Figure E.4 if $\gamma_{11}^s = 1$

Effect of ξ^s on x^s and Effect of η^s on y^s	Correlation between x and y	Proportion of Explained Variance
1	1	1
.9	.81	.66
.8	.64	.41
.7	.49	.24
.6	.36	.13
.5	.25	.06

variables of interest which are not directly observed. The variables x and y are the observed variables. Now imagine that the correlation between the theoretical variables is equal to 1. This means that there is a perfect relationship. Let us see what will happen to the correlation between the observed variables if the relationship between the theoretical variables and the observed variables becomes worse and worse. This means that we will assume more and more measurement error or less and less reliability. The correlation between the observed variables will become smaller as the reliability gets worse. This trend is demonstrated in Table E.2. This table shows that the correlation between the observed variables is only equal to the correlation between the variables of interest if the relationship between the theoretical variables and the observed variables is perfect. That is the only case in which the relation between the observed variables is exactly identical to the relationship between the theoretical variables. As soon as the relationship becomes defective (when measurement error arises) the observed relationship is not identical anymore to the theoretical relationship. The size of the relationship can be computed by the decomposition equation (E.4)

$$\rho_{y_1 x_1} = \lambda_{y11}^s \gamma_{11}^s \lambda_{x11}^s \qquad (E.4)$$

The table also shows that the discrepancy increases rapidly. This means that ignoring the fact that measurement error might exist between the observed and the theoretical variables can lead to very serious errors in the interpretation of the results. In the previous chapter we have shown that measurement errors probably also prevented the fit of the school career model of chapter 4 to the data. The table above shows that observed correlations can only be seen as correlations between the variables of interest if the measurement errors are extremely small. In the major part of this book we have made the assumption of error-free measurement in order to simplify the discussion of the approach. In chapter 15 we have indicated however that such errors are an important obstacle in finding the correct model for a causal process. For many fields in the social sciences one can not make the assumption of error-free measurement and one has to take errors into account in the model. In the section on path analysis we have already seen that this is possible because models with unmeasured variables can be identified and even be tested if enough indicators are available. We will not discuss this approach any further here because it would lead to a large number of other topics which are beyond this text.

For the moment it is sufficient to say that the LISREL approach makes it possible to estimate and test models of the type of Figure E.3, while the models of this book can be analyzed as well with this approach. All these models can be analyzed with the same program using the same approach which has been discussed here. All other approaches reviewed in this chapter can not deal with this array of models, or only in a very inefficient way. It is fair to say that this is the most important advantage of the LISREL approach.

In the past, the strong assumptions made have been the major disadvantage of the LISREL approach. These assumptions were introduced to derive simple estimation and testing procedures. In this respect we can mention:
—linearity
—additivity
—identical parameters for all cases
—independent observations
—interval measurement
—multivariate normality
Recently several of these assumptions have been relaxed as a result of new developments. So far no serious efforts have been made within this context to develop approaches for nonlinear or nonadditive models. Also the assumption of independent observations has not been relaxed so far. On the other hand many efforts have been made to relax the assumptions of interval measurement, multivariate normality of the variables and the assumption of identical parameters for all cases.

Starting with the last assumption, the previous chapter showed that it is possible to split up a sample in several groups and test whether the parameters are the same and, if not, to relax this assumption. This possibility exists within the LISREL program since the appearance of LISREL IV in 1978.

With respect to the measurement level assumptions, a lot of work has been done recently, partly within the LISREL context and partly outside it. Within LISREL it is nowadays possible to analyze data sets with categorical variables as well if it is reasonable to assume that these variables are in fact continuous and normally distributed but mistreated by the measurement instruments which have turned these continuous variables into categorical variables. Some details of this approach have been given in chapter 9.

If these assumptions seem to be unrealistic one can always turn to the loglinear modelling approach mentioned before or one can rely on other approaches which try to rescale the categorical variables in such a way that the correlations become maximal. The last approach assumes that all variables have a linear relationship and tries to find the scale values which satisfy this assumption as good as possible.

The third assumption which has been relaxed is the assumption of multivariate normality. Within the LISREL context this was done by providing alternative estimation procedures which do not require multinormality. In this text these procedures have already been mentioned, namely the ULS and GLS estimation procedure. The disadvantage of these estimators is that very little is known about their behavior under conditions which deviate considerably from multivariate normality and under conditions of small samples. With respect to the Maximum Likelihood estimator there is at least the elaborate study of Boomsma which indicates under what conditions this procedure is robust.

Outside the LISREL context interesting work has been done as well. Since around 1980 Browne and Sapiro are working on estimation and testing procedures which do not require prior specification of the distribution of the variables. Using the Generalized Least Squares procedure which we have discussed before they have been able to show that in some sense optimal estimates can be obtained by adjusting the weight matrix within the GLS method taking into account the skewness in the data. In this way an attractive estimation and testing procedure has been developed for the general class of covariance structure models which is also covered by LISREL. This development is very promising because it liberates this approach from the unattractive assumption of multivariate normality. The difficulty at this moment however is the extreme amount of computer space which is required to apply this method. Due to these technical problems this method is yet only feasible for very small models. But it is not unlikely that these procedures will become feasible for practical use on large computers in the future. By now a program already exists which provides such "asymptotic distribution free" (ADF) estimates called BENWEE. A less demanding "two stage asymptotic distribution free" procedure has also been developed recently (EQS). It is not very likely that these programs will substitute LISREL. But it may be expected that the suggested procedures will be built into the LISREL program if they turn out to be feasible on the new computers and useful in practice.

Some General Remarks

This chapter has given an overall picture of the several approaches which have been developed in the past. The LISREL approach grew out of several traditions and is presently the most general approach. A major advantage of the

LISREL procedure is the availability of a testing procedure. The only problem is, as we have seen, the number of assumptions which has to be made. But it was also indicated that these assumptions have been relaxed more and more during the past 5 years. It is likely that these developments will continue in the near future. This will make the LISREL approach the most general method for the analysis of causal hypotheses or covariance structure models on the basis of nonexperimental data. In our view the LISREL approach deserves a similar place in the social science methodology for nonexperimental research as is given to the analysis of variance for experimental research.

Further Reading

The cross-table analysis as it was discussed in the past can be found in Greenwood (1945) and Chapin (1947). The more recent developments using loglinear modelling have been described in a very simple way by Gilbert (1981), in a more elaborate and technical way by Upton (1978) and Fienberg (1977) and in a more complete way by Bishop, Fienberg and Holland (1975).

The correlational approach was originally developed by Simon (1954) and Blalock (1962, 1964). A nice example can be found in Goldberg (1966). The path analysis was originally developed for biological research by Sewell Wright (1934). In sociology, this approach was introduced by Duncan (1966), Land (1969) and Boudon (1965). The models with unobserved variables have been introduced by Costner (1969) and Blalock (1969b).

The econometric approach can be found in many different econometric textbooks which we have mentioned before. For a historical perspective we refer to H.M. Blalock Jr.'s "Causal models in the social sciences" (1971). The first indications of the LISREL approach can be found in the proceedings of the conference on Structural Equation Models edited by Goldberger and Duncan (1973). This text requires already some knowledge of matrix algebra.

A discussion of the problems with respect to testing in the path analysis approach can be found in Saris, Den Ronden and Satorra (1984). The more recent developments with respect to the measurement scales and alternative estimation procedures are described in the latest version of the LISREL manual (Jöreskog and Sörbom, 1983) and in recent extensions of this manual.

However, there are no simple introductions to the full possibilities of the LISREL approach. Perhaps the best reference to be made is the more recent summarizing article written by Jöreskog where he discusses several applications of LISREL (1978). We can also mention the introductions written by Bentler (1980), Bielby and Hauser (1977) and Saris(1980). More elaborate introductions requiring more knowledge can be found in Kenny (1979) and Dwyer 1983.

The distribution free approaches are discussed and compared in an article by Bentler (1983). A more complete description of the distribution free approach can be found in Browne (1982)and Shapiro (1983), but these papers are very technical.

In the text the approach of Wold (1979) has not been mentioned, although he claims that he provides an alternative approach with less restrictions for the same problems for which LISREL has been developed. However, Wold's approach has several drawbacks as can be seen most clearly in the work of Dijkstra (1981). Unfortunately this book requires a lot of statistical knowledge from the reader.

Appendix

Statistical Tables

Appendix A

The Normal Distribution*

Appendix B

The χ^2 Distribution**

Appendix C

The Power of the .05 Level Likelihood Ratio Test for a Given Non-Centrality Parameter (λ)***

Appendix D

The Non-Centrality Parameter (λ) required for a .05 Level test with a Given Power. ***

---

*Reproduced with permission of Penguin Books from K.A. Yeomans, "Introducing Statistics", Vol. II, London, 1975

**Reproduced with kind permission of MacMillan Publishing Company from R.A. Fisher, "Statistical Methods for Research Workers", New York, 1948

***Reprinted from G.E. Haynam, Z. Govindarajulu and F.C. Leone, "Tables of the Cumulative Chi-square Distribution", in: H.L. Harter and D.B. Owen (eds.), "Selected Tables in Mathematical Statistics", Providence, 1973, with the permission of the Institute of Mathematical Statistics, California State University

306

Appendix A
The Normal Distribution

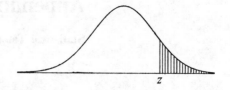

z

z		0	1	2	3	4	5	6	7	8	9
0.0	0	5000	4960	4920	4880	4841	4801	4761	4721	4681	4641
0.1		4602	4562	4522	4483	4443	4404	4364	4325	4286	4247
0.2		4207	4168	4129	4091	4052	4013	3974	3936	3897	3859
0.3		3821	3783	3745	3707	3669	3632	2594	3557	3520	3483
0.4		3446	3409	3372	3336	3300	3264	3228	3192	3156	3121
0.5		3085	3050	3015	2981	2946	2912	2877	2843	2810	2776
0.6		2743	2709	2676	2644	2611	2579	2546	2514	2483	2451
0.7		2420	2389	2358	2327	2297	2266	2236	2207	2177	2148
0.8		2119	2090	2061	2033	2005	1977	1949	1922	1894	1867
0.9		1841	1814	1788	1762	1736	1711	1685	1660	1635	1611
1.0		1587	1563	1539	1515	1492	1469	1446	1423	1401	1379
1.1		1357	1335	1314	1292	1271	1251	1230	1210	1190	1170
1.2		1151	1131	1112	1094	1075	1057	1038	1020	1003	9853
1.3	0.0	9680	9510	9342	9176	9012	8851	8692	8534	8379	8226
1.4		8076	7927	7780	7636	7493	7353	7215	7078	6944	6811
1.5		6681	6552	6426	6301	6178	6057	5938	5821	5705	5592
1.6		5480	5370	5262	5155	5050	4947	4846	4746	4648	4551
1.7		4457	4363	4272	4182	4093	4006	3920	3836	3754	3673
1.8		3593	3515	3438	3363	3288	3216	3144	3074	3005	2938
1.9		2872	2807	2743	2680	2619	2559	2500	2442	2385	2330
2.0		2275	2222	2169	2118	2068	2018	1970	1923	1876	1831
2.1		1786	1743	1700	1659	1618	1578	1539	1500	1463	1426
2.2		1390	1355	1321	1287	1255	1222	1191	1160	1130	1101
2.3		1072	1044	1017	9903	9642	9387	9138	8894	8656	8424
2.4	0.00	8198	7976	7760	7549	7344	7143	6947	6756	6569	6387
2.5		6210	6037	5868	5703	5543	5386	5234	5085	4941	4799
2.6		4661	4527	4397	4269	4145	4025	3907	3793	3681	3573
2.7		3467	3364	3264	3167	3072	2980	2890	2803	2718	2635
2.8		2555	2477	2401	2327	2256	2186	2118	2052	1988	1926
2.9		1866	1807	1750	1695	1641	1589	1538	1489	1441	1395
3.0		1350	1306	1264	1223	1183	1144	1107	1070	1035	1001
3.1	0.000	9676	9354	9043	8740	8447	8164	7889	7622	7364	7114
3.2		6871	6637	6410	6190	5977	5770	5571	5377	5190	5009
3.3		4834	4665	4501	4342	4189	4041	3897	3758	3624	3495
3.4		3369	3248	3131	3018	2909	2803	2701	2602	2507	2415

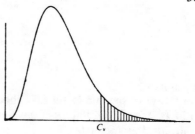

Appendix B
The χ^2 Distribution

Degrees of freedom	p=0.50	0.30	0.20	0.10	0.05	0.02	0.01
1	0.455	1.074	1.642	2.706	3.841	5.412	6.635
2	1.386	2.408	3.219	4.605	5.991	7.824	9.210
3	2.366	3.665	4.642	6.251	7.815	9.837	11.341
4	3.357	4.878	5.989	7.779	9.488	11.668	13.277
5	4.351	6.064	7.289	9.236	11.070	13.388	15.086
6	5.348	7.231	8.558	10.645	12.592	15.033	16.812
7	6.346	8.383	9.803	12.017	14.067	16.622	18.475
8	7.344	9.524	11.030	13.362	15.507	18.168	20.090
9	8.343	10.656	12.242	14.684	16.919	19.679	21.666
10	9.342	11.781	13.442	15.987	18.307	21.161	23.209
11	10.341	12.899	14.631	17.275	19.675	22.618	24.725
12	11.340	14.011	15.812	18.549	21.026	24.054	26.217
13	12.340	15.119	16.985	19.812	22.362	25.472	27.688
14	13.339	16.222	18.151	21.064	23.685	26.873	29.141
15	14.339	17.322	19.311	22.307	24.996	28.259	30.578
16	15.338	18.418	20.465	23.542	26.296	29.633	32.000
17	16.338	19.511	21.615	24.769	27.587	30.995	33.409
18	17.338	20.601	22.760	25.989	28.869	32.346	34.805
19	18.338	21.689	23.900	27.204	30.144	33.687	36.191
20	19.337	22.775	25.038	28.412	31.410	35.020	37.566
21	20.337	23.858	26.171	29.615	32.671	36.343	38.932
22	21.337	24.939	27.301	30.813	33.924	37.659	40.289
23	22.337	26.018	28.429	32.007	35.172	38.968	41.638
24	23.337	27.096	29.553	33.196	36.415	40.270	42.980
25	24.337	28.172	30.675	34.382	37.652	41.566	44.314
26	25.336	29.246	31.795	35.563	38.885	42.856	45.642
27	26.336	30.319	32.912	36.741	40.113	44.140	46.963
28	27.336	31.391	34.027	37.916	41.337	45.419	48.278
29	28.336	32.461	35.139	39.087	42.557	46.693	49.588
30	29.336	33.530	36.250	40.256	43.773	47.962	50.892

For degrees of freedom greater than 30, the expression $\sqrt{2\chi^2} - \sqrt{2\nu - 1}$ may be used as a normal deviate with unit variance, where ν is the number of degrees of freedom.

308

Appendix C
The Power of the .05 Level Likelihood Ratio Test for Given Values of the Non-Centrality Parameter (λ)

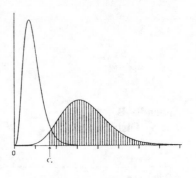

Degrees of Freedom	$\lambda=0.200$	0.400	0.600	0.800	1.000	1.200	1.400	1.600	1.800	2.000
1	0.073	0.097	0.121	0.145	0.170	0.195	0.219	0.244	0.269	0.293
2	0.065	0.081	0.098	0.115	0.133	0.151	0.169	0.187	0.206	0.225
3	0.062	0.075	0.088	0.101	0.116	0.130	0.145	0.161	0.176	0.192
4	0.060	0.071	0.082	0.093	0.105	0.118	0.131	0.144	0.157	0.171
5	0.059	0.068	0.078	0.088	0.099	0.109	0.121	0.133	0.145	0.157
6	0.058	0.066	0.075	0.084	0.093	0.103	0.114	0.124	0.135	0.146
7	0.057	0.065	0.073	0.081	0.090	0.099	0.108	0.118	0.127	0.138
8	0.057	0.064	0.071	0.079	0.087	0.095	0.103	0.112	0.121	0.131
9	0.056	0.063	0.069	0.077	0.084	0.092	0.100	0.108	0.116	0.125
10	0.056	0.062	0.068	0.075	0.082	0.089	0.097	0.104	0.112	0.121
11	0.055	0.061	0.067	0.074	0.080	0.087	0.094	0.101	0.109	0.117
12	0.055	0.061	0.066	0.072	0.079	0.085	0.092	0.099	0.106	0.113
13	0.055	0.060	0.066	0.071	0.077	0.083	0.090	0.096	0.103	0.110
14	0.055	0.060	0.065	0.070	0.076	0.082	0.088	0.094	0.101	0.107
15	0.055	0.059	0.064	0.070	0.075	0.081	0.086	0.092	0.099	0.105
16	0.054	0.059	0.064	0.069	0.074	0.079	0.085	0.091	0.097	0.103
17	0.054	0.059	0.063	0.068	0.073	0.078	0.084	0.089	0.095	0.101
18	0.054	0.058	0.063	0.067	0.072	0.077	0.082	0.088	0.093	0.099
19	0.054	0.058	0.062	0.067	0.072	0.076	0.081	0.087	0.092	0.098
20	0.054	0.058	0.062	0.066	0.071	0.076	0.081	0.086	0.091	0.096
22	0.054	0.057	0.061	0.065	0.070	0.074	0.079	0.083	0.088	0.093
24	0.053	0.057	0.061	0.065	0.069	0.073	0.077	0.082	0.086	0.091
26	0.053	0.057	0.060	0.064	0.068	0.072	0.076	0.080	0.085	0.089
28	0.053	0.056	0.060	0.063	0.067	0.071	0.075	0.079	0.083	0.087
30	0.053	0.056	0.059	0.063	0.066	0.070	0.074	0.078	0.082	0.086
32	0.053	0.056	0.059	0.062	0.066	0.069	0.073	0.077	0.080	0.084
34	0.053	0.056	0.059	0.062	0.065	0.069	0.072	0.076	0.079	0.083
36	0.053	0.056	0.059	0.062	0.065	0.068	0.071	0.075	0.078	0.082
38	0.053	0.055	0.058	0.061	0.064	0.067	0.071	0.074	0.077	0.081
40	0.053	0.055	0.058	0.061	0.064	0.067	0.070	0.073	0.077	0.080
42	0.053	0.055	0.058	0.061	0.064	0.067	0.070	0.073	0.076	0.079
44	0.053	0.055	0.058	0.060	0.063	0.066	0.069	0.072	0.075	0.078
46	0.052	0.055	0.058	0.060	0.063	0.066	0.069	0.072	0.075	0.078
48	0.052	0.055	0.057	0.060	0.063	0.065	0.068	0.071	0.074	0.077
50	0.052	0.055	0.057	0.060	0.062	0.065	0.068	0.071	0.073	0.076
55	0.052	0.054	0.057	0.059	0.062	0.064	0.067	0.069	0.072	0.075
60	0.052	0.054	0.056	0.059	0.061	0.063	0.066	0.068	0.071	0.074
65	0.052	0.054	0.056	0.058	0.061	0.063	0.065	0.068	0.070	0.073
70	0.052	0.054	0.056	0.058	0.060	0.062	0.065	0.067	0.069	0.072
75	0.052	0.054	0.056	0.058	0.060	0.062	0.064	0.066	0.068	0.071
80	0.052	0.054	0.056	0.057	0.059	0.061	0.063	0.066	0.068	0.070
85	0.052	0.054	0.055	0.057	0.059	0.061	0.063	0.065	0.067	0.069
90	0.052	0.053	0.055	0.057	0.059	0.061	0.063	0.065	0.067	0.069
95	0.052	0.053	0.055	0.057	0.059	0.060	0.062	0.064	0.066	0.068
100	0.052	0.053	0.055	0.057	0.058	0.060	0.062	0.064	0.066	0.067

Degrees of Freedom	$\lambda = 2.200$	2.400	2.600	2.800	3.000	3.500	4.000	4.500	5.000	5.500
1	0.317	0.341	0.364	0.387	0.410	0.465	0.516	0.564	0.609	0.650
2	0.244	0.264	0.283	0.302	0.321	0.369	0.415	0.460	0.503	0.545
3	0.208	0.225	0.241	0.258	0.275	0.316	0.358	0.400	0.440	0.480
4	0.185	0.200	0.214	0.229	0.244	0.282	0.320	0.358	0.396	0.433
5	0.169	0.182	0.195	0.209	0.222	0.257	0.292	0.327	0.363	0.398
6	0.157	0.169	0.181	0.193	0.206	0.237	0.270	0.303	0.336	0.369
7	0.148	0.159	0.170	0.181	0.192	0.222	0.252	0.283	0.314	0.346
8	0.141	0.151	0.161	0.171	0.182	0.209	0.237	0.267	0.296	0.326
9	0.134	0.144	0.153	0.163	0.173	0.198	0.225	0.253	0.281	0.309
10	0.129	0.138	0.147	0.156	0.165	0.190	0.215	0.241	0.268	0.295
11	0.125	0.133	0.141	0.150	0.159	0.182	0.206	0.230	0.256	0.282
12	0.121	0.129	0.137	0.145	0.153	0.175	0.198	0.221	0.246	0.271
13	0.117	0.125	0.132	0.140	0.148	0.169	0.191	0.213	0.237	0.261
14	0.114	0.121	0.129	0.136	0.144	0.164	0.184	0.206	0.229	0.252
15	0.112	0.118	0.125	0.133	0.140	0.159	0.179	0.200	0.221	0.244
16	0.109	0.116	0.122	0.129	0.136	0.155	0.174	0.194	0.215	0.236
17	0.107	0.113	0.120	0.126	0.133	0.151	0.169	0.188	0.209	0.229
18	0.105	0.111	0.117	0.124	0.130	0.147	0.165	0.184	0.203	0.223
19	0.103	0.109	0.115	0.121	0.127	0.144	0.161	0.179	0.198	0.217
20	0.102	0.107	0.113	0.119	0.125	0.141	0.157	0.175	0.193	0.212
22	0.098	0.104	0.109	0.115	0.121	0.135	0.151	0.168	0.185	0.203
24	0.096	0.101	0.106	0.111	0.117	0.131	0.146	0.161	0.178	0.194
26	0.094	0.098	0.103	0.108	0.113	0.127	0.141	0.156	0.171	0.187
28	0.092	0.096	0.101	0.106	0.111	0.123	0.137	0.151	0.165	0.181
30	0.090	0.094	0.099	0.103	0.108	0.120	0.133	0.146	0.160	0.175
32	0.088	0.093	0.097	0.101	0.106	0.117	0.130	0.142	0.156	0.170
34	0.087	0.091	0.095	0.099	0.104	0.115	0.126	0.139	0.152	0.165
36	0.086	0.090	0.094	0.098	0.102	0.112	0.124	0.136	0.148	0.161
38	0.085	0.088	0.092	0.096	0.100	0.110	0.121	0.133	0.145	0.157
40	0.084	0.087	0.091	0.095	0.099	0.109	0.119	0.130	0.142	0.154
42	0.083	0.086	0.090	0.093	0.097	0.107	0.117	0.128	0.139	0.151
44	0.082	0.085	0.089	0.092	0.096	0.105	0.115	0.125	0.136	0.148
46	0.081	0.084	0.088	0.091	0.094	0.104	0.113	0.123	0.134	0.145
48	0.080	0.083	0.087	0.090	0.093	0.102	0.111	0.121	0.131	0.142
50	0.079	0.082	0.086	0.089	0.092	0.101	0.110	0.119	0.129	0.140
55	0.078	0.081	0.084	0.087	0.090	0.098	0.106	0.115	0.124	0.134
60	0.076	0.079	0.082	0.085	0.088	0.095	0.103	0.112	0.120	0.130
65	0.075	0.078	0.080	0.083	0.086	0.093	0.101	0.109	0.117	0.125
70	0.074	0.076	0.079	0.082	0.084	0.091	0.098	0.106	0.114	0.122
75	0.073	0.075	0.078	0.080	0.083	0.089	0.096	0.103	0.111	0.119
80	0.072	0.074	0.077	0.079	0.082	0.088	0.094	0.101	0.108	0.116
85	0.071	0.074	0.076	0.078	0.080	0.086	0.093	0.099	0.106	0.113
90	0.071	0.073	0.075	0.077	0.079	0.085	0.091	0.098	0.104	0.111
95	0.070	0.072	0.074	0.076	0.078	0.084	0.090	0.096	0.102	0.109
100	0.069	0.071	0.073	0.075	0.078	0.083	0.089	0.094	0.101	0.107

Degrees of Freedom	λ = 6.000	6.500	7.000	7.500	8.000	8.500	9.000	9.500	10.000	11.000
1	0.688	0.722	0.754	0.782	0.807	0.830	0.851	0.869	0.885	0.913
2	0.584	0.621	0.655	0.687	0.717	0.745	0.770	0.794	0.815	0.852
3	0.518	0.555	0.589	0.623	0.654	0.683	0.711	0.737	0.761	0.804
4	0.470	0.505	0.540	0.573	0.604	0.635	0.663	0.690	0.716	0.762
5	0.433	0.467	0.500	0.533	0.564	0.594	0.623	0.651	0.677	0.726
6	0.403	0.435	0.468	0.500	0.530	0.560	0.589	0.617	0.644	0.693
7	0.378	0.409	0.441	0.471	0.502	0.531	0.560	0.587	0.614	0.664
8	0.357	0.387	0.417	0.447	0.476	0.505	0.533	0.561	0.587	0.638
9	0.338	0.367	0.397	0.425	0.454	0.482	0.510	0.537	0.564	0.614
10	0.323	0.351	0.379	0.407	0.435	0.462	0.489	0.516	0.542	0.592
11	0.309	0.336	0.363	0.390	0.417	0.444	0.471	0.497	0.523	0.572
12	0.297	0.322	0.349	0.375	0.401	0.428	0.454	0.479	0.505	0.554
13	0.285	0.310	0.336	0.361	0.387	0.413	0.438	0.463	0.488	0.537
14	0.275	0.300	0.324	0.349	0.374	0.399	0.424	0.448	0.473	0.521
15	0.267	0.290	0.314	0.338	0.362	0.386	0.411	0.435	0.459	0.506
16	0.258	0.281	0.304	0.327	0.351	0.375	0.398	0.422	0.446	0.492
17	0.251	0.273	0.295	0.318	0.341	0.364	0.387	0.410	0.434	0.480
18	0.244	0.265	0.287	0.309	0.331	0.354	0.377	0.399	0.422	0.467
19	0.238	0.258	0.279	0.301	0.323	0.345	0.367	0.389	0.412	0.456
20	0.232	0.252	0.272	0.293	0.315	0.336	0.358	0.380	0.402	0.445
22	0.221	0.240	0.260	0.280	0.300	0.320	0.341	0.362	0.383	0.426
24	0.212	0.230	0.249	0.268	0.287	0.307	0.327	0.347	0.367	0.408
26	0.204	0.221	0.239	0.257	0.275	0.294	0.314	0.333	0.353	0.392
28	0.197	0.213	0.230	0.247	0.265	0.283	0.302	0.321	0.340	0.378
30	0.190	0.206	0.222	0.239	0.256	0.273	0.291	0.309	0.328	0.365
32	0.184	0.200	0.215	0.231	0.248	0.265	0.282	0.299	0.317	0.353
34	0.179	0.194	0.209	0.224	0.240	0.256	0.273	0.290	0.307	0.342
36	0.175	0.189	0.203	0.218	0.233	0.249	0.265	0.281	0.298	0.332
38	0.170	0.184	0.198	0.212	0.227	0.242	0.257	0.273	0.289	0.322
40	0.166	0.179	0.193	0.207	0.221	0.236	0.251	0.266	0.282	0.314
42	0.163	0.175	0.188	0.202	0.216	0.230	0.245	0.260	0.275	0.306
44	0.159	0.172	0.184	0.197	0.211	0.225	0.239	0.253	0.268	0.298
46	0.156	0.168	0.180	0.193	0.206	0.219	0.233	0.247	0.262	0.291
48	0.153	0.165	0.177	0.189	0.202	0.215	0.228	0.242	0.256	0.285
50	0.150	0.162	0.173	0.185	0.198	0.210	0.223	0.237	0.250	0.278
55	0.144	0.155	0.166	0.177	0.188	0.200	0.213	0.225	0.238	0.264
60	0.139	0.149	0.159	0.170	0.181	0.192	0.203	0.215	0.227	0.252
65	0.134	0.144	0.153	0.163	0.174	0.184	0.195	0.206	0.218	0.242
70	0.130	0.139	0.148	0.158	0.168	0.178	0.188	0.199	0.210	0.232
75	0.127	0.135	0.144	0.153	0.162	0.172	0.182	0.192	0.202	0.224
80	0.124	0.132	0.140	0.149	0.157	0.167	0.176	0.186	0.196	0.216
85	0.121	0.128	0.136	0.145	0.153	0.162	0.171	0.180	0.190	0.210
90	0.118	0.126	0.133	0.141	0.149	0.158	0.166	0.175	0.184	0.203
95	0.116	0.123	0.130	0.138	0.146	0.154	0.162	0.171	0.179	0.198
100	0.114	0.120	0.127	0.135	0.142	0.150	0.158	0.166	0.175	0.193

Degrees of Freedom	λ=12.000	13.000	14.000	15.000	16.000	17.000	18.000	19.000	20.000	21.000
1	0.934	0.950	0.963	0.972	0.979	0.985	0.989	0.992	0.994	0.996
2	0.883	0.908	0.928	0.944	0.957	0.967	0.974	0.980	0.985	0.989
3	0.840	0.871	0.896	0.917	0.934	0.948	0.959	0.968	0.975	0.981
4	0.802	0.837	0.866	0.891	0.912	0.929	0.943	0.955	0.964	0.972
5	0.768	0.806	0.838	0.866	0.890	0.910	0.927	0.941	0.952	0.962
6	0.738	0.777	0.812	0.843	0.869	0.891	0.911	0.927	0.940	0.951
7	0.710	0.751	0.788	0.820	0.849	0.873	0.895	0.913	0.928	0.941
8	0.685	0.727	0.765	0.799	0.829	0.856	0.879	0.898	0.915	0.930
9	0.661	0.704	0.743	0.779	0.810	0.838	0.863	0.884	0.903	0.919
10	0.639	0.683	0.723	0.760	0.792	0.822	0.848	0.870	0.890	0.908
11	0.619	0.663	0.704	0.741	0.775	0.806	0.833	0.857	0.878	0.897
12	0.601	0.645	0.686	0.724	0.759	0.790	0.818	0.843	0.866	0.885
13	0.583	0.628	0.669	0.707	0.743	0.775	0.804	0.830	0.854	0.874
14	0.567	0.611	0.653	0.692	0.727	0.760	0.790	0.817	0.842	0.863
15	0.552	0.596	0.638	0.677	0.713	0.746	0.777	0.805	0.830	0.853
16	0.538	0.581	0.623	0.662	0.699	0.733	0.764	0.793	0.819	0.842
17	0.524	0.568	0.609	0.648	0.685	0.720	0.751	0.781	0.807	0.831
18	0.512	0.555	0.596	0.635	0.672	0.707	0.739	0.769	0.796	0.821
19	0.500	0.543	0.584	0.623	0.660	0.695	0.728	0.758	0.785	0.811
20	0.489	0.531	0.572	0.611	0.648	0.683	0.716	0.747	0.775	0.801
22	0.468	0.509	0.549	0.588	0.625	0.661	0.694	0.725	0.754	0.781
24	0.449	0.489	0.529	0.568	0.605	0.640	0.674	0.705	0.735	0.763
26	0.432	0.471	0.510	0.548	0.585	0.620	0.654	0.686	0.716	0.745
28	0.417	0.455	0.493	0.531	0.567	0.602	0.636	0.668	0.699	0.727
30	0.402	0.440	0.477	0.514	0.550	0.585	0.619	0.651	0.682	0.711
32	0.389	0.426	0.463	0.499	0.534	0.569	0.603	0.635	0.666	0.695
34	0.377	0.413	0.449	0.485	0.520	0.554	0.587	0.620	0.650	0.680
36	0.366	0.401	0.436	0.471	0.506	0.540	0.573	0.605	0.636	0.665
38	0.356	0.390	0.425	0.459	0.493	0.526	0.559	0.591	0.622	0.652
40	0.347	0.380	0.414	0.448	0.481	0.514	0.547	0.578	0.609	0.639
42	0.338	0.371	0.403	0.437	0.469	0.502	0.534	0.566	0.596	0.626
44	0.330	0.361	0.394	0.426	0.459	0.491	0.523	0.554	0.584	0.614
46	0.322	0.353	0.385	0.416	0.448	0.480	0.511	0.542	0.572	0.602
48	0.314	0.345	0.376	0.407	0.438	0.470	0.501	0.531	0.561	0.591
50	0.308	0.337	0.368	0.398	0.429	0.460	0.491	0.521	0.551	0.580
55	0.292	0.320	0.349	0.378	0.408	0.438	0.467	0.497	0.526	0.554
60	0.278	0.305	0.333	0.361	0.389	0.418	0.446	0.475	0.503	0.531
65	0.266	0.292	0.318	0.345	0.372	0.400	0.428	0.456	0.483	0.511
70	0.256	0.280	0.305	0.331	0.357	0.384	0.411	0.438	0.465	0.491
75	0.246	0.270	0.294	0.319	0.344	0.369	0.395	0.422	0.448	0.474
80	0.238	0.260	0.283	0.307	0.332	0.356	0.381	0.407	0.432	0.458
85	0.230	0.252	0.274	0.297	0.320	0.344	0.369	0.393	0.418	0.443
90	0.223	0.244	0.265	0.287	0.310	0.333	0.357	0.381	0.405	0.429
95	0.217	0.237	0.257	0.279	0.301	0.323	0.346	0.369	0.393	0.416
100	0.211	0.230	0.250	0.271	0.292	0.314	0.336	0.359	0.381	0.404

Degrees of Freedom	λ=22.000	23.000	24.000	25.000	26.000	27.000	28.000	29.000	30.000	31.000
1	0.997	0.998	0.998	0.999	0.999	0.999	1.000	1.000	1.000	1.000
2	0.992	0.994	0.995	0.996	0.997	0.998	0.999	0.999	0.999	0.999
3	0.985	0.989	0.991	0.993	0.995	0.996	0.997	0.998	0.998	0.999
4	0.978	0.982	0.986	0.989	0.992	0.994	0.995	0.996	0.997	0.998
5	0.969	0.976	0.981	0.985	0.988	0.991	0.993	0.994	0.996	0.997
6	0.961	0.968	0.975	0.980	0.984	0.987	0.990	0.992	0.994	0.995
7	0.952	0.961	0.968	0.974	0.979	0.983	0.987	0.989	0.992	0.993
8	0.942	0.952	0.961	0.968	0.974	0.979	0.983	0.986	0.989	0.991
9	0.932	0.944	0.954	0.962	0.969	0.975	0.979	0.983	0.986	0.989
10	0.923	0.935	0.946	0.955	0.963	0.970	0.975	0.980	0.984	0.987
11	0.913	0.926	0.938	0.949	0.957	0.965	0.971	0.976	0.980	0.984
12	0.903	0.918	0.931	0.942	0.951	0.959	0.966	0.972	0.977	0.981
13	0.893	0.909	0.922	0.935	0.945	0.954	0.961	0.968	0.973	0.978
14	0.883	0.900	0.914	0.927	0.938	0.948	0.956	0.964	0.970	0.975
15	0.873	0.891	0.906	0.920	0.932	0.942	0.951	0.959	0.966	0.971
16	0.863	0.881	0.898	0.913	0.925	0.936	0.946	0.954	0.962	0.968
17	0.853	0.872	0.890	0.905	0.918	0.930	0.941	0.950	0.957	0.964
18	0.843	0.863	0.881	0.898	0.912	0.924	0.935	0.945	0.953	0.960
19	0.834	0.855	0.873	0.890	0.905	0.918	0.930	0.940	0.948	0.956
20	0.824	0.846	0.865	0.883	0.898	0.912	0.924	0.935	0.944	0.952
22	0.806	0.828	0.849	0.867	0.884	0.899	0.912	0.924	0.935	0.944
24	0.788	0.812	0.833	0.853	0.870	0.886	0.901	0.914	0.925	0.935
26	0.771	0.795	0.818	0.838	0.857	0.874	0.889	0.903	0.915	0.926
28	0.754	0.779	0.802	0.824	0.843	0.861	0.877	0.892	0.905	0.917
30	0.738	0.764	0.788	0.810	0.830	0.848	0.865	0.881	0.895	0.908
32	0.723	0.749	0.773	0.796	0.817	0.836	0.854	0.870	0.885	0.898
34	0.708	0.734	0.759	0.782	0.804	0.824	0.842	0.859	0.875	0.889
36	0.694	0.720	0.746	0.769	0.791	0.812	0.831	0.848	0.865	0.879
38	0.680	0.707	0.732	0.756	0.779	0.800	0.820	0.838	0.854	0.870
40	0.667	0.694	0.720	0.744	0.767	0.789	0.809	0.827	0.845	0.861
42	0.654	0.682	0.708	0.732	0.756	0.777	0.798	0.817	0.835	0.851
44	0.642	0.669	0.696	0.720	0.744	0.766	0.787	0.807	0.825	0.842
46	0.630	0.658	0.684	0.709	0.733	0.755	0.777	0.797	0.815	0.833
48	0.619	0.646	0.673	0.698	0.722	0.745	0.766	0.787	0.806	0.824
50	0.608	0.635	0.662	0.687	0.711	0.734	0.756	0.777	0.796	0.814
55	0.582	0.610	0.636	0.662	0.686	0.710	0.732	0.753	0.773	0.792
60	0.559	0.586	0.612	0.638	0.662	0.686	0.709	0.731	0.751	0.771
65	0.538	0.564	0.590	0.616	0.640	0.664	0.687	0.709	0.730	0.750
70	0.518	0.544	0.570	0.595	0.620	0.644	0.667	0.689	0.710	0.731
75	0.500	0.526	0.551	0.576	0.600	0.624	0.647	0.670	0.691	0.712
80	0.483	0.508	0.533	0.558	0.582	0.606	0.629	0.651	0.673	0.694
85	0.468	0.493	0.517	0.541	0.565	0.589	0.612	0.634	0.656	0.677
90	0.453	0.478	0.502	0.526	0.549	0.573	0.595	0.618	0.639	0.661
95	0.440	0.464	0.488	0.511	0.534	0.557	0.580	0.602	0.624	0.645
100	0.428	0.451	0.474	0.497	0.520	0.543	0.565	0.587	0.609	0.630

Degrees of Freedom	λ=32.000	33.000	34.000	35.000	36.000	37.000	38.000	39.000	40.000	41.000
1	1.000	1.000	1.000	1.000	1.000	1.000	1.000	1.000	1.000	1.000
2	1.000	1.000	1.000	1.000	1.000	1.000	1.000	1.000	1.000	1.000
3	0.999	0.999	0.999	1.000	1.000	1.000	1.000	1.000	1.000	1.000
4	0.998	0.999	0.999	0.999	0.999	1.000	1.000	1.000	1.000	1.000
5	0.997	0.998	0.998	0.999	0.999	0.999	0.999	1.000	1.000	1.000
6	0.996	0.997	0.998	0.998	0.999	0.999	0.999	0.999	1.000	1.000
7	0.995	0.996	0.997	0.997	0.998	0.998	0.999	0.999	0.999	0.999
8	0.993	0.995	0.996	0.997	0.997	0.998	0.998	0.999	0.999	0.999
9	0.991	0.993	0.994	0.996	0.996	0.997	0.998	0.998	0.999	0.999
10	0.989	0.991	0.993	0.994	0.995	0.996	0.997	0.998	0.998	0.999
11	0.987	0.989	0.991	0.993	0.994	0.995	0.996	0.997	0.998	0.998
12	0.984	0.987	0.990	0.992	0.993	0.994	0.996	0.996	0.997	0.998
13	0.982	0.985	0.988	0.990	0.992	0.993	0.995	0.996	0.996	0.997
14	0.979	0.983	0.986	0.988	0.990	0.992	0.994	0.995	0.996	0.997
15	0.976	0.980	0.984	0.986	0.989	0.991	0.992	0.994	0.995	0.996
16	0.973	0.977	0.981	0.984	0.987	0.989	0.991	0.993	0.994	0.995
17	0.970	0.975	0.979	0.982	0.985	0.988	0.990	0.992	0.993	0.994
18	0.966	0.972	0.976	0.980	0.983	0.986	0.988	0.990	0.992	0.993
19	0.963	0.969	0.973	0.978	0.981	0.984	0.987	0.989	0.991	0.993
20	0.959	0.965	0.971	0.975	0.979	0.983	0.985	0.988	0.990	0.992
22	0.952	0.959	0.965	0.970	0.975	0.979	0.982	0.985	0.987	0.989
24	0.944	0.952	0.959	0.965	0.970	0.974	0.978	0.981	0.984	0.987
26	0.936	0.944	0.952	0.959	0.964	0.970	0.974	0.978	0.981	0.984
28	0.927	0.937	0.945	0.953	0.959	0.965	0.970	0.974	0.978	0.981
30	0.919	0.929	0.938	0.946	0.953	0.960	0.965	0.970	0.974	0.978
32	0.910	0.921	0.931	0.940	0.947	0.954	0.960	0.966	0.970	0.974
34	0.901	0.913	0.923	0.933	0.941	0.949	0.955	0.961	0.966	0.971
36	0.893	0.905	0.916	0.926	0.935	0.943	0.950	0.956	0.962	0.967
38	0.884	0.897	0.908	0.919	0.928	0.937	0.945	0.951	0.957	0.963
40	0.875	0.889	0.901	0.912	0.922	0.931	0.939	0.946	0.953	0.959
42	0.866	0.880	0.893	0.905	0.915	0.925	0.933	0.941	0.948	0.954
44	0.858	0.872	0.885	0.897	0.908	0.919	0.928	0.936	0.943	0.950
46	0.849	0.864	0.877	0.890	0.902	0.912	0.922	0.930	0.938	0.945
48	0.840	0.855	0.870	0.883	0.895	0.906	0.916	0.925	0.933	0.941
50	0.831	0.847	0.862	0.875	0.888	0.899	0.910	0.919	0.928	0.936
55	0.810	0.827	0.843	0.857	0.871	0.883	0.895	0.905	0.915	0.924
60	0.790	0.807	0.824	0.839	0.853	0.867	0.879	0.891	0.901	0.911
65	0.770	0.788	0.805	0.821	0.836	0.850	0.864	0.876	0.887	0.898
70	0.751	0.769	0.787	0.804	0.819	0.834	0.848	0.861	0.873	0.885
75	0.732	0.751	0.769	0.787	0.803	0.818	0.833	0.847	0.860	0.872
80	0.714	0.734	0.752	0.770	0.787	0.803	0.818	0.832	0.846	0.858
85	0.697	0.717	0.736	0.754	0.771	0.788	0.803	0.818	0.832	0.845
90	0.681	0.701	0.720	0.738	0.756	0.773	0.789	0.804	0.818	0.832
95	0.666	0.685	0.705	0.723	0.741	0.758	0.775	0.790	0.805	0.819
100	0.651	0.671	0.690	0.709	0.727	0.744	0.761	0.777	0.792	0.806

Degrees of Freedom	λ = 42.000	43.000	44.000	45.000	46.000	47.000	48.000	49.000	50.000
1	1.000	1.000	1.000	1.000	1.000	1.000	1.000	1.000	1.000
2	1.000	1.000	1.000	1.000	1.000	1.000	1.000	1.000	1.000
3	1.000	1.000	1.000	1.000	1.000	1.000	1.000	1.000	1.000
4	1.000	1.000	1.000	1.000	1.000	1.000	1.000	1.000	1.000
5	1.000	1.000	1.000	1.000	1.000	1.000	1.000	1.000	1.000
6	1.000	1.000	1.000	1.000	1.000	1.000	1.000	1.000	1.000
7	1.000	1.000	1.000	1.000	1.000	1.000	1.000	1.000	1.000
8	0.999	1.000	1.000	1.000	1.000	1.000	1.000	1.000	1.000
9	0.999	0.999	0.999	1.000	1.000	1.000	1.000	1.000	1.000
10	0.999	0.999	0.999	0.999	1.000	1.000	1.000	1.000	1.000
11	0.999	0.999	0.999	0.999	0.999	1.000	1.000	1.000	1.000
12	0.998	0.999	0.999	0.999	0.999	0.999	1.000	1.000	1.000
13	0.998	0.998	0.999	0.999	0.999	0.999	0.999	1.000	1.000
14	0.997	0.998	0.998	0.999	0.999	0.999	0.999	0.999	1.000
15	0.997	0.997	0.998	0.998	0.999	0.999	0.999	0.999	0.999
16	0.996	0.997	0.997	0.998	0.998	0.999	0.999	0.999	0.999
17	0.995	0.996	0.997	0.997	0.998	0.998	0.999	0.999	0.999
18	0.995	0.996	0.996	0.997	0.998	0.998	0.998	0.999	0.999
19	0.994	0.995	0.996	0.997	0.997	0.998	0.998	0.998	0.999
20	0.993	0.994	0.995	0.996	0.997	0.997	0.998	0.998	0.999
22	0.991	0.993	0.994	0.995	0.996	0.996	0.997	0.998	0.998
24	0.989	0.991	0.992	0.993	0.995	0.995	0.996	0.997	0.997
26	0.986	0.989	0.990	0.992	0.993	0.994	0.995	0.996	0.997
28	0.984	0.986	0.988	0.990	0.992	0.993	0.994	0.995	0.996
30	0.981	0.984	0.986	0.988	0.990	0.992	0.993	0.994	0.995
32	0.978	0.981	0.984	0.986	0.988	0.990	0.992	0.993	0.994
34	0.975	0.978	0.981	0.984	0.986	0.988	0.990	0.991	0.993
36	0.971	0.975	0.979	0.982	0.984	0.986	0.988	0.990	0.992
38	0.968	0.972	0.976	0.979	0.982	0.984	0.987	0.988	0.990
40	0.964	0.969	0.973	0.976	0.979	0.982	0.985	0.987	0.989
42	0.960	0.965	0.970	0.973	0.977	0.980	0.983	0.985	0.987
44	0.956	0.961	0.966	0.970	0.974	0.978	0.980	0.983	0.985
46	0.952	0.958	0.963	0.967	0.971	0.975	0.978	0.981	0.984
48	0.948	0.954	0.959	0.964	0.968	0.972	0.976	0.979	0.982
50	0.943	0.950	0.955	0.961	0.965	0.970	0.973	0.977	0.980
55	0.932	0.939	0.946	0.952	0.957	0.962	0.967	0.970	0.974
60	0.920	0.928	0.936	0.942	0.949	0.954	0.959	0.964	0.968
65	0.908	0.917	0.925	0.932	0.939	0.946	0.951	0.957	0.961
70	0.895	0.905	0.914	0.922	0.930	0.937	0.943	0.949	0.954
75	0.883	0.893	0.903	0.912	0.920	0.928	0.935	0.941	0.947
80	0.870	0.881	0.891	0.901	0.910	0.918	0.926	0.933	0.939
85	0.858	0.869	0.880	0.890	0.900	0.908	0.917	0.924	0.931
90	0.845	0.857	0.869	0.879	0.889	0.899	0.907	0.915	0.923
95	0.833	0.845	0.857	0.868	0.879	0.889	0.898	0.907	0.915
100	0.820	0.833	0.846	0.857	0.868	0.879	0.888	0.897	0.906

Appendix D
The Non-Centrality Parameter (λ) for Given Power Levels of the .05 Level Likelihood Ratio Test

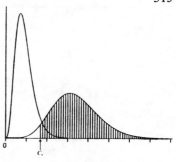

Power

Degrees of Freedom	0.10	0.12	0.14	0.16	0.18	0.20	0.22	0.24	0.26	0.28
1	0.43	0.59	0.76	0.92	1.08	1.24	1.40	1.57	1.73	1.89
2	0.63	0.86	1.08	1.30	1.52	1.73	1.94	2.15	2.36	2.57
3	0.78	1.06	1.33	1.59	1.85	2.10	2.34	2.59	2.83	3.07
4	0.91	1.23	1.54	1.84	2.12	2.40	2.68	2.95	3.21	3.48
5	1.03	1.39	1.72	2.05	2.36	2.67	2.97	3.26	3.55	3.83
6	1.13	1.52	1.89	2.24	2.58	2.91	3.23	3.54	3.85	4.16
7	1.23	1.65	2.04	2.42	2.78	3.13	3.47	3.80	4.13	4.45
8	1.32	1.77	2.19	2.59	2.97	3.34	3.69	4.05	4.39	4.73
9	1.41	1.88	2.32	2.74	3.14	3.53	3.91	4.27	4.63	4.99
10	1.49	1.98	2.45	2.89	3.31	3.71	4.10	4.49	4.86	5.23
11	1.57	2.09	2.57	3.03	3.46	3.88	4.29	4.69	5.08	5.46
12	1.64	2.18	2.68	3.16	3.61	4.05	4.47	4.88	5.28	5.68
13	1.71	2.27	2.79	3.29	3.76	4.21	4.64	5.07	5.48	5.89
14	1.78	2.36	2.90	3.41	3.90	4.36	4.81	5.25	5.67	6.09
15	1.84	2.45	3.00	3.53	4.03	4.51	4.97	5.42	5.86	6.29
16	1.91	2.53	3.10	3.64	4.16	4.65	5.13	5.59	6.04	6.48
17	1.97	2.61	3.20	3.76	4.28	4.79	5.28	5.75	6.21	6.66
18	2.03	2.69	3.30	3.87	4.41	4.92	5.42	5.91	6.38	6.84
19	2.09	2.76	3.39	3.97	4.52	5.05	5.56	6.06	6.54	7.01
20	2.15	2.84	3.48	4.07	4.64	5.18	5.70	6.21	6.70	7.18
22	2.26	2.98	3.65	4.27	4.86	5.43	5.97	6.50	7.01	7.51
24	2.36	3.12	3.81	4.46	5.08	5.66	6.22	6.77	7.30	7.82
26	2.46	3.25	3.97	4.64	5.28	5.89	6.47	7.04	7.58	8.12
28	2.56	3.37	4.12	4.82	5.48	6.10	6.70	7.29	7.85	8.41
30	2.66	3.50	4.27	4.99	5.67	6.31	6.93	7.53	8.12	8.68
32	2.74	3.61	4.41	5.15	5.85	6.51	7.15	7.77	3.37	8.95
34	2.84	3.73	4.55	5.31	6.03	6.71	7.37	8.00	8.61	9.21
36	2.92	3.84	4.68	5.46	6.20	6.90	7.57	8.22	8.85	9.46
38	3.00	3.95	4.81	5.61	6.37	7.08	7.77	8.44	9.08	9.71
40	3.08	4.04	4.93	5.75	6.52	7.25	7.96	8.64	9.30	9.94
42	3.15	4.15	5.05	5.89	6.68	7.43	8.15	8.84	9.51	10.17
44	3.23	4.25	5.17	6.03	6.83	7.60	8.34	9.04	9.73	10.40
46	3.31	4.34	5.29	6.17	6.99	7.77	8.52	9.24	9.94	10.62
48	3.38	4.44	5.40	6.30	7.14	7.93	8.70	9.43	10.15	10.84
50	3.45	4.53	5.52	6.43	7.28	8.10	8.87	9.62	10.35	11.05
55	3.63	4.76	5.79	6.74	7.64	8.49	9.30	10.08	10.83	11.57
60	3.80	4.98	6.05	7.04	7.98	8.86	9.70	10.51	11.30	12.06
65	3.96	5.19	6.30	7.33	8.30	9.22	10.09	10.93	11.74	12.53
70	4.11	5.39	6.54	7.61	8.61	9.56	10.46	11.33	12.17	12.99
75	4.26	5.58	6.78	7.88	8.91	9.89	10.82	11.72	12.59	13.43
80	4.41	5.77	7.00	8.14	9.20	10.21	11.17	12.09	12.99	13.85
85	4.55	5.95	7.22	8.39	9.49	10.52	11.51	12.46	13.38	14.27
90	4.69	6.13	7.43	8.64	9.76	10.83	11.84	12.82	13.76	14.67
95	4.82	6.30	7.64	8.88	10.03	11.12	12.16	13.16	14.12	15.06
100	4.95	6.47	7.84	9.11	10.29	11.41	12.47	13.50	14.48	15.44

Power

Degrees of Freedom	0.30	0.32	0.34	0.36	0.38	0.40	0.42	0.44	0.46	0.48
1	2.06	2.22	2.39	2.56	2.74	2.91	3.09	3.27	3.46	3.65
2	2.78	2.99	3.20	3.41	3.62	3.83	4.05	4.27	4.50	4.73
3	3.30	3.54	3.78	4.02	4.26	4.50	4.75	5.00	5.25	5.50
4	3.74	4.00	4.26	4.53	4.79	5.05	5.32	5.59	5.86	6.14
5	4.12	4.40	4.68	4.96	5.25	5.53	5.82	6.11	6.40	6.69
6	4.46	4.76	5.06	5.36	5.66	5.96	6.26	6.57	6.88	7.19
7	4.77	5.09	5.41	5.72	6.04	6.35	6.67	6.99	7.31	7.64
8	5.06	5.40	5.73	6.06	6.39	6.72	7.05	7.38	7.72	8.06
9	5.34	5.68	6.03	6.37	6.72	7.06	7.41	7.75	8.10	8.46
10	5.59	5.95	6.31	6.67	7.02	7.38	7.74	8.10	8.46	8.83
11	5.84	6.21	6.58	6.95	7.32	7.68	8.06	8.43	8.80	9.18
12	6.07	6.45	6.83	7.22	7.59	7.97	8.35	8.74	9.12	9.51
13	6.29	6.69	7.08	7.47	7.86	8.25	8.65	9.04	9.43	9.83
14	6.51	6.92	7.32	7.72	8.12	8.52	8.93	9.33	9.74	10.15
15	6.71	7.13	7.55	7.96	8.37	8.78	9.19	9.61	10.02	10.44
16	6.91	7.34	7.77	8.19	8.61	9.03	9.45	9.88	10.30	10.73
17	7.11	7.55	7.98	8.42	8.84	9.27	9.71	10.14	10.57	11.01
18	7.30	7.75	8.19	8.63	9.07	9.51	9.95	10.39	10.83	11.28
19	7.48	7.94	8.39	8.84	9.29	9.74	10.19	10.64	11.09	11.54
20	7.66	8.13	8.59	9.05	9.50	9.96	10.42	10.88	11.33	11.80
22	8.00	8.49	8.97	9.45	9.92	10.39	10.87	11.34	11.82	12.30
24	8.33	8.83	9.33	9.82	10.31	10.80	11.29	11.78	12.27	12.76
26	8.65	9.17	9.68	10.19	10.69	11.20	11.70	12.20	12.71	13.22
28	8.95	9.48	10.01	10.53	11.05	11.57	12.09	12.61	13.13	13.65
30	9.24	9.79	10.33	10.87	11.41	11.94	12.47	13.00	13.53	14.07
32	9.52	10.09	10.65	11.20	11.74	12.29	12.83	13.38	13.92	14.48
34	9.80	10.38	10.95	11.51	12.08	12.63	13.19	13.75	14.31	14.87
36	10.07	10.66	11.24	11.82	12.39	12.96	13.53	14.10	14.67	15.25
38	10.33	10.93	11.53	12.12	12.70	13.29	13.87	14.45	15.03	15.62
40	10.57	11.18	11.79	12.40	12.99	13.59	14.18	14.78	15.37	15.97
42	10.81	11.44	12.06	12.68	13.29	13.90	14.50	15.10	15.71	16.32
44	11.05	11.70	12.33	12.96	13.58	14.19	14.81	15.43	16.04	16.67
46	11.29	11.94	12.59	13.23	13.86	14.49	15.11	15.74	16.37	17.00
48	11.52	12.18	12.84	13.49	14.13	14.77	15.41	16.05	16.69	17.33
50	11.74	12.42	13.09	13.75	14.40	15.05	15.70	16.35	17.00	17.65
55	12.29	12.99	13.69	14.38	15.06	15.73	16.41	17.08	17.75	18.43
60	12.81	13.54	14.26	14.97	15.68	16.38	17.08	17.77	18.47	19.17
65	13.31	14.07	14.81	15.55	16.28	17.00	17.72	18.44	19.16	19.89
70	13.79	14.57	15.34	16.10	16.85	17.60	18.34	19.08	19.83	20.57
75	14.25	15.06	15.85	16.63	17.41	18.17	18.94	19.70	20.47	21.23
80	14.70	15.53	16.34	17.15	17.94	18.73	19.52	20.30	21.09	21.87
85	15.13	15.99	16.83	17.65	18.46	19.27	20.08	20.88	21.69	22.49
90	15.56	16.43	17.29	18.13	18.97	19.80	20.62	21.45	22.27	23.09
95	15.97	16.86	17.74	18.61	19.46	20.31	21.15	22.00	22.84	23.68
100	16.37	17.28	18.18	19.07	19.94	20.81	21.67	22.53	23.39	24.25

Power

Degrees of Freedom	0.50	0.52	0.54	0.56	0.58	0.60	0.62	0.64	0.66	0.68
1	3.84	4.04	4.25	4.46	4.67	4.90	5.13	5.38	5.63	5.89
2	4.96	5.20	5.44	5.69	5.95	6.22	6.49	6.78	7.07	7.38
3	5.76	6.03	6.30	6.58	6.86	7.16	7.46	7.77	8.10	8.44
4	6.42	6.71	7.00	7.30	7.61	7.93	8.25	8.59	8.94	9.31
5	6.99	7.30	7.61	7.93	8.26	8.59	8.94	9.30	9.67	10.05
6	7.51	7.83	8.16	8.50	8.84	9.19	9.56	9.93	10.32	10.72
7	7.97	8.31	8.66	9.01	9.37	9.74	10.11	10.51	10.91	11.33
8	8.41	8.76	9.12	9.48	9.86	10.24	10.64	11.04	11.46	11.90
9	8.82	9.18	9.55	9.93	10.32	10.71	11.12	11.54	11.98	12.43
10	9.20	9.57	9.96	10.35	10.75	11.16	11.58	12.01	12.46	12.92
11	9.56	9.95	10.34	10.75	11.16	11.58	12.01	12.46	12.92	13.40
12	9.91	10.31	10.71	11.13	11.55	11.98	12.42	12.88	13.36	13.85
13	10.24	10.65	11.07	11.49	11.92	12.37	12.82	13.29	13.78	14.28
14	10.56	10.98	11.41	11.84	12.28	12.74	13.21	13.68	14.18	14.69
15	10.87	11.30	11.73	12.18	12.63	13.09	13.57	14.06	14.57	15.09
16	11.16	11.60	12.05	12.50	12.97	13.44	13.92	14.43	14.94	15.48
17	11.45	11.90	12.36	12.82	13.29	13.77	14.27	14.78	15.31	15.85
18	11.73	12.19	12.65	13.13	13.61	14.10	14.60	15.12	15.66	16.21
19	12.00	12.47	12.94	13.42	13.91	14.41	14.93	15.45	16.00	16.56
20	12.27	12.74	13.22	13.71	14.21	14.72	15.24	15.78	16.33	16.91
22	12.78	13.27	13.77	14.27	14.79	15.31	15.85	16.41	16.98	17.57
24	13.26	13.77	14.28	14.80	15.33	15.87	16.43	17.00	17.59	18.20
26	13.73	14.25	14.78	15.31	15.86	16.42	16.99	17.57	18.18	18.80
28	14.18	14.71	15.25	15.80	16.36	16.93	17.52	18.12	18.74	19.38
30	14.61	15.16	15.71	16.28	16.85	17.44	18.04	18.65	19.28	19.94
32	15.03	15.59	16.16	16.73	17.32	17.92	18.53	19.16	19.81	20.48
34	15.44	16.01	16.59	17.18	17.78	18.39	19.01	19.66	20.32	21.00
36	15.83	16.41	17.00	17.61	18.22	18.84	19.48	20.14	20.81	21.51
38	16.21	16.81	17.41	18.03	18.65	19.29	19.94	20.61	21.29	22.00
40	16.57	17.18	17.80	18.42	19.06	19.70	20.37	21.05	21.75	22.47
42	16.93	17.55	18.18	18.82	19.46	20.12	20.80	21.49	22.20	22.94
44	17.29	17.92	18.56	19.21	19.86	20.54	21.22	21.93	22.65	23.40
46	17.64	18.28	18.93	19.58	20.25	20.94	21.63	22.35	23.09	23.85
48	17.98	18.63	19.29	19.96	20.64	21.33	22.04	22.76	23.51	24.28
50	18.31	18.97	19.64	20.32	21.01	21.71	22.43	23.17	23.93	24.71
55	19.11	19.80	20.49	21.20	21.91	22.64	23.39	24.15	24.94	25.75
60	19.88	20.59	21.31	22.03	22.77	23.53	24.30	25.09	25.90	26.74
65	20.61	21.35	22.09	22.84	23.60	24.38	25.17	25.99	26.82	27.68
70	21.32	22.08	22.84	23.61	24.40	25.20	26.01	26.85	27.71	28.60
75	22.00	22.78	23.56	24.36	25.17	25.99	26.82	27.68	28.56	29.47
80	22.66	23.46	24.26	25.08	25.91	26.75	27.61	28.49	29.39	30.32
85	23.30	24.12	24.94	25.78	26.62	27.49	28.37	29.27	30.19	31.15
90	23.92	24.76	25.60	26.46	27.32	28.20	29.10	30.03	30.97	31.95
95	24.53	25.38	26.24	27.12	28.00	28.90	29.82	30.76	31.73	32.73
100	25.12	25.99	26.87	27.76	28.66	29.58	30.52	31.48	32.47	33.48

Power

Degrees of Freedom	0.70	0.71	0.72	0.73	0.74	0.75	0.76	0.77	0.78	0.79
1	6.17	6.32	6.47	6.62	6.78	6.94	7.11	7.28	7.47	7.65
2	7.71	7.87	8.05	8.22	8.41	8.59	8.79	8.99	9.20	9.42
3	8.79	8.98	9.17	9.36	9.56	9.77	9.98	10.20	10.42	10.66
4	9.69	9.88	10.09	10.29	10.51	10.73	10.95	11.19	11.43	11.68
5	10.46	10.66	10.88	11.10	11.32	11.55	11.79	12.04	12.29	12.56
6	11.15	11.36	11.59	11.82	12.05	12.29	12.54	12.80	13.07	13.34
7	11.77	12.00	12.23	12.47	12.72	12.97	13.23	13.50	13.77	14.06
8	12.35	12.59	12.83	13.08	13.33	13.59	13.86	14.14	14.42	14.72
9	12.90	13.14	13.39	13.65	13.91	14.18	14.45	14.74	15.04	15.34
10	13.41	13.66	13.92	14.18	14.45	14.72	15.01	15.30	15.61	15.92
11	13.90	14.15	14.42	14.69	14.96	15.25	15.54	15.84	16.15	16.47
12	14.36	14.62	14.89	15.17	15.45	15.74	16.04	16.35	16.67	17.00
13	14.80	15.07	15.35	15.63	15.92	16.22	16.52	16.84	17.17	17.50
14	15.23	15.50	15.79	16.08	16.37	16.67	16.99	17.31	17.64	17.99
15	15.64	15.92	16.20	16.50	16.80	17.11	17.43	17.76	18.10	18.45
16	16.03	16.32	16.61	16.91	17.22	17.54	17.86	18.20	18.55	18.90
17	16.42	16.71	17.01	17.32	17.63	17.95	18.28	18.62	18.98	19.34
18	16.79	17.09	17.39	17.70	18.02	18.35	18.69	19.04	19.39	19.76
19	17.15	17.45	17.76	18.08	18.40	18.74	19.08	19.43	19.80	20.17
20	17.50	17.81	18.12	18.45	18.78	19.11	19.46	19.82	20.19	20.57
22	18.18	18.50	18.82	19.16	19.50	19.84	20.20	20.57	20.95	21.34
24	18.83	19.15	19.49	19.83	20.18	20.53	20.90	21.28	21.67	22.08
26	19.45	19.78	20.13	20.48	20.83	21.20	21.58	21.97	22.37	22.78
28	20.04	20.39	20.74	21.09	21.46	21.84	22.22	22.62	23.03	23.45
30	20.62	20.97	21.33	21.69	22.07	22.45	22.85	23.26	23.67	24.11
32	21.17	21.53	21.90	22.27	22.65	23.05	23.45	23.87	24.29	24.74
34	21.71	22.08	22.45	22.83	23.22	23.62	24.04	24.46	24.90	25.35
36	22.23	22.60	22.99	23.37	23.77	24.18	24.60	25.03	25.48	25.94
38	22.74	23.12	23.51	23.91	24.31	24.73	25.16	25.59	26.05	26.51
40	23.22	23.61	24.00	24.41	24.82	25.24	25.68	26.12	26.58	27.06
42	23.70	24.10	24.50	24.91	25.33	25.76	26.20	26.65	27.12	27.61
44	24.17	24.57	24.98	25.40	25.82	26.26	26.71	27.17	27.65	28.14
46	24.63	25.04	25.45	25.88	26.31	26.75	27.21	27.68	28.15	28.66
48	25.08	25.50	25.92	26.34	26.78	27.24	27.70	28.17	28.66	29.17
50	25.52	25.94	26.37	26.80	27.25	27.71	28.18	28.66	29.16	29.67
55	26.59	27.02	27.46	27.91	28.37	28.84	29.33	29.83	30.34	30.87
60	27.60	28.05	28.50	28.97	29.44	29.93	30.43	30.95	31.48	32.02
65	28.58	29.04	29.50	29.98	30.47	30.98	31.49	32.02	32.57	33.13
70	29.51	29.99	30.47	30.96	31.46	31.98	32.50	33.04	33.60	34.18
75	30.41	30.90	31.39	31.89	32.41	32.94	33.48	34.04	34.61	35.20
80	31.29	31.78	32.29	32.80	33.33	33.87	34.43	35.00	35.59	36.19
85	32.13	32.64	33.16	33.69	34.23	34.78	35.35	35.93	36.53	37.15
90	32.95	33.47	34.00	34.54	35.09	35.66	36.24	36.84	37.45	38.08
95	33.75	34.28	34.82	35.37	35.94	36.52	37.11	37.72	38.34	38.99
100	34.53	35.07	35.62	36.18	36.76	37.35	37.95	38.57	39.21	39.87

Power

Degrees of Freedom	0.80	0.81	0.82	0.83	0.84	0.85	0.86	0.87	0.88	0.89
1	7.85	8.05	8.27	8.49	8.73	8.98	9.24	9.53	9.83	10.16
2	9.64	9.87	10.12	10.37	10.64	10.93	11.23	11.55	11.89	12.26
3	10.91	11.16	11.42	11.70	12.00	12.30	12.63	12.98	13.35	13.74
4	11.94	12.21	12.49	12.79	13.10	13.43	13.77	14.14	14.53	14.95
5	12.83	13.12	13.41	13.72	14.05	14.39	14.76	15.14	15.55	16.00
6	13.63	13.93	14.24	14.56	14.90	15.26	15.64	16.04	16.47	16.93
7	14.35	14.66	14.99	15.32	15.67	16.05	16.44	16.85	17.30	17.77
8	15.03	15.35	15.68	16.03	16.39	16.78	17.18	17.61	18.07	18.56
9	15.66	15.99	16.33	16.69	17.06	17.46	17.87	18.32	18.79	19.29
10	16.25	16.58	16.94	17.30	17.69	18.09	18.52	18.98	19.46	19.98
11	16.81	17.16	17.52	17.89	18.29	18.70	19.14	19.61	20.10	20.63
12	17.34	17.69	18.07	18.45	18.85	19.28	19.73	20.20	20.71	21.25
13	17.85	18.22	18.59	18.99	19.40	19.83	20.29	20.78	21.29	21.85
14	18.34	18.72	19.10	19.50	19.92	20.37	20.83	21.33	21.86	22.42
15	18.82	19.19	19.59	20.00	20.43	20.88	21.35	21.86	22.39	22.97
16	19.27	19.66	20.06	20.48	20.91	21.37	21.86	22.37	22.92	23.50
17	19.72	20.11	20.52	20.94	21.39	21.85	22.34	22.87	23.42	24.02
18	20.15	20.55	20.96	21.39	21.84	22.32	22.82	23.35	23.91	24.52
19	20.56	20.97	21.39	21.83	22.28	22.77	23.27	23.81	24.38	25.00
20	20.97	21.38	21.81	22.25	22.72	23.21	23.72	24.27	24.85	25.47
22	21.75	22.17	22.61	23.07	23.55	24.05	24.58	25.14	25.74	26.38
24	22.49	22.93	23.38	23.85	24.34	24.86	25.40	25.98	26.59	27.24
26	23.21	23.65	24.12	24.60	25.10	25.63	26.19	26.78	27.40	28.07
28	23.89	24.35	24.82	25.31	25.83	26.37	26.94	27.54	28.18	28.87
30	24.56	25.02	25.50	26.01	26.53	27.09	27.67	28.28	28.94	29.64
32	25.19	25.67	26.16	26.67	27.21	27.77	28.37	29.00	29.66	30.38
34	25.81	26.30	26.80	27.32	27.87	28.45	29.05	29.69	30.37	31.09
36	26.41	26.91	27.42	27.95	28.51	29.09	29.71	30.36	31.05	31.79
38	27.00	27.50	28.02	28.56	29.13	29.73	30.35	31.01	31.72	32.47
40	27.55	28.06	28.59	29.14	29.72	30.32	30.96	31.63	32.35	33.11
42	28.11	28.62	29.16	29.72	30.31	30.92	31.57	32.25	32.98	33.75
44	28.65	29.17	29.72	30.29	30.88	31.51	32.16	32.86	33.59	34.38
46	29.17	29.71	30.26	30.84	31.45	32.08	32.75	33.45	34.20	35.00
48	29.69	30.23	30.80	31.38	32.00	32.64	33.31	34.03	34.78	35.59
50	30.20	30.75	31.32	31.91	32.53	33.18	33.87	34.59	35.36	36.18
55	31.42	31.99	32.58	33.19	33.83	34.50	35.21	35.96	36.75	37.60
60	32.59	33.17	33.78	34.41	35.07	35.77	36.49	37.26	38.08	38.95
65	33.71	34.31	34.93	35.58	36.26	36.97	37.72	38.51	39.35	40.24
70	34.78	35.40	36.04	36.70	37.40	38.13	38.90	39.71	40.57	41.49
75	35.82	36.45	37.11	37.79	38.50	39.25	40.04	40.87	41.75	42.69
80	36.82	37.47	38.14	38.84	39.57	40.34	41.14	41.99	42.89	43.85
85	37.79	38.46	39.14	39.86	40.60	41.39	42.21	43.08	44.00	44.98
90	38.74	39.41	40.12	40.84	41.61	42.41	43.25	44.13	45.07	46.07
95	39.66	40.34	41.06	41.81	42.58	43.40	44.25	45.16	46.11	47.14
100	40.55	41.25	41.98	42.74	43.53	44.36	45.23	46.15	47.13	48.17

Power

Degrees of Freedom	0.90	0.91	0.92	0.93	0.94	0.95	0.96	0.97	0.98	0.99
1	10.51	10.90	11.32	11.81	12.35	13.00	13.77	14.75	16.11	18.37
2	12.66	13.09	13.58	14.12	14.73	15.45	16.31	17.40	18.91	21.40
3	14.17	14.65	15.16	15.74	16.41	17.17	18.10	19.26	20.87	23.52
4	15.41	15.91	16.46	17.07	17.77	18.58	19.55	20.78	22.47	25.25
5	16.47	17.00	17.57	18.21	18.94	19.78	20.80	22.08	23.84	26.73
6	17.42	17.97	18.56	19.23	19.99	20.86	21.92	23.25	25.06	28.05
7	18.29	18.85	19.47	20.15	20.93	21.84	22.93	24.30	26.17	29.25
8	19.09	19.67	20.30	21.01	21.82	22.75	23.87	25.28	27.20	30.36
9	19.84	20.43	21.08	21.81	22.64	23.60	24.75	26.19	28.16	31.40
10	20.54	21.15	21.82	22.56	23.41	24.39	25.57	27.04	29.06	32.37
11	21.21	21.83	22.51	23.28	24.14	25.15	26.35	27.86	29.92	33.30
12	21.84	22.47	23.17	23.95	24.84	25.86	27.09	28.63	30.73	34.17
13	22.45	23.09	23.81	24.61	25.51	26.55	27.80	29.37	31.51	35.01
14	23.03	23.69	24.42	25.23	26.15	27.21	28.48	30.08	32.26	35.82
15	23.59	24.26	25.00	25.83	26.76	27.84	29.14	30.76	32.97	36.59
16	24.13	24.82	25.57	26.41	27.36	28.46	29.77	31.42	33.67	37.34
17	24.66	25.35	26.12	26.97	27.94	29.05	30.39	32.06	34.34	38.06
18	25.17	25.88	26.65	27.52	28.50	29.63	30.98	32.68	34.99	38.77
19	25.66	26.38	27.17	28.04	29.04	30.18	31.56	33.28	35.62	39.44
20	26.14	26.87	27.67	28.56	29.57	30.73	32.12	33.86	36.24	40.11
22	27.07	27.82	28.64	29.55	30.58	31.78	33.20	34.99	37.42	41.38
24	27.95	28.71	29.56	30.49	31.55	32.77	34.23	36.06	38.55	42.59
26	28.80	29.58	30.44	31.40	32.48	33.73	35.22	37.09	39.63	43.76
28	29.60	30.41	31.29	32.26	33.37	34.64	36.17	38.07	40.66	44.87
30	30.39	31.21	32.10	33.10	34.23	35.53	37.08	39.02	41.66	45.95
32	31.14	31.98	32.89	33.91	35.06	36.38	37.96	39.94	42.62	46.99
34	31.88	32.73	33.66	34.69	35.86	37.21	38.82	40.83	43.56	48.00
36	32.58	33.45	34.40	35.45	36.64	38.01	39.64	41.69	44.46	48.97
38	33.28	34.16	35.12	36.19	37.40	38.79	40.45	42.53	45.34	49.92
40	33.93	34.83	35.80	36.89	38.12	39.53	41.22	43.33	46.18	50.82
42	34.59	35.50	36.49	37.59	38.83	40.27	41.98	44.12	47.02	51.72
44	35.23	36.15	37.16	38.27	39.54	40.99	42.73	44.90	47.83	52.60
46	35.85	36.79	37.81	38.94	40.22	41.70	43.46	45.65	48.63	53.46
48	36.47	37.41	38.45	39.59	40.89	42.39	44.17	46.39	49.41	54.31
50	37.06	38.02	39.07	40.23	41.55	43.06	44.87	47.12	50.17	55.13
55	38.51	39.50	40.58	41.78	43.13	44.69	46.56	48.88	52.02	57.11
60	39.89	40.90	42.02	43.25	44.65	46.25	48.16	50.55	53.77	58.99
65	41.21	42.25	43.39	44.66	46.09	47.74	49.70	52.15	55.45	60.80
70	42.48	43.55	44.72	46.02	47.49	49.17	51.18	53.68	57.07	62.54
75	43.70	44.80	46.00	47.33	48.83	50.56	52.61	55.17	58.63	64.22
80	44.89	46.01	47.23	48.59	50.13	51.89	53.99	56.60	60.13	65.84
85	46.04	47.18	48.43	49.82	51.38	53.18	55.32	57.99	61.59	67.41
90	47.15	48.32	49.59	51.01	52.60	54.44	56.62	59.34	63.01	68.93
95	48.23	49.42	50.72	52.17	53.79	55.66	57.88	60.65	64.38	70.41
100	49.29	50.50	51.82	53.29	54.94	56.85	59.11	61.92	65.72	71.85

Bibliography

ALWIN, D.F. and R.M. HAUSER(1975) The Decomposition of Effects in Path Analysis. American Sociological Review, 40, pp. 37–47

ALWIN, D.F. and D.J. JACKSON (1981) Application of Simultaneous Factor Analysis to Issues of Factorial Invariance. In: Jackson D.J. and E.F. Borgatta (eds.): Factor Analysis and Measurement in Sociological Research, pp. 249–280; Beverly Hills: Sage

ANDERSON, N.H.(1974) Information Integration Theory : a Brief Survey. In: D.H. Krantz, R.C. Atkinson, R.D. Luce, P. Suppes (eds.): Contemporary Developments in Mathematical Psychology, vol. 2; San Francisco: Freeman

ARMINGER, G.(1979) Factor Analyse. Teubner Studienskripten

ASHER, H.B.(1976) Causal Modeling. Beverly Hills : Sage

AXELROD, R.(Ed .)(1976) Structure of Decision: The Cognitive Maps of Political Elites. Princeton: Princeton University Press

BAGOZZI, R.P.(1982) Evaluating Structural Equation Models with Unobservable Variables and Measurement Error: A Comment. In: Fornell C. (ed.): A Second Generation of Multivariate Analysis, vol. 2, pp. 317–331; New York: Praeger

BASMAN, R.L.(1963) The Causal Interpretation of Nontriangular Systems of Economic Relations. Econometrica 31, pp. 439–448

BENTLER, P.M.(1980) Multivariate Analysis with Latent Variables Causal Modeling. Annual Review of Psychology 31, pp. 419–456

BENTLER, P.M. and D.G. WEEKS (1980) Linear Structural Equations with Latent Variables. Psychometrika 45, pp. 289–308

BENTLER, P.M. and D.G. BONETT (1980) Significance Tests and Goodness of Fit in the Analysis of Covariance Structures. Psychological Bulletin 88, pp. 588–606

BENTLER, P.M. (1983) Simultaneous Equation Systems, as Moment Structure Models: with an Introduction to Latent Variable Models. In: De Leeuw J., W.J. Keller and T. Wansbeek (eds.): Interfaces between Econometrics and Psychometrics, pp. 13–43; Amsterdam: North Holland Publishing Company

BENZÉCRI,J.P. (1973) Analyse des Données. Paris:Dunod

BETHLEHEM, J.G and W.J. KELLER (1983) A Generalized Weighting Procedure based on Linear Models. In: Proceedings of the American

Statistical Association Meetings, pp.70–75; Toronto: Section on Survey Research

BETHLEHEM, J.G. and H.M.P KERSTEN (1982) The Nonresponse Problem. Survey Methodology 7, no.2, pp.130–156

BIELBY, W.T. and W.T. HAUSER (1977) Structural Equation Models. Annual Review of Sociology 3

BIRNBAUM I. (1981) An Introduction to Causal Analysis in Sociology. London: McMillan Press

BISHIR, J.W. and D.W. DREWES (1970) Mathematics in the Behavioral and Social Sciences. New York: Harcourt, Brace and World Inc.

BISHOP, Y.M.M., S.E. FIENBERG and P.W. HOLLAND (1975) Discrete Multivariate Analysis: Theory and Practice. Cambridge Mass.: MIT Press

BLALOCK, H.M. (1962) Four-Variable Causal Models and Partial Correlations. American Journal of Sociology 68, pp.182–194

BLALOCK, H.M. (1964) Causal Inferences in Non Experimental Research. Chapel Hill: University of North Carolina Press

BLALOCK, H.M. (1967) Causal Inferences, Closed Populations and Measures of Association. American Political Science Review 61, pp.130–136

BLALOCK, H.M. (1969 a) Theory Construction : from Verbal to Mathematical Formulations. Englewood Cliffs : Prentice-Hall

BLALOCK, H.M. (1969 b) Multiple Indicators and the Causal Approach to Measurement Error. American Journal of Sociology 75, pp.264–272

BLALOCK, H.M. (Ed .) (1971) Causal Models in the Social Sciences. Chicago: Aldine Atherton

BLALOCK, H.M. (Ed .) (1974) Measurement in the Social Sciences: Theories and Strategies. London: McMillan

BLOK, H. and W.E.SARIS (1980) Relevante Variabelen bij het Doorverwijzen na de Lagere School: een Structureel Model. Tijdschrift voor Onderwijs Research 5, pp.63–80

BOOMSMA, A. (1982) The Robustness of LISREL against Small Sample Sizes in Factor Analysis Models. In: Jöreskog K.G. and H.Wold (eds.): Systems Under Indirect Observation: Causality, Structure, Prediction, Part 1, pp.149–173; Amsterdam: North Holland Publishing Company

BOOMSMA, A. (1983) On the Robustness of LISREL (Maximum Likelihood Estimation) Against Small Sample Size and Non-Normality. Amsterdam: Sociometric Research Foundation

BOUDON, R. (1965) A Method of Linear Causal Analysis : Dependence Analysis. American Sociological Review 30, pp.365–374

BOUDON, R. (1967) L'Analyse Mathématique des Faits Sociaux. Paris: Plon

BOUDON, R. (1968) A New Look at Correlation Analysis. In: H.M. Blalock and A.B. Blalock (eds.): Methodology in Social Research, pp.199–235; New York: McGraw-Hill

BROWNE, M.W. (1975) Generalized Least Squares Estimators in the Analysis of Covariance Structures. In: Aigner D.J. and A.S. Goldberger (eds.): Latent Variables in Socio-Economic Models, pp.205–226; Amsterdam: North Holland

BROWNE, M.W. (1982) Covariance Structures. In: Hawkins, D.M. (ed.): Topics in Applied Multivariate Analysis; Cambridge: Cambridge University Press

CAMPBELL, D.T. and J.C. STANLEY (1963) Experimental and Quasi Experimental Designs for Research. Chicago: Rand McNally

CHAPIN, F.S. (1947) Experimental Design in Sociological Research. New York: Harper

CARMINES, E.G. and R.A. ZELLER (1979) Reliability and Validity Assessment. Beverly Hills: Sage

CHRIST, F.S. (1966) Econometric Models and Methods. New York: Wiley

COCHRAN, W.G. (1977) Sampling Techniques. New York: Wiley

COOK, T.D. and D.T. CAMPBELL (1979) Quasi-Experimentation: Design and Analysis Issues for Field Settings. Chicago: Rand McNally

COOMBS, C.H. (1964) A Theory of Data. New York: Wiley

COSTNER, H.L. and R.L. LEIK (1964) Deductions from Axiomatic Theory. American Sociological Review 29, pp.819–835

COSTNER, H.L. (1969) Theory, Deduction and Rules of Correspondence. American Journal of Sociology 75, pp.245–263

COSTNER, H.L. and R. SCHOENBERG (1973) Diagnosing Indicator Ills in Multiple Indicator Models. In: Goldberger A.S. and O.D. Duncan: Structural Equation Models in the Social Sciences, pp.167–199; New York: Seminar Press

DAWES, R.M. (1972) Fundamentals of Attitude Measurement. New York: Wiley

DEVLIN, S.J., R. GNANADESIKAN and J.S. KETTENRING (1975) Robust Estimation and Outlier Detection with Correlation Coefficients. Biometrika 62,3, pp.531–545

DIJKSTRA, T.K. (1981) Latent Variables in Linear Stochastic Models: Reflections on "Maximum Likelihood" and "Partial Least Squares" Methods. Amsterdam: Sociometric Research Foundation

DRAPER, N. and H. SMITH (1966) Applied Regression Analysis. New York: Wiley

DOORN L.,VAN, W.E. SARIS and M. LODGE (1983) Discrete or Continuous Measurement: What Difference Does it Make ? Kwantitatieve Methoden 10, pp.104 – 121

DUNCAN, O.D. (1966) Path Analysis : Sociological Examples. American Journal of Sociology 72, pp.1 – 16

DUNCAN, O.D. (1975) Introduction to Structural Equation Models. New York: Academic Press

DWYER, J.N. (1983) Statistical Models for the Social and Behavioral Sciences. Oxford: Oxford University Press

FIENBERG, S.E. (1977) The Analysis of Cross-Classified Categorical Data. Cambrdige Mass.: MIT Press

FINNEY, J.M. (1972) Indirect Effects in Path Analysis. Sociological Methods and Research 1, pp.175 – 186

FISHER, F.H. (1969) Causation and Specification in Economic Theory and Econometrics. Synthese 20, pp.489 – 500

FISHER, F.H. (1970) A Correspondence Principle for Simultaneous Equation Models. Econometrica 38, pp.73 – 92

FISHER, R.A. (1935) The Design of Experiments. London: Oliver Boyd

FISHER,R.A. (1948) Statistical Methods for Research Workers. New York:MacMillan Publ.Comp.

FORNELL, C. (Ed .) (1982) A Second Generation of Multivariate Analysis. New York: Praeger

FORNELL, C. and D.F, LARCKER (1982) Structural Equation Models with Unobservable Variables and Measurement Error: Algebra and Statistics. In: Fornell C. (ed.): A Second Generation of Multivariate Analysis, vol.2, pp. 331 – 348; New York: Praeger

FORNELL, C. and D.F. LARCKER (1982) Evaluating Structural Equation Models with Unobservable Variables and Measurement Error. In: Fornell C. (ed.) A Second Generation of Multivariate Analysis, vol.2, pp.289 – 317; New York: Praeger

GEWEKE, J.F. and K.M. SINGLETON (1980) Interpreting the Likelihood Ratio Statistic in Factor Models when the Sample Size is Small. Journal of the American Statistical Association 75, pp.133 – 137

GIFI, A. (1981) Non linear Multivariate Analysis. Leiden: Department of Data Theory, University of Leiden

GILBERT,G.N. (1981) Modelling Society: an Introduction to Loglinear Analysis for Social Researchers. London: Allan and Unwin

GNANADESIKAN, R. and J.R. KETTENRING (1972) Robust Estimates, Residuals and Outlier Detection with Multiple Response Data. Biometrics 29, pp.81 – 124

GOLDERG, A.S. (1966) Discerning a Causal Pattern among Data on

Voting Behavior. American Political Science Review 60, pp. 913 – 922

GOLDBERGER, A.S. (1964) Econometric Theory. New York: Wiley

GOLDBERGER, A.S. (1970) On Boudon's Method of Linear Causal Analysis. American Sociological Review 35, pp. 97 – 101

GOLDERGER, A.S. and O.D. DUNCAN (Eds .) (1973) Structural Equation Models in the Social Sciences. New York: Seminar Press

GOLDERGER, A.S. (1973) Structural Equation Models: an Overview. In: Goldberger A.S. and O.D. Duncan (eds.): Structural Equation Models in the Social Sciences, pp. 1 – 18; New York: Seminar Press

GOODMAN, L.A. (1972) A Modified Multiple Regression Approach to the Analysis of Dichotomous Variables. American Sociological Review 37, pp. 28 – 46

GOODMAN, L.A. (1973) Causal Analysis of Data from Panel Studies and Other Kinds of Surveys. American Journal of Sociology 78, pp. 1135-1199

GREENWOOD, E. (1945) Experimental Sociology: a Study in Method. New York: King's Crown Press

GRUVEUS, G.T. and K.G. JÖRESKOG (1970) A Computer Program for Minimizing a Function of Several Variables. Research Bulletin, Princeton E.T.S., pp. 10 – 14

GURR, T.R. (1974) The Neo Alexandrians: a Review Essay on Data Handbooks in Political Science. American Political Science Review 68, pp. 243 – 252

GUTTMAN, L. (1977) What is not What in Statistics. The Statistician 26, pp. 81 – 107

HAMBLIN, R. (1974) Social Attitudes: Magnitude Measurement and Theory. In: Blalock, H.M. (ed.): Measurement in the Social Sciences, pp. 61 – 121; London: McMillan

HANSEN, M.N., W.N. HURWITZ and W.G. MADOW (1953) Sample Survey Methods and Theory. Volume 1: Methods and Application. Volume 2: Theory. New York: Wiley

HANUSHEK, E.A. and J.E. JACKSON (1977) Statistical Methods for Social Scientists. London: Academic Press

HAYNAM, G.E.,GOVINDARAJULU Z. and LEONE F.C. (1973) Tables of the Cumulative Chi-square Distribution. In Harter H.L. and D.B.Owen (eds): Selected Tables in Mathematical Statistics. Providence, Rhode Island: American Mathematical Society

HAUSER, R.M. and A.S. GOLDBERGER (1971) The Treatment of Unobservable Variables in Path Analysis. In: Costner, H.L. (ed.): Sociological Methodology 1971, pp. 81 – 117; San Francisco: Jossey-Bass

HAWKES, R.K. (1971) The Multivariate Analysis of Ordinal Measures.

American Journal of Sociology 76, pp.908–926

HAYS, W. (1973) Statistics for the Social Sciences, 2nd ed. London: Holt, Rinehart and Winston

HEISE, D.R. (1969) Problems in Path Analysis and Causal Inference. In: Borgatta, E.F. (ed.): Sociological Methodology 1969, pp.38-73; San Francisco: Jossey-Bass

HEISE, D.R. (1970) Causal Inference from Panel Data. In: Borgatta, E.F. and G.W. Bohrnsted (eds.): Sociological Methodology 1970, pp.3–27; San Francisco: Jossey-Bass

HEISE, D.R. (1975) Causal Analysis. New York: Wiley

HEISE, D.R. and G.W. BOHRNSTEDT (1970) Validity, Invalidity and Reliability. In: Borgatta, E.F. (ed.): Sociological Methodology 1970, pp.104-130; San Francisco: Jossey-Bass

HILL, M.O. (1974) Correspondence Analysis: a Neglected Multivariate Method. Applied Statistics 23, pp.340–354

HOEL, P.G. (1971) Introduction to Mathematical Statistics. New York: Wiley

HOELTER, J.W. (1983) The Analysis of Covariance Structures. Sociological Methods and Research 11, pp.325–344

HOLSTI, O.R. (1969) Content Analysis for the Social Sciences. Reading: Addison Wesley

HYMAN, H. (1955) Survey Design and Analysis: Principles, Cases and Procedures. Glencoe: Free Press

JACKSON, D.J. and E.F. BORGATTA (Eds .) (1981) Factor Analysis and Measurement in Sociological Research. Beverly Hills: Sage

JESSEN, R.J. (1978) Statistical Survey Techniques. New York: Wiley

JOHNSON, N.L. and S. KOTZ (1970) Continuous Univariate Distributions. New York: Houghton Mifflin

JOHNSTON, J.J.(1972) Econometric Methods. New York: McGraw Hill

JONG, U. DE, J. DRONKERS and W.E. SARIS (1982) Veranderingen in Schoolloopbanen tussen 1965 en 1977: Ontwikkelingen in de Nederlandse Samenleving en Haar Onderwijs. Mens en Maatschappij, 57, pp.26–39

JÖRESKOG, K.G. (1967) Some Contributions to Maximum Likelihood Factor Analysis. Psychometrika 32, pp.443–482

JÖRESKOG, K.G. (1969) A General Approach to Confirmatory Maximum Likelihood Factor Analysis. Psychometrika 34, pp.183–202

JÖRESKOG, K.G. (1970) A General Method for Analysis of Covariance Structures. Biometrika 57, pp.239–251

JÖRESKOG, K.G. (1971) Statistical Analysis of Sets of Congeneric Tests. Psychometrika 36, pp.109–133

JÖRESKOG, K.G. and A.S. GOLDBERGER (1972) Factor Analysis by Generalized Least Squares. Psychometrika 37, pp. 243−260

JÖRESKOG, K.G. (1973) A General Method for Estimating a Linear Structural Equation System. In: Goldberger and Duncan (eds.): Structural Equation Models in the Social Sciences, pp. 85−112; New York: Seminar Press

JÖRESKOG, K.G. (1974) Analyzing Psychological Data by Structural Analysis of Covariance Matrices. In: Krantz, D.H. a.o. (eds.): Contemporary Developments in Mathematical Psychology, vol. 2; San Francisco: Freeman

JÖRESKOG, K.G. and D. SÖRBOM (1977) Statistical Models and Methods for the Analysis of Longitudinal Data. In: Aigner, D.J. and A.S. Goldberger (eds.): Latent Variables in Socio-Economic Models, pp. 285−326; Amsterdam: North Holland Publishing Company

JÖRESKOG K.G. (1978) Structural Analysis of Covariance and Correlation Matrices. Psychometrica 43, pp. 443−477

JÖRESKOG ,K.G. and D. SÖRBOM (1979) Advances in Factor Analysis and Structural Equation Models. Cambrdige, Mass.: Abt Associates

JÖRESKOG, K.G. and D. SÖRBOM (1983) LISREL VI Users Guide Uppsala: Department of Statistics, University

KENNY, D.A. (1975) Cross-Lagged Panel Correlation: a Test for Spuriousness. Psychological Bulletin 82, pp. 887−903

KENNY, D.A. (1979) Correlation and Causality. New York: Wiley

KIM, J.O. and G.D. FERREE (1981) Standardization in Causal Analysis. Sociological Methods and Research 10(2), pp. 187−210

KISH, L. (1965) Survey Sampling. New York: Wiley

KNUTH, D.E. (1979) TEX and METAFONT, New Directions in Typesetting. Providence: American Mathematical Society/Digital Press

KOOPMANS, T. (1973) Identification Problems in Economic Model Construction. In: Blalock, H.M. (ed.): Causal Models in the Social Sciences, pp. 159−178; Chicago: Aldine Atherton

KRIPPENDORF, K. (1980) Content Analysis: an Introduction to its Methodology. Beverly Hills: Sage

KRUSKAL, W.H. and J.M. TANUR (Eds .) (1978) International Encyclopedia of Statistics. New York: Free Press

KRUSKAL, W.H. (1978) Tests of Significance. In: Kruskal, W.M. and J.M. Tanur (eds.) International Encyclopedia of Statistics, pp. 944−958; New York: Free Press

LAND, K.C. (1969) Principles of Path Analysis. In: Borgatta, E.F. (ed.): Sociological Methodology 1969, pp. 3−37; San Francisco: Jossey Bass

LAWLEY D.N. and A.E. MAXWELL (1971) Factor Analysis as a Statistical Method, 2nd ed. London: Butterworth

LARZELERE, R.E. and S.A. MULAIK (1977) Single Sample Tests for Many Correlations. Psychological Bulletin 84, pp. 557–569

LEHMAN, E.L. (1978) Hypothesis Testing. In: Kruskal W.H. and J.M. Tanur (eds.): International Encyclopedia of Statistics, pp. 441–449; New York : Free Press

LEWIS-BECK, M.S. (1974) Determining the Importance of an Independent Variable: a Path-Analytic Solution. Social Science Research 3, pp. 95–107

LODGE, M., J. TANNENHAUS, D. CROSS, B. TURSKY, M.A. FOLEY and M. FOLEY (1976) The Calibration and Cross Model Validation of Ratio Scales of Political Opinion in Survey Research. Social Science Research 5, pp. 325–347

LODGE, M. and B. TURSKY (1979) Comparison between Category and Magnitude Scaling of Political Opinion Employing SRC/CPS Items. American Political Science Review 73, pp. 50–66

LODGE, M. (1981) Magnitude Scaling: Quantitative Measurement of Opinions. Beverly Hills: Sage University Paper nr. 25

MALINVAUD, E. (1970) Statistical Methods of Econometrics. Amsterdam: North Holland Publishing Company

MARSDEN, P.V. (Ed.) (1981) Linear Models in Social Research. Beverly Hills: Sage

MARSDEN P.V. (1981) Conditional Effects in Regression Models. In: Marsden P.V. (ed.): Linear Models in Social Research, pp. 97–116; Beverly Hills: Sage

MCDONALD, R.P. (1978) A Simple Comprehensive Model for the Analysis of Covariance Structures. British Journal of Mathematical and Statistical Psychology 31, pp. 59–72

MCFATTER R.M. (1979) The Use of Structural Equation Models in Interpreting Regression Equations Including Suppressor and Entrance Variables. Applied Psychological Measurement 3, pp. 123–125

MCGINNES, R. (1966) Review of Causal Inferences in Non-Experimental Research. Social Forces 44, pp. 584–586

MEDLEY, D.M. and H.E. MITZEL (1967) Measuring Classroom Behavior by Systematic Observation. In: Gage, N.L. (ed.): Handbook of Research on Teaching, pp. 247–328; Chicago: Rand McNally

MORRISON, D.G., R. MITCHELL, J.N. PADEN a.O. (1972) Black Africa: a Comparative Handbook. New York: Free Press

MUTHÉN, B. (1984) A General Structural Equation Model with Dichotomous, Ordered Categorical and Continuous, Latent Variable Indicators. Psychometrica 49, pp. 115–133

OLSSON, U. (1979 a) Maximum Likelihood Estimation of the Polychoric
Correlation Coefficient. Psychometrika 44, no.4, pp.443–460

OLSSON, U. (1979 b) On the Robustness of Factor Analysis against Crude
Classification of the Observation. Multivariate Behavioral Research 14,
pp.485–500

OLSSON, U., F. DRASGOW and N.J. DORANS (1982) The Polyserial
Correlation Coefficient. Psychometrika 47, no.3, pp.337–347

OPP, K.D. and P. SCHMIDT (1976) Einführung in die
Mehrvariabelenanalyse : Grundlagen der Formulierung und Prüfung
komplexer Sozialwissenschaftlicher Aussagen. Reinbek: Rowolt

POPPER, K.R. (1959) The Logic of Scientific Discovery. New York : Basic
Books

RAJ, D. (1968) Sampling Theory. New York: McGraw Hill

RILEY, M.W. (1963) Sociological Research : a One Case Approach. New
York: Harcourt, Brace, World

ROBINSON, J.P., J.G. RUSK and K.B. HEAD (1968) Measures of
Political Attitudes. Ann Arbor: University of Michigan, Institute of
Survey Research (ISR)

ROBINSON, J.P. and P.R. SHAVER (1969) Measures of Social
Psychological Attitudes. Ann Arbor: University of Michigan, Institute
of Survey Research (ISR)

SARIS, W.E., C. BRUINSMA, W. SCHOOTS and C. VERMEULEN
(1977) The use of Magnitude Estimation in Large Scale Survey
Research. Mens en Maatschappij, 52, pp.369–395

SARIS, W.E., W.M.de PIJPER and P. ZEGWAART (1979) Detection
of Specification Errors in Linear Structural Equation Models. In:
Schuessler K.F. (ed.): Sociological Methodology 1979, pp.151–171;
San Francisco: Jossey Bass

SARIS W.E. (1980) Linear Structural Relationships. Quality and Quantity
14, pp.205–225

SARIS, W.E., P. NEIJENS and L. VAN DOORN (1980) Scaling Social
Science Variables by Cross Modality Matching. Methods and Data
Newsletter 5, pp.3–22

SARIS, W.E. and H. BLOK (1982) Het Onderwijzersadvies nader
bekeken. Tijdschrift voor Onderwijsresearch 7, pp.49–60

SARIS, W.E. and A. SATORRA (1984) The Likelihood Ratio Test
of Structural Equation Models. In: Sociometric Research 1984;
Amsterdam: Sociometric Research Foundation, (forthcoming)

SARIS, W.E., J. den RONDEN and A. SATORRA (1984) Testing
Structural Equation Models. In: Cuttance P.F. and J.R. Ecob
(eds.): Structural Modeling; Cambridge: Cambridge University Press
(forthcoming)

SATORRA, A. and W.E. SARIS (1982) The Accuracy of a Procedure for Calculating the Power of the Likelihood Ratio Test as used within the LISREL Framework. In: C.P. Middendorp (ed.): Sociometric Research 1982, pp.129–190; Amsterdam: Sociometric Research Foundation

SATORRA, A. and W.E. SARIS (1985) The Power of the Likelihood Ratio Test in Covariance Structure Analysis. Psychometrica: (forthcoming)

SCHMIDT, P. (1977) Zur Praktischen Anwendung von Theorien : Grundlagenprobleme und Anwendung auf die Hochschuldidaktik. Dissertation, University of Mannheim

SHAPIRO, A. (1983) Asymptotic Distribution Theory in the Analysis of Covariance Structures: an Unified Approach. South African Statistical Journal 17, pp.33–81

SIK-JUM LEE and P.M. BENTLER (1980) Some Asymptotic Properties of Constrained Generalized Least Squares Estimation in Covariance Structure Models. South African Statistical Journal 14, pp.121–136

SIMON, H.A. (1952) On the Definition of the Causal Relation. Journal of Philosophy 49, pp.517–528

SIMON, H.A. (1954) Spurious Correlation : a Causal Interpretation. Journal of the American Statistical Association 49, pp.467–479

SMITH, R.B. (1972) Neighbourhood Context and College Plan: an Ordinal Path Analysis. Social Forces 51, pp.199–217

SMITH, R.B. (1974) Continuities in Ordinal Path Analysis. Social Forces 53, pp.200–229

SOM, R.K. (1973) A Manual of Sampling Theory. London: Heinemann

SOMERS, R.B. (1968) An Approach to Multivariate Analysis of Ordinal Data. American Sociological Review 33, pp.971–977

SOMERS, R.B. (1974) Analysis of Ordinal Rank Correlation Measures based on the Product Moment Model. Social Forces 53, pp.229–246

SÖRBOM, D. (1975) Detection of Correlated Errors in Longitudinal Data. British Journal of Mathematical and Statistical Psychology 28, pp.138–151

SPECHT, D.A. (1975) On the Evaluation of Causal Models. Social Science Research, pp.113–133

SPEIER, M. (1973) How to Observe Face-to-Face Communication : a Sociological Introduction. Pacific Palisades, Collorado: Good Year Publishing

STEGMÜLLER, W. (1960) Das Problem der Kausalität. In: Topitsch, F. (ed.): Probleme der Wissenschaftstheorie, pp.171–190; Wien

STEVENS, S.S. (1957) On the Psychological Law. Psychological Review 64, pp.153–181

STEVENS, S.S. (1975) Psychophysics : Introduction to its Perceptual

Neural and Social Prospect. New York: Wiley

STROTZ, R.H. (1960) Interdependence as a Specification Error. Econometrica 28, pp. 428 – 442

STROTZ, R.H. and H. WOLD (1969) Recursive versus Nonrecursive Systems: an Attempt at Synthesis. Econometrica 28, pp. 417 – 427

SUPPES, P. (1970) A Probabilistic Theory of Causality. Amsterdam: North Holland Publishing Company

SWAMINATHAN, H. and J. ALGINA (1978) Scale Freeness in Factor Analysis. Psychometrika 43, pp. 581 – 583

TAYLOR, C.L., M.C. HUDSON a .O. (1972) World Handbook of Political and Social Indicators. New Haven: Yale University Press

THEIL, H. (1971) Principles of Econometrics. New York: Wiley

TORGERSON, W.S. (1958) Theory and Methods of Scaling. New York: Wiley

TUKEY, J.W. (1954) Causation, Regression and Path Analysis. In: Kempthorne, O. a.o. (eds.): Statistics and Mathematics in Biology, pp. 35 – 66; Ames: Iowa State College Press

UPTON, J.G. (1978) The Analysis of Cross-Tabulated Data. New York: Wiley

VETTER, H. (1972) Statische und Dynamische Kausalanalyse. Zeitschrift für Sozialpsychologie 3, pp. 13 – 22

WALLPOLE, R.E. (1974) Introduction to Statistics, 2nd ed. New York: McMillan

WERTS, C.E. and R.L. LINN (1971) Path Analysis, Psychological Examples. Psychological Bulletin 74, pp. 193-212

WHEATON, B., B. MUTHÉN, D. ALWIN and G. SUMMERS (1977) Assessing Reliability and Stability in Panel Models with Multiple Indicators. In: Heise, D.R. (ed.): Sociological Methodology 1977, pp. 84 – 136; San Francisco: Jossey Bass

WILEY, D. (1973) The Identification Problem for Structural Equation Models with Unmeasured Variables. In: Goldberger and Duncan, (eds.): Structural Equation Models in the Social Sciences, pp. 69 – 83; New York: Seminar Press

WILSON, T.P. (1974 a) On Interpreting Ordinal Analogues to Multiple Regression and Path Analysis. Social Forces 53, pp. 196 – 199

WILSON, T.P. (1974 b) Reply to Somers and Smith. Social Forces 53, pp. 247 – 251

WILSON, T.P. (1974 c) Measures of Association for Bivariate Ordinal Hypotheses. In: Blalock, H.M. (ed.): Measurement in the Social Sciences: Theories and Strategies pp. 327 – 34; London: McMillon

WOLD, H. (1980) Model Construction and Evaluation when Theoretical Knowledge is Scarce : An Example of Partial Least Squares. In:

332

Kmenta J, and J.B. Ramsey (eds.): Evaluation of Econometric Models, pp. 47–74; New York: Seminar Press

WOLD, H. (1982) Soft Modeling: the Basic Design and Some Extensions. In: Jöreskog K.G. and H. Wold (eds.): Systems under Indirect Observation: Causality, Structure, Prediction, Part 2, pp. 1– 54; Amsterdam: North Holland Publishing Company

WONNACOTT, R.J. and T.H. WONNACOTT (1970) Econometrics. New York: Wiley

WONNACOTT, T.H. and R.J. WONNACOTT (1980) Introductory Statistics. New York: Wiley

WRIGHT, S. (1934) The Method of Path Coefficients. Annals of Mathematical Statistics V, pp. 161–215

WRIGHT, S. (1960) Path Coefficients and Path Regressions : Alternative or Complementary Concepts ? Biometrics 16, pp. 189–202

YAMANE, T. (1967) Elementary Sampling Theory Englewood Cliffs: Prentice-Hall

YEOMANS, K.A. (1975) Introducing Statistics. London: Penquin

Index *

* The index indicates only the page number of the definition of the concept.